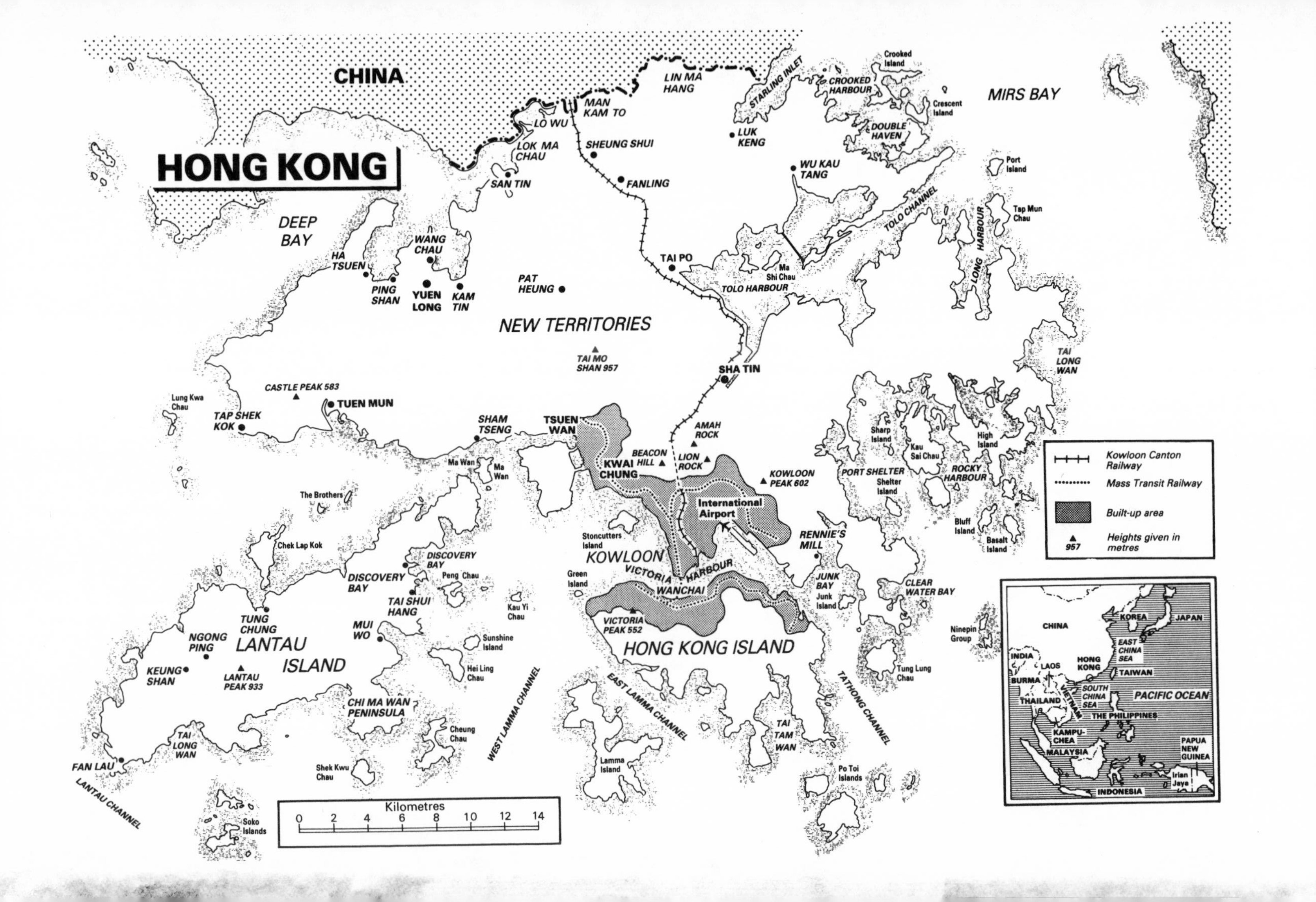

HONG KONG
CHINA
MIRS BAY
DEEP BAY
LIN MA HANG
STARLING INLET
Crooked Island
CROOKED HARBOUR
Crescent Island
DOUBLE HAVEN
MAN KAM TO
LO WU
LOK MA CHAU
SAN TIN
SHEUNG SHUI
FANLING
LUK KENG
WU KAU TANG
Port Island
Tap Mun Chau
TOLO CHANNEL
LONG HARBOUR
HA TSUEN
PING SHAN
WANG CHAU
YUEN LONG
KAM TIN
PAT HEUNG
TAI PO
Ma Shi Chau
TOLO HARBOUR
NEW TERRITORIES
TAI MO SHAN 957
SHA TIN
TAI LONG WAN
CASTLE PEAK 583
TUEN MUN
Lung Kwa Chau
TAP SHEK KOK
SHAM TSENG
TSUEN WAN
AMAH ROCK
BEACON HILL
LION ROCK
KWAI CHUNG
KOWLOON PEAK 602
Ma Wan
The Brothers
International Airport
Sharp Island
Kau Sai Chau
High Island
PORT SHELTER
Shelter Island
ROCKY HARBOUR
Bluff Island
Basalt Island
Kowloon Canton Railway
Mass Transit Railway
Built-up area
957
Heights given in metres
Chek Lap Kok
DISCOVERY BAY
Peng Chau
Stoncutters Island
KOWLOON
RENNIE'S MILL
VICTORIA HARBOUR
WANCHAI
Green Island
JUNK BAY
Junk Island
CLEAR WATER BAY
TAI SHUI HANG
Kau Yi Chau
TUNG CHUNG
MUI WO
Sunshine Island
VICTORIA PEAK 552
Ninepin Group
NGONG PING
LANTAU ISLAND
HONG KONG ISLAND
KEUNG SHAN
LANTAU PEAK 933
Hei Ling Chau
Tung Lung Chau
CHI MA WAN PENINSULA
WEST LAMMA CHANNEL
EAST LAMMA CHANNEL
TATHONG CHANNEL
TAI LONG WAN
Cheung Chau
TAI TAM WAN
FAN LAU
Shek Kwu Chau
Lamma Island
Po Toi Islands
LANTAU CHANNEL
Soko Islands
Kilometres
0
2
4
6
8
10
12
14
CHINA
KOREA
JAPAN
EAST CHINA SEA
INDIA
HONG KONG
TAIWAN
LAOS
BURMA
VIETNAM
SOUTH CHINA SEA
PACIFIC OCEAN
THAILAND
THE PHILIPPINES
KAMPU-CHEA
MALAYSIA
PAPUA NEW GUINEA
Irian Jaya
INDONESIA

KEVIN RAFFERTY

CITY ON THE ROCKS

HONG KONG'S UNCERTAIN FUTURE

VIKING

VIKING
Published by the Penguin Group
Viking Penguin, a division of Penguin Books USA Inc.,
40 West 23rd Street, New York, New York 10010, U.S.A.
Penguin Books Ltd, 27 Wrights Lane, London W8 5TZ, England
Penguin Books Australia Ltd, Ringwood, Victoria, Australia
Penguin Books Canada Ltd, 2801 John Street,
Markham, Ontario, Canada L3R 1B4
Penguin Books (N.Z.) Ltd, 182–190 Wairau Road,
Auckland 10, New Zealand

Penguin Books Ltd, Registered Offices:
Harmondsworth, Middlesex, England

First American Edition
Published in 1990 by Viking Penguin,
a division of Penguin Books USA Inc.

10 9 8 7 6 5 4 3 2 1

Library of Congress Catalog Card Number 89-40782
ISBN 0-670-80205-0

CIP data available

Printed in the United States of America

To Michelle
With thanks and love

CONTENTS

List of Illustrations

All the photographs were taken by the author

1 THE SLAUGHTER OF SIX MILLION HOPES

IT was more like a carnival than a protest march. Vast crowds swarmed into the centre of the city, laughing, smiling, enjoying themselves. Fathers, some of them in uniform, carried children on their heads for a better view and risked ice-cream droppings on their shoulders. Every tree sprouted cheerful watchers. Every litter-bin had a body precariously balanced on top. Every roadside bollard seemed to jiggle under swaying, craning people. Every pedestrian road-bridge groaned under football-match sized crowds, jolly, waving, cheerful. The traffic which normally clogs the eight-lane highway – articulated buses, lorries, cars and carts – melted away. Only a few bicycles survived to weave a crazy path through the masses.

As the marchers tramped into sight, the police got to their feet, stubbed out their cigarettes, put aside their playing cards and formed a human chain three and four deep blocking the road against demonstrators, since the municipal authorities had forbidden the protest. But it was a half-hearted barrier. With little more than a push and a shove, the students surged through. They linked arms, waved their banners, showed off headbands with messages, shouted slogans like 'Hello Mr Democracy'. Most moving of all, they sang *The Internationale* as the onlookers joined in and clapped and cheered them, before swelling their ranks to complete the joyous journey to the immense square at the heart of the capital.

The youths had captured the mood of the country. Hundreds of thousands of people: students, workers, housewives, children and babes in arms, crowded the square, urging the bemused policemen to join in. This was not Western Europe or Japan or Eastern Europe, all of which have had a taste of popular mass demonstrations. It was Peking in May 1989, the People's Republic of China, at Tian'anmen, Gate of Heavenly Peace, where almost forty years before Mao Zedong had proclaimed the victory of the Communist revolution and where today the Chairman's larger-than-life picture still watches over the heart of China's empire. It was a clever idea to sing the Party's own hymn -- yet the united soaring chorus of massed voices was symbolic of who really represented the people.

The spate of discontent was sparked off by the death in mid-April of Hu Yaobang, the chirpy, sparrow-like former Secretary-General of the Communist Party who was unceremoniously sacked in 1987 by the country's strongman, Deng Xiaoping. Hu's faults lay in singing out of tune by advocating greater freedom and failing to suppress student calls for democracy. Several days after his cremation, crowds clustered around the flower-decked Monument to the People's Heroes bearing his portrait. On campuses in Peking and other cities students put up wall posters demanding democracy, press freedom and an end to corruption.

The students held mammoth rallies. They paraded outside Zhongnanhai, former playground of the mandarins and princes of the Ming and Ching dynasties where today the Communist elite is ensconced elegantly in the name of the equality of man. On the eve of the historic summit visit by Soviet President Mikhail Gorbachev, a small group of students began a hunger strike in the square itself to call attention to their demands, and they were joined by tens of thousands of other students and workers who clustered around to protect them from the security forces. The Chinese government could not use the square for its planned ceremonial reception for Gorbachev. At various times more than a million Chinese jam-packed the square. The mood of anger and distrust towards the Communist leadership extended right to the top. 'Let Tzu Hsi retire!'; the reference to the Dowager Empress Tzu Hsi (Ci Xi), regarded as the corrupt symbol of the declining years of the Ching (Qing) dynasty, might to a foreigner seem obscure, but it was quickly understood by the Chinese as pointing a finger directly at supremo Deng Xiaoping himself. Some demonstrators also pointedly smashed bottles: Deng's name in Chinese sounds like the words for 'little bottle'. The strongman was openly and rudely referred to as 'Shorty'. Some students pointed out that Deng himself had sacked Hu and had shut down the Democracy Wall in 1979. Others recalled that Deng had been Mao Zedong's principal assistant in 1957 in the notorious 'Hundred Flowers' campaign, when Mao declared: 'You have to let the poisonous weeds sprout before you can pull them out.'

Another general complaint was that China's leaders are all old and out of touch. One student wall-poster claimed: 'Required qualifications to be a State leader: minimum age 80: maximum educational level, primary school; no brain.'

Other leaders were singled out by name for ridicule. The protesters openly called for the resignation of Premier Li Peng and the supposedly liberal Party Secretary-General Zhao Ziyang was accused of corruption – his son is known to operate a profitable business in southern China. One report listed a string of privileged posts occupied by the well-connected. Fuelling the discontent was the acknowledged fact that Communist Party leaders at both national and provincial level have used China's recent economic reforms for their own enrichment. 'Party bosses have become the leading millionaire cadres,' complained several protesting students. 'It is hard to point to a single leader who has clean hands,' added a former student now working for a government department.

For six weeks protests filled the streets of the capital in a remarkable outpouring of popular feeling against a discredited regime. It was remarkable, peaceful, united, unarmed, orderly, naïve, exuberant, a direct challenge from the masses to the claim of the Communist Party to enjoy what in Chinese history has been called 'the Mandate of Heaven'. Some members of the security forces fraternized and joined the demonstrators. The authorities refused to offer concessions. Party Secretary-General Zhao Ziyang visited hunger strikers in the square and in hospital and murmured 'We came too late' – for which he later became a hero to the masses. The authorities minus Zhao declared martial law, which brought a further rash of protests, massive demonstrations, grimmer-faced than before but still orderly and peaceful, and wall posters depicting Li Peng as Hitler reincarnated. The protesting people took over buses and lorries to block the main roads against 100,000 troops sent to Peking.

The declaration of martial law was only a flexing of muscles. The Communist rulers initially sent a mass of young unarmed troops in to try to quell the dissent and take over the square. But these were literally overwhelmed by the crowds, angrier now, who commandeered the troops' own vehicles to strengthen their barricades. They lectured and hectored the young soldiers, who looked crestfallen and shamefaced, asking why they were attacking their own people. Then they fed their would-be persecutors. This was all too much for the old men of the Communist Party in Zhongnanhai: 'Put an end to this dissent,' they ordered. After darkness on Saturday 3 June the brutal crackdown began. There was no nonsense of tear gas or water cannon or plastic bullets, or live ones in the air: the People's Liberation Army was turned against the Chinese people with tanks and armoured carriers and real guns fired in earnest.

There were some heroic scenes, the joining of hands by students and workers, the bravery of demonstrators lining up to take the place of fallen colleagues before the soldiers' guns, a lone student playing matador to a line of tanks, Chinese who spoke out. Professor Yang Xianyi, a Communist Party member, was asked on the BBC World Service if he weren't being too critical of Deng and the leadership. 'I am not being critical. I am condemning arch-criminals, the worst criminals in Chinese history,' he responded. Bob Hawke, Australia's Prime Minister, tried unsuccessfully to choke back tears as he described at a memorial service for the dead in Canberra's Parliament House what had happened. Children and young girls were among those slaughtered: 'Armoured-personnel carriers and tanks then ran backwards and forwards over the bodies of the slain until they were reduced to pulp, after which bulldozers moved in to push the remains into piles which were then incinerated by troops with flame-throwers.' According to western sources, 7,000 people were killed. In August Amnesty International gave a lower figure of at least 1,300 civilian's killed in the immediate crack-down, but accused Peking of carring out 'judicial killings' since June.

This was not how the Chinese leaders justified the blood on their hands. Western reporters who had given graphic – and themselves brave – frontline descriptions and pictures of the slaughter had also written many woolly-headed stories inflating puffs of rumours into front-page articles about massive closed-door struggles within the Chinese leadership, of army units fighting one another, taking sides in a gigantic struggle between liberals and hardliners, of Deng Xiaoping on his deathbed and of, as one London newspaper billboard put it, 'First shots fired in civil war.'

Wishful thinking: when Deng appeared on 9 June, surrounded by a solid phalanx of generals, he was in no mood to apologize or compromise. He praised the troops as 'China's Great Wall of Iron and Steel'. He thanked and congratulated the army for saving China from the 'counter-revolutionaries' who had tried to overthrow the Communist Party and declare a capitalist republic. Other official media described the slain demonstrators as 'gangsters', 'ruffians' and 'bourgeois elements'. The elderly leaders paused for a moment's silence in memory of the brave soldiers who had died putting down the unarmed civilians (some of the fallen soldiers were shot by mistake by their colleagues). The Communist propaganda machine launched a barrage of television and radio reports praising the PLA action. Wives and children of soldiers who had died were displayed on television as the families of 'martyrs'. Deng and colleagues then let loose the security forces and secret police on to the university campuses and centres of dissent to round up hundreds of demonstrators who had not fled. It was a systematic attempt to eradicate dissent. Those arrested faced a swift, secret trial without a defence lawyer followed by a bullet in the head. Deng was widely reported to have said that a million dead would be a small price to pay in a nation of one billion; a grim savagery.

Significantly missing from the Chinese line-up was reformer-in-chief Zhao Ziyang, later sacked from his job of Communist Party Secretary-General and from all his other Party posts for his 'mistakes', including 'conniving' with pro-democracy demonstrators. Far from being dead, Deng Xiaoping was at the helm again, with a little help from his old buddies of the 'Long March' of more than fifty years before. The interesting thing about their intervention was that they had by-passed or scrapped the machinery of both Party and state to make their intervention and order the crackdown. Deng himself holds no government job and is not a member of the main Party body, the Standing Committee of the Politburo. He is China's 'Strongman' through being chairman of the Party's Military Affairs Commission, his only job, and clearly the only one that counts in China. Apart from Yang Shangkun, State President, supposedly a ceremonial job, and Prime Minister Li Peng, commonly regarded as having no power base of his own, all the other leaders who approved the crackdown are retired or hold merely advisory positions.

The message was grim and clear enough. China had taken several steps backwards to the darker ages where 'Big Brother' state watched and regulated everything. Constant propaganda urged people to spy on their neighbours and even on family members who had protested or shown sympathy for democracy demonstrators and to report them to the authorities. The secret police again came out openly on streets and in workplaces, watching and reporting. Party cadres and members were urged to study Deng's thoughts. Some eminent China-watchers shrugged and declared that this was not *really* an unusual or even especially brutal crackdown. Only a few thousand had been killed, and China's billion people were used to living under a regime of fear.

Television shots of the public massacre in the heart of the Chinese empire had made horror-movie pictures, transmitted by television satellite into hundreds of millions of living rooms round the world. But in most places for most people the pictures presented a distant struggle, cinema-screen scenes of a faraway land, grim but with few further implications for their personal lives. One place was different: in the tiny British crown colony of Hong Kong nearly six million people watched the pictures of massacre in horror and with deep personal loathing.

Hong Kong *is* different. The majority of Hong Kong inhabitants are themselves Chinese. Hong Kong is physically part of China. Almost half of its people fled from China's Communist regime and most of the rest are children of such refugees. Hong Kong at the moment is a British colony with a very different, unabashedly capitalist, way of life and a much higher standard of living than that in mainland China. Yet Hong Kong really is a slice of China in western disguise. And on the stroke of midnight, as 30 June passes into 1 July 1997, Britain has promised to give back the whole of Hong Kong to Communist China.

For the Hong Kong masses, the protests in China were a signal for unexpected political awakening. Previously any gathering of 500 people to discuss a political issue in the colony was a monster-sized rally. Liberals like Martin Lee Chu-ming QC tried to awaken interest in China's plans for ruling Hong Kong and to denounce their shortcomings, largely in vain. Yet even before the People's Liberation Army had begun shedding blood, Hong Kong Chinese had woken up to their Chinese inheritance. The declaration of martial law brought unprecedented protests in the British colony too. The Tian'anmen Square massacre sent the whole colony into mourning.

To be sure, there was an element of self-interest, a fearful growing realization that in 1997 Hong Kong would be part of this China; but there was also a popular surge of feeling for the young Chinese on the mainland who had dared to speak up for basic rights supposedly guaranteed in China's constitution. Up to a million Hong Kong people put aside their Sunday pastimes and took to the streets, taking over the whole of the Hong Kong centre, forming a massive petition and prayer of protest. What was the more remarkable was that one of the marches was in the middle of a typhoon with the Number 8 signal up, meaning 'batten down all hatches and stay indoors'. When the news of the deaths came, Hong Kong people demonstrated in grief, wearing black armbands or dressed in black and white, Chinese mourning colours. The Cenotaph on a small green patch in the very centre of Hong Kong was swathed in floral tributes and black flags to the Chinese martyrs for freedom. In front was placed a banner just like a Chinese flag, but it was black with white stars.

A general strike was called. The stock exchange did not close its doors for fear of what the rest of the world might think (the colony's reputation having been irrevocably damaged when it closed its stock market for four days during the October 1987 crash), but instead, stockbrokers joined 20,000 other financial colleagues in a lunchtime demonstration. They had extra reason for mourning as the stock market dropped 25 per cent. More impressive, according to veteran China-watcher Jesuit Father Laszlo Ladany, was that the Christians and liberals marched shoulder to shoulder with Hong Kong's influential pro-Communist trade union workers. Pro-Communist newspapers denounced China's action. Employees at Peking's own Bank of China fixed a banner from their headquarters window apologizing for the Chinese crackdown. Leaders of Chinese enterprises in Hong Kong placed newspaper advertisements condemning the violence. United unified Hong Kong, Right and Left, Catholic and Communist, all protested against Peking's action.

The old men in Zhongnanhai were unmoved. Indeed the Chinese propaganda machine turned threateningly against Hong Kong. State television described Hong Kong as a 'hostile foreign force' for providing money to Peking students. Twice in three days the Peking official media singled out Hong Kong for backing 'unlawful activities' aimed at subverting the Chinese government and toppling its system. According to Ladany 'there were also suggestions from Chinese hardliners that the whole protest movement was a Hong Kong-inspired plot'. If not Hong Kong on its own, the hardliners accused, then the colony was doing it with the support of the United States. China's state television declared that Hong Kong and the USA had 'exploited the patriotic sentiment of the students to create turmoil'.

The question after the bloodshed and turmoil was obvious enough. Could Britain go ahead and hand over Hong Kong to China's not-so-tender mercies in 1997? The initial reaction from London was that the promise to hand over Hong Kong was part of a sacred treaty and could not be overturned. The British government was quick to point out that Peking had promised in the agreement that the colony would not be absorbed into China, but would be permitted to maintain its autonomous existence for at least fifty years after 1997 as a special administrative region under Chinese sovereignty, and was specifically allowed – indeed commanded – to maintain its capitalist way of life.

Several days after the massacre an up-and-coming member of the government, William Waldegrave, Minister of State at the Foreign Office, expressed his hand-wringing faith in China. The *Independent* newspaper reported (8 June 1989):

> Mr Waldegrave suggested that the need to show trust towards Peking imposed a constraint on Britain's response to events in China and their implications for the colony. 'Throughout the darkest days in China of the Cultural Revolution, when there was slaughter going on, they stuck to treaties,' said Mr Waldegrave. 'China could at any time during the last how many years, have simply invaded Hong Kong, and we could not have resisted. There is something deep in the Chinese state which says treaties should be kept.'

Hong Kong pleas to the government of Margaret Thatcher were greeted with little more than sympathy and cups of tea with British leaders in 10 Downing Street, London, or Government House, Hong Kong. If Britain would not go back or renegotiate the Sino-British agreement then Hong Kong Chinese demanded the right to live in Britain. From the very top of society to the ordinary people came a united plea for a safe refuge. Dame Lydia Dunn, a leading businesswoman and senior member of the executive council (equivalent to a cabinet), questioned the morality of handing over 'British citizens to a regime that did not hesitate to use its tanks and forces on its own people'. And a young girl student spoke for the majority when she pleaded that 'it is immoral to hand over Hong Kong to a murderer'.

Thatcher said 'No'. In the House of Commons she declared that 'it would not be right to suggest that [Chinese entitled to Hong Kong British passports] should automatically have the right of abode here'. Foreign Secretary Sir Geoffrey Howe repeated the message on a visit to Hong Kong, though he did admit that if he were in the position of the Hong Kong Chinese he too would be seeking to emigrate. The best that Britain would promise was that it would look at introducing a more democratic system of government in Hong Kong and press Peking to live up to its promise to allow Hong Kong a separate way of life without interference from the Communist mainland.

Hong Kong in 1989 was a remarkable and indeed unique city, international, rich, almost as wealthy in per capita terms as Britain itself, but with a strangely paternal and colonial system of government. Hong Kong's way of life was in stark, and sometimes mocking, contrast to that in the giant People's Republic, with a freedom and tolerance unknown across the border. Without the peculiar historical legacy of its British colonial past, the city should have been looking forward to its greatest years of prosperity, harmony and happiness. Instead it was living on the edge of fear. Even before the Communist crackdown in Peking, there had been an exodus of mobile Hong Kong middle classes, anxious not to be ruled by Communists directly or indirectly. Lawyer Martin Lee said that entrusting

Hong Kong to China would be like handing over 5.5 million Jews to Germany after the Second World War. In Tian'anmen Square China's troops had also slaughtered six million hopes. But London and Peking seemed determined to press on.

What *is* Hong Kong? How did it come to be in this position, and what are its prospects for the future?

2 A Very Chinese International City

From more than a hundred miles out it is visible, a shining, beckoning jewel on a dark and distant shore. On some clear summer nights you can see its lights from the air two hundred miles away. This is little short of amazing, a modern-day miracle of magic, like seeing the lights of Liverpool or Paris from London, or seeing Washington DC from New York. As the pilot takes the aircraft lower and closer, attracted by the lights as a moth to the flame, it becomes clear that it *is* a dark and inhospitable shore. The lights come in highly concentrated patches. Between them are gloomy stretches of water and high granite hills, steep and precarious enough to defy all but the most ingenious and inventive of twentieth-century builders. Down, down . . . the aircraft roars as the captain rumbles the flaps out and uses the spoilers to regulate the speed and angle of descent. It's quite usual to jolt against wisps of cloud, even in relatively clear skies, so that the whole experience is like some badly coordinated dream: lights appear and are promptly swallowed by dark cloud. Down, down, the aircraft goes and the dream accelerates. Islands appear and just as quickly disappear; an incongruous navy of boats comes into view, huge tankers and ocean liners, majestic mistresses of the ocean, down to small junks tossed about by every wave; skyscrapers seem perched impossibly on the edges of hillsides (or is it a Cubist painting?); then more clouds snatch away the sights before you can realize that they are real. Then suddenly the aircraft starts to make a steep right-handed turn and the hills and skyscrapers and lights are marching in a rush to meet its outstretched wingtip. Is this the rude ending of a dream before waking, or is it a real-life emergency?

'No', says Captain Martin Willing, a senior Boeing 747 pilot with Cathay Pacific Airways, 'This is quite normal.' At every other sophisticated modern airport in the world the instrument landing system (ILS) leads the pilot to a safe landing, straight on to the runway. But here, things are so cramped that the ILS is guiding the pilot not to the runway but to a painting on a nearly-vertical hillside. This is hardly a masterpiece, just a huge square divided into big red and white checks, but it is a life-saver. When he sees the chequerboard from a minimum height of 675 feet, the pilot has to take his aircraft in a sharp 47.2 degree turn to starboard (the right-hand side), and then he will be able to achieve the runway safely less than a minute later. So down the aircraft roars in one of the most exciting yet scary landings in the world. The kaleidoscopic dream is speeded up for an exhilarating final 45–55 seconds. On the starboard side skyscrapers seem to float up right out of the sea. One of them is topped by the neon advertising sign which consists of the word 'CITIZEN' and then some Chinese characters, totalling 328 feet, or 100 feet longer than a jumbo jet, and made from 3.5 miles of glass tubing. You hardly have a chance to read it. On the port side (the left) the view isn't quite so spectacular, mainly because the aircraft is still turning and the passenger there is peering over the hilltops at blocks of flats regimented like neat soldiers on a route-march across the country.

By the time the craft begins to straighten up, it seems to be doing a dance with death. A whole honeycomb city appears: washing on a line almost waiting to be picked up by the wingtip; a double-decker bus below so close it looks like the small prey of this hungry eagle: for a millisecond you have a grandstand view of a basketball game; traffic, buildings, people whizz past the window almost close enough to say 'hello'. Then the aircraft lands. The thrills are not quite over. The pilot opens the throttle sharply in reverse, to avoid joining the ocean liners and small boats in the water. WELCOME TO HONG

KONG (Heung Gong in the local Cantonese, or 'Fragrant Harbour' – and immediately you notice the effluent stench of the Kai Tak nullah, an open drain alongside the runway). The crazy, jumbled-up images of the final minutes of the flight, the dazzling blur of lights, water, ships, islands, hills, buildings that seem to defy gravity, are only part of the mixture that is Hong Kong, one of the most international and probably the most exciting city in the world.

Physically, you wouldn't expect to find a place like Hong Kong located where it is, still less to discover a great modern metropolis. It is an awkward size and shape, naturally carbuncled with hills that mean that nothing is ever smooth. Like Caesar's Gaul it is divided into three parts: hilly Hong Kong island, acquired from China in 1841; the tiny 11-square-kilometre tip of the Kowloon peninsula, taken in 1861; and the rather more sprawling 'New Territories' leased from China for ninety-nine years in 1898. But in all a mere 1,070 square kilometres.

For most of its 150-year history, Hong Kong has been defying doomsayers who claim that it shouldn't exist and hasn't any future. One of the most famous and earliest remarks was that of the then British Foreign Secretary, Lord Palmerston, who, on hearing that Captain Charles Elliot RN had secured Hong Kong for Britain, derided it as 'a barren Island with hardly a House upon it' and forthwith dismissed Elliot. An unnamed correspondent for *The Times* (London) newspaper, writing in the edition of 13 April 1841, was long-winded but equally scathing, saying of Hong Kong:

> It is one of a group of islands about 35 miles from Macao; it is formed of granite rock, with scarcely a vestage [*sic*] of vegetation, except for a few spots used as garden by the poor fishermen who inhabit it. It has one recommendation – that of beautiful water, from a fall of some extent. It is surrounded by islands and mud banks in many of the approaches. The bay, or, as some call it, the harbour, is by

no means large, and is open to the heavy seas thrown in by the south west winds, when the anchorage is extremely dangerous. The whole island is not more than 6 or 7 miles in length, and about 2 in breadth (although I perceive *The Globe* with its usual regard to truth, makes it 14), nor a building of any description, except the hovels I have mentioned.

If our trade in future is to be confined to this miserable island, the loss by accident to laden boats, during a voyage of 120 or 130 miles from Canton, through a difficult and dangerous navigation, will be very great. A worse situation could not have been selected for trade, and that is the reason why the Chinese have so readily ceded it. It may be considered as a banishment from the more civilised parts of the empire by the Chinese authorities, who have insulted, insulted and tricked and cajoled us.

Physically, Hong Kong *is* an unlikely place for any settlement to thrive. The harbour is deep and sheltered for much of the year, but the territory is still exposed to typhoons which can whip winds of hurricane force (sustained speeds at least of 118 km per hour and gusts of 220 km an hour or more). Such winds are capable of uprooting trees, besides dumping torrential rains. The granite hills begin to rise almost from sea level, making building difficult. Gouging out of the hillside and levelling off the land is an expensive process. So today on Hong Kong island the main settlements follow the narrow coastal corridors, which have been expanded by reclamation from the sea. On the flatter Kowloon peninsula, almost every square millimetre of ground is multi-occupied. The acres of rolling farmland that used to distinguish the New Territories have long gone. Small pig farms and vegetable gardens are these days the mainstay of farming there. Eight new towns with spick and span regiments of tall flats and factories have gobbled up much of the wide open space. Some of Hong Kong's 235 outlying islands do offer ruggedness if not genuine wilderness. There are still some secret spots where it is possible to hide from the rest of the world, but they are few and the hustling world is never far away. Even from the sanctuary of the Mai Po marshes near the border with China the sparkling skyscraper towers of the new towns are visible.

Kai Tak airport itself is the first lesson in Hong Kong's disadvantages and in the ingenuity used in overcoming them. It is built on reclaimed land and has a narrow finger of runway jutting into the sea. The approach may be exciting for passengers, but it is decidedly uncomfortable for residents living crowded cheek-by-jowl under the screaming jets' approach. Watch from the ground, and it does look as if the hungry bird of prey will seize at least a washing line and perhaps a bus and a couple of cars as well as it swoops towards land. After 21.00 hours (9 pm) pilots are advised not to use runway 13, landing over congested Kowloon City, but to fly the opposite way through the Lei Yue Mun gap. That flight path is more straightforward and provides picturesque views between islands and through the shipping in the harbour approaches. But it is often more dangerous because of the prevailing winds and tricky thermals. A new airport on one of the outer islands would be one of *the world's* most expensive building projects.

Hong Kong's physical unattractiveness is made worse by the climate. Winters are admittedly mild, with the temperature rarely dropping below 8 degrees Centigrade in the urban areas. Whenever there are reports of frost forming on higher ground, long queues of vehicles process towards the spot, with eager occupants anxious to see and touch this strange phenomenon. But damp, rheumatic springs are followed by hot and sweaty summers in which the temperature is a relentless 32 to 34 degrees (more than 90 degrees Fahrenheit) and humidity levels are commonly above 90 per cent. Shoes or clothes left unattended collect mildew quickly. Victoria Peak, the pinnacle of Hong Kong society, is frequently covered by muggy clouds, so that inhabitants have to run air-conditioners and dehumidifiers round the clock to be comfortable. High rainfall is another feature of Hong Kong summers. Some of it is brought by the typhoons sweeping in from the sea, which can easily shut Hong Kong down for a day or more and then dump several hundred millimetres of rain in their wake to impede the business of getting back to normal.

On top of all this, there is a shortage of natural resources. The 1,070 square kilometres (404 square miles) of the Hong Kong territory offer virtually no minerals, no forests, no obvious resources to tap, apart from the harbour. Ironically, in spite of the drenching rain and the sea, there isn't enough drinking water.

For all these handicaps and vile attributes, Hong Kong today is a thriving metropolis of about 5.8 million people. The population would undoubtedly have topped 7 or perhaps 10 million but for the fact that the government long ago closed the doors to new arrivals. The overall density of population is 5,154 per square kilometre (13,614 per square mile), virtually the highest in the world. The population density of Singapore, for example, is 4,115 per square kilometre (10,870 per square mile) and that of supposedly crowded Western Europe drops to about 400 per square kilometre (1,000 per square mile). Some parts of urban Kowloon in Hong Kong are the most congested places on earth. Mong Kok used to have the doubtful privilege, but now the honour belongs to nearby Sham Shui Po, 165,445 people per square kilometre. That's not counting the infamous Walled City (see chapter 11), the honeycomb city on the final approach to Kai Tak, where 33,000 inhabitants were crammed together at a density of more than a million per square kilometre until the government began to rehouse them.

Nor is Hong Kong some poor third world country where people are starving on the street. Indeed, going by per capita figures, Hong Kong by 1990 is leaping towards the upper ranks of the so-called developed or industrialized countries. Annual income is about US$10,000 per person, placing the territory ahead of the poorer countries of Europe, such as Spain (per capita income $5,000 in the mid-1980s) and Ireland. Successive financial secretaries have boasted that given normal progress –

by normal Hong Kong standards that is – the territory will pass the UK in just two years' time. Per capita income in the UK is about US$11,000 a head. Hong Kong long ago surpassed China and India. The world's two biggest countries are straining to raise their per capita incomes to a mere $400 a year. One of the mysteries and at the same time one of the achievements of the twentieth century is how Hong Kong came to achieve this high standard of living with such paucity of resources.

The only resource Hong Kong has in abundance is its people, hard-working, hungry to improve themselves and become rich. This is what has really driven Hong Kong over the past forty years. Even a cursory look around the territory demonstrates that the local Chinese, who make up 98 per cent of the total population, have virtually no hangups when it comes to making money. The proliferation of hawkers on every main shopping street shows this. Many of them stand warily behind unlicensed carts and quickly dart away whenever they spot a policeman coming their way. They offer anything and everything from cooked local foods and toy trinkets like yo-yos that light up to leather belts for HK$25 (£2), silk ties for HK$10 or 'designer' sports shirts with famous brand labels that quickly come ungummed for HK$20.

In industry and commerce, many entrepreneurs literally started with nothing and became multi-millionaires in a decade or so. The most famous is probably Li Ka-shing, who left school at 13, and at 22 started his own factory making plastic goods; today, he's king of the Hong Kong property scene and has the world as his oyster. The classic start involved setting up a factory, perhaps in his or her own home, making whatever was the latest fad for export. One year in the 1960s it seemed as if all Hong Kong's factories were making wigs; the next they switched *en masse* to plastic flowers, and the next year to making toys. Some things never change. A vast majority of Hong Kong's almost 50,000 manufacturing establishments employ ten or fewer workers. It is still the dream of every young Chinese to have his own business, not to work for someone else.

In parentheses, this fierce independence causes problems as

businesses grow beyond a certain size and need many managers who can no longer be ordered around autocratically as the old unlettered tycoons expect to do. It also remains to be seen whether the younger generation of entrepreneurs' sons, increasingly educated at Harvard, Yale, Berkeley or Massachusetts Institute of Technology, will be able to put their business school training into practice and actually delegate responsibility in a large modern company as their fathers never could; whether their modern education will have squashed their flair and entrepreneurial vision; and indeed whether they will be able to get on with their fathers, used to doing sums on the backs of envelopes and taking 'seat of the pants' decisions.

Almost every bright young man still cherishes the old dreams of making his own fortune. A young quality control manager in a watch factory, a man with a degree from a western university, clearly did. As soon as he had saved enough capital, he said, he would leave his existing employer and go off and set up his own factory. 'That has always been my dream – to prove that I can do it.'

An important ingredient underpinning the entrepreneurial success of Hong Kong is a unique system of government. Businessmen don't have to worry about sudden political changes. That is because the place has an unusual colonial government, paternal even by the standards of modern colonies. Limited elections only came recently and there are no politics nor political parties. Foreigners often talk of Hong Kong's '*laissez-faire* economy' and sometimes refer to the colony as a tax haven, but such assertions cause government officials to bubble with indignation. They point out, quite correctly, that the government doesn't just allow Hong Kong to rule itself. The authorities have come to play an important part in certain sections of economic and social life.

By the late 1980s half of the population lived in government-owned flats. On average a new housing unit is opened every 7.5 minutes of the working day. Increasingly the government has enforced a battery of health and safety regulations, as well as laws regulating the number of hours that can be worked to ensure that workers get enough leisure time. One leading industrialist claims that it is easier to employ workers just across the border in China 'because they don't have as many controls and we can get enough hours of overtime out of them. In Hong Kong it's getting very difficult to meet crucial Christmas shipments because of restrictions on overtime working,' he grumbles. The government could certainly do more. Pollution laws are still slack and the Hong Kong environment has been damaged, probably irreparably.

What the government has set out to do is to lay down the basic infrastructure and provide conditions in which business can flourish. From the start, the government took the view that it wasn't the business of civil servants to try to be involved in business. For a time immediately after the war the government *was* involved in directing exports and imports and actively controlling large chunks of the economy. Eric Himsworth, in charge of trade immediately after the Second World War, said it was a conscious decision for the government to get out of business as quickly as possible and leave it to private enterprise.

Most utilities such as transport, power, telecommunications and communications are supplied by the private sector, regulated by the government – but not water supplies nor the airport, which are still run by the public sector. Apart from seeing that the basic infrastructural services are provided, the government makes it relatively easy for companies to set up. It can be done in less than a morning. Port facilities are superb and customs quick and simple so that goods can move in and out of Hong Kong speedily, apart from the strictly controlled substances like narcotics and firearms. Tax rates are deliberately low, on the principle that budding entrepreneurs know best how to spend their own money and should make their own mistakes.

A vital factor underpinning the whole system is the British legal tradition of open courts and common law. This means that citizens are free to go about their business with a minimum of government interference, and need not fear the long arm of the law descending on them merely because they have offended some government dignitary. This freedom certainly marks Hong Kong out from neighbouring China, where changes of state policy have been frequent, each time some new slogan or 'ism' has attracted the rulers. It also means that Hong Kong is free from the peculiar favouritism that infects many communist states, where children of leading figures can get important jobs or favours, while enemies can quickly be stripped of their wealth or privilege. Indeed it is a major break with Chinese tradition that in Hong Kong *guanxi* (connections), commonly practised in China, are not an exclusive recipe for success.

All this together provides a natural environment encouraging competition and good service. D. K. Patel, a senior manager of the Hongkong and Shanghai Banking Corporation, says that Hong Kong is one of the few places in the world where a matter of weeks after an order has been placed, say for shirts or dresses, they can be ready on the racks in the shops abroad. 'Everything moves like clockwork in Hong Kong,' he says. 'When the goods are finished, usually they are packed neatly under polythene and labelled according to the store's own requirements – so that they can actually be wheeled on racks out of the delivery van and straight through the shop's doors for immediate sale.' He contrasts this with the environment in many other neighbouring countries. 'Hong Kong no longer offers cheap goods produced by cheap labour, but American or European stores that pin their faith just in cheap labour find that that's not enough. It's no good having garments sitting partially completed in a foreign country while the buttons or the zippers are held up by customs waiting for forms to be completed properly or for duty to be paid.' Such hiccups do not occur in Hong Kong.

This environment favourable to business has propelled tiny Hong Kong into the top twelve trading powers in the world and spawned a host of industries in which Hong Kong leads the world. It is the world's largest exporter of clothing. It is also the leader in watch production, churning out 270 million pieces a year.

Hong Kong is not the world's largest toy producer, but it is the largest exporter. The territory also leads in some less well-known products including exports of candles and of artificial plastic firewood! It is the busiest container port in the world.

The zest for money-making is not limited to manufacturing industry. Increasingly, Hong Kong is turning out billionaires whose fortunes have been made in service sectors, such as property, tourism, banking and finance. Hong Kong sometimes boasts it is 'the world's third largest financial centre (after London and New York)'. In terms of stock market activity, the size of local banking institutions or the weight of money in the market, Hong Kong is puny compared to Tokyo. The Tokyo stock market is the biggest in the world and Japanese banks are also the world's giants. Where Hong Kong does score is in the number and variety of the financial institutions that have opened offices in the territory. Altogether there are about 500 of them, including 165 licensed banks (with more than 1,000 offices), 250 registered deposit-taking companies, more than 30 licensed deposit-taking companies (equivalent to merchant banks), more than 100 fund management companies and almost 900 stockbroking firms, plus lawyers, accountants, insurance agents and other financial concerns. All these activities together boost Hong Kong's claims to be an *international* centre, while Tokyo is a *Japanese* centre.

Demand for internationally accepted excellent facilities has produced other assets, including some of the best hotels in the world, supreme telecommunications and superb air links, so that Hong Kong vies with Sinagpore to be the best communications centre in the Asia-Pacific region. In surveys by such magazines as *Institutional Investor* Hong Kong regularly has at least three hotels in the world's top ten, the Oriental Mandarin right in the centre of Hong Kong island, the Regent, a new glass palace on the Kowloon waterfront, and the old favourite, the Peninsula. Critics charge that such hotels are expensive and that the people who do the surveys are not representative, but those polled are people who demand the best. Hong Kong's hotels are judged by whether they meet the very highest standards of the world, and they have succeeded. But there are also hundreds of cheaper establishments, some offering beds for only a few dollars a night.

Excellence feeds upon itself. Good hotels have encouraged other services, such as food and wine, that are among the best in Asia, and offer further support to the growing tourism industry. Hong Kong now receives nearly six million visitors a year and is able to play upon its reputation as an exotic city on the doorstep of China, a capitalist paradise on the edge of the world's largest communist state, a living, mysterious city of the Orient, a tax-free shoppers' paradise and a crossroads between east and west.

Any visitor is spoilt for choice. Almost everything he or she wants is concentrated within two areas of about a square mile each – on Hong Kong island and, just across the water, on the overcrowded neon tip of the Kowloon peninsula. Hong Kong Central District is the more elite of the two. The new buildings of the Landmark complex and its neighbours house classy upmarket shops selling brand-name goods that bring a sparkle into the eyes of any fashion-conscious international visitor. Nathan Road, the central spine of Kowloon, known more popularly as 'The Golden Mile', is a hotch-potch, but typical of Hong Kong's whirling kaleidoscope. Here the classy shops sit cheek-by-jowl with garish boutiques piled high with merchandise, and with the barrows of street hawkers whose eyes dart from the customers to the next corner to check there is no policeman on the prowl. Hong Kong must be one of the few places in the world where real Gucci, fake Gucci and plastic Gucci goods sit side by side. Some hawkers are fly rip-off merchants. But on other barrows are piles of factory overruns, goods with genuine designer-labels going for a fraction of their normal export price because they have some slight fault, or – if you're really lucky – simply because the shipment missed the export boat. Hong Kong seems to sparkle with gold or diamond jewellery shops, while every other store seems filled with electronic goods, cameras, stereo equipment, televisions, radios and watches.

For clothes, there are literally thousands of shops, though the days of Hong Kong's twenty-four-hour made-to-measure suits are over, and anyone who looks for one must be prepared to see it fall off his back after a few wearings. However, Hong Kong still sometimes tries to set records. The lack of local sheep means that it can't totally compete with Australia: in Melbourne in 1982 a group of 65 people made a full three-piece suit in 1 hour 34 minutes 33.42 seconds; and that included everything from shearing the wool off the sheep's back, carding, spinning and weaving it, cutting and finally stitching the suit. But a Hong Kong tailor did recently run close with a suit made to measure from a bolt of cloth in just over an hour.

One of the most remarkable establishments is a small shop in an arcade off Nathan Road. In its windows it displays smiling pictures of Britain's Duke of Kent, Australian Prime Minister Bob Hawke, former US Secretary of state Henry Kissinger and military men with generals' red tabs. It boasts name-cards and letters from well-known figures in the world of politics, entertainment and journalism, including notes from former British Prime Minister Edward Heath, from the office of the Prince of Wales, from former British Foreign Secretary and Nato Secretary-General Lord Carrington, and from Mr Denis Thatcher, all offering thanks for suits, blazers or shirts made for them. But the shop hardly looks like a high-class tailoring establishment; it seems more like the set for some trouser-dropping farce; the Indian proprietor rushes to offer a bottle of beer while customers keep popping out from behind the makeshift curtains that form fitting rooms. The shop is known as 'Sam's Tailor' and the suits bear the proud motto 'Her Majesty's Forces' Tailors'. It is difficult to identify precisely who Sam is, since several men answer to that name, the original Sam from Bombay and his sons who now effectively run the business. None of them will disclose his full name. The business is run by Indians but the tailors are Chinese. Judging by the constant clamour of customers, Sam's is a roaring success. At about HK$1,500 (£115 or $190) for a two-piece suit, Sam is considerably cheaper than

London's Savile Row. The notables whose photographs and letters litter the windows and shelves in Sam's shop generally don't have to suffer the scrum of the shop. Sam will go to their hotels. He boasts that if a customer is satisfied, he can send repeat orders through the mail and new suits will be sewn and shipped anywhere in the world. Occasionally one of the Sams even goes to London to drum up business there. Sam is part of Hong Kong folklore, not least because, as a former army officer recalls, 'In the old days he was much more than a mere tailor. He was a sort of secondary banker to the young army and police officers. Not only would he cash a cheque for you, but if you were short of cash, he'd advance $200 for you until pay-day.'

Young subalterns now with field marshal's batons in their knapsacks have remained loyal to Sam. Bankers, perhaps because they spend most of their time on Hong Kong island, prefer to go to Man Hing Cheong in the Oriental Mandarin Hotel or to Baromon in Swire House, both more classy and expensive. Sam discreetly refuses to identify his rivals, saying: 'Choosing a tailor is rather like choosing a doctor – if you've got someone who you trust, stick to him.' As there are more than 7,000 custom tailors in Hong Kong, he's glad to have so many satisfied customers.

The shopping attractions of Hong Kong are legion and legendary, so much so that one British magazine sent a reporter over for a weekend to see whether he could recoup the cost of the fare by buying goods in Hong Kong more cheaply than at home. He made his task more difficult by living high on the hog, taking a chauffeur-driven Rolls-Royce from the airport, staying in the Peninsula Hotel and treating himself to champagne suppers. Even with these extra expenses he failed by a matter of less than US$100 to meet the cost of the trip in savings on the price of the goodies he bought. Back home of course he probably got clobbered by customs for a much larger sum; most countries retain stingy import restrictions that prevent a happy tourist from making the most of Hong Kong's bargains at one visit.

Hong Kong isn't merely a cheap shoppers' paradise. It is both Asia's market-place and the next-door-neighbour of big brother China, offering a rich selection of goods from all over Asia. Indian shopkeepers have encouraged sales of merchandise from the subcontinent. There are also shops specializing in Thai, Korean, Philippine and Indonesian goods. Hollywood Road shops offer pricey antiques from all over Asia. But the richest cornucopia comes from China itself. Peking has shown more merchant sense in Hong Kong than it has in its own country. In China, the state-owned and state-run department stores have a lot to learn about ideas that the customer comes first, and certainly about marketing. Peking's department stores are drab and uninteresting, especially to someone who has visited Hong Kong. But the Chinese Communist department stores in Hong Kong are chock-a-block with everything from patent medicines and special supposedly aphrodisiac potions made from animal penises to duck-down pillows, rich silks and Chinese artefacts, some of them rare and beautiful and others, regrettably, cheap and nasty modern copies of dazzling originals. One store even offers computer eye-tests and guarantees to produce new spectacles in an hour.

The attractions are not limited to shopping. Apart from the grander hotels the territory also has plenty of cheaper ones, ranging from the clean, cheap and respectable variety to flop-houses where rooms can be rented by the hour. One very respectable traveller arrived in Hong Kong late one evening in October, the busiest month for visitors. She found all the recognized hotels full; the eminently respectable and clean YWCA had just given its last bed. So, with some relief since it was nearly midnight, she was grateful to find a small hotel near Causeway Bay. It was so cheap that she stayed there a second night and wondered why the bill, rendered daily, was much more expensive the second day than the first. Gradually light dawned: 'I realized that it was a Hong Kong love hotel, where men would bring their girls for a few hours of pleasure. Charges were by the hour. I then understood why I had been greeted with such funny looks on my arrival: they were not used to seeing single women arriving alone.' There are plenty of hotels offering rooms by the hour and not all their clients are illicit lovers. Some married Hong Kong Chinese couples use Kowloon love-nests to seek a few hours of peace and quiet from their over-crowded homes, children and in-laws.

Hong Kong still has its fair share of red light activities. For those who can read Chinese characters, the delights on offer are freely advertised, sometimes poetically, but leaving no doubt for those seeking the pleasures of the flesh. It is impossible to walk far in Tsim Sha Tsui off Nathan Road without seeing photographs displaying acres of naked female flesh and being accosted by touts and hustlers on the doorsteps urging entry to the bright light shows. Some bars have even achieved fame and a sort of respectability. The 'Bottoms Up' bar in Tsim Sha Tsui, run by a former Windmill girl, Pat Sephton, has topless bar girls and figured fleetingly in a James Bond film *The Man with the Golden Gun*. In 1986 it celebrated its tenth birthday, quite a record for Hong Kong where such establishments readily change hands. Other bars with fancy names like Pussycat Bar, Hot Lips, leave little doubt about how they want to entice customers.

But there's always the old warning to the customer: 'Beware'. It applies particularly to the bars. Sitting close to a hostess in a darkened bar doesn't always come cheap. Letters frequently appear in the Hong Kong press filled with the moans of visiting tourists who have paid US$100 for a single tepid drink of beer and not got more than a few words of broken English from their 'middle-aged' painted companions in return.

Shopping in Hong Kong also has its perils, sometimes literally. One visiting tourist caused a camera-shop owner to go to the trouble of fetching some goods from the shelf. Having examined them the tourist asked the price and then, after bargaining, decided not to buy. This didn't please the shopkeeper one bit and he took decisive action. He jumped across the counter and thrust a ball point pen up the nose of the erstwhile, might-have-been valued customer. Violent assaults like this don't happen too often. But the customer is quite right to take every precaution and to double-check at every point of the transaction to make sure the goods are as good as promised, have all the accessories, are the latest models and offer a worldwide and not merely a local guarantee.

Another attraction of Hong Kong is the splendid variety of its restaurants, from the elegant candle-lit *haute cuisine* dining-rooms in the top hotels right down to scruffy-looking backstreet café tables. Altogether Hong Kong has about 19,000 restaurants and cafés, giving it probably the highest ratio of restaurants per capita of any city in the world. Such dedication is not completely surprising, considering the central role of food in Chinese life. When you greet someone in Cantonese, you don't say 'How are you?', but 'Have you eaten?'. Eating places include a restaurant in the New World Centre complex which can seat 7,000 people at a time and claims to be the biggest in the world. Standard cuisine is the local Cantonese cooking, but virtually every other variety of food in the world is available in Hong Kong, from regional Chinese specialities like Pekinese, Shanghainese, Mongolian, Chiu Chow and Sichuan to Indian, Indonesian, Korean, Malaysian, Philippine, Thai, Vietnamese and western food of all kinds, including McDonalds and other popular American fast foods. In 1989 plans were announced for a traditional British fish and chip shop. The Chinese cooking in Hong Kong may be unlike that available in Chinese restaurants and takeaways in Australia, Europe or the USA. Tourists from countries accustomed to Chinese restaurants that have adopted and adapted to local ways sometimes grumble that Hong Kong restaurants don't serve the extra side-orders of chips or fortune cookies available back home. Prices range from less than US$4 a head for filling Cantonese dim sum (literally tit-bits) lunch in an unpretentious café to hundreds of US dollars a head at a western-style meal, depending on the fineness of the wine. Other treats available in Hong Kong include Shanghainese hairy crabs that are only 'in season' for a few weeks in autumn: locals rave over them. But Hong Kong restaurants also offer a great trade in (to a westerner) repulsive items such as snake, dog, lizard, live baby mice – which are said to be good for ulcers – and bear's paw. Some locals also boast that they like (the illegal) monkey's brains, best taken from the skull of a freshly slaughtered animal. Some of these treats are illegal, but that doesn't stop them being available to the connoisseurs prepared to pay the price of what – to them – are delicacies. This exotica serves as a reminder that the Hong Kong the tourists commonly look for is by no means the whole picture. Most visitors will not share Chinese tastes in exotic foods, but Hong Kong offers more than enough to do that is exciting and new. A list of a hundred favourite things would not be exhaustive though it would undoubtedly be exhausting.

It would include a trip on the Peak Tram, the funicular railway built in 1888 that takes passengers up to Victoria Peak (1,805 feet, 554 metres above sea level) affording a splendid panoramic view, rain or mist permitting, of the whole of Hong Kong, stretching down to the harbour and airport and the hills of China beyond Kowloon. Photographs of Hong Kong taken from the Peak over the years provide the best evidence of how the colony has changed and grown from a small, cosy British colonial outpost to a frenetic, throbbing modern metropolis. The basic operation of the Peak Tram has not changed since its foundation, but the system was modernized in 1989 to carry more passengers. It operates by means of 5,000-foot steel cables which are wound on drums. The opening of the tramway allowed the vertical spread of Hong Kong and saw the start of house-building in the cooler Peak area, previously virtually inaccessible since the only way to reach it was on foot or in sedan chairs.

At lower levels, two of the delights of Hong Kong are the trams and the 'Star' Ferry, which offers a crossing between Hong Kong island and Kowloon. The trams, which operate only on Hong Kong island, follow the north shoreline. For HK60 cents (US8 cents) these double-deckers have seats for 48 passengers, but actually carry three times as many at rush hour. From the upper deck the tram offers the best possible view of *all* the sights, tourist spots and the crowded ordinary living conditions of urban Hong Kong. Until 1980, when the Mass Transit Railway was opened, the 'Star' Ferry offered the main means of transport between Hong Kong and Kowloon. These days the underground railway has snatched away many of the passengers, especially those in a hurry, but the 'Star' Ferry still carries more than 100,000 passengers a day on the 1.5 km trip across the harbour, taking about eight minutes. The cost in 1989 was HK$1 on the first class upper deck and 60 cents on the second class lower deck, more than fives times cheaper than the Mass Transit Railway. It is called the 'Star' ferry because the ten 33.5-metre-long green and white 'double-ended' vessels (meaning they can be steered from two separate wheelhouses one at each end) all have the word 'Star' in their names, which include *Morning* and *Evening Star*, *Shining Star* and *Celestial Star*. The 'Star' Ferry Company was started on 1 May 1898 when it bought the Kowloon Ferry Company from a self-made Indian businessman, Zorabjee Nowrajee, who had originally come from Bombay as a cook.

Sometimes it seems as if Hong Kong exists only to claim its own chapter in the *Guinness Book of Records*. The colony revels in activities which are the biggest or best in the world. The Ocean Park claims it is the world's largest oceanarium, including a huge marine mammal theatre seating 4,000 people, and a pool capable of taking killer whales. The aquarium at Ocean Park is the biggest in the world, containing two million litres of seawater. Attractions also include an amusement park with a huge rollercoaster, the 'Dragon', two and a half minutes of fun at 50 miles an hour. The park also boasts the world's longest escalator ride, 225 metres long, able to take 4,000 passengers an hour each way on a trip up the hillside with its 30-degree incline.

For cinema buffs Hong Kong has much to offer. It has one of the biggest film industries in the world, producing 130 films a year to win the reputation of 'Hollywood of the Far East'. Sir Run Run Shaw, now in his eighties, is still its dominating mogul as film-maker and cinema-owner. Hong Kong films have gained popularity not only in South East Asia, but also in the Chinese communities of the USA and Europe. Shaw's films have been criticized for being all in the same sort of mould, not surprising since he once expressed the grandfatherly view that 'the cinema offers air-conditioned darkness'. He has few pretensions to art. Asked what was his best film, Shaw replied 'the ones that made the most money'. In the early 1970s Bruce Lee 'kick flick' kung-fu films won Hong Kong an international audience. Lately, new film-makers have arrived, including Raymond Chow, aiming at the mass market. A so-called New Wave consists of younger directors and producers with a social conscience. One of the most prominent is Ann Hui. Her *Boat People*, a film about the Vietnamese fleeing from the horrors of post-war Vietnam to overcrowded Hong Kong, caused a storm at the 1983 Cannes Film Festival, when it was first removed on the orders of the French government afraid for its relations with Hanoi, only to be smuggled in and shown as a *film surprise*.

One of the biggest occasions in Hong Kong is a day at the races. Some critics have even said that the race course in Hong Kong is the only place where Chinese and expatriates, rich and poor, all rub shoulders together. There are two courses, the old course at Happy Valley on Hong Kong island that dates back to the early days of the infant British settlement, and the new at Sha Tin, in the New Territories. Whereas Happy Valley is cramped and in the middle of the urban areas, Sha Tin is built on reclaimed land and is one of the most modern racing tracks in the world. Among its attractions is the giant screen in front of the grandstand that shows pictures of the horses as they flash round the other side of the track. The screen can also be used for providing immediate details of the state of the betting, the results, or urgent news from anywhere. The Happy Valley race course has room for 40,000 spectators at a time, and Sha Tin can accommodate 70,000 people. And the stands are always full. The reason is that the race course offers practically the only form of legalized betting in Hong Kong – apart from the Mark

Six lottery which is actually run by the Royal Hong Kong Jockey Club. (Hong Kong has no formal gambling casino, except for the stock market. Mahjong games for money go on all the time in spite of the ban on gambling: the click of the tiles can be heard in many parts of Hong Kong at afternoon parlour sessions played by grandmothers, and in the evenings by rich businessmen playing for big stakes. One pillar of the establishment, a prominent personality, claims that HK$100,000 or more a night changes hands at a single mahjong game.) On the race tracks the Hong Kong populace at large makes up for its deprivation. Apart from those actually present at the race course, tens of thousands more cluster round the numerous betting shops all over Hong Kong to hear how the race is going.

Together the Hong Kong people punt US$3,100 million a year on the horses, or about US$450 for every man, woman and child. This makes the Jockey Club's legal betting revenue probably the highest in the world. The territory has eighteen newspapers devoted exclusively to horse-racing news and another eighty have big sections on the sport. The betting system is backed by what Jockey Club officials claim is the world's most sophisticated racing computer system, often called upon to handle 1,500 bets a second. In the thirty minutes before a race, operators receive 30,000 calls from punters. Everyone claims to be a winner from the Jockey Club activities. More than 80 per cent of the takings go back to the lucky winners. The government takes a large slice in taxes of almost HK$3 billion a year, about 8 per cent of its total revenues. And the Jockey Club supports various charities to the tune of more than HK$220 million a year; it built Ocean Park and helps fund ballet, the Arts Festival, youth clubs and schools for the handicapped.

The oddity is that though the races are exciting and the followers are the keenest in the world, the quality of local horses is poor. An absence of local feedstock and the climate means that it's impossible to breed good horses locally. Any really top class horse would race away with the field. But the carefully engineered handicapping system ensures that this doesn't happen and that the races are exciting to the very finish.

The fanatical following of the race track provides yet more evidence that Hong Kong works and plays probably harder than any other place in the world – and all the time is trying to make money. In industry and exporting the place has a string of firsts, biggest, bests, tops in the world. In 1987 another record was chalked up when Hong Kong became the world's largest container terminal, surpassing Rotterdam, with New York a distant third. By 1990 Hong Kong will have the world's tallest bronze statue of Buddha atop Muk Yu Hill on Lantau island, 26.4 metres high on a plinth of 33.95 metres. In total the Buddha will be bigger than the 31-metre-tall statue of Christ overlooking Rio de Janeiro. Hong Kong claims it has more Rolls-Royce cars per kilometre of road than any other territory. In 1987 Hong Kong boasted the world's largest wall sign, a Marlboro Cowboy giant (advertising cigarettes) 80 feet tall by 40 feet wide. In spite of its small size Hong Kong has the fourth largest consumption of brandy in the world, almost 9 million bottles a year, and most of that is VSOP or expensive XO quality (at up to £50 a bottle); in per capita brandy consumption Hong Kong undoubtedly comes top of the world. A flick through the pages of the Hong Kong telephone book also reveals a city that would win prizes for ingenious names: there is a string of Cheerful companies, many Good Lucks as well as Good Joy, Good Friends and Good Hopes and some unique ones like Ping Pang Piano Factory, Tin Tin Motor Company, Real No Squeak Shoes, Right Time Construction Co., Smart Rich Co., Smooth Investment Co.

Hard work, the booming economy and trade, the open environment, the British colonial 'hands off' government, the rule of law, the widespread use of the (international) English language, its unique position on the edge of China but not part of it, have all turned Hong Kong into Asia's *international* city. Its only rival is Tokyo, but Tokyo, in spite of the vaster size of the Japanese economy, remains a narrow chauvinistic place. But this international reputation sits oddly: it's also important not to be fooled by Hong Kong. Under the western gloss it is a very

Chinese city. Westerners are welcome, but 98 per cent of the people are Chinese. Although the local citizens have embraced western-style capitalism, realizing that it is their passport to a more comfortable life, Hong Kong should not be seen as a western society. Deep down, traditional Chinese practices remain rooted in the heart of the society. Former Chief Secretary and Financial Secretary Sir Philip Haddon-Cave claims that Hong Kong has the only *living* evolving Chinese culture. In China itself the Communists have crushed the religious festivals and ceremonies that are an essential part of Chinese life. In Taiwan and Singapore big-brotherly governments have sanitized some of the practices. In Hong Kong tradition remains supreme. There are always ceremonies going on, sometimes quietly on street corners and unnoticed except by those who know what to look for.

The obvious external signs of Hong Kong's Chinese religious beliefs are the temples. Many of the most celebrated are not old. The Wong Tai Sin temple in the district of the same name was newly opened in 1973, replacing a fifty-year-old temple on the same site. At Joss House Bay it is claimed that various temples to Tin Hau have existed since 1266, but the current one is of recent origin. At the Tin Hau temple at Stanley a bell and drum used by a pirate to send messages to his fleet in the late 1700s sound the daily opening and closing, but the actual temple is much renovated. Regardless of the age of the buildings, the temples are deeply rooted in the community. There is always someone making offerings, and at the festival times – which are many – the places of worship are filled to overflowing. The oldest temple still standing in Central Hong Kong is the Man Mo temple on Hollywood Road, which goes back to the 1840s. The temple is dedicated to Man Cheong, god of literature and guardian of civil servants or mandarins, and to Kwan Kung (or Mo), the god of war. But there is a dark clutter of religious statues rarely seen in western churches or temples. Guarding the temple are brass symbols of the Eight Immortals, seven men and a woman, representing the different conditions of life: male, female, lord, peasant, age, youth, poverty and wealth. Symbolism is all-important. It also has two brass deer which symbolize longevity, and there's a shrine to Pao Kung, the god of justice, and an altar to Shing Wong, the city god.

An important activity in the Man Mo temple, as indeed in many temples, is going to have your fortune told. In the Man Mo temple you shake the sticks until a number comes up, and then go next door to the Litt Shing Kung (All Saints) temple to consult a soothsayer. The presiding goddess over this temple is Kwan Yum (or Kuan Yin), the Buddhist goddess of mercy, who is customarily supposed to save people from misery by giving them compassionate glances.

Other favourite Hong Kong gods are Tin Hau, possibly the most popular and colourful of all, as goddess of the sea; Wong Tai Sin, renowned for being generous with granting the wishes of his worshippers, notably, it is said, in racing tips and curing ill-health; Kwan Tai, god of war and source of righteousness; Hung Shing, god of the south seas and a weather prophet; and Tam Kung, a local child god reputedly able to heal the sick and control the weather. But there are many other gods and goddesses. The Chinese calendar is based on a twelve-year lunar cycle, with each year represented by a different animal. This is supposedly to commemorate a race among the animals to reach the Buddha. First to arrive was the Rat, followed by the Ox, Tiger, Rabbit (Hare), Dragon, Snake, Horse, Sheep (Goat), Monkey, Cock, Dog and Pig. But the year is additionally described according to the five elements. This means that there are sixty years altogether in a full cycle. The four-temple complex in Public Square Street in Kowloon and other temples display sixty small figures called Tai Sui or gods of the year. Parents bring tiny children to worship the god of their particular year. Altogether Hong Kong has several hundred Chinese temples, about half of which are Buddhist. Most of the rest are Taoist, but some, and indeed the most popular, are mixed or *miu*. If asked, Hong Kong people would probably say they are Buddhists, but many of them also pray in front of Taoist altars.

On festival occasions Taoist priests will dress in traditional red robes with black silk hats. Gods proliferate – earth god, city god, god of pregnant women, god of wealth . . .

Unlike in Christianity, there are few set patterns for Chinese religious worship. Certain events, most notably funerals, may be dictated by the priests of the temple, but for the most part worshippers come and go, offering incense and prayers as they feel moved. The Chinese festivals are popular and celebrated with great joy. Barbara E. Ward notes 'Hardly a month passes without two or three major occasions that large numbers of people in different parts of the territory feel bound to celebrate; the minor ones are uncountable' (in *Chinese Festivals* by Joan Law and Barbara E. Ward, published in 1982 by the South China Morning Post). Nowadays, festival organizers have made use of modern techniques such as sometimes spectacular electric lights and microphones.

Among the most colourful festivals illustrating the gusto of Hong Kong religious feeling is that of the Dragon Boats, held on the fifth day of the fifth moon of the Chinese lunar year (early June). The festival is supposed to celebrate Wat Yuen, a minister to the king of one of China's warring states and also one of China's greatest poets. He lived more than 2,400 years ago. Some historians say that the dragon boats go back further, to Hong Kong's pre-Chinese past, when crocodile worship was widespread. Apparently Wat Yuen gave his king good advice, but this was rejected and he was dismissed. Desperate, he composed his most beautiful poem by the banks of a river, summarizing his life and ideals, and then threw himself into the water. The people searched in vain for him and then, when they couldn't find him, threw rice into the water, in the hope that the fishes would eat that rather than his body. In commemoration of this, boats decorated to look like dragons take to the waters and people eat dumplings of sticky rice wrapped in leaves.

Dragon boat races have been developed into colourful international competitions. Chinese mythology differs from that of the west in that the dragons are beneficent creatures rather than malevolent or hostile ones. They are beasts made up of a mixture of other creatures including a camel's head, a deer's horn, a cow's ears, a snake's neck, a frog's belly, a carp's scales, a hawk's claws and a tiger's paws. The dragon boats are long, thin vessels. Local versions are from 12 to 37 metres long and carry 20 to 48 paddlers, plus a drummer who beats time and an oarsman on the stern to steer. But for international races the boats have a maximum crew of 22 and are 11.58 metres long, 1.07 wide and 0.46 metres deep. Heads and tails of the boats are detachable and are kept in the local temples. Each year new heads must be made and ceremoniously given life. In a ceremony of 'opening the light' the eyes must be painted with a dot of vermilion paint mixed with blood from the comb of a brown chicken. When this has been done the dragon is regarded as 'alive' and has to be ceremonially and respectfully treated. According to Barbara Ward it must be 'presented with incense and candles, and protected from anything that might endanger its essentially *yang* (masculine) character, such as contact with women'. Dragon boat races are held in many parts of Hong Kong including Stanley, Shau Kei Wan, Tai Po and Sai Kung.

Another important festival is on day 15 of moon 7, Yue Laan or the Festival for the Hungry Ghosts (normally in late August or early September by the Gregorian calendar). The seventh moon is a dangerous time for people who believe in ghosts since the gates of the underworld are then opened and the ghosts are free to roam at will. The ghosts in question are people who have died without the proper ceremonies. The festival involves placating them with the same sorts of offering that the gods and worthy ancestors are given, mainly food, paper clothing and spirit money. The food is later given away and the money and clothing are burnt. Incense is offered and there are days and nights of opera, to entertain the ghosts.

Another festival falling in April, in moon 2 and sometimes in moon 3 is the Ching'Ming festival. The words mean clear and bright, referring to the weather. People visit the family graves and sweep them, clean and repaint the inscriptions and then offer incense and red candles plus rice, wine and tea, and they burn paper clothing and spirit money. The whole family then kneels down to pay respect to the spirits. Having paid their respects, they have a graveside picnic, a sort of sharing the food with the dead.

But the most important festival, one that sums up the Hong Kong Chinese spirit, is the Lunar New Year festival occurring in late January or early February according to the western solar calendar. Echoes of the Chinese sentiments are found in the west in such things as New Year resolutions. However, the Chinese do things much more elaborately. Barbara Ward writes, 'Morally the key note is renewal. The old year goes, and with it go old misfortunes and old wrongs; the new year comes and brings the chance for starting afresh. Socially, it signifies reunion, the end of strife, the renewal of harmony. Personally and in business one hopes to pay off one's debts, tidy up all loose ends, and turn over a new leaf.' Starting on the twentieth day of the twelfth moon, house-cleaning starts and housewives begin to stock up on food. Chinese are forbidden to use a knife or to do any work for the first two days of the new year, so food must be prepared in the final ten days of the old year. On day 24 of moon 12 the Kitchen God (sometimes called the Stove God) is supposed to leave for heaven, where he will report on the family's behaviour to the Jade Emperor. His picture is burned outside the kitchen to send him on his way; but before that he is offered incense and candles and given a meal of sticky sweet things which are smeared to his mouth to make sure that he says sweet and flattering things.

Another task that must be done before the new year is repayment of debts; employees are normally given their annual bonus before the end of the year. Just before new year the Hong Kong Chinese put up red strips of paper with auspicious characters written on them wishing wealth, long life and, on junks, favourable winds. Also on the final day of the old year brilliantly coloured Door Gods, represented as generals in full array, are installed on houses and flats to keep the demons away. Flower markets do a roaring trade and are open until beyond midnight.

People go to buy peach and kumquat trees. Peach is popular since the wood is supposedly an enemy of the demons and the peach symbolizes long life; while the small trees laden with tiny kumquat oranges are traditional new year purchases because the Chinese characters for the tree are the same as those for 'gold' and 'lucky'. On New Year's eve takes place the special family dinner at which everyone has to be present. Dead family members also have places laid for them, complete with bowl and chopsticks. Parents give children red packets containing *laisee* or lucky money. Collection of *laisee* continues throughout the new year and a married person greeted by an unmarried female relative or friend is supposed to hand over a packet of it. The children of Hong Kong have a traditional rhyme 'May the new year be happy and wealthy for you/And bring us a big load of *laisee* too.' There is no formal public celebration of the new year, though all the temples are packed. The celebration is very much a family festival, illustrating belief about the continuity of life in the Chinese cosmos. New Year is also the one time when Hong Kong virtually ceases its hectic pursuit of work and wealth, though only for a couple of days.

To the Chinese, living human beings are only part of a complex world. Nature is alive and the elements of nature have their own forces; so, too, the dead have powers. Some students of Hong Kong's Chinese claim that fear of the dead amounts to an obsession. Ancestor-worship is based on dread that the predecessors might come back if they are not properly treated. Even sophisticated modern Chinese, including those who have been converted to Christianity and those who proudly profess agnosticism or atheism, show this lingering respect for Chinese beliefs, though they may pass it off as respecting tradition. Many Chinese Christians will go to their local church, but also go to the temple.

Traditional practices are celebrated most vigorously at New

Year, but religious observance goes on throughout the year. An ordinary visitor, preoccupied with his own affairs, might not notice them, but there are small shrines everywhere on the streets of Hong Kong. Sometimes they are marked by a small niche in the wall where, seemingly for no reason at all, there are a few joss sticks or fruit or sweets. Sometimes paper offerings are burnt on the streets when the moon is new or full. When someone has died or is buried, his departure is marked by the burning of paper houses, cars and fake paper money. Some of these paper representations of his worldly goods are so lovingly made that they might be considered minor works of art. They are sent up in smoke so that he will be well provided for in heaven. The same principle governs the writing of names of people taking part in village festivals. Participants' names are written on a long paper scroll, then sent to heaven on the back of a paper horse which is burnt. Villagers anxiously check to make sure that their name is read out, as the calling of the name is the calling to the gods of the people who should be blessed. Inside houses and shops, local shrines are common. To a westerner the shrine to the kitchen god may look peculiar. It has a red light before it and each day the god is given new offerings and joss-sticks; but there is no image, not even a picture of the kitchen god; instead his name is written in gold characters on red paper.

The Chinese cosmos extends far beyond the gods and living and dead ancestors. To quote from a German clergyman, the Reverend F. J. Eitel, writing in 1873, the Chinese 'look upon nature not as a dead inanimate fabric, but as a living breathing organism. They see a golden chain of spiritual life running every form of existence and binding together, as in one living body, everything that subsists on heaven above or on earth below . . . The whole system of feng shui is based upon this emotional concept of nature' (Eitel, *Feng Shui; or The Rudiments of Natural Science*). *Fung shui*, or less common today *feng shui* (the words literally mean wind and water) is very much alive in present-day Hong Kong. The system is in the ancient Chinese classics but was only developed into a complete system in the Sung dynasty in the twelfth and thirteenth centuries AD. The modern aim is to ensure that nature is in harmony with man. Even today, whenever buildings are put up or new offices taken over, *fung shui* experts are consulted to ensure that harmony prevails. When the Regent Hotel was built on a prime site on the Kowloon side of the harbour, there was fear that the building might cut off the view of the sweep of the harbour. The expert gave his opinion that the nine dragons of Kowloon (Kowloon means nine dragons and refers to the hills around) wouldn't be able to see their way through to the harbour to bathe. The problem was solved by building a huge glass atrium through which the harbour can be seen, a huge publicity scoop as well as a dragon-pleaser. When the Hongkong Bank was ready to move into its new headquarters building in 1985, the *fung shui* men had to be consulted. They decreed that the two bronze lions, Stephen and Stitt, should be moved back to guard the new bank's steel and glass palatial headquarters at 4 a.m. on a Sunday; further, to prevent either beast being jealous, the job had to be done using two cranes simultaneously. When the lions were formally welcomed to the bank they had to be treated properly and with due ceremony that included the bank's directors, all of them pillars of the local community, going round and patting the bronze lions. One branch of McDonald's fast-food chain was advised to keep a tank of piranha fish by the door to help *fung shui*.

Hong Kong Chinese frequently keep goldfish in prominent places. These are supposed to help bring good luck. It's common to see pictures in houses placed at a slant rather than straight: this is so that the ghosts bringing bad luck won't be able to rest there but will slide off. Many Chinese won't have mirrors in public places in their homes, but on the other hand, mirrors can also be used as a device to deflect bad *fung shui*. This is seen most amusingly right in Central Hong Kong. The US Consulate General building has reflective glass on its main windows. These reflections cast back to the offices of the Hong Kong Legal Department. Fearing that bad *fung shui* is being reflected on to them, large numbers of clerks in the department have installed small hexagonal *bhat gwa* mirrors so that any bad influences or spirits will reflect back off them to where it came from. The famous kung-fu film star Bruce Lee, known to Chinese as Siu Lung or 'Little Dragon', moved into Kowloon Tong, an area popular, indeed trendy, with rich young Chinese, but unpopular among older ones because it is in a valley and all valleys have bad *fung shui*. The film star placed a *bhat gwa* mirror on a tree outside the house to improve the *fung shui*, but a typhoon blew down the tree and broke the mirror. So Lee was unprotected. Some Chinese even say that the nine dragons or *kow loon* were jealous of his success and struck him down when he was unprotected and still young.

Concern about the importance of being in harmony with nature is very much a living thing in today's Hong Kong. In ordinary offices you may see small statues of galloping red horses – put there to improve the *fung shui*. Doors may be re-hung – because it was bad luck the way they were placed. Even the British concern, Marks and Spencer, consulted the experts and in consequence its Mong Kok store has several features unknown in Europe, including fish tanks containing fifteen huge bug-eyed goldfish, eight strategically placed lights over the main entrance and four wooden turtles behind the 'light control' bra collection, all to improve the *fung shui*. After a number of jockeys had been injured, one of them fatally, at Sha Tin race course, a procession of Buddhist monks held a special prayer meeting to ask for blessing and the removal of bad luck.

Even US-trained young Chinese businessmen will consult the *Chinese Almanack* to find an auspicious day on which to do business. Businessmen in particular are keen to see that their cars bear the right numbers. Anything with the number 8 in it is good, since the word sounds like the Cantonese for 'prosperity'. The number 2 means 'easy', 3 means 'living' and 9 stands for 'perpetual'. Combination of numbers may enrich a meaning. The number 1 on its own has no special significance, but 1 and 3 together mean 'whole life' (though 4 is an unlucky number signifying death). Thus 138 stands for 'wealthy and prosperous all life long'. Businessman Stephen Codron tells how a car dealer offered to sell him a vehicle with a plate bearing the numbers 2958. 'He obviously thought I was only an ignorant foreigner, but I knew enough that that plate meant "continuous business with no money" and I would be a laughing stock among my Chinese friends. I told him to find something better and he came up with 782, meaning "always prosperity in business". So far it has proved accurate.' Names can also be critical. Sir David Wilson, who became Governor of Hong Kong in April 1987, took advice and changed the transliteration of his name into Chinese characters. If he hadn't done so, he would have been known in Cantonese as Ngai Tak-Ngai, a very bad name since the first 'Ngai' can mean 'false' or 'counterfeit' and the second can suggest a story of 'two ghosts knocking at the door', an extremely unlucky idea. So instead he became Wai Yik-Shun meaning 'to defend and protect with faith and trust', much more appropriate.

The need for good *fung shui* extends right to the grave. Chinese fear the ability of the dead to influence the living and certainly to make them miserable. Some families design elaborate passports for their dead complete with proper Chinese seals and a visa allowing entry to the underworld.

To outsiders it is a closed world, difficult to penetrate. The Chinese don't accept strangers easily. Though they may work with them, Chinese and non-Chinese generally keep apart. This is not surprising, since Chinese call Westerners *gweilos*, literally pale ghosts, meaning that they are beyond the pale of Chinese civilization. It is a continuation of the traditional belief that China is the centre of the world.

It's no use pretending that this Hong Kong is a place of social or economic equality, or that it is all pretty. Hong Kong has more than its share of super-rich. There are hundreds of local Chinese who could put a million US dollars or more into a suitcase at short notice. But mere millionaires are small beer in Hong Kong; the really rich are in the billionaire league, like Li

Ka-shing, the man who started off making plastic flowers and is today the controller of property and trading concerns that account for about 20 per cent of the local stock market capitalization, and Sir Yue-Kong Pao, still the world's biggest private shipowner as well as the owner of a big empire on dry land. Both are worth more than 2 billion US dollars. Some people delight in flaunting their wealth luridly and outrageously. Quite the most ostentatious are a middle-ageing Chinese couple, Brenda and Kai-bong Chau, who are literally the most gilded of Hong Kong's beautiful people. They are to be found, when not entertaining in grand style on the town, high on the Peak, though not on the popular side overlooking the harbour. The Chaus' house, chosen because the *fung shui* was good, has a clear view of the ocean and the sunset which, when the mood is good, can be golden. The house is – appropriately – called 'Villa d'Oro', and almost everything inside is painted gold or gilded, including gold-plated taps in the bathroom, gold coins set into the lavatory seat, a gilded mirrored ballroom of 1,000 square feet, a dinner service done in gold. The Chaus have turned it into a gaudy art form and love showing it off as proof of Hong Kong style. 'Gold is very normal; you see it in Indian palaces and at Versailles,' coos Brenda Chau, whose father was the founder of the Kowloon Motor Bus Company and had six wives. She met her husband at Cambridge University. They even have a gold-painted Rolls-Royce Phantom and a liveried chauffeur to match. But because, says Kai-bong, wife Brenda has different moods, they also have a champagne-pink Rolls-Royce (a Silver Cloud). The chauffeur for that has a pink outfit to match. But so does Mrs Chau: besides a variety of matching pink dresses she also has a full-length pink mink coat, and takes pride in dressing up in it to show her rich style.

The super-rich, the rich and the moderately rich together are numerous, but they are probably less than 1 per cent of the total population. For most Hong Kong people the living is not so easy. If you peer into the upper air of urban Kowloon, the private apartments seem like a mass of tiny cages built on top of one another, each with a splash of individuality, their own waving washing lines, plus a few plant pots and a bird. The Chinese love their birds, and in the early morning two sights are common: old folk going to the parks and open spaces to perform their *Tai Chi Chuan* exercises, and old men carrying their birds in cages for their early morning constitutional, talking to the birds as they go. Government housing has helped many people, but large numbers are still vulnerable. One old man in Kowloon in the late 1980s was paying HK$170 a month for an upper-deck bunk that consisted of just enough space to sleep, screened off with cardboard and old newspaper. This was his 'home'. Street sleepers can be seen on both sides of Hong Kong's harbour, and the crabby hands of beggars thrusting towards tourists are a constant part of the jostling throng at the busy Mass Transit Railway stations. One of the best known of Hong Kong's street sleepers never appears to beg, but shuffles her slow wizened way through Central District clutching her few possessions. She is neatly dressed in a blue or red or grey dressing-gown, often with a headscarf. She rarely talks and seems to live in a dream world. Some locals say she was a young woman from a wealthy family who fell head over heels in love with a young Japanese who was then killed in the war. She never recovered, but old servants are still loyal and continue to bring her food, so she does not have to beg.

In spite of the housing programme there are still almost 400,000 people living in squatter hutchments on hillsides. Here they are the ready prey both for the Triad gangs (who may charge up to HK$20,000 for purchase of a tiny scrap of a place to live) and for the government clearance squads who determine when squatter settlements should no longer exist. The government has tidied up many of the squatter areas, reinforcing the land with concrete and insisting on fire breaks. So today the encampments are protected from sudden death by mudslips during the rainy season or rapidly spreading outbreaks of fire. The government has laid on water supplies and sanitary facilities, so that in spite of the squalor the squatters do manage to build homes out of their hutches. Many families have televisions and refrigerators.

The Triads are another grim reminder that the down side of Hong Kong life is unpleasant and dangerous. In the past Triads were romanticized. The movement has obscure origins going back centuries, but achieved its strength in the eighteenth and nineteenth centuries when it developed – or was rationalized – into a movement to rid China of its 'foreign' (Manchu) rulers. Eminent figures like Sun Yat-sen were members. With the fall of the Manchus and the setting up of the Republic of China in 1911, the Triads had achieved their proclaimed cherished goal and there should therefore be no reason for their continuing to exist. But with the breakdown of China in the 1920s and 1930s into warlordism, Triad leaders saw excellent profits to be made from the pickings. Today it's not so easy to describe the operations of the Triads. This is not only because of their secrecy, but also because there is no central organization and no one 'Mister Big' figure running the whole show. Altogether there are about fifty to sixty Triad gangs in Hong Kong, but of these only seventeen are active and only a handful are really well organized. Of a total of 120,000 Triad members, somewhere between 15,000 and 20,000 are active. Police describe their operation and organization as being rather like Mafia or US gangs during the Prohibition era. They are powerful and bound by secret rituals demanding loyalty under pain of death. The 14K gang has achieved international notoriety by winning control of the heroin trade in northern Europe. Another gang, Dai Hoon or Big Circle, a group of disaffected Red Guards who fled to Hong Kong during the Cultural Revolution, has even challenged the 14K on its own drug turf, though Dai Hoon doesn't have the typical Triad rituals. Triads are also very influential in the seamy world of call girls, nightclubs, gambling, loan sharking and restaurants, where they can operate protection rackets. Other areas of their activity include interior decorating and the wholesale markets. For a while in the 1970s the Hong Kong government was proclaiming that it had the Triads on the run. This hope was proved to be merely a boast in the mid-1980s when special government reports revealed that the Triads had regained some of their old strength, and cries of alarm were heard again in official circles.

There's very little that is really romantic about the Triads and their oaths, still less about some of their methods. In December 1988 a young hairdresser was murdered by Triad members plunging barbecue forks into his body. Some Triad gangs thought they could act with impunity: at least one lion dance was performed publicly by youths wearing the characters of the Wo Shing Wo gang on their shirts. In British police circles there was alarm that the exodus of people from Hong Kong would strengthen Triad activity in Chinese societies in the west; there was also a reluctance to employ Hong Kong police officers to help because of the claim that the colony's police force had been infiltrated by the Triads. Police in Hong Kong angrily denied such claims. But in 1988 and 1989 the Hong Kong authorities, stung by foreign criticism, renewed their efforts to break the Triads. An amnesty was offered to Triad members prepared to renounce their oaths to a special independent tribunal. Police said the scheme was aimed at people trapped on the outer fringes of Triad activity like hawkers and youths lured by the glamour of the gangs. If a person renounced the Triads then any such activity indulged in before the renunciation would be forgiven, unless it related to serious crimes like rape or murder. Police claim that youngsters, sometimes as young as ten years old, are bullied into joining the Triad gangs and then are too afraid to speak out or leave.

The pernicious influence of the Triads and the very vicious side of Hong Kong's underworld has led at least some neutral observers to assert that China's virtues outweigh Hong Kong's vices. 'I prefer China to Hong Kong,' says one westerner who has spent considerable time in both places. 'At least in China you don't have 12- and 13-year-old girls sold into sexual slavery. It happens in Hong Kong.'

But for most ordinary Hong Kong Chinese the special excitement of the place is the perpetual dream of breaking out of poverty and becoming rich, as Li and hundreds of others did. And if they can't make it themselves, they can hope that their children, boosted by a modern education, will succeed. In the balmy days of the early and mid-1980s, when the stock market was booming, the crowds anxiously scanning the latest prices on boards round the city weren't limited to normal 'City' types, but also included ordinary Chinese like newspaper hawkers and amahs (maids) clad simply in black pyjama suits. They'd gambled their money there too. Everyone has a stake in Hong Kong's future. It is a daily miracle that this tiny colony has come so far, especially considering the ordinariness of its people. Virtually all of Hong Kong's inhabitants are refugees. A few of them were rich businessmen in Shanghai, and some of those – so the legends say – fled with gold bars strapped to their Rolls-Royces. But the majority are peasants or from peasant stock, people who a generation ago were toiling in the sweaty paddy fields and on the duck farms of Guangdong province.

Perhaps the most remarkable of Hong Kong's miracles is the political one – how a tiny crowded territory on the end of Communist China has not only avoided being absorbed by China but has developed a flourishing lifestyle that seems to mock everything that Communist China stands for. Even without the boastful opulence of the Chaus, there is an enormous gap between rich and poor in Hong Kong. Hong Kong thrives on capitalism where China abhors it. Gambling, horse racing, prostitution, blue movies, sexy bars, free speech and press all flourish in Hong Kong and are strongly disapproved of in China itself. That's without considering the fact that Hong Kong is still a colony of an ailing western power. China itself of course profits from Hong Kong. It is probably the single biggest investor in the territory, with a proliferation of department stores, banks and businesses. These all generate foreign exchange to keep China's own economy ticking over. The big country also gains hard currency earnings by selling Hong Kong essential supplies of food and water. Hong Kong has come to depend on China – literally – to keep it alive. If China turned off the taps or stopped food supplies, Hong Kong would die. When in early 1989 there was a dispute at the border and lorry drivers went on strike for a day, food and vegetable prices in Hong Kong shot up by up to 30 per cent. Equally, China has been recently learning from Hong Kong about how the rest of the world works. Hong Kong offers a door through which China can obtain technology and sensitive items which are barred to it as a Communist country. More mundanely, Hong Kong can offer simple training – from how a modern office works to how big management decisions involving millions of dollars should best be taken and how marketing and advertising of goods should be done professionally.

Some Hong Kong officials and businessmen dreamed that this system could continue for ever, since it is clearly in the interests of both Hong Kong and China. Sir John Bremridge, Financial Secretary from 1981 to 1986, cheerfully claimed that in Hong Kong China had discovered the long-sought secret of the philosopher's stone – it was making gold (fully convertible Hong Kong dollars) from sales of cabbage. Lord Kadoorie, Hong Kong's first-ever member of the House of Lords, described eloquently how Hong Kong was the window through which China could learn about the twentieth century and its technology without corrupting its own system. Again, therefore, there was the incentive for China to retain the status quo.

Such hopes were echoed by some senior colonial administrators who hoped that growing links between the territory and the Chinese motherland might lead Peking to leave things as they were. Perhaps some business-as-usual agreement could be reached by sleight of hand. Let the British relinquish their colonial claims quietly and let China allow Hong Kong to go its own sweet way for everyone's benefit. It was a nice theory – and, to a westerner, a persuasive argument. Unfortunately, it failed to take account of harsh *realpolitik*, especially as that relates to Communist China. Successive Chinese governments, both Nationalist and Communist, have regarded colonial Hong Kong as an insult to the integrity of China. Deng Xiaoping's dream was to put right the colonial wrongs and reunify China. Britain was no longer powerful enough to stand up to such a man. Margaret Thatcher went to Peking in December 1984 to sign a death warrant for colonial capitalist Hong Kong.

3 A Raucous Kaleidoscope of Sights, Sounds and Smells

From the Peak of Hong Kong island you get, weather permitting, a glossy picture-postcard panoramic view of the territory, clustered around one of the best and most picturesque natural harbours in all the world. Only those of Rio de Janeiro in Brazil and Sydney in Australia can compete with Hong Kong, and Hong Kong is definitely much more dynamic. The silver sands of Rio, the flotilla of pleasure craft in Sydney harbour, lend an air of leisure and relaxation to those cities. Hong Kong, however, is dedicated to work, manufacturing, trade, finance, banking, making money; its ships, whether shining ocean-going liners, oil-sleek tankers, boxy container vessels or humble paint-peeling Chinese junks, seem to be in a hustle to get someplace else. The harbour is fringed on both sides by tall tower blocks that rise from the very water's edge. Occasionally one is pulled down, but another quickly takes its place, bigger, more sparkling than ever. There is just one tiny flat finger of land poking into the harbour that doesn't contain a tower block, and that is Kai Tak airport, daringly located in the heart of the city.

Hong Kong island is the oldest part of the British settlement and also the most mixed and varied, representative of the hurly burly, the excitement and the contradictions of life in the colony. From the height of the Peak, everything below seems both ordered and orderly, having its own neatly arranged place. That carefully manicured view is reinforced by the fact that up on the Peak life is pleasant indeed. The air is cooler than down below at sub-tropical sea level. There are leafy lanes and paths where children can cycle safely. And, if the clouds and mist stay away, there's an unrivalled view of the rest of the world beyond.

The Peak is the peak in more ways than one: not just a high viewpoint, but also the very pinnacle of Hong Kong society. Before the Second World War, a government permit was needed to live there. That policy was relaxed, and today ordinary Hong Kong people and tourists of every race, shape, size and colour come here for an afternoon's stroll, to admire the view, or to walk arm-in-arm away from the claustrophobic environment of their cramped homes. Stopping to look is one thing, but living on the Peak is quite another. There is no longer any government fiat, but to all but the superwealthy the Peak is still closed – by price. Housing costs are on a par with those of London's Mayfair or with mid-town Manhattan. Rent of a reasonable sized flat of say 200 square metres may run to US$5,000 or more a month. Buying a place to live would be a cool matter of more than a million US dollars, and that would only fetch a flat, not a house. Peak properties at the Peak proper with the full harbour panorama run to several millions in anyone's money.

Not all the newly rich Chinese have accepted their birthright to live on the Peak. Some like Macao casino operator Stanley Ho, who lives on Repulse Bay Road, and shipping and property magnate Sir Yue-Kong Pao, out at Deep Water Bay, have opted for equally spacious living but with private beach access. The Peak still has more than its fair share of westerners. These include young men from the Hongkong Bank and from the old-established trading companies, which have retained old Peak properties, plus a new generation of whiz-kids working for foreign banks and brokerages, probably inhabiting duplex apartments or flats in the foothills. These favoured occupants frequently have the benefit of an in-house swimming pool and live a special, treasured existence, hardly having to mingle with the *hoi polloi* down below. Such young westerners enjoy a standard of living that few apart from the very highest-flying could dream of back in their home countries. At least one servant will dance attendance at dinner parties. The wife will only have to soil her hands with cooking if she wishes to. Children of course will be taken care of by the amah, an old Chinese woman if the family is lucky or well-connected, but more likely one or more Filipinas (of whom there were more than 45,000 in Hong Kong by the late 1980s). 'We couldn't manage without our two Filipina amahs,' says a Briton in his thirties working for an American financial institution.

> Sometimes we have to hire an extra girl for evenings when we have more than 10 people to dinner. Life is much more hectic than back home. Generally I don't get back until seven in the evening because we have to see how the London markets have opened. That gives time for a quick G+T [gin and tonic] or two before getting showered and changed for dinner. My wife is also exhausted by this time. Though the girls look after our two children, aged three and nearly five, during the day and babysit at night, my wife likes to bathe them and read them a bedtime story. If we have people to dinner she doesn't normally cook herself, but it is a hard enough job to supervise and make sure the Filipinas get the recipes right. They are wonderful but don't always understand western food, particularly if it is fancy stuff to impress a business contact. We entertain at home or eat out at least four and sometimes six nights a week. On Sundays, the amahs' day off, we usually take a boat out if it's fine. So Sunday evening is really the only time we have to ourselves to put our feet up and watch a video, knowing we won't be interrupted by a call from London or New York. It seems we hardly have time to think. Thank goodness breathing is done on automatic pilot.

He and many of his colleagues will be US dollar millionaires before they leave the territory.

Those who live on the Peak are insulated from the niggling hardships that the rest of Hong Kong has to suffer. The summer days, stretching effectively from early May until late September, are long and hot and sweaty. That's no sweat for those on the Peak since the dehumidifiers and air conditioners can be run round the clock (with the enormous bill of course picked up by the company). For the journey into the office it's unlikely that the Western whiz-kid (or his Chinese counterpart) will have to suffer the indignities of anything as unrefined as a bus queue. Some denizens of the Peak use the Peak Tram, but most have a car (normally on the company of course) and possibly a driver. Their daily route from home to the office and back thus takes them exclusively along a route that gives them only the western gloss of Hong Kong.

Down the twists and turns of the Peak and along the steep slope to sea level is Hong Kong's business and banking district, known as Central. This is one of the achievements of British rule, since a century ago the land on which most of this activity takes place did not even exist. In the 1840s the first road of the new baby British settlement was Queen's Road. The sea lapped gently within earshot. Today the sea has been pushed 100 metres further back. Des Voeux Road, Connaught Road, each roaring traffic-choked thoroughfares, the waterfront promenades and ferry jetties, have all sprung up on new land. This is the territory of expensive skyscraper buildings where, it seems, each new creation is the most expensive ever in the history of the world. Among the buildings are the Mandarin Oriental Hotel, reckoned by many businessmen to be the best in the world, occupying a modest twenty-five storey wedge between Connaught Road and Des Voeux Road. Opposite it is the fifty-two storey Jardine House (formerly known as Connaught Centre) with its distinctive round windows like portholes, 'the house of a thousand orifices' some Chinese have nicknamed it, or 'Hong Kong Stilton', according to British wags. Next door is the stately sweep of Exchange Square, with its two tall towers and one smaller one, a handsome mixture of granite and glass that houses the new state-of-the-art computer-organized trading floor of the Stock Exchange of Hong Kong. Opened in the mid-1980s, the building is home for many of the biggest names in international business, including the Hong Kong offices of six of the ten biggest banks in the world. Its owners, the Hongkong Land Company, claim that the facilities and communications systems of Exchange Square are among the best in the world. 'It joins an "exclusive club" of sophisticated new-system buildings – the other dozen "members" all being in the United States,' said a Hongkong Land press release. The boast of being the best was the least that Hongkong Land could do, since the company paid a mere HK$4.755 billion for the 13,400-square-metre site in 1982, just before the property market crashed, making it a world record sum for a single site.

But if it's world records that are being sought, the new Hongkong Bank headquarters situated between Des Voeux Road and Queen's Road, with its address of 1, Queen's Road, Central, set quite a few. The bank gives the cost as HK$5 billion, but that doesn't include the land, since the bank already owned the site (on a 999-year lease) or the financing or expensive furnishing costs. In all, the Hongkong Bank is almost certainly the world's first billion-US-dollar building. The building itself is unique. Its devotees describe it as handsome and its critics decry it as a monstrosity. But it is by no means the tallest building in Hong Kong. Just across the road between Garden Road and Cotton Tree Drive on the periphery of what has traditionally been accepted as the Central business district, the Bank of China has stolen a march on the Hongkong Bank and on everyone else in Hong Kong. The Peking-controlled bank built Hong Kong's tallest building, the world's fifth biggest. In fact, this is the tallest building in the world outside the USA. At seventy-two storeys, reaching a height of 315 metres (or 370 if the two 'chopsticks' on top are counted), at a total cost of HK$2 billion including the land price, it is a 'snip'. The bank paid a controversial HK$1 billion 'friendship price' for the land at the height of the property boom, just when the Land Company was shelling out more than four times as much for its Exchange Square site. The architect was New York-based American Chinese I. M. Pei, whose father was the first manager of the Bank of China in Hong Kong. The architect's firm say the design for the building is rooted in classical Chinese philosophy and iconography. They describe its structure as 'similar to the trunk of the bamboo propelled ever higher by each new growth'. But local Chinese worry that its angular shape may mean that the *fung shui* is bad. Topping out of the building (the ceremony to mark the completion of the superstructure) was done on 8 August 1988, the eighth day of the eighth month of the eighty-eighth year, a combination designed to ensure the best possible luck, since 'eight' in Cantonese is a homonym for the word that denotes prosperity.

Little ever stands still in Hong Kong, and even before the Bank of China building was due to be opened in late 1989 local entrepreneur Gordon Wu announced plans for a hotel in Wanchai that he boasted would be ninety storeys high.

It is quickly obvious that in Central Hong Kong there are few old, or even elderly, buildings. One reason is that Hong Kong itself is not very old, but it's more relevant to say that in this money-conscious city, there are few dollars and cents in being old. Hong Kong is not a place renowned for being sentimental: when something more modern and efficient can be created, the old will be torn down. At the start of the 1980s a distinguished landmark of Central was the Hong Kong Club building, a modest structure tiered like a wedding cake and dating back to the closing years of the last century. Some historically conscious citizens started a damp squib of a campaign urging preservation of the building, but this soon fizzled out. The old club was expensive to maintain; a new block with more compact rooms, lower ceilings and additional floors available for rent was a much more attractive proposition. After the destruction of the old club just a few token old buildings can still be seen. Parts of St John's (Anglican) Cathedral date back to 1847. The church occupies the only freehold land in Hong

Kong. All other land is leasehold, with some property on 999-year leases, but most modern ones being granted for 99 years. On the eastern fringes of Central at the start of the road to the Peak is Flagstaff House, built in 1845 as an army headquarters but now preserved and converted into a tea museum.

Murray Barracks, once an officers' mess and later used by the occupying Japanese army as its headquarters during the Second World War, used to stand lower down on Queensway and Cotton Tree Drive. But it was removed and is intended to be rebuilt on Stanley peninsula. The only other moderately historical building preserved in Central Hong Kong is the old Supreme Court, begun in 1903 and converted in the mid-1980s into the Legislative Council building. With the move of the Bank of China headquarters there will apparently be little new scope for rebuilding in the Central area. Most buildings are already touching their maximum 'plot ratio' – the amount of floor space that can be built on a particular site, governed partly by the capacity of the infrastructure such as telephones, electricity, water supplies and sewers. But if confidence is maintained Hong Kong will keep changing just like a kaleidoscope, through land reclamation, through the Central area expanding both east and west as well as through relaxed plot ratios. As evidence of Central Hong Kong's rapidly changing face, in 140 years there have been four different buildings on the site of the present Gloucester Tower of the Landmark.

The biggest single private landlord in Central Hong Kong is the Hongkong Land Company, which is responsible for about half a million square metres (more than 5 million square feet) of prime space, including Exchange Square, Jardine House, Prince's Building, Alexandra House and the twin-tower Landmark. The Landmark is one of the world's most modern shopping and office complexes. The first few floors of the twin forty-seven-level complex are opened up for a 2,000-square-metre atrium bordered by more than a hundred shops. Among the high-class boutiques are Gucci, Lanvin, Cacherel, Dior, Louis Vuitton. It is possible to buy almost anything here, from shirts, suits and dresses to accessories like ties, shoes, bags, jewellery, watches, perfume – almost anything provided it's high fashion and expensive.

In the central atrium a fountain happily splashes away; its water tuned to respond and jump according to the noise levels around. But the fountain can be turned off and boarded up to provide a stage for plays or concerts. The Landmark is generally regarded as one of the more imaginative success stories of Hong Kong. Immediate considerations of dollars and cents of rental income were set aside to create a public meeting place. Generally it has worked out, and there's more coordination and unity about the Landmark than about other older, sometimes more glitzy, Hong Kong shopping palaces. Of course this allows the Land Company to select only prime candidates, who will, of course, pay the very highest rents. On most days the Louis Vuitton Landmark shop actually has a queue outside, members of Japanese tourist groups being allowed in a few at a time, eagerly seeking the ubiquitous status symbol without paying the princess's ransom involved in buying in Tokyo.

In spite of Hong Kong's dedication to money-making the government has managed to preserve some small areas of space for contemplation. Halfway up the Peak are the Zoological and Botanical Gardens. These owe their origin to Governor Sir John Bowring (1852–6) who decided that a wildlife park should be built to preserve Hong Kong's flora and fauna. In Cantonese the gardens are still called after Bowring, popularly known as 'Peng Fau' (Head Soldier). They are called 'Peng Fau Fa Yuen' (the head soldier's flower garden). The gardens are close to Government House, the modest residence of the Queen's representative. It's perhaps a sign of the times that the present-day head soldier of Hong Kong (since the Governor is still commander-in-chief of the garrison) is a neighbour of the inhabitants of 'mid-levels', a ledge on which the homes of expatriates whose companies don't provide rental allowances and young middle-class Chinese who haven't yet made it to the top perch uncomfortably. They pay US$1,500 or more a month in rent for 100 square metres of apartment space, offering perhaps a peep of Hong Kong's famous harbour view. It is another sign of the times that the Governor's own view has been drastically curbed by the new buildings. Sir Edward Youde, who died in office in December 1986, commented that in previous times a Hong Kong Governor could look out of his window and judge the state of the economy and trade by the number of ships in the harbour; but these days the governor can't see the whole of the harbour. But he does have tennis courts and a private garden, little luxuries that other mid-level inhabitants can't afford, plus ample parking for his Rolls-Royce, Daimlers and other cars. For ordinary people a mere parking space has to be paid for, at US$150 a month or so.

Down at ground level, the government has shown itself to be boringly bureaucratic, especially when it comes to planning. Until the mid-1970s, one of the favourite snapshots of Hong Kong was the greensward of the Cricket Club with a game in progress right under the nose of a huge colour picture of China's Chairman Mao Zedong hanging from the Bank of China building. The Cricket Club moved out and the local council took over the land to build a park. It ripped up the pitch and replaced it with concrete fringed by plants and trees. In the late 1980s the government set about building an instant eyesore in the centre of the city, a double-decker road along Connaught Road, the last main thoroughfare before the sea passing just outside the front doors of the Mandarin Oriental Hotel. There was a feeble campaign to suggest that the road should be cut or sunk below ground level so as not to spoil the view, but 1987 saw the start of the construction. The waterfront piers leading to Hong Kong's ferry terminals are mostly tatty and tacky, so the government lost an important opportunity of creating a stylish harbour front that would match the natural beauty. Anyone looking towards the sea from the lower floors of the Hongkong Bank has a distinctly forgettable view. At this level the fine perspective of the harbour and ships is obscured; instead there is the concrete of Statue Square (where there is only a single statue, that of Sir Thomas Jackson, chief manager of the Hongkong Bank a century ago), the patch of grass around the Cenotaph, the top of a car park and the shabby Star Ferry terminal. Apart from the Macao ferry pier, which has been glassily redeveloped with a hotel, an office tower and a concourse laden with shops, the various piers range from boring to ramshackle and ripe for redevelopment. The local Urban Council has hardly set a distinguished example. Right along the Central waterfront it has built walkway-cum-concrete-park, raised for much of the stretch between the Star Ferry and Western, so that a pedestrian on the pavement looking out to sea sees only a blank wall. On Sundays the whole of Central is filled with the twittering singsong sparrowlike voices of thousands of Filipina maids who have nowhere else to go on their day off, after they have been to church. They cook, eat, play music and gossip away the day. At nights the concrete sheltered area near the General Post Office is occupied by a few huddled hulks whose only home is a cardboard box they carry with them.

Spiralling prices of land and office space in the Central district have pushed more and more Hong Kong companies to move out of the area and into adjoining Wanchai. The Communist trading group, China Resources, built a huge skyscraper headquarters and showroom on reclaimed land in Wanchai, and the Chinese Ministry of Foreign Affairs took space there for its visa-issuing office. Also in Wanchai are the Sun Hung Kai Building, the new Supreme Court, the Hong Kong Academy for the Performing Arts and the new Convention and Exhibition Centre. Old Wanchai was renowned as the 'rest and recreation' centre for visitors, particularly soldiers seeking a respite from their official duties. Here Suzie Wong (the prostitute with a heart of gold of the film *The World of Suzie Wong* fame) lived (in the Luk Kwok Hotel). The Luk Kwok of the 1970s and 1980s prided itself on being a 'family' hotel, rather smart and posh for the likes of modern-day Suzie and her sisters – but then it fell to the demolition men. The Wanchai bars that never close are still in existence, and most look seedy. In all, Wanchai's old-time reputation for the good time looks like being squeezed. Already the area is winning a reputation as an upmarket place for dining out. With new business coming in from Central, it may be a matter of time before much of the Wanchai that many visitors have known and loved comes under the demolition jack-hammer.

Settlement of Hong Kong island has followed the thin coastal strip, almost perforce, since the terrain quickly begins to rise steeply. Adjoining Wanchai is Causeway Bay. This displays an interesting blend of old and new. Among the quaint old practices is the sounding of the 'Noonday Gun' across the road from the Excelsior Hotel. This task falls to Jardine Matheson and Co., the old (still) British-run company that was in existence before Hong Kong became British. The gun is fired every day at noon precisely, as well as at midnight on 31 December to mark the coming of the New Year (when it's a black tie and dinner-jacket occasion). It is celebrated in Noel Coward's line: 'In Hong Kong, they strike a gong and fire a noon-day gun, to reprimand each inmate who's in late.' No one knows the true origin of the practice. According to one legend the gun was originally fired as a salute to one of Jardine's opium boats; the colonial authorities took it amiss and so perversely insisted that Jardine fire the gun every day. In front of the gun is the Royal Hong Kong Yacht Club, where some of Hong Kong's 6,000 pleasure craft lie at anchor waiting for the weekend. Causeway Bay also offers a crowded mooring place and typhoon shelter for many local sampans. On land, Causeway Bay is jam-packed with humanity from about 10 in the morning until after 10 at night when the shops close. The area was given a new lease of life in 1973 when the cross-harbour road tunnel was opened, giving an alternative means of transport between Hong Kong and Kowloon apart from the Star Ferry and vehicular ferries across the harbour. It boasts some classy shops including branches of the old-established Lane Crawford (now a part of Sir Yue-Kong Pao's empire), of China Products and a handful of Japanese department stores, Daimaru, Matsuzakaya and Sogo. In between are shops of every shape and size filled with glittering goods as only Hong Kong shops can be, including the latest in cameras, televisions and videos, stereo and hi-fi, watches, jewellery, garments. The area vies with Kowloon's 'Golden Mile' for the tourist dollar. Just so the tourists and the local Chinese can make a full day of it there are also plenty of restaurants, including a whole street called 'Food Street' that boasts about thirty establishments with altogether more than 2,000 dishes on the menu – from best American steak and Japanese teppanyaki to most varieties of Chinese fare.

Food plays a large part in the lives of the Chinese, especially of the Cantonese who make up the vast majority of Hong Kong's population. Local experts boast that the Cantonese, like the French, believe in living to eat rather than eating to live. But according to the Chinese it's not acceptable to eat any food at any time. It is vitally important to have a diet in which *yin* (negative) and *yang* (positive) foods are in balance. On top of this, to Chinese, there are five basic tastes, and these also have to be satisfied, but not to excess. The five are sweetness (for the spleen); sourness (for the liver); hotness (the lungs); bitterness (the heart); and saltiness (the kidneys). Ancient Chinese pharmacopoeia goes back for several thousand years, and 600 years ago Hu Sihui, Imperial Dietician ('food doctor official' as his title is expressed in Chinese) to the Yuan Dynasty, laid down formal dietary guidelines from the specific – 'people with heart disease should avoid saltiness and eat more beans and dog meat' – to the general – 'after a full meal do not wash your hair, avoid sex like an arrow, avoid wine like an enemy'. In Causeway Bay local Chinese customers predominate, whereas in the more popular tourist area of Tsim Sha Tsui in Kowloon some of the restaurants have over-adapted in their anxiety to win the tourist dollars. Chinese food has many varieties, from *dim-sum* (literally meaning 'to touch the heart' but in fact titbits) eating places where you pay for what you order from trolleys hurriedly pushed past, to sumptuous multi-course banquets. In Causeway Bay there is also the additional attraction of a sampan dining cruise starting from the typhoon anchorage. Hire a sampan – price negotiable around HK$100 an hour – order food fresh from other sampans and see it cooked in front of you. It is also possible to be attended by sweet and sour music. An anonymous writer for the local tourist association got quite carried away by the occasion, and described the music as 'a melodic caterwauling which sounds like a combination of the Beatles and Cantonese opera'. The writer warmed to the task, adding: 'Along with the wine, wok-fried seafood and the waves, you've got song. It's the famous Causeway Bay ladies. If they figure that they're the equivalent of the Sung Dynasty sing-sing girls, they're a few dynasties too late (and a lot older). But the selection is irresistible. They have a carte of musical selections: everything from *Can't Buy Me Love* to *Happy Birthday* to *Moscow Nights* and *Waterloo Bridge* – but after the first line in English, the rest comes in Cantonese. Their voices are lusty, the accompaniment (banjo, tambourine and drums) unique, and the melodies coming out over the sea are like none heard before or since.'

The Chinese revere their drink as well as their food, and traditions going back centuries are to be found at the Luk Yu Tea-house in Stanley Street, a seedy street in Central. The tea-house in fact dates back only to 1930 and has been in Stanley Street since 1975. But it has great stylishness, with its huge black fans suspended from high ceilings and turning idly (since the place is air-conditioned), with its solid wooden chairs inlaid with marble, with its kettle-warming stands at various points on the floor, and with its burnished brass spittoons and coat hooks near each marble-topped table. Stained glass murals and framed scrolls decorate the walls. Mirrored marble private booths mark it out as a place of quiet business. Tea-drinking is even more important to the Chinese than it is to tea-drinking westerners. China is after all the country that discovered the refreshing qualities of the drink. According to legend, 5,000 years ago Emperor Shen Nung was relaxing under a camellia tree watching some water boiling when a breeze blew several leaves into the cauldron. The aroma caught his attention and he drank the first cup of tea. Since that time the Chinese have made an art out of tea-drinking, Lu Tu, a Tang dynasty connoisseur who lived in the eighth century AD, wrote a 'Tea Classic' on the proper techniques for making the finest tea; hence the Cantonese version of his name lives on at Hong Kong tea-house. Some Hong Kong tea-drinkers will pay thousands of dollars for a pound of their favourite leaf. They have plenty of places where they can enjoy their drinks, but most are small and humble compared with the Luk Yu.

But tea-drinking isn't just an excuse for gossiping or idle aesthetic exercise. Aficionados point out that a cup of tea is a chemical treasury containing 20 amino acids, 12 sugars, six organic acids, 30 polyphenolic bodies and up to 5 per cent caffeine and theophylline. This theophylline, say the experts, is an active ingredient in the relaxation of bronchioles: it speeds up the heartbeat and aids digestion. The Chinese are ever a highly practical people. Tea-houses also serve as an important place for business, much as coffee-houses served the London insurance and stockbroking markets several centuries ago. In fact the tea-house is *more* important, since it is also a place for settling disagreements. The Chinese have never trusted the formality of courts of law and would prefer to settle differences quietly over tea. Today business is still done in the private booths of the Luk Yu tea-house, and a deal struck over the tea-cups is as binding as a solemn western handshake or signed and sealed formal agreement. Incidentally, the tapping of fingers on the table is not a signal that a deal has been struck, but is an old courtesy, an acknowledgement that someone has done the kindness of pouring a cup of tea. The history-conscious Cantonese say that it commemorates a visit by a Qing dynasty emperor who went to a tea-house *incognito* and took his turn pouring the tea. His companions wanted to perform the traditional *kowtow* for the service, but that would have given him away, so he told them they could tap three fingers on the table, one representing the bowing head and the other two the arms.

It's a relief to get out of the wall-to-wall crowds of Causeway

Bay to the nearby Victoria Park, named after the British Queen whose statue is still at the entrance. From about 5 in the morning the park is busy, one of many popular spots all over Hong Kong for old folk to do their *Tai Chi Chuan* exercises. These are generally done in slow motion from a semi-crouching position and have a balletic quality. Many of the movements have their own flowery names such as 'catching a peacock's tail' and 'finding a needle at the bottom of the sea'. To a watching Westerner, it might all seem slightly absurd, but *Tai Chi* has its own history. Followers claim that it is most healthful, especially in combating modern stress. According to popular history, about a thousand years ago Cheung Sam-fung, a Taoist priest, watched a snake curling up to fend off the attacks of a predatory bird, until the bird tired and the snake struck and killed it. The priest copied the snake and modelled on its movements a system of self-defence, *Tai Chi* (literally 'great ultimate fist'). This was useful for priests who were barred from carrying weapons but faced the perils of robbers. Slow motion is supposed to improve balance; the semi-crouch position gives greater muscle control; while deep breathing stimulates blood circulation and helps relax the body.

Causeway Bay and the surrounding areas still show some traces of a Chinese existence that goes back long before the tourists and their travellers' cheques. The Tin Hau Temple across from Victoria Park traces its history to 1747. In Pennington Street there are traditional Chinese medicine shops and pawnshops and a tea-house offering herbal '24-flavoured tea'. There's also a shop renowned for making paper effigies for funerals. Next door is the badly named Happy Valley, mecca for the gambling Hong Kong community with its race course tightly packed in among tall blocks of flats. Five different segregated cemeteries line the road opposite the race course, all dating from the 1840s and 1850s, for Muslims, Catholics, Jews, Parsees and – the largest one, called the Colonial Cemetery – for westerners. After this perhaps it is appropriate that Happy Valley also accommodates the most macabre sight in Hong

Kong – the Tiger Balm Gardens (now renamed the Aw Boon Haw Gardens after their founder), a sort of Chinese Disneyland of wonders, much more grotesque than anything Disney could have thought up. The garden is filled with colourful statues of Chinese figures. Buddhas, gods, fairies, dragons, generals and a whole garish zoo of animals live there. One of the most gruesome scenes shows 'judgement in hell'. For the sinners the punishments include tongues torn out, bodies ripped in half and other grim punishments. Aw Boon Haw and his brother invented the recipe for the famous Tiger Balm, billed as a cure-all for everything from headaches to bruising and even – it is reported – snake-bites. The balm still sells well, not only in Hong Kong but throughout all parts of Asia where there is a substantial Chinese population.

The centre of Hong Kong island is hilly and wooded, and much of the land is given over to country parks. The eastern coastal stretches of the island have scattered settlements, such as at Shek-O where some expatriates keep country homes. In the last few years there has been a revival and much new building on the south side of the island, especially in three places all bearing resounding British names: Aberdeen, Repulse Bay and Stanley. These are of course the names that the British colonists inflicted upon them. Heung Tsai (little Hong Kong) was renamed Aberdeen in 1848 as tribute to the Secretary of State for the Colonies, the Earl of Aberdeen. Its bay provides anchorage for about 20,000 of the estimated 70,000 Hong Kong people who live on boats. At one time there may be 2–3,000 junks and sampans in Aberdeen Bay. From a distance they look attractive and romantic, but when you climb on board, most prove to be chaotic, rickety and rather smelly and slummy. They are guarded by fierce dogs and generally festooned with washing. The Hong Kong government has been trying to lure the boat-dwellers from the sea by building housing estates, opening schools and reclaiming the harbour land. There are two main tribes of boat people, the Tanka (literally the 'egg people' because they used to pay taxes in eggs) and the Hoklo.

Fishing is their main occupation, but tourism offers a useful supplement. Sampan-rides through the harbour are popular; so is a visit by sampan to the aptly named Jumbo floating restaurant – big enough to take several busloads of tourists – where customers are invited to choose their own fresh fish, still swimming in large tanks. Aberdeen also has a number of boatyards where junks are built. Besides sampans – propelled by a person in the prow using a pole – Hong Kong's inshore waters are populated by faster, bigger, motorized launches, properly known as Walla-Wallas. Even locals argue about whether this name derives from the chugging noise of the engine or from the first boat of the kind owned by a man from Walla Walla, Washington, in the USA. Walla-Wallas, which can seat forty people, are used for ferrying sailors to ships anchored in the roads.

The neighbouring area of Stanley (also named after a nineteenth-century Secretary of State for the Colonies) has a strong seafaring history. It was a haunt of pirates long before the British arrived. Today it is the home of the Hong Kong Sea School, which trains boys in seamanship. It is also renowned for its markets, offering a wide variety of goods, notably fashionable clothes that can be picked up for a fraction of the price they would fetch in Europe or even in a Hong Kong department store. At weekends Stanley and nearby Repulse Bay (named after a British warship HMS *Repulse*) are crowded by both westerners and local Chinese. They tend to be segregated, with the westerners in the markets or on their boats and the Chinese filling every square millimetre of the beach.

Segregation of the Chinese and the visitors is a continuing fact of Hong Kong life and is almost by mutual consent. At workplaces, of course, there are many Chinese working for western companies headed by expatriates. In recent years, since rich Chinese like Li Ka-shing and Yue-Kong Pao have taken over big once-British business concerns, there have been increasing numbers of expatriate managers working for Chinese bosses. Sometimes affectionate friendships result. Among the younger people in particular there's been a breaking down of traditional racial barriers. But it is still a matter of concern for a Chinese family if their son or daughter is tempted to marry a foreigner. A white stranger is traditionally described as *gweilo*, literally 'pale ghost'. This, originally a term of great insult, has come to be regarded almost as an expression of endearment, widely used by foreigners of themselves. But the term still suggests the great divide: to the Chinese, China is still the centre of the earth. To the Cantonese everyone else is a ghost of some kind or another: black or brown strangers are *morlau* or black ghosts. The attitude borders on racism.

Hong Kong island itself still remains very Chinese. Ironically, the area where traditional Chinese practices are most entrenched is close to the very spot where the first British colonists landed in 1841. Possession Point, now some distance inland, is in the heart of the Western district (known in Chinese as Sai Ying Pun). The film *The World of Suzie Wong* was largely shot in Western because Wanchai was thought to be too modern and un-Chinese. There's no monument to the original take-over of Hong Kong apart from the names of Possession Street and of Belcher Street, named after the captain of HMS *Sulphur*, whose crew became the first British sailors officially to set foot on Hong Kong. Though the bulldozers are on the way, tearing out old buildings in the name of progress, the western district remains almost the last concentrated bastion of traditional Chinese artisans. It is the world of the Man Mo temple, reeking of incense and with worshippers muttering mantras to gods in dark corners. It is an area in which there is a surprise on virtually every street corner. If you peer into the darkness of the shops, you can find rice merchants, jade carvers, fan-makers, people making costumes for Chinese street opera, ivory carvers, fortune-tellers, shops selling ginseng, snake-wine, hundred-year-old eggs, funeral wreathes and Chinese herbal medicines and herbs, including potions based on recipes several thousand years old. Among the profusion of specialists are mahjong makers, offering a wide range of products from modern plastic to the most delicately carved ivory at exquisite prices.

There are carvers of Chinese name-stamps called chops. Even today many Hong Kong Chinese carry a personal chop as an essential part of their belongings. Individually carved with the name in Chinese characters, it serves as the equivalent of a signature. Using his or her chop, which may be made of stone, ivory, jade or wood, a person can draw money from the bank or acknowledge receipt of documents.

Down at ground level in Western, many of Hong Kong's Chinese banks have their headquarters on or around Des Voeux Road West. In the area known as Nam Pak Hong (North-South trading houses) is a series of shops that exude exotic though slightly fusty smells. These come from traditional and much cherished Chinese produce like dried mushrooms, dried sharks' fins, birds' nests, abalones and snakes. At first sight there is something old-fashioned and Dickensian about the dingy interiors stocked with bags and chests of goods, but these are often big businesses, employing both the traditional abacus and modern electronic calculators, and with traders continuously on the telephone striking deals.

The Chinese areas on the fringes of Central and in Western are a higgledy-piggledy land of disorganization and disorder. Streets, lanes and little alleyways veer off sharply in odd directions. Soon the ground begins to rise steeply in a series of not quite parallel lanes climbing towards the mid-levels. Many are named after nineteenth-century British politicians or forgotten administrators, such as Caine, Elgin, Graham, Lyndhurst, Peel, Pottinger, Seymour, Shelley, Staunton. Beside every road there are tiny shops, virtual one-man factories in miniature where cobblers, key-cutters, carpenters and other artisans ply their trade. You must go on foot and look into the nooks and crannies to appreciate the full richness and variety. The streets and the houses look mean and insignificant, but they have their own individuality and some of them are surprisingly old by Hong Kong standards, boasting their own balustrades or delicate pieces of carving in iron or wood. Searching for the oddities and eccentricities is one way of distracting yourself from the effort of the climb. Some of the area has already succumbed to the nastier temptations of the modern age. The antique shops in Hollywood Road are mostly tarted up and charge tourists high prices for their wares. If you know what you are looking for and can tell a Tang dynasty horse from a fake you might find something worthwhile to take home, though probably at a price. Where Ladder Street meets Hollywood Road, there is the 'thieves market', also called 'Cat Street'. There are arguments about the name and whether it was derived from 'cat burglars' or 'cathouses' (brothels) or was a derivation from pidgin English 'catchee' (to buy). In shops and stalls by the roadside goods are piled indiscriminately: you may find cheap bric-à-brac or you may find genuine antiques that make the search worthwhile.

Those with sharp eyes may also spot evidence of continuing deep Chinese religious feelings. On Staunton Street, just before it reaches Peel Street, is a small shrine to the City God, the guardian of city dwellers, who is supposed to speak on behalf of a dead person to the ten judges who sit and decide punishment for the sins of the dead. Dotted in the various places are shrines to earth gods (*Tsu Ti*) who protect small communities, listen to the gossip and keep a record of births, marriages and deaths; it's easy to miss them since they are small and may only be marked by spent incense sticks and the smoke they have left behind.

At the Western end of Hollywood Road, cheek by jowl are several shops making the huge wooden coffins that the Chinese are proud to keep under their beds ready for the day that they need them, a dry-cleaner-cum-jeweller's shop, a butcher's and a shop selling funeral decorations. From inside gloomy houses there is the unmistakable clickety-clack of mahjong tiles. On the streets ancient people watch the world go by, or sit drinking tea, or look after tiny tots whose skin is as smooth and unlined as the old folks' faces are engraved like a complicated relief map of Hong Kong island. In some alleyways there are small hutchments of the really poor people, dirty, dank and unhygienic, little more than orange boxes or cardboard lined with yellowing newspaper. The shiny passage of a Rolls-Royce for a split second reflects the squalor, before it purrs away. Hong Kong is a very unequal society, perhaps the most unequal on earth, though not until you get to congested Kowloon do you see the equality of inequality, with row upon row of poor caged apartments. But on Hong Kong island there are plentiful reminders. For example, abutting the modern plate-glass of Sogo department store in Causeway Bay is a decaying, crowded apartment block. A window box of flowers, flags of washing, dying plants, a plaintively chirruping bird, testify to the individualism and humanity that have not been quite smashed by the wretched living conditions. Birds are important to the ordinary Cantonese, companions to be taken – in their cages – for an early morning constitutional, just as an American or European would take his or her pet dog. Into Kowloon on Causeway Bay tea-houses birds are taken to sing to each other while their owners talk. Hui Hing, who has run a bird shop – well, more of a stall, since it is only 11 feet 10 inches long by 3 feet deep – in Western for forty years, says that birds may cost as little as HK$20 or as much as HK$15,000 for strong fighting birds.

Even in the Chinese Western district, the twentieth century is pressing on apace. The area resounds to the sounds of bulldozers and jackhammers as Hong Kong's business and banking district extends remorselessly westwards. Hui Hing's birds find it hard to make their songs heard above the din. And the shop may die with the Hui parents; their children have found more lucrative occupations. Along the waterfront of Hong Kong island are the traditional routes to the rest of the territory, to the so-called 'outlying islands' (though many of them are within sight and only twenty minutes to an hour away by ferry), to Macao, and also to Kowloon, which once was the start of one of the world's great railway adventures – from Hong Kong through Canton and China to join up with the Trans-Siberian Railway through Mongolia and the Soviet Union to Western Europe. Today only the tower of the Kowloon railway terminus stands next to the Star Ferry, a forlorn amputated finger from the past. The railway headquarters has moved several hundred metres away to Hung Hom, and from there there are daily through trains to Canton in Chinese livery.

These days too there are a variety of ways of getting across the Hong Kong harbour to Kowloon: they include the old trusted 'Star' Ferry and vehicular ferries, but there is also the Cross-Harbour Tunnel at Causeway Bay or, since 1980, the Mass Transit (underground) Railway which whisks passengers from Hong Kong to Kowloon in a mere three minutes, in carriages with stainless steel seats – easier to sluice down, it is said. Another cross-harbour tunnel with road and MTR links at Lei Yue Mun to the east of Causeway Bay opened in late 1989. On both sides of the 'Star' Ferry are living memorials to an older age: ancient rickshaw-pullers sitting in front of their machines, now idle except for posing for tourists or pulling visitors on an expensive ride round the local block.

The MTR and the 'Star' Ferry deposit their passengers in Tsim Sha Tsui, at the tip of the Kowloon peninsula and surely the biggest, gaudiest shopping extravaganza the world has known. Not for nothing is Nathan Road known as the 'Golden Mile'. It hardly seems imaginable that until after the Second World War Nathan Road was a tree-lined boulevard that acquired the nickname of 'Nathan's Folly' because no one thought it would ever be developed. It was a picnic place for idle Sundays. Nowadays Nathan Road is decorated in gaudiest cluttered neon – though the signs don't flash, as their proximity to Kai Tak airport could involve dangerous disturbance to incoming aircraft. There's an absence here of the really skyscraping buildings that mark Hong Kong's Central District. All buildings in Tsim Sha Tsui and adjoining areas are restricted to about seventeen storeys because of the closeness of the airport and the soil on which they are built. It gives a curiously truncated look: these temples of Mammon cut off in the middle of their money-making prime. In the last ten years the Golden Mile has become so crowded that new glittering pleasure and spending palaces have opened on reclaimed land at Tsim Sha Tsui East: there there are several more shopping malls and luxury hotels displaying all that the greediest collector of twentieth-century goods and services could ever dream of. It's an area where the stranger should beware. Many of the shops have their fair share of hustlers, who will push the unwary visitor into unwise purchases of cameras, clothes (whether high fashion or cheap T-shirts), shoes, silk, Chinese antiques or artefacts. The best rule is to go to one of the big department stores, to a shop displaying the 'red junk' logo of the Hong Kong Tourist Association, or to know what you are looking for and the price you should pay for it.

In spite of government efforts to control them, money changers, particularly in Tsim Sha Tsui, represent one of Hong Kong's worst bargains. Under government pressure they have to display their rates, but the apparently attractive exchange rate on the board is that for the money changers' selling of US dollars, while most tourists want to buy Hong Kong dollars. There's also a hefty commission charge.

In Tsim Sha Tsui East are Club Volvo and China City, which claim to be the biggest entertainment centres in the world. Club Volvo has a huge dance lounge (6,510 square metres, 70,000 square feet). That is equivalent to two football fields joined together. The visitor doesn't have to worry about walking over this vast area; he will be driven to his personal 'relaxation zone' in a full-sized but battery-powered replica of an old open-top Rolls-Royce. Myriad lights twinkle overhead. Those who've made the trip claim it is rather like going along the runway at an international airport, but upside down. The club was started in 1984. One of the founders was Mrs Loretta Fung, sister of Mrs Anna Chennault, widow of the legendary General Claire Chennault, who started the 'Flying Tigers' in China during the Second World War. For a club that seems the ultimate in capitalist decadence, Volvo has strong Chinese connections. The ribbon-cutting opening ceremony was performed by, among others, Wang Guangying, chairman of the China-backed Everbright group, and Li Chuwen, then vice-director of Xinhua, the New China News Agency. The attractions for customers include a thousand hostesses, dressed in traditional silk cheongsams slit to the thigh, and specially selected for their beauty, poise and conversational skills. The hostesses are supervised by a hundred 'mama-sans' who carry walkie-talkies to respond speedily to their customers' requests. Digital clocks linked to computers are placed over the seating areas and begin to operate immediately a hostess joins the customer – for conversation and restrained flirtation. The drinks don't come cheaply. A bottle of cognac costs more than US$100. Girls can be taken out for a full night on the town for about $150. Fans of Club Volvo claim it's a better bargain than being ripped off by the hustlers of Wanchai or Kowloon bars. For Japanese customers the club maintains quiet and private areas. If customer support is anything to go by, Volvo claims a big success: daily turnover topped HK$700,000 in 1987. The club has had its ups and downs, including a firebombing attempt by the 14K Triad gang only hours before its opening. Some other nightclubs tried to lure girls away through full-page advertisements; Club Volvo counter-attacked by offering mama-sans at other clubs HK$1 million if they deserted and brought forty women with them. In late 1987 the club announced it was planning a public offering of 25 per cent of its shares, an attempt which brought objectors, claiming the Club Volvo was selling a 'Mickey Mouse' share that would bring discredit to the local market. (The stock market listing did not materialize.)

Night-club entertainment has clearly been developed by male chauvinists. A Club Volvo manager said: 'Lady guests may accompany men; no ladies on their own.' Club Volvo's decor has been described as 'imaginative' and having 'the style and tone of a kind of high class Star Wars bordello'. By comparison China City – which has 300 hostesses of different nationalities – has created a lush patio including an aviary full of lovebirds. Tony Lai, manager of China City, once boasted that 'compared with us, every other night club in Hong Kong is just a small store. We're the supermarkets of the night life business.'

Another, very different building that richly illustrates the jam-packed variety of Tsim Sha Tsui is considerably older. Chungking Mansions was built in 1962, at the time that Hong Kong's building restrictions were relaxed. From the basement, full to the brim with shops offering a huge range of goods, to the topmost floors where cheap lodging houses and travel agents are crammed together, Chungking Mansions epitomizes the hustle and bustle of Hong Kong's seedier side. The basement floor, for example, shouldn't be given over to shops of any kind. It was supposed to be a car park, but cars were never parked there. The regulations were broken from the very start. Sometimes the block is known as 'Little India' because of the predominance of Indian-owned shops offering clothes, bags, trinkets and knick-knacks of all shapes and sizes and gaudiness. On the ground floor there is a huge nightclub which once figured in crime reports involving Triad gangs. As you climb to the top you pass more shops, a range of curry restaurants, several floors of apartments and then the cheap hotels. Here everything and everyone works hard for a living. In the curry restaurants several proprietors begin looking at the clock after 9.30 p.m., as they are anxious to turn the space over to sleeping accommodation. In 1985 a reporter from the *South China Morning Post* summed up the attractions of Chungking Mansions: 'To stay there can cost as little as HK$20 a night – depending on what you want. To eat, even less – depending on what you can stomach. And marijuana sells for about HK$300 – depending on your bent.' Once a grand sight in Tsim Sha Tsui, by the late 1980s the mansions had become infamous rather than famous. As the *Morning Post* reporter put it, it had become a 'mecca of cheap guest houses, curry restaurants, bustling shops, crime and shady small business'. Lack of proper cleaning and supervision made the building not so much a mere eyesore, more a menace to public health. Local inhabitants said that even many of the prostitutes had been driven out by the deteriorating conditions. Illegal structures littered the outside ground floors. Inefficient air-conditioners poured lukewarm drops of water and hot air all over the place. Irregular garbage collection led to corridors and stairwells being strewn with rubbish. Going up to one of the curry restaurants presented the difficult choice of riding in a shaky, dirty, smelly lift that seemed ready to give up the ghost at the next moment, or trying to climb a virtually impenetrable mush of garbage on the stairs. Then in 1987 the authorities started a clean-up. Illegal structures were removed and regular rubbish collection was arranged, so that the mansion was no longer an immediate threat to health. But it remains a patched-up memorial to the get-rich-quick property dealers of the 1960s.

For all these deficiencies, Chungking Mansions has many supporters. For young tourists it offers a cheap place to stay. If they are prepared to put up with crumbling plaster, cockroaches, dirty mattresses and dormitory living, and to guard their possessions with their lives, a room can be had for a few US dollars a night there. With air-conditioning of a sort and privacy, it would still cost less than a fifth of the price of the cheapest nearby first-class hotel, and less than 8 per cent of the cost of a single room at the Peninsula Hotel, or the modern Regent Hotel, both of them fewer than a hundred metres away.

In spite of all its cheap drabness, Chungking Mansions offers to the careful observer lovely serendipitous little surprises that come just when you despair of the caked dirt of ages. The mansions has more than 600 different units of shops, hotels, apartments, offices and factories in its five blocks. On the eleventh floor of one of the blocks is the home of a small, rather shrivelled Chinese man and his wife and family. Au Yue Shan's flat is cramped and unattractive. The moment you enter you are likely to cough, having disturbed the fine, light layer of dust that covers everything. The reason is that the flat is also an ivory-carving factory. Au himself sits in one nook like an ancient elf, watched over by the family cat, carving chunks of ivory into the most delicate jewelled shapes. Sometimes Au allows other workers to do some of the basic carving, but he reserves the final touches and polishing for himself. He's been doing the work ever since he was 13, and he started this business in 1972. He likes the location of Chungking Mansions, 'since it is very central and close to all the shops that buy my work'. Au carvings can be seen in many Tsim Sha Tsui shop windows at very fancy prices, reflecting the fineness of his work. International alarm over the fate of the African elephant now threatens the livelihood of Au and Hong Kong's other 1,500 ivory carvers. The colony's biggest markets for carvings, Japan and the USA, in June 1989 prohibited imports of raw or worked ivory from Hong Kong. The belated decision to protect the African elephant from extinction through a total ban on dealings in its tusks will, if effective, remove the market for a Hong Kong business worth almost HK$700 million a year. The colony's traders had cleverly got round regulations against poached ivory by buying crudely worked ivory from the Gulf, sometimes from workshops they had themselves set up in Dubai. This gave international documentation to the tusks whatever their origin, legitimate or not. Au's tragedy is that he is a simple craftsman threatened with extinction. The international ivory traders can move on to some other lucrative business.

Encountering the Aus is a reminder that this area of Kowloon, besides being a tourist paradise, is also home for millions of ordinary Chinese as well as something of the world's workshop. The Aus' quarters are cramped, but a good deal less so than those of many other Hong Kong citizens. Away from the tourist tracks and deeper into Kowloon the area begins to resemble an unpleasant 'urban jungle'. Here and there are surprises that can delight the eye. The Yau Ma Tei typhoon shelter looks picturesque with its clusters of boats, but the shelter is also famous for its floating brothels. These one-woman loveboats offer pleasure diced with danger, not least because people on neighbouring boats don't relish their games of mahjong being interrupted. In Temple Street in Yau Ma Tei there are famous night markets that only come to life when the sun goes down and their lights go on. Where Kansu and Reclamation Streets meet is Hong Kong's famous jade market. At the Yau Ma Tei car park are professional letter-writers. Shanghai Street is decked out with shop after shop selling items for brides. Also in Yau Ma

Tei there is a complex of temples dedicated to Tin Hau, the protector of fishermen, to Shing Wong, the City God, and to the gods of earth and mercy.

Further inland into Kowloon the surprises are fewer, but some still survive. In the crowded Sau Mau Ping housing estate is a temple to the monkey god, a much-loved rascal and favourite of Chinese children. He was once described as 'a kind of oriental Santa Claus, Charlie Chaplin and Mickey Mouse reincarnated into one'. And at Wong Tai Sin there is the famous temple of the same name. To an outsider it is no great work of art, and it was built in the 1970s, but it is an important community centre. It is also a favourite place for fortune-telling, particularly popular with racing punters anxious for guidance on which horse to back.

But apart from these pleasant spots, urban Kowloon is a densely packed jungle in which apartments, factories, roads and traffic all fight with people for space. The average Kowloon inhabitant has just 9 square feet of territory to himself. Most residents defiantly try to stake out their claims to individuality with garlands of plants, lines of washing, or a cage containing a canary or other songbird to brighten up a shabby, cramped existence. As you look up at the solid walls of flats with bars to keep out robbers, they appear very much like personalized prisons packed one on top of another. Factories and homes jostle for space and neither have sufficient room to breathe. Yet this is very much how the Hong Kong industrial and economic miracle started. In home-made backyard factories, Hong Kong refugees with little more than brave entrepreneurial dreams in their heads used their quick wit and willingness to work all hours of the day and night to good effect. They quickly learnt about world market demands and realized that, uninhibited by a 'permit raj' government, they could move faster than any rivals. It was the classic capitalist situation, competition leading to the survival of the fittest. Although the territory has long moved beyond making only simple things like wigs and plastic flowers, most Hong Kong exports still involve super-quick assembly-line operations. This is true of most toys and watches, where the trick is to assemble the goods quickly and add the latest fads whether they be motors, computer aids, 'Cabbage Patch' or 'Ninja' features. Visit Hong Kong toy factories in Kwun Tong or the New Territories and you will see piles of dolls' eyes like frog-spawn staring at you from one basket, hair for wigs from another. In the textile trades, gigantic leaps have been made, and operators now sit at video screens able to move a cursor or press a button to produce a whole cut pattern virtually at a finger-tip. It is a shock to go from such a clean computerized environment to the mad world on the doorstep, with lorries, buses and aircraft all roaring past.

Government action has brought big changes in housing. When a fire in 1954 left thousands of people homeless, the government had to take action. It moved rapidly and started building tower blocks of apartments. Today 2.8 million people, or almost half of the total population, live in apartments built by the government. The government housing authority manages more than half a million rental flats on 122 housing estates, one of the world's largest public housing stocks. New flats are being built at about 40,000 a year. It's easy to be critical. The early Mark I and Mark II flats built in the mid-1950s and early 1960s suffer from cramped space and have communal bathing, laundry and toilet facilities. Because of the shortage of space, cooking is done in the corridor. The fug of stale food smells lingers in the air.

Attitudes on the estates vary. Some people are glad that they have a roof over their heads, a job, a TV set, refrigerator and most mod cons, knowing that their relatives in China don't live as well as this. The more socially conscious condemn the government for not doing enough and for the extremes of living conditions between the overcrowded poor in Kowloon and the fat cats on the Peak or on private beach-fronted properties. What worries the politically conscious is that the biggest, fattest cats of Hong Kong are the firmest friends of Communist China across the border, soon to be their master. The government, and the more optimistic apartment-dwellers, respond that there was an impossible amount to do in a short time. Hong Kong's is after all a refugee population. The Mark I and Mark II flats are now being pulled down. The new blocks are lighter and airier, with private facilities, separate kitchens and an average of 4 to 5 square metres per adult. It's not much by western standards, still less by those of the fat cats, but there is the constant hope that the children, thanks to their education, will break out and be able to enjoy a standard of living that their parents can only dream of.

The battle is not yet won. Almost 400,000 people still live in what are called 'tolerated squatter settlements', hillside hutchments that have been 'improved' through providing communal lavatories and showers and concrete pathways so that the whole camp does not slip away with the mud in annual torrential rains. The housing struggle will go on until the next century, simply because Chinese family patterns are changing. Previously three generations would live together; now the nuclear family is emerging. Children want to be on their own with their own families. Demands for housing are continuing to grow, even though the refugee flow has been staunched by the draconian measure of handing back illegal immigrants to China.

It is a humbling experience to visit the ordinary homes of Kowloon sardine-tin dwellers, especially after the palaces of the Peak. The young British banker up there may feel he is master of all he surveys: there, the pecking order is decided by how much of a harbour view the inhabitant has. There's little such luxury in overcrowded Kwun Tong, Mong Kok and Sham Shui Po. Here the choice is between the washing and the walls of a neighbour's flat or perhaps a glimpse of the choking fumes from the traffic rumbling many storeys below, In one Kwun Tong estate, a Mark II twelve-storey version (scheduled to be pulled down in 1990), the view is shrouded by other buildings and by neighbours' washing. Except on the clearest days you need an electric light to distinguish who is sitting across the same room from you. The gloom might be described as that of a nineteenth-century slum, but for the eerie glow cast by the television set. There's no space wasted, for example, on lavatory, or bathroom, or kitchen – simply because the flat does not have any of these facilities.

The Lam family who live here came from China in the 1950s and is conscious that it is not the worst off in Hong Kong. People who live on squatter estates and are at the mercy of the Triad gangs have a lot less security. The Lam parents and the seven of their nine children left at home are crammed into the three small rooms. Some sleep in bunks, some on the floor and the two smallest boys find a space to sleep on the balcony that is used during the day for cooking. The earnings of the family are pooled, and Mrs Lam worries about what will happen when another child marries and leaves or when they get old. They travel by bus and complain that the MTR is too expensive, but this is a two-television family, having one large black-and-white model and a smaller colour set. They have a telephone, and the living room is littered with the brand-name products advertised on television. There is no proper storage space to hide the plethora of household aids and beauty products. Immediately we arrive a giant bottle of Coca-Cola is brought out to wish us well.

Cantonese-speaking Mrs Lam is not very talkative. Her horizons are clearly limited. When asked if anyone in the neighbourhood had really become rich, she thought and replied that one husband and wife had become hawkers, sold fish and had earned enough to buy their own flat. Our interpreter interjected that the area in which the 'rich' couple lived was hardly a step up from the Kwun Tong housing estate.

The opportunity of going from rags to riches is supposed to be the biggest asset of the Hong Kong *laissez-faire* system, but in the modern age even the moderately poor like the Lams never get within reach of a handle with which to haul themselves up to the level of owning a cheap Japanese car, let alone a Mercedes. The quality of the local schooling is poor, and there are never enough resources to get a head start in business. One of the daughters, by dint of studying at night school, had managed to get five 'O'-level passes, but is now stuck trying to find a job – in the police or government service – which will justify her qualifications and pay her the higher salary deserved for all the effort. The Lam children have had more education than their parents and have more grumbles. The eldest daughter living at home had recently returned from China and in slightly hesitant English she thoughtfully summed up the differences between the two societies. 'China is not as primitive as it used to be. The environment is better than Hong Kong and the food is adequate. But there is not the freedom.' As for the British, the daughter had no good words, because, she said, she had seen how the expatriates live and how the Hong Kong Chinese are left vulnerable. In housing and in jobs, she thought, there was a need for some kind of protection. 'Hong Kong is supposed to be rich. Why should we be left poor?'

In the more modern Kowloon estates to which the Lams will soon be moved there is more space per head, private cooking and bathing facilities, better planning and shopping facilities. But the family still worries about whether it will be able to afford the higher rents in the new place, since they will have to pay almost 20 per cent of the family income instead of less than 10 per cent. Fares to work will also be higher. Even on the most modern estates in the new towns life is cramped. The statistics say that Hong Kong has almost caught up in per capita income terms with the United Kingdom. But clearly the evidence in Hong Kong is that some people are much more unequal than others.

In spite of the inequalities it is difficult to find Hong Kong revolutionaries. Local leftists would elsewhere be described as liberals with a social conscience. The aspiration to be rich and successful is all-pervasive. A social worker with Caritas, the Roman Catholic charity, explained that there is a difference in attitudes between Asians and westerners: 'Here, in Asia, people look on a capitalist with envy, but then work hard to emulate him; in the West, the mentality is to look on a successful man with hatred and try to fight him and knock him out.'

Everywhere Hong Kong is busy with the initiative and energy to make money, whether in modern or traditional markets. In overcrowded Sham Shui Po is the huge 'golden' arcade full of computers and computer parts and accessories at rock-bottom prices. Police raids for pirated goods interrupt but don't stop the shops. It is an unlikely spot for such a modern business, slap in the middle of a typical jostling, hustling very Chinese area. Just round the corner are street markets including stalls offering snake medicines. One Chinese friend claims to have seen a stallholder bite the head off a live cobra to get fresh snake blood. 'We Chinese insist that things are fresh', he says with pride.

Cramped living quarters help to explain the Hong Kong people's love of eating out. In the past few years they have taken to western-style fast food. By the late 1980s Hong Kong boasted the world's largest Pizza Hut, serving a customer every ten seconds. The territory has many flourishing McDonalds hamburger restaurants, which cater to one person per second.

Luckily Hong Kong doesn't stop at Kowloon, but has been able to draw on the broad acres of the so-called New Territories which comprise 90 per cent of the total land area. When political negotiations started between Britain and China over Hong Kong's future, some fanciful notions were expressed that perhaps it would be possible that British Hong Kong – meaning the bits ceded to Britain in perpetuity – could not be returned to China, but must be maintained as British. The multi-millionaire Stanley Ho, who holds the gambling franchise for Macao, was one of those who thought this would be possible, provided Kai Tak airport was counted in British Hong Kong and provided that British Hong Kong had access to the Kwai Chung container port (conversations with the author during the negotiations). To anyone actually patrolling the boundaries of British Hong Kong today, it was a far-fetched idea. Hong Kong slips quietly from Kowloon into the New Territories. Boundary Street, the actual boundary between the theoretically ceded territory of Kowloon and the theoretically leased territory of the New

Territories, is virtually the same on one side as on the other, packed with offices, houses, shops and playing fields. Kai Tak airport is built on reclaimed land, but British officials drawing their lines on the map reckoned that part of it at least came within the area of leased territory rather than the ceded Kowloon.

The New Territories are the most rapidly changing part of Hong Kong. Eight so-called 'new towns' are springing up in various parts of the once rolling green fields. Already three of them, Tsuen Wan, Sha Tin and Tuen Mun house 1.5 million people. Other settlements at Tai Po, Fanling and Yuen Long, where nearly 400,000 people live today, are being developed into new towns. Other developments are in hand at Junk Bay on the Sai Kung peninsula and at Tin Shui Wai in the north-western New Territories. All told, by the late 1990s the population of the New Territories will be nearly 3.5 million people, compared with 1.8 million in the mid-1980s and fewer than half a million at the start of the 1970s. Old lifestyles are being swept away. The government in the 1980s greatly restricted pig farming, though it refused to ban it completely in spite of its contribution to the growing pollution problem. A generation ago the New Territories were largely given over to paddy farming. Today the developed New Territories offer a better life for a wide range of people, with more room for housing, greater personal space and light and air and recreation facilities.

They also offer expanded space for properly zoned industrial facilities. At the start there was resistance to the development. Original inhabitants didn't like to see the environment destroyed or the way of life disrupted. Some of the newcomers too didn't like being displaced to homes far distant from the places they knew and loved. Where this also entailed long journeys to work, the comments were especially bitter. But gradually, as the towns are being properly developed, with their own recreation areas, shopping and transport become easier and the new inhabitants of the New Territories are discovering that it's a better life, especially for bringing up children. There may even be room for growing children to study at home for their higher education, a simple enough need, but a luxury in heavily congested Kowloon. Initially the new towns were greatly criticized. Legislative Councillor Hui Yin-fat called them 'cemeteries with lights on'. He now concedes that progress has been made, but says that the government has been slow to install social amenities. One of the saddest sights of Kai Tak airport is that of students sitting on the floor of the concourse reading their books. Kai Tak offers a comfortable air-conditioned environment for studying – even though there aren't enough seats.

Tuen Mun, one of the burgeoning new towns, used to be a fishing village. In 1959 its most important building was put up, the Ching Chung Koon temple dedicated to Liu Tong Bun, who was born in 789 AD and is one of the Taoist Eight Immortals (people with legendary reputations who have been deified and have the power to become invisible and to bring the dead back to life). The temple includes important relics of Liu, including his magic devil-slaying sword and fly-switch. In front of the altar is a thousand-year-old jade seal. The temple also contains many Chinese art treasures and almost 4,000 books on the history of Taoism. The large complex is unusual, since it also offers a home for old people with no relatives or means of support. But today Tuen Mun has been enveloped by modern buildings. Factories include the YKK zipper concern and toymaker Playmates (which is staying even when its manufacturing moves to China). Tall blocks of flats offer homes that are palaces compared with the airless cages of Kowloon.

Another success story is Sha Tin, a decade ago a quiet place where water buffaloes pulled ploughs through the rice paddies and from which fishing smacks put out to sea. The Lion Rock hills cut Sha Tin off from the rest of Hong Kong, though the place was always well known, since it is located near Amah Rock. This clump of granite supposedly resembles a woman with a baby on her back. According to legend it commemorates the wife of a fisherman who went to sea but didn't return. She waited for him day after day for a year, until the gods took pity on her and turned her into stone. The rock today is a place of pilgrimage for Chinese women.

By the early 1990s Sha Tin will house half a million people. In spite of regiments of housing blocks reaching thirty-six storeys it is not just an urban jungle, but a town with facilities including parks, cinemas, Japanese department stores, a seventeen-storey hotel and the famous modern race course. Indeed, its more fanciful supporters boast that Sha Tin is so attractive that it has become a place where Kowloon-dwellers spend holiday week-ends by the sea. People pull up chairs to watch the daily music show at the fountain of the New Town Plaza; it dances to western and Chinese orchestral music.

In the New Territories it is still possible to see old Chinese ways at their most traditional and colourful. It will be a pity if they disappear completely and all that remains of them is the Sung dynasty village at Lai Chi Kok amusement park; that village recreates the China of a thousand years ago. G. R. Sayer, historian of Hong Kong, saw the New Territories through rather romantic glasses when he wrote: 'Tales of its beauty and enchantment were passed back across Kowloon hills – tales of paved mountain paths, walled villages of the plain, sequestered shrines, rocky pools of crystal water, cliff and shelving strand, plateau and majestic peak, silent bays, silver sand . . .' The San On district of China's Guangdong province, of which the New Territories was a large part a century and more ago, was infested by pirates and bandits, and its own clans were frequently warring among themselves. But it is an area with a longer history of settlement than Hong Kong island itself and stretching back for 5,000 years. The very name of Kowloon has interesting legends attached to it. According to these, a boy emperor fleeing to what is now Kowloon noticed that there were eight hills, so he called them the 'eight dragons'. However, a servant gently corrected him, pointing out that the Emperor was also regarded as a dragon – so they should be called the nine dragons, or in Chinese *Gau Loong* (Kowloon). Thanks to constant construction, reclamation and flattening of hills, it is no longer possible to count the dragons. Near Kai Tak airport there is a park that has a memorial to the boy emperor. He met his death in Hong Kong. Mongol invaders were threatening, and to avoid being captured the chief minister took the eight-year-old-boy in his arms and jumped into the sea, thus ending the Sung dynasty.

Some of the New Territories villages have a history going back to the Sung Dynasty (AD 960–1279). The area is also home for a number of interesting temples. The so-called Temple of Ten Thousand Buddhas at Sha Tin actually has 12,800 Buddha statues of carved wood and sculpted clay. It is reached only after a steep and depressing climb up a concrete path, up a hillside littered with rubbish (431 steps, says one guidebook). After another gentler, shorter climb, there is another temple of Man Fat, dedicated to its founder the monk Yuet Kai, whose body, covered with gold, sits inside the temple.

In rural parts of Hong Kong some old Chinese practices, long abandoned in China, continue. It is still possible for example to see traditional walled villages. In many of these houses are packed closely together and all face in the same direction – towards what the Chinese traditionally always called south, whatever the compass said. The front of the house would be determined by the *fung shui* but always known as the south or 'red bird'; the left-hand side would be east or 'green dragon'; the right, west or 'right tiger'; and the rear, the north or 'black warrior', sometimes 'tortoise'. Watch towers or walls would be built because of the serious fighting between villages. This continued long after the British extended their rule. Houses frequently had a wall in front of them and traditionally didn't have windows. Both devices were intended to deter evil spirits. Chinese believe that spirits cannot move except in straight lines. Sometimes the defensive measures were supported by strategically placed mirrors – evil spirits are supposedly ugly and afraid of seeing themselves.

Many of the old villages are still inhabited by people who all bear the same family name. The New Territories were dominated by the five great clans, of whom the Tangs (Dangs) were the first to arrive in the twelfth century. The seventeenth-century fortified Kat Hing Wai village, still inhabited by Tangs, though with television aerials topping the fortifications, is now a tourist attraction. But in various places there are old ancestral halls of other clans, the Haws, Pangs, Lins and Mans. Some date back five or six centuries, and today form small patches of history in a rapidly changing environment.

In some places in the New Territories it is also possible to see large stone urns in clusters, normally on hillsides. They contain the bones of people who died many years ago. Traditional Chinese have never favoured cremation, even though it is becoming the rule in China. Buried bodies are exhumed after ten years or so (because of pressure of land, after seven in urban Hong Kong). Families polish the bones and put them in these earthen pots to await burial in their final resting-place – which would of course be determined by the *fung shui* (and by whether the descendants had saved enough money for a suitable final home). A proper grave would be in the shape of a Greek letter omega.

The New Territories still has its green spaces, including country parks and hiking trails. The government boasts that 70 per cent of the territory is countryside. Tai Mo Shan, the highest point (957 metres), is in the middle of the New Territories. The Mai Po marshes close to the Chinese border are a bird sanctuary. But it is the people who prove the most interesting aspect of the area. Some of the rural dwellers of the New Territories were quick to realize the advantages of a British passport, and Chinatown in London's Soho is largely populated by Hong Kong Chinese from the rural areas, who migrated before the London government created a second-class British passport issued in Hong Kong. Many migrants could only speak Cantonese and some of them still haven't learnt English. But the New Territories also has people who have been the most resistant to change, including farmers who till little garden-sized plots of land or keep pigs. Camera-shy Hakka women wearing black pyjama suits and oversized hats can also be seen working in the fields and in the markets as well as on construction sites all over Hong Kong. The matriarchal tribe originally came from northern China generations ago and their very name Hakka (or 'guest people') shows their outsider status even today.

Hong Kong's land ends where the territory meets the Shum Chum river, on the other side of which the yellow-starred red flag of China flutters. But there are other parts of the territory – in all 235 islands ranged around the colony. Most of them are small, but the three biggest are Lantau, Lamma and Cheung Chau. All of the islands have their own special character. Cheung Chau, the smallest of the large islands, is noted for its annual 'bun festival', celebrated every May to exorcise wandering ghosts. The island, on which motor vehicles are forbidden, used to be a haunt of pirates. Today most of the people are fishermen. But there is also a large expatriate community that prefers the rural pleasantness of the island. Lamma is also attractive, nicknamed the 'stone age island' because some of Hong Kong's earliest archaeological remains have been discovered there. Just across the East Channel from Aberdeen, Lamma has only 6,000 people on its five square miles. Most of the people here are also fishermen, although Europeans have discovered the island. Many of the other islands are deserted and some of them have particular legends about them or local reputations. Some have romantic names like Crooked Island, Crescent Island, Sunshine Island, the Brothers, Shelter Island, Bluff Island.

On Peng Chau, an inhabited island east of Lantau, the wild coastline has orange and brown rocks. The island is still noted for rattan ware and ceramics. On Ping Chau, out in Mirs Bay east of the New Territories, there once was a flourishing population of 3,000, but now only three people, including the caretaker of the island, live there; there's been an exodus to Tai Po in the New Territories and to London in the UK. Meanwhile the island's cattle run wild. On Tap Mun, a little to the south-west of Ping Chau, there is a special Tin Hau temple dedicated to the goddess of the sea. Many places have such temples, but this one, more than a hundred years old, is visited by fishermen from all around, as it is the last temple before the open sea. When the winds roar, they are magnified through a crack on the altar of the temple, and the howls are interpreted as a warning of storms. On Crooked Island, Kat o Chau, there is rich green vegetation, and the people are mainly Hoklo fishermen, dressed in traditional black. On Ap Chau, west of Crooked Island, the 500 fishermen and their families all belong to the True Jesus Church, which has its headquarters in Taiwan. These zealous Christians are liable to go into fits of ecstasy during their services. The island has no electricity.

Lantau is the biggest of all the islands, actually bigger than Hong Kong island itself, but has fewer than 30,000 inhabitants, compared to a million on Hong Kong. The word Lantau in Cantonese means 'broken head', a reference to the two-headed Lantau Peak which reaches a height of 934 metres in the middle of the lizard-shaped island. Its mountainous terrain is the easy explanation for the sparse settlements. The island is something of a retreat for priests of more than one religion. There is an important Buddhist monastery called Po Lin (Precious Lotus) at which the world's largest statue of Buddha is being built (22.4 metres high on a 34-metre plinth). Visitors can stay there in spartan conditions. Adjoining the monastery are tea-gardens. Roman Catholic Trappist monks have also set up a monastery in a spot ideal for their uninterrupted contemplative farming life. The farm and its plump cattle supply fresh milk for some of Hong Kong's hotels. Located on the east of the island, it is only accessible by four-wheel drive vehicle along a dirt track; the best means of approach is from the beach, followed by a walk that takes an hour and a half. For how long Lantau will preserve its peacefulness is an open question. Expatriates and modern middle-class Chinese have already established a beachhead at so-called Discovery Bay, popularly known as Disco Bay, a 1,500-acre site, accessible by regular hovercraft from near the Star Ferry pier. But the island would develop rapidly if ambitious plans for a new international airport on nearby Chek Lap Kok island go ahead. These call for a bridge to Lantau to be built, and Lantau's peace will be shattered by the scream of jet engines.

4 Barbarians Invade the Celestial Kingdom:

The Birth of the Hong Kong Colony

> 'You shouldn't say Hong Kong is being handed *back* to China. Hong Kong as we know it never belonged to China. It is a British creation. Say Hong Kong is being given to China.' (A retired Hong Kong government secretary and former member of the executive council)

Hong Kong has not always been a favoured spot, a cosmopolitan city, a tourist attraction, an international financial centre, one of the world's top twelve trading territories, the sophisticated modern gateway to China, a haven for poor, tattered refugees and smart entrepreneurs seeking their fortunes, or any of the other things it became by the 1980s. Perhaps the most famous quote in Hong Kong's history is that of Lord Palmerston, British Foreign Secretary in 1841, who expostulated 'A barren Island with hardly a House upon it . . .', when he learnt of Britain's new possession. Palmerston was being unkind, but not unduly harsh. Hong Kong island proper had had a small fishing settlement for hundreds of years and its hinterland, known today as the New Territories, was occupied by farming villages. Archaeologists have discovered a Han tomb in Sham Shui Po dating back to the first century AD, and other evidence suggests that there were human settlements in the area as far back as 4000 BC. But nineteenth-century Hong Kong was so insignificant that officials in the provincial capital of Canton (Guangzhou) less than a hundred miles away up the Pearl river knew little of its existence. The 1822 edition of the provincial gazetteer of Xin'an county, which included Hong Kong, failed to mark the existence of the island. It was simply a place of poor fisherfolk, and its waters were the haunt of pirates. (See *New Peace County: A Chinese gazetteer of the Hong Kong region* by Peter Y. L. Ng, Hong Kong University Press, 1983.) Translation of one entry in the gazetteer reads laconically: 'Pirates arrived at dawn and looted until noon.'

Bringing Hong Kong under the British flag and jurisdiction was achieved, more or less, simply because Britain was the most powerful trading nation in the world and had the Royal Navy to enforce its sway. The surprise was, perhaps, that it took so long for the power to get a toehold in China. The British were not the first Europeans to seek a presence there. Portuguese ships had reached Canton in 1514, and Lisbon established a colony at Macao in 1557. The Portuguese had the China trade to themselves for a century, until the entry of the Dutch. Not until 1596 did two British Elizabethan merchant adventurers, Richard Allot and Thomas Broomfield, set off for China armed with the Queen's Commission and letter 'to the most high and sovereign prince, the most puissant Governor of the great kingdom of China, the chiefest Emperor in those parts of Asia, and the islands adjoining and the great monarch of the oriental regions of the world . . .'. The Queen commended to the Emperor the desires of the merchants 'of sayling to the regions of your empire for traffiques sake' and hoped that 'by this intercourse and traffique, no loss, but rather most exceeding benefits, will redound to the princes and subjects of both kingdoms, and thus help and enrich one another'. What the Chinese would have made of this letter, written in Latin and in English, will never be known, since the merchants' ship was lost without trace before it could reach China.

The next British encounter with China was not very satisfactory either. In 1637 four English ships commanded by Captain Weddell, who carried a letter of introduction from Charles I, arrived in Macao. The Portuguese were unwilling to encourage rivals, and when Weddell was forced to deal with the Chinese he was repelled in the Pearl river. The Portuguese then bundled him out of Macao, so he sailed away empty-handed, expelled 'outt of the Citty and the Country, even by Fire and Sword as one May well say', according to one of the merchants.

Nevertheless, Britain's remorseless growth as the world's leading trading nation continued, and China was inexorably drawn into its orbit. Two centuries after the Portuguese had arrived, Britain's East India Company established its base with a permanent factory in Canton. By the late eighteenth and early nineteenth centuries trade was considerable and Britain's share was greater than those of all other countries combined. But life was uncomfortable for the traders actually in China. They were there on sufferance and lived a precarious existence. Attempts to open China's doors wider met incomprehension and resistance towards the 'untutored barbarians'.

The clash of attitudes between ancient China and the brash modern nation from the west was displayed clearly in 1793 and 1794 when Britain mounted a diplomatic expedition, under Lord Macartney to the Emperor's court. Emperor Ch'ien-lung (Qian Long) regarded himself as ruler at the centre of the world. His China had enjoyed more than two thousand years of civilization and he clearly looked down his nose at the intruders. His grandson wrote that it was 'plain that these barbarians always look upon trade as their chief occupation and [are] wanting in any high purpose'. Macartney eventually gained an audience with the Emperor, but achieved none of the purposes for which he had set out. The actual meeting was delayed while the Chinese unsuccessfully demanded that the British envoy must perform the ceremonial *kowtow* – that is, press his head to the floor nine times on being ushered into the imperial presence. To the British this was unthinkable: they suggested that Macartney should greet the Chinese Emperor in the same manner as he greeted his own sovereign, by going down on one knee and kissing the royal hand. But the Chinese saw the British sovereign as a lesser creature, and his envoy was regarded as the representative of a vassal state bearing tribute to the Celestial Empire, the King of Heaven, the sanctuary of the world – as China saw itself. In the end, the matter of the *kowtow* was settled by Macartney going down on one knee and bowing his head when the Chinese courtiers *kowtowed*. But China was clearly sore. A subsequent envoy, Lord Amherst, went all the way to China in 1816 and 1817 without being able to meet the Emperor.

The British emissaries were not overly impressed by the products of 2,000 years of Chinese civilization. Macartney himself in his journal made it plain that he regarded Chinese behaviour as frequently disgusting.

> 'The people, even of the first rank, though so fond of dress as to change it usually several times a day, are yet in their persons and customs frowzy and unclean . . . they wear but little linen and what they do wear is extremely coarse and ill-washed. They seldom have recourse to pocket handkerchiefs, but spit about the rooms without mercy, blow their noses in their fingers, and wipe them with their sleeves, or upon anything near them. The practice is universal, and what is still more abominable, I one day observed a Tartar of distinction call his servant to hunt in his neck for a louse that was troublesome to him.'

Another British observer noted that servants had the job of searching for vermin on their masters, and that when vermin were caught 'they very composedly put [them] between their teeth'. The Chinese, noted the visitors, were 'unacquainted with the use of soap'. Nor were the British pleased about housing standards. John Barrow regarded the accommodation offered to him as 'fitter for hogs than for human creatures'. He noted that the state officers at the French King's court at Versailles lived like princes compared with the grand councillors in China, who had no glass in their windows, no looking-glasses, no paintings; instead of doors the Chinese had bamboo-fibre screens, and instead of beds they had wooden planks or bricks covered with mats. Rooms in the best residences were open to the rafters of the roof, floors were composed of bricks or clay, and windows were covered in oiled paper, silk gauze or shells of pearls. And Barrow grumbled, 'there is not a water-closet nor decent place of retirement in all China'. As for the ordinary people, they lived miserably, subject to the system of 'squeeze' – extortion – employed by poorly paid officials in order to survive on their pittances.

Lack of respect was mutual. The Chinese courtiers and people at large laughed at the British manner of dress, with their tight-fitting trousers and powdered wigs, all extremely uncomfortable when the temperature rose above 30 degrees Centigrade in the summer. China's rulers closed their eyes to the strides that Britain had made in science and technology. In his edict to the British king George III, the Emperor dismissed the request of Britain to have a permanent ambassador in the Chinese capital. 'Therefore oh King, as regards your request to send someone to remain at the capital, apart from not being in harmony with the regulation of the Celestial Empire, such a course, we feel very strongly, would be of no advantage to your country.' The Emperor acknowledged the sending of envoys to 'kowtow and to present congratulations and also to present the local products', but saw all this as a demonstration of humility and loyalty to himself, the ruler of all the countries 'within our four seas' (meaning the whole world). The Emperor concluded: 'You, oh King, should simply act in conformity with our wishes by strengthening your loyalty and swearing perpetual obedience so as to ensure that your country may share the blessings of peace.' The Emperor acknowledged the presents he had been sent, such as astronomical instruments and recent scientific inventions, but did not see them as the implements of an advancing civilization. Shown how an air pump worked, he merely commented that it was perhaps 'good enough to amuse children'. Macartney presented the Emperor with 'elegant easy carriages', much smoother than his own transport; but they were never used because the Chinese would not permit a coachman to sit *above* their sovereign. Evidently too the Chinese did not take notice of the sixty-four-gun man-of-war, the *Lion*, in which Macartney and his entourage arrived.

China was prepared to concede that the British and other Europeans might need China's goods, including tea, porcelain, silks and rhubarb. But for themselves they had 'never valued ingenious articles' and therefore had not 'the slightest need' of manufactured goods from England. As to trade, the Emperor decreed that 'Our Celestial Empire possesses all things in prolific abundance', glossing over the fact that China had traded with other countries and bought musical clocks and toys from France and Germany, and had traditionally bought furs and skins from Mongolia and Tibet. There were also longstanding trade links between the Arabs and China.

Rebuffs did nothing to stop the expanding European powers' interest in China; on the contrary. The Dutch, learning of Macartney's failure, sent a mission to China in 1795, and they were prepared to *kowtow*. And they did so, thirty times in the thirty-seven days that they stayed in Peking (Beijing), including one occasion on which the Minister Plenipotentiary's wig fell off. The Emperor burst into laughter. Neither the Dutch nor the Russians, who followed in 1805, had any more joy than did Macartney in getting concessions. But trade continued apace. The British East India Company's agency at Canton, established in the seventeenth century, traded extensively, though under vexatious restrictions. The East India Company's supercargoes (officers responsible for the care and selling of the cargoes of merchant ships) had to deal with the Hoppo (a corruption of the Chinese name for the imperial superintendent of customs) and the committee of Chinese merchants known as the Co-hong, which was under the supervision of the Hoppo. Even when a system of fees and duties and tariffs was established to govern the trade, the Chinese squeezed the unwelcome visitors for all they were worth. By the nineteenth century the foreign merchants were increasingly unhappy about their Canton confinement.

E. J. Eitel, a German clergyman, who became an authority

on both Hakka and Cantonese dialects and who was private secretary to Hong Kong Governor Sir John Pope Hennessy and later Inspector of Schools in Hong Kong, summed up the first two centuries of British trade with China in the following way:

> The relations between the Chinese Government and the East India Company had been conducted on the express understanding, which for two centuries was tacitly acquiesced in by the Company, that China claims the sovereignty overall under heaven; that trade, whether retail or wholesale is a low degrading occupation, fit only for the lower classes beneath the contempt of the Chinese gentry, literati and officials; but that the Emperor of China, as the father of all human beings, is merciful even to barbarians, and as their existence seems to depend upon periodical supplies of silk, rhubarb and tea, the Emperor permits the foreign traders at Canton to follow their base instincts and allow them to make money for themselves by this trade, subject to official surveillance restrictions and penalties. At the same time, though permitted to reside at intervals in the suburbs of Canton, foreigners must not suppose that they are the equal even of the lowest of the Chinese people; they must not presume to enter the city gates under any pretext whatever, or travel inland, nor take into their service any natives except those belonging to the Pariah caste of the boat population (known as Ham-shui), forbidden by law to live on shore or to compete at literary examinations. So long as the Company's Supercargoes and other foreign merchants resorting to Canton silently accepted the degrading status thus assigned to them, and tacitly acknowledged the political supremacy and the Heaven-bestowed jurisdiction of the Chinese Government, things went on tolerably and trade continued in spite of all restrictions. (*Europe in China*)

The 'factories' that the foreigners were allowed to set up had to serve as all-purpose warehouses, offices and living quarters. There were thirteen of them in all, packed into a narrow 300-metre front, each about 100 metres in length. There were merchants from Austria, Denmark, Spain and Sweden, and some Parsees, all with their own factories; but the main powers were the Dutch, the French, the Americans – called 'flowery flag devils' by the Chinese – and, most powerful of all, the East India Company, whose establishment was called 'The Factory' and employed more men than its rivals. Besides the other restrictions detailed by Eitel the foreign merchants were only permitted to reside at Canton during the October to May trading season. European women were not allowed into the factories. So Portuguese Macao was the base to which foreigners repaired.

Ordinary Chinese found the Europeans a great subject for amusement. A favourite Chinese pastime was to come and stare at the *fan-quis* in their funny clothes, with their long noses and strange pale eyes. Even the educated were puzzled by the strangeness of the foreigners, and one Chinese scholar said they reminded him of the water buffaloes in the rice fields. They moved 'like prancing Manchu ponies', he noted, rather than gliding as the mandarins did in their flowing gowns. The mandarins would not soil themselves by direct contact with the traders. That job was left to the *hong* merchants, and some of these Chinese benefited fabulously from the association. One of the most famous, nicknamed Howqua, had a fortune estimated in the 1830s at $25 million, a huge sum for those days, especially when it is remembered that the Hoppo had to have his cut. Conversations were normally carried on in pidgin (corruption of 'business') English. In law, as we have seen, the foreigners' lives were strictly confined, but bribes allowed them to taste some of the delights of Canton, though not the flower boats – floating brothels – if they valued their lives.

The foreign merchants themselves did little to bring about any understanding with the local people. Eitel concedes that

> with very rare exceptions, none of those foreigners seemed able to learn the Chinese language nor even to conceive any appreciation of Chinese history, philosophy or literature, besides shewing utter incapacity to comprehend the principles of Chinese polity, morality and etiquette. Nor did these barbarians exhibit any symptoms of religious life, so far as the Chinese could observe, to whom they appeared to have no soul whatever above dollars and sensual pleasures.

By the 1830s, when William IV had come to the British throne, the situation was ripe for change. China had begun to worry about the outflow of silver bullion foreign exchange. In earlier days the flow of silver had been the opposite way, largely because of British imports of tea. 'Tea tempers the spirits, harmonizes the mind, dispels lassitude, and relieves fatigue; awakens thought and prevents drowsiness, lightens and refreshes the body and clears the perceptive faculties', poets had said of the beverage which had been China's national drink since the sixth century, but which did not reach Britain until 1699. But by the 1820s, sales were up to 20 or 30 million pounds' weight a year, a good business all round, including for the British exchequer, which collected £3 million a year in taxes, enough to cover half the cost of the Royal Navy. It was a problem to find goods to offer in exchange to the Chinese, so that the British foreign exchange reserves were not depleted. An attempt was made to sell manufactured goods, mainly woollens, but the Chinese had no use for wool: poor people wore padded cotton and the rich preferred silks and furs. As one Communist Chinese history of the period says, 'the Chinese social economy as a whole was natural economy combining individual farming with household handicrafts . . . most of the peasants' clothing and other daily necessities were produced at home. They had no particular need of, nor did they have the money to buy, the manufactured goods of foreign capitalism' (*The Opium War*, Foreign Languages Press, Peking, 1976). This Chinese history points out that from 1781 to 1793 the total value of British goods exported to China was 16.87 million silver dollars, only a sixth of the value of China teas that went to Britain. 'Foreign ships coming into Guangdong province had to bring more in silver dollars than in goods.'

The solution (for the British) was opium. The opium poppy was no stranger to China, having been introduced in the early eighth century by Turks and Arabs and eaten raw as medicine. By the seventeenth century the Chinese had begun to smoke it mixed with tobacco. Sales of the drug were the solution to the silver outflow. Everyone on the British side benefited. The East India Company was given the monopoly of manufacture and sales of opium in India. The colonial government of British India collected huge taxes (these came to £1 million in 1829–30, or one-tenth of total revenues). Since the East India Company would not sell an illegal product in China itself, the sales were made in India to the merchants. These foreign traders made immense fortunes in carrying the opium to China and selling it there. Numerous imperial edicts from 1729 onwards forbade the sale or consumption of opium and detailed strict penalties for those caught infringing the law. But they were widely disregarded, and the mandarins connived at imports of the 'foreign mud' for their own profit. An English missionary, G. Tradescant Lay, asserted that 'In China, every man is a smuggler in opium from the Emperor downwards ... opium here is only contraband in the letter. It is an article that bears a duty which, to render as high as possible in traffic, comes in the shape of a prohibition.' The foreign merchants professed no worries about the effects of the drug, though they did not generally take it themselves. For them it offered profit. By 1820, nearly 5,000 chests were imported per year, a figure which rose to 20,000 by the 1830s and had almost doubled again by the end of the decade. By the early 1830s the trading firm of Jardine Matheson alone was selling 6,000 chests and making £100,000 a year from the drug. In 1836 the value of opium imports reached $18 million, making it the world's most valuable single commodity. 'Opium is like gold; I can sell it any time', said one of the merchants. Immense bribes were paid to poorly paid officials, but still the trade was hugely profitable.

The early 1830s saw the dawn of the free trade movement in the west. The East India Company was beginning to lose its control over foreign merchants. Until this time, no foreigner could land at Canton without a passport from the British East India Company. But the expanding foreign community was beginning to talk of 'international and reciprocal responsibility', and murmuring seditions against trade monopolies as 'commercial inequities', as Eitel expressed it. The foundation of companies like Jardine Matheson in the early 1830s also played an important role. William Jardine was a lowland Scot and a former ship's surgeon, known as the 'iron-headed old rat', who had only a single chair in his office – for himself – so that visitors were not encouraged to linger. His co-founder, James Matheson, was more genteel than Jardine, coming from a family of clergymen and army officers in Sutherland. (In tune with the spirit of the times, they employed the bearded Pomeranian clergyman Karl Gutzlaff as interpreter. He was frequently found handing out religious pamphlets as opium chests were unloaded; and he saw the trade in the drug as a means of opening China to Christianity.) By the 1830s these merchants were increasingly powerful and rich figures on the China coast. More to the point, they were also well connected at home in Britain (where they both later became Members of Parliament). They had strong links with men dedicated to free trade who had begun to enter the British Parliament after the 1812 Reform Act.

As an example of the merchants' growing assertiveness, at the end of May 1831 a meeting of British subjects in China, with William Jardine presiding, decided 'to appeal to the home country' against the policy of yielding to the caprices of native authorities. It was the first open sign of pressure that eventually bore fruit. In 1833 the hated monopoly of the East India Company in China was dissolved. Henceforth, the merchants could conduct their Canton agency business openly and freely.

Eitel comments that 'in this general free trade movement you see above the dark horizon the first streak of light, heralding the advent of the future free port of Hong Kong'.

But Hong Kong did not come into being as a British colony and free port without a struggle and without a clash between the Chinese authorities and British warships – which demonstrated that the Chinese Emperor was no longer the master even of the waters around his own home, let alone the four seas. Both countries hastened to bring about this denouement.

The opening shots were fired in 1834. Foreign Secretary Palmerston appointed Lord Napier of Meristoun, a Presbyterian and a Scottish landowner, to be Chief Superintendent of Trade of Canton, where he was to live and look after the interests of the British merchants. His instructions told him to respect China's laws and customs and to be moderate and circumspect. However, Palmerston obviously anticipated a possible need for an iron fist under the velvet glove. His instructions told Napier not to use menacing language or to look for the help of the Royal Navy 'unless, in extreme cases, the most evident necessity' demanded it. These were difficult, if not impossible, instructions to carry out, given that Jardine and the rest of the merchants wanted Britain to take a firm hand with China, to disabuse the Emperor of the notion that England 'depended upon them for food and raiment, and that the Emperor was the only monarch of the universe'. Napier too had set himself a high goal, to open up 'the wide field of the Chinese Empire to the British Spirit and Industry'. He immediately challenged several cherished Chinese customs, arriving at Canton without permission and daring to send a letter – not a 'petition' – to the local viceroy.

The viceroy blamed the Co-hong for not restraining and dealing with Napier. He used Chinese characters that called Napier 'Laboriously Vile'. He railed:

> if the Barbarian headman throws in private letters, I, the Viceroy, will not receive or look at them . . . Nations have their laws; it is so everywhere. Even England has its law;

> how much more the Celestial Empire! How flaming bright are its great laws and ordinances. More terrible than the awful thunderbolt. Under this whole bright heaven who dares to disobey them? . . . Should the said Laboriously Vile oppose and disobey, it will be because the Hong merchants have mismanaged the affair. In that case I shall be obliged to report against them.

In another edict the viceroy declared that the Laboriously Vile must leave Canton immediately or the *hong* merchants would be punished severely. 'These are the orders. Tremble hereat! Immensely tremble.' Napier, egged on by the merchants, prepared for firm action. He was not impressed by the threats, holding the Chinese defences in contempt. 'What could an army of bows and arrows and pikes and shields do against a handful of British veterans?'

But the upshot was that the British retired hurt at the end of the first round. A Chinese edict declared that there could be no peace while Laboriously Vile was in China, so all commercial transactions between Chinese and English were prohibited until Napier's departure. The Chinese employed by the English were ordered to leave immediately and shopkeepers were forbidden to sell goods to the English, who would be prevented from approaching Canton by a strong guard of soldiers. The British superintendent decided on a show of force and called up two frigates; the viceroy immediately fortified Chinese positions on the river so that Napier had little option but to withdraw. By this time the British superintendent was suffering from fever and applied through his doctor for permission to withdraw to Macao, at the same time taking the frigates to Lintin island. This was a face-saving device, but the Chinese viceroy insisted that he should go by Chinese boat instead of British cutter. He was escorted out like a prisoner accompanied by gongs and firecrackers. He died in the Portuguese colony on the night of 11 October 1834. Trade resumed at Canton upon Napier's ignominious withdrawal.

For the time being Napier's hard-line policy died with him. The Duke of Wellington took over as Foreign Secretary; he regarded Napier's venture disapprovingly, describing it as 'an attempt to force upon the Chinese an unaccustomed mode of communication with an authority with whose power and of whose nature they had no knowledge, which commenced its proceedings by an assumption of power hitherto unadmitted'. The new government sought to establish 'conciliatory methods' as prescribed by the East India Company. James Matheson of Jardine Matheson, by this time the first president of the British Chamber of Commerce in Canton, described the policy as one of 'submissiveness and servility'. But in spite of this British goodwill, events were moving inexorably towards further clashes between the British traders and the Chinese authorities, who still imagined that the whole world lay within their sway.

In the late 1830s the Chinese authorities were concerned about opium. The outflow of silver to pay for opium had increased. Chinese sources say that 'the most conservative estimate is that at least 100 million dollars' worth, one-fifth of the total amount of silver in circulation in China, was drained from the country in the twenty years 1821–40 before the Opium War. This means there was, on the average, an annual loss of 5 million dollars in silver, one-tenth of the Ching (Qing) government's annual revenue.' Some Chinese were also worried about increasing addiction to the drug. The Communist historians assert indignantly:

> At first only aristocrats, officials, landlords and rich merchants smoked the drug. Later, all kinds of hangers-on of the ruling class, such as eunuchs, yamen runners, sedan-chair bearers, soldiers, Buddhist monks and nuns, Taoist priests and city prostitutes, became addicts. According to an estimate of 1835, over 2 million people took to smoking the drug. (*The Opium War*)

The Emperor Tao-Kuang (Dao Guang) was advised that 'opium

is nothing less than a flowing poison; it leads to extravagant expenditure, is a small evil, but as it utterly ruins the minds and morals of the people it is a dreadful calamity.' He was impressed by advice from Lin Tse-hsu (Lin Zexu), Governor-General of Hubei and Hunan, who advocated that tough anti-opium measures adopted in central China should be applied throughout the empire to bring an end to the consumption of opium.

After nineteen interviews between Lin and the Emperor, the sovereign wept, apparently exclaiming: 'How alas can I die and go to the shades of my imperial fathers and ancestors, until these dire evils are removed!' He appointed Lin to Canton as High Commissioner. There the new man immediately set to work with a will. Among his early actions, he wrote to Queen Victoria, who had just succeeded to the British throne. He informed her that

> the Way of Heaven is fairness to all: it does not suffer us to harm others in order to benefit ourselves . . . I am told that in your own country opium smoking is forbidden under severe penalties. This means you are aware of how harmful it is . . . so long as you do not take it yourselves, but continue to make it and tempt the people of China to buy it, you will be showing yourself careful of your own life, but careless of the lives of other people, indifferent in your greed for gain to the harm you do to others; such conduct is repugnant to human feelings and at variance with the Way of Heaven . . . I now give you my assurance that we mean to cut off this powerful drug for ever. What is here forbidden to consume, your dependencies must be forbidden to manufacture, and what has already been manufactured Your Majesty must immediately search out and throw to the bottom of the sea, and never again allow such a poison to exist . . . you will be showing that you understand the principles of Heaven . . . by respectful obedience to our commands.

Lin told the Queen that all the opium in China was being destroyed and that foreign ships arriving with the drug would be set on fire.

He also took a stern line with the foreign merchants, reminding them via the Co-hong that it was only through the Emperor's kindness that they were allowed to trade at all. China, he declared, did not need foreign goods, whereas foreigners could not survive without tea or rhubarb for their health. Lin was an impressive figure in many ways. A contemporary foreign merchant, Wells Williams, gave his view: 'Of all the Chinamen I have ever seen, Lin was decidedly the finest looking and the most intelligent. He was indeed a superior man, and if only he had been better informed he might have brought the difficult business entrusted to him to a much more creditable issue than he did; but this his ignorance and the conceit that accompanies ignorance prevented.'

At first the foreigners did not take Lin seriously, believing that all officials had their price. James Matheson described the repeated prohibitions as 'so much waste paper'. But the new man showed a firmer hand. He had thousands of offenders imprisoned and at least one person a day executed for dealing in the drug. Next Lin demanded that the foreigners hand over all their opium. To help them comply he imprisoned two Chinese merchants, cut off food and water supplies to the factories, and prepared to blockade them.

Captain Charles Elliot, who had taken over as Superintendent of Trade, gave in and collected 20,000 chests of the drug, valued at almost £3 million, to hand over to Lin. The Chinese Commissioner expressed himself pleased by the 'real sincerity and faithfulness' of the British and encouraged other foreigners to be like them. Lin duly destroyed the opium by having it thrown into trenches covered with water and then decomposed by adding a mixture of salt and lime. A Chinese coolie who tried to smuggle a few ounces of the drug from the restricted enclosure was beheaded on the spot.

Lin was encouraged in his firm attitude by his belief that

neither the British navy nor any other barbarian sailors would be able to compete with China. Their ships, he predicted, would be unwieldy in the Chinese inshore waters. In addition, he asserted, the English soldiers had legs so firmly bound that they had no freedom to move.

Unfortunately for him, though, destroying the opium actually helped the trade. Prices rose sharply and ships began racing to India for new supplies. The Commissioner returned to his ruthless methods. But the clashes that followed were sparked off not by opium but by an incident on 7 July 1839 at Tsim Sha Tsui (the tip of the Kowloon peninsula opposite Hong Kong island). Canton under a vigorous Lin was a difficult place for the foreign merchants, so their vessels had withdrawn down the Pearl river. Since Portuguese Macao was reluctant to get involved in a dispute with China by offering shelter, the ships found safe anchorage off the small island of Hong Kong. Chinese villagers clashed with a shore party from the foreign ships, and, as G. R. Sayer puts it, 'during the course of [the fight] a Chinese, Lin Wei Hi, lost or was alleged to have lost, his life' (*Hong Kong: Birth, Adolescence and Coming of Age*, Oxford University Press, 1937). Lin demanded that the British should hand over the murderer to him for justice, a demand that caused Elliot a problem because he didn't know who was actually responsible. He had hurried to the village in which the incident had happened, paying $1,500 in compensation to the dead man's family, a further $400 as a sweetener against extortion by local officials, and $100 to villagers who had suffered in the affray. He received an acknowledgement that the death had been accidental. But Lin by now had the bit between his teeth and reacted to Elliot's refusal to hand over the murderer by demanding that all the fresh opium must be surrendered for destruction. When the Commissioner decided to visit Macao accompanied by several hundred troops an alarmed Elliot advised the British merchants and their families to leave Macao and board the merchant ships at Hong Kong. There were no Royal Navy vessels in Chinese waters, and the Portuguese, loath to offend the Chinese, were unwilling to offer protection to the British.

Lin was confident when he entered Macao in September 1839. He was able to get a close look at the Europeans and was not impressed. He said:

> They look like actors, playing the part of foxes, hares and other such animals on stage . . . their hair is very curly but they keep it short, not leaving more than an inch or two to curl. They have heavy beards, much of which they shave, leaving one curly tuft, which at first sight creates a surprising effect. Indeed, they do look like devils; and when the people of these parts call them 'devils' it is no empty term of abuse.

In this confident and superior mood, Lin issued a notice calling upon the Chinese of Kowloon and Hong Kong to cut off all supplies to the English. This was an attempt to force the foreigners to go back to Canton and submit to the authorities there, or to go home. Unfortunately for him, the Royal Navy, in the shape of the twenty-eight-gun frigate HMS *Volage*, arrived off Hong Kong, to find a hundred British families unable to get supplies and a line of men-of-war junks at anchor below a fully manned battery. Attempts to get food for the British were unsuccessful. When they warned about the strength of their arms, the Chinese threatened to fire on them. Elliot, 'greatly provoked' and unable to get supplies, ordered Captain Smith, in command of HMS *Volage*, to open fire. The brief engagement showed that Chinese confidence in their own superiority was grossly misplaced. The outgunned and out-manoeuvred Chinese junks were severely damaged. They would have been totally destroyed, had not sunset intervened, and Elliot refused Captain Smith permission to finish off the Chinese fleet the next morning. Pressure on supplies was relieved, but not Lin's determination to bring the foreigners to heel. But that was not the story the Chinese sent back to Peking. Lin claimed that a 'victory over superior forces' had been won. The Emperor himself encouraged firm action. He noted in his customary vermilion ink in the margin of Lin's report: 'You and your colleagues will never get into trouble with me for taking too high-handed a line. My only fear is lest you should show weakness and hesitation.' Lin kept up the pressure. He again demanded that the murderer of the Chinese peasant be handed over, and decreed that failure to obey would bring about the destruction of the English fleet. Elliot quickly instructed the *Volage* and another frigate, the *Hyacinth*, to go to the Bocca Tigris (Tiger's Mouth or the Bogue; Humen to Chinese) where the Pearl river narrows, to deal with the Chinese fleet of men-of-war and fireboats assembling there.

Elliot nevertheless hesitated before firing the first shot. Serving officers continually complained of his lack of decisiveness. Attempts to negotiate were rejected. An uncertain Elliot was persuaded by Captain Smith that the lives of the British families were in danger; and to withdraw as if frightened by the Chinese would insult the traditions of the Royal Navy. On 3 November 1839 the *Volage* and the *Hyacinth* sailed towards the Chinese fleet with guns blazing. Within an hour four junks had been sunk and the rest were badly damaged. The Chinese admiral Kwan's flagship was waterlogged. At this point Elliot called off the action with only one British sailor wounded and with minor damage to the rigging of a British vessel. The admiral could be seen through the smoke brandishing his sword, and Elliot described him 'manifesting a resolution of behaviour honourably enhanced by the helplessness of his efforts'. Elliot withdrew to allow the Chinese to retreat into the river. Commissioner Lin claimed that the heroic admiral had forced the English warships to retire.

In spite of this taste of British fire-power, Commissioner Lin strove to convince the Emperor that matters were still under control. He reported to Peking six fresh victories over the barbarians, described in Chinese histories as the Six Smashing Blows against the English warships. Chi'shan (Xishan in Pinyin; Keshan or Kishan in Manchu), China's Governor-General of Chihli (Zhili), predicted accurately the course of the next few years when he wrote in August 1840: 'Our military affairs are in the hands of civil officials, who are very likely admirable calligraphists but know nothing of war.'

In spite of all Lin's vigorous measures, by 1840 both the legal and the opium trades were again flourishing. The Emperor began to be impatient and demanded 'measures to root out this evil once and for all'.

Back in London Palmerston had again became Foreign Secretary, and was convinced of the need to take a tough line against the Chinese. He decided to issue war orders *before* tackling Parliament, and in February 1840 he instructed the Governor-General of India to organize 4,000 troops and 16 warships and send them to the Pearl river under the command of Rear-Admiral Sir George Elliot, cousin of Charles Elliot. Palmerston was fortunate to live before the age of telecommunications, but eventually news of preparations in India reached Britain and Palmerston had to face a full-scale debate in early April. A powerful speech was made by the thirty-year-old William Ewart Gladstone, who declared that Palmerston was planning 'an iniquitous war'. Opposition leader Sir Robert Peel had decided to ignore the question of the opium traffic, but Gladstone went straight to the point. 'A war more unjust in its origins, a war more calculated in its progress to cover this country with permanent disgrace, I do not know, and I have not read of,' he asserted, reminding Palmerston that 'the opium smuggled into China comes exclusively from British ports', naming Bengal and Bombay. All that was required, he argued, was to nip the opium traffic in the bud on British soil. But Thomas Babington Macaulay, Secretary of State for War, delivered a ringing speech in praise of empire, proclaiming that Britons:

> belonged to a country which had made the farthest ends of the earth ring with the fame of her exploits in redressing the wrongs of her children; that made the Dey of Algiers humble himself to her insulted Consul; that revenged the horrors of the black hole on the fields of Plassey; that had

> not degenerated since her great Protector vowed that he would make the name of Englishmen as respected as ever had been the name of Roman citizens . . .

Palmerston won the day, and by June, as he had planned, British and Indian troops assembled off the Ladrones Islands (south west of Hong Kong, and south east of Macao). The fleet consisted of 3 line-of-battle ships with 72 guns, 15 frigates and sloops and 4 armed steamers of the East India Company, plus transports bringing a mixed contingent of troops including the 18th (Royal Irish) and 26th (Cameronians) regiments of foot, the 49th regiment, the Bengal Volunteers, Madras Artillery, and sappers and miners.

George Elliot was made Senior Plenipotentiary, with his cousin Charles as his junior. Palmerston had set out the terms of the expedition in a formal note, dated 20 February 1840, addressed to the 'Minister to the Emperor of China'. It demanded restoration of goods extorted from British subjects, satisfaction for the affront to Elliot, security for British traders, and payment of *hong* debts to the British merchants. The way of securing the future for British traders was either through the cession of an island, or through a detailed treaty providing for factories to be set up on the mainland. 'Satisfaction for the past and security for the future,' were his overall aims. He complained that the opium laws had been enforced against foreigners but not against the Chinese. Lin responded to the British naval build-up by offering rewards for the capture of British ships, or seizure of Englishmen, combatants or not, dead or alive.

By the beginning of July the British fleet had sailed north and was at anchor off Tinghai (Dinghai) on Chusan (Zhoushan) island, north east of the town of Ningpo (Ningbo). Lord Jocelyn, military secretary to the China mission, went aboard the junk of the Chinese admiral to summon the town to surrender. Jocelyn quickly noted that even the admiral had been taking the forbidden drug: 'He was an old man and bore in his face the marks of opium.' The Chinese fleet failed to obey British demands to surrender. Commodore Sir James Gordon Bremer, the commander of the British fleet, waited beyond the time allowed, but then opened fire. After barely a few minutes the Chinese fled, their admiral was taken from his vessel having lost a leg, and British soldiers landed at Chusan to find it deserted, with only 'a few dead bodies, bows and arrows, broken spears and guns remaining the sole occupants of the field'. Around the town of Tinghai itself was a deep ditch and the gates were locked and barricaded. The ramparts were strewn with rockets and arrowheads and packets of quicklime ready to be thrown into the eyes of the barbarians. But the place was deserted apart from people in the temple burning incense, and a few inhabitants who *kowtowed* before the barbarian army. A placard in front of some houses read 'Spare our lives'.

Thus was the first great British victory over the Chinese achieved. Tinghai succumbed to looting by both Chinese and British troops. The Emperor lost patience and dismissed Commissioner Lin, having presumably found it hard to understand how, if Lin were scoring great victories, the barbarians could successfully attack China's ports. His temper was not helped by receiving Palmerston's letter, which Elliot, after two fruitless attempts, had finally delivered by entrusting it to the Governor-General of Chihli. To do this he had sailed to the mouth of the Peiho river near Tiensin, (Tianjin) only 100 kilometres from Peking. This Governor-General, a Manchu, was then posted to Canton to investigate Lin's behaviour. He personally believed that the British must be treated with circumspection and allowed to continue indulging their passion for trading. He was no doubt influenced by the reports of an envoy he had sent to inspect the British fleet, who informed him that the British steamships could 'fly across the water, without wind or tide, with the current, or against it'. In addition, the British cannon were 'mounted on stone platforms' and could 'be turned in any direction'. Meanwhile Captain Charles Elliot was in full command of British forces, his cousin having resigned because of ill health. By now Charles Elliot had the backing of a considerable military force. New Commissioner Kishan prepared for peace, dismantled the defence works at Canton, promised resumption of trade and the prospect of indemnity. He was therefore disappointed by further British demands for cession of a 'large and properly situated' offshore island, plus the use of two other ports besides Canton, Amoy (Xiamen) and Foochow (Fuzhou).

The new Commissioner tried to buy time, knowing that the Emperor could not agree to the new demands. But the British reaction was a successful action on 7 January 1841 to capture the forts on either side of the entrance to the Bogue, an achievement which would open up the Pearl river right up to Canton to British shipping. The contest lasted a mere two hours, and a handful of British soldiers were wounded, while an estimated 500 Chinese were killed. At this point Kishan surrendered to British demands.

The outline agreement provided for an indemnity of $6 million for the opium seized by Lin, for the cession of Hong Kong and the re-establishment of British merchants at Canton. It was known as the Convention of Chuenpi, agreed on 20 January 1841, but never signed. Both sides were unhappy. The Emperor rejected Kishan's 'concessions'. He was tired of discussions and wanted to see the British annihilated. The Emperor's cousin I-Shan took over with the title of Rebel-Quelling General. Kishan was tried and sentenced to death, but then exiled, like Lin, to the wilderness of Turkestan. Meanwhile in England the government also wanted more. Queen Victoria wrote to her uncle, the King of the Belgians, that 'the Chinese business vexes us much, and Palmerston is deeply mortified at it. All we wanted might have been got, if it had not been for the unaccountably strange conduct of Charles Elliot . . . who completely disobeyed his instructions and *tried* to get the *lowest* terms he could.' Palmerston too commented: 'It seems to me that Captain Elliot is disposed to act upon an erroneous principle in his dealings with the Chinese and to use too much refinement in submitting to their pretensions . . . After all our naval power is so strong that we can tell the Emperor what *we* mean to hold rather than that *he* should say what he would cede.' So Elliot too was dismissed (and ended his career as British Consul-General in Texas). Both sides prepared for fresh battle.

The Emperor instructed I-Shan to 'extirpate the barbarians'. Elliot himself struck the first blow. Unaware of his dismissal but anxious not to be idle in the face of the Chinese build-up of forces, he ordered the fleet to break through the Bogue and sail to Whampoa. The Chinese continued to encourage Canton mobs to attack and plunder the factories and set fire to them. Some American merchants were dragged off too. Their protests that they were not British were rejected on the grounds that if not British they should 'speak a different language and wear a different dress'. Rewards of $50,000 alive or $30,000 dead were offered for Elliot, Bremer and J. R. Morrison (the interpreter).

On 24 May 1841 British land forces began their assault on Canton under Major-General Sir Hugh Gough. The town surrendered even before the general could call up his heavy guns. I-Shan had not proved much of a rebel-queller. He encouraged his own troops to kill armed civilians who might be the enemies of the Manchus within the Chinese defence forces. But he proved nimble of brain in his reports to the Emperor, claiming that the people of Canton, 'weeping and wailing, sending up loud cries to heaven, have choked every pathway and earnestly begged that peaceful arrangements should be entered into'. He even presented the option of coming to terms as a possible diplomatic ploy to induce the British fleet to leave the Pearl river – when the Chinese would be able to 'renew the fortifications and seek another occasion for attacking and destroying the barbarians at Hong Kong'. But this time Gough, unlike Elliot, was not prepared to relax or trust the Chinese.

Elliot's designated successor Sir Henry Pottinger arrived in China on 10 August 1841 determined not to stand any nonsense, and announcing his opinion that it was for 'the Queen of England to pronounce what port or portions of the sea coast of China shall be added to Her Majesty's Dominions'. Before Pottinger arrived, a small number of British troops separated from their fellows had been defeated in the village of Sanyuan-Li, a triumph still celebrated in China. But quickly the British went into action and moved up the coast, took Amoy (Xiamen) with 2 killed and 15 wounded, reoccupied Tinghai, captured Chinhai and then took Ningpo. The last city was sacked because of Chinese ill-treatment of some British prisoners. When the British carried the attack through Shanghai, Chinkiang and a blockade of the Grand Canal to the gates of Nanking (Nanjing), 'the southern capital', this really caused alarm to the Imperial Court, which was then prepared to discuss terms. The fear was that if the British took Nanking they would control the heart of China's richest region and could directly threaten Peking itself. Attempts were made at haggling, but in the face of Pottinger's sternness the Chinese gave way and the Treaty of Nanking was signed on 29 August 1842, ending the war and confirming the surrender of Hong Kong to Britain. In addition, Amoy, Foochow, Ningpo, Shanghai and Canton – henceforward known as the five treaty ports – were opened to British trade; an indemnity of $21 million was agreed; the rule that the foreign traders' business must be conducted through the *hong* merchants was abandoned; and an official British representative was accepted in China. Part of the indemnity was supposed to go towards repaying the traders for the confiscated and destroyed opium. Pottinger also tried to get China to legalize opium. But despite the preoccupation with the drug, there was not a single word about opium in the treaty as signed.

Pottinger had also disregarded instructions in retaining Hong Kong. The Earl of Aberdeen, Foreign Secretary in Peel's Tory government, which had assumed power in September 1841, opposed retention of the island. But Pottinger responded that 'This settlement has already advanced too far to admit of its being restored to the authority of the Emperor consistently with the honour . . . of Her Majesty's Crown.' As a supplement to the main treaty, negotiations at the Bocca Tigris produced the Treaty of the Bogue, by which foreigners were granted exemption from the laws of China and could only be prosecuted in courts of their own nationality.

Thus the naval power of Britain took its first tiny bite of Chinese territory. The small island of Hong Kong was only thirty-five square miles in area and had been derided by Palmerston and Queen Victoria. In fact those who had visited the island had pleasant memories. Captain Henry Ellis, secretary to Lord Amherst during his abortive mission of 1816, was greatly struck by the 'picturesque' situation of Hong Kong, where the ships dropped anchor for the purpose of watering. He noted the lights on the water and the sound of gongs as local fishermen made their offerings to the gods for protection. Perhaps more important, he was impressed by the fact that these natives were relatively friendly, writing that they were 'active, lively and intelligent, not alarmed at strangers . . . the dislike of Europeans [being] confined to Canton'.

The actual treaty says:

> It being obviously necessary, and desirable, that British subjects should have some port whereat they may careen and refit their ships, when required, and keep Stores for that purpose, His Majesty the Emperor of China cedes to Her Majesty the Queen of Great Britain the Island of Hong Kong, to be possessed in perpetuity by Her Britannic Majesty, Her Heirs, and Successors and to be governed by such laws and regulations as Her Majesty the Queen of Great Britain shall see fit to direct.'

Hong Kong was obviously intended as a colony where foreigners could do business without interference from the Chinese and their ways, which were assumed to be full of corruption, avarice and oppression. But China did not give up its haughty claim to be supreme over all foreign nations. A mere four months after the Nanking Treaty, on 24 December 1842, the Emperor issued an edict ordering I-Il-Po, who had signed the treaty for China, 'to meet Pottinger and immediately explain to him that the Celestial Dynasty has for its principle, in governing all foreigners without its pale, to look upon them with the same feeling of universal benevolence with which she looks upon her own children'.

Though opium was the *particular* cause that had triggered the rather nasty little series of wars, new Hong Kong Governor Pottinger pointedly claimed that modern international trade, rather than opium, was at the heart of the British quarrel. In a public proclamation dated July 1842 he asserted that the real points of issue between Britain and China were: first, that English merchants had for two centuries suffered ill-treatment at the hands of Canton officials, and that Commissioner Lin in 1839 had confined and threatened an English officer and English merchants; secondly, that the ministers at Peking, 'men without truth and good faith', had concluded a truce and peace terms but suddenly changed their minds and begun the war again; thirdly, that high Chinese officials had tortured and killed shipwrecked Englishmen and reported the actions to the Emperor as victories won in battle; finally, that authorities in Canton had profited by the foreign trade and extorted illegal payments, and at the same time presented a false picture of what was going on to the Emperor. In consequence, continued Pottinger, what England demanded in justice was compensation for losses, a friendly trading partnership between the two countries on terms of equality, and possession of the island as a base for commerce where merchants could live securely without worrying that the Chinese might renew the offensive against them.

As the foreign merchants saw it, the British victories and the foundation of Hong Kong as a British territory had taught the Chinese a lesson – one that the merchants had been urging for some years. Back in 1836 James Matheson, Jardine's partner, had published *The Present Position and Prospects of the British Trade with China*, in which he described the Chinese as a 'truculent, vainglorious people'.

For the Chinese the cession of Hong Kong was the first of a series of 'unequal treaties' forced on them by foreign powers. Both the Kuomintang (Nationalists) and the Communist

People's Republic hold this view, and they have remembered the slurs. The authors of *The Opium War*, published by the Foreign Language Press (Peking, 1976), have no doubts about the British game plan:

> The British bourgeoisie felt it imperative to seek new and bigger markets for their goods in order to shake off the crisis [of over production] and gain more profit. Having consolidated their control over their Indian colony, they shifted the spearhead of their aggression to China, a country with vast territory, rich resources and a big population, so as to force open its door and extend their tentacles to rob and enslave the Chinese people.

For historians with a Communist world-view there are small consolations. The Chinese historians claim that the so-called British victories were really walkovers since the Ching (Qing) dynasty generals lacked the guts for a fight and mostly retreated or ran away. The only big victory of the campaign in these Chinese eyes was the occasion on which the 'Sanyuanli people trounced the invaders'. What, according to British historians, was the defeat of a small detachment of British who had become separated from the main force became in Chinese writings the first victory of the people over the evil of imperialism.

According to the authors of *The Opium War*, villagers caught the British force of 2,000 eating breakfast, impeded their retreat and then surrounded the routed British army in Sufang fort. All the loyal Chinese joined in. Women and old people fought with hoes and rakes and 'the children supported the peasant fighters by shouting battle cries'; the British then had to call on officials and gentry loyal to the Ching dynasty to persuade the masses 'by rhetoric and trickery' to disperse. The other consolation, in Communist eyes, was that 'the opium war of 1840–42 marked both the beginning of modern Chinese history and the start of the Chinese people's bourgeois-democratic revolution against imperialism and feudalism'. Former Chairman Mao Zedong himself named the Opium War as the first stage of the 'struggle by the Chinese people against imperialism and its lackeys'. Even in the latter half of the twentieth century the struggle evokes quick sensitivities. Quoting from an American opium trader who described a siege of the Canton factories 'by the mob', the Communist historian interpolates his own bracket immediately after the word 'mob' – 'a slanderous reference to the Chinese people'.

Eitel gives the most ringing declaration of faith and hope in Hong Kong, as perhaps only a German convert to the confident Victorian British Empire could be.

> The Island of Hong Kong was even in its pre-British time an eccentric vantage point. It never was so much of an integral portion of Asia as to be of any practical moment to the Chinese political or social organism. Its very name was unknown to the topographers or statesmen of China and men had to come from the Far West to give it a name in the history of the East. Its situation at the farthest south-east point of the Chinese Empire, in line with the British Possessions in Africa, India and North-America, constituted it a natural Anglo-Chinese outstation in the Pacific. Hong Kong never belonged naturally either to Asia or to Europe, but was plainly destined in God's providence to form the connecting link for both . . .
>
> The evolution of the Colony of Hong Kong was in reality the product of a quasi marriage-alliance between Europe and Asia, concluded at Canton (after AD 1634) between the East India Company and the Chinese Government. But this international union carelessly entered upon was characterized, in the course of the next two centuries, by a deep-seated and growingly manifested incompatibility of temper, such as made Anglo-Chinese international life at Canton a burden too heavy to be borne by either nation. British free trade notions based on the assumption of international equality could not remain in wedlock with China's

iron rule of monopoly based on the claim of political supremacy over the universe . . . That divorce was solemnly and emphatically pronounced, though with patent unwillingness, by Commissioner Lin (AD 1839) acting on behalf of Asia, whereupon Captain Elliot, acting as the representative of Europe, secured Hong Kong as a cradle for the offspring of that unhappy union (born AD 1841), that is to say for the Colony whose divine destiny it is to reconcile its parents hereafter in a happier reunion by due subordination of Asia to Europe . . .

This conception of Hong Kong as the vantage point from which the Anglo-Saxon race has to work out its divine mission of promoting its civilization of Europe in the East, and establishing the rule of constitutional liberty on the continent of Asia and on the main of the Pacific, is not a mere fancy . . . (*Europe in Asia*).

5 A Smug Hastings in the East: 1841–1950

Hong Kong before the Second World War was 'snobby and provincial. If Shanghai was London, then Hong Kong was Hastings.' (Lord Kadoorie)

Infant Hong Kong grew quickly and lustily, in spite of its disadvantages. Canton newspapers drew attention to these and ridiculed the problems of setting up normal life in Hong Kong. A spoof paper, the *Wang Tung Argus No. 2*, was put out by the Canton Press in May 1841 declaring that 'a premium of one thousand dollars will be paid to any person who shall devise means for feeding Cattle on granite rock, or raising crops from the sands of the sea shore; as both materials are to be found in good abundance on the new settlement'.

But the life of the new possession had begun. On 25 January 1841, Captain E. Belcher, commanding the survey ship HMS *Sulphur*, landed at 8.15 a.m. on Hong Kong, and, he said, 'being "bona fide" first possessors, Her Majesty's health was drank with three cheers on Possession Mount.' The next day Commodore Bremer and a squadron arrived to take formal possession and hoist the Union flag. It was to be another twenty-nine months before the Treaty of Nanking was ratified and Hong Kong could be declared a Crown colony on 26 June 1843. Tory Foreign Secretary Lord Aberdeen ordered Pottinger in June 1842 that 'this island should be considered a mere military position and that all buildings etc not required in that light, should be discontinued'. But that kind of injunction was already too late. By October 1841 a flourishing town had already grown up, numbering 15,000 people, most of them local Chinese. In that month the first carriage and four was seen on Queen's Road, and brought a local cheer. One of the first acts of Elliot and Bremer in February 1841 was to proclaim that Hong Kong island was now part of Queen's dominions inhabited by subjects of the Queen of England, and they 'hereby promised protection, in Her Majesty's greatest name against all enemies whatever and they are further secured in the free exercise of their religious rites, ceremonies and social customs and in the enjoyment of their lawful private property interests'. Elliot promised that Hong Kong would be a free trade port, a promise that Pottinger reiterated.

In 1841 the first buildings, including godowns (warehouses), Chinese stalls, European bungalows and houses of all descriptions had already begun to rise. Alexander Matheson of Jardine Matheson erected the first stone and brick house. The very first permanent building, appropriately enough, was Jardine Matheson's godown for storing opium. All this activity prompted mainland stonemasons, bricklayers, carpenters and scaffold-builders to come to Hong Kong, and they were quickly followed by Chinese provision dealers, furniture dealers, joiners, cabinet makers and even curio shops. All this happened while Lord Aberdeen and the government in London were dithering about whether Hong Kong should be a permanent settlement!

The early history of Hong Kong involved a constant struggle to put the colony on its feet, against the obstacles of indifferent government within, lawlessness on the streets and piracy in the waters, and the continuing unfriendly attitude of the Chinese authorities. Government and administration of the territory was never smooth. G. R. Sayer captures some of the personal animosities in the ruling elite at the end of the era of Sir John Bowring, Governor from 1854 to 1859:

> It is true that the Chief Justice, who under an earlier regime had been suspended for suspected indulgence in intoxicating liquor, had returned to the bench; but the

> Attorney General had now been dismissed for accusing the Registrar-General of associating with pirates: the Registrar-General in turn hinted that the Captain Superintendent of Police had a financial interest in brothels; while the acting Colonial Secretary had been charged by a local editor with receiving a bribe in connection with the opium monopoly: the Lieutenant Governor with taking commission on the stall-rents at the Central Market; and the Governor himself had been pilloried in another newspaper for giving privileged treatment in the matter of government contracts.

Hong Kong was always a raucous, rumbustious place. Even as late as March 1859 *The Times* administered a reproof, saying that Hong Kong 'is always connected with some fatal pestilence, some doubtful war, or some discreditable internal struggle. So much so that the name of this noisy, bustling, quarrelsome, discontented and insalubrious island may not inaptly be used for a euphonous synonym for a place not mentioned in polite societies.'

By February 1855 Lord Palmerston was back in power in London, this time as Prime Minister. And he had been pondering action against a China that was still unhappy about the foreign presence in the country. 'The Time is fast coming,' wrote the new Prime Minister,

> we shall be obliged to strike another Blow in China. These half civilized governments such as those in China, Portugal and Spanish America all require a Dressing every eight or ten years to keep them in order. Their minds are too shallow to receive an Impression that will last longer than some such Period and warning is of little use. They care little for words and must not only see the Stick but actually feel it on their Shoulders before they yield.

The excuse was provided by an incident involving the *Arrow*, a ship owned by a Chinese but registered in Hong Kong and under the command of a British captain. Police at Canton had boarded the vessel, pulled down the British ensign and arrested the entire crew, an action regarded by the British as illegal under the terms of the Treaty of the Bogue of 1843. The Chinese denied that the *Arrow* was a foreign vessel, as it had been built in China and was owned by a Chinese. Governor Bowring saw the incident as the opportunity to use the Navy to strike at Canton and establish the right of foreign residence there. Even though the *Arrow*'s Hong Kong registration had in fact expired, Bowring argued that it should still be regarded as British, since it *had been* registered in Hong Kong, had a British captain and was flying a British flag. When the Chinese failed to apologize Bowring called the Royal Navy into action and the four barrier forts guarding the approaches to Canton were bombarded and taken. Sporadic fighting continued for some weeks as the navy tightened its grip on the Pearl river.

In London there was uproar against Bowring's high-handed action. Lord Derby forsook his normal preoccupation with race horses and pheasant-shooting to organize the attack. The Lords, including thirteen bishops, voted in favour of the government (who of course backed Bowring), but in the Commons the Palmerston administration was defeated. Palmerston went to the country. He had read the mood of the nation well and increased his majority. The British people obviously sided with Admiral Sir Charles Napier, who claimed in the Commons he didn't know why there was so much fuss about Bowring demanding an apology. 'Good God! There was nothing extraordinary in that. If a man knocked another's hat off and then knocked him down, surely an apology would be required.' Palmerston was free to pursue his strong policy. He approached the Earl of Elgin (son of the seventh Earl who had brought the 'Elgin Marbles' to London from Greece) as special envoy, and sent him to Hong Kong and China.

In China irregular warfare continued for some time. The British held back from a full-scale campaign because they were handicapped by the outbreak of the Mutiny in India. Elgin arrived in Hong Kong in mid-1857 with instructions to demand compensation, the restoration of treaty rights, the establishment of a British minister or ambassador in Peking and also 'permission to be secured for Chinese vessels to resort to Hong Kong from all parts of the Chinese Empire without distinction'. It was the end of 1857 before the military expedition was ready. Besides the 5,000 British troops, it included 1,000 Frenchmen; the French had joined after the murder in Kwangsi (Guanxi) of a French priest had aroused outrage in Paris. Suggestions that his heart had been fried and eaten and his body chopped up and thrown with rubbish to the animals on the streets added to French fury. Canton was captured and looted, but an uncomfortable Elgin called a halt. He revealed his feelings in writing to his wife, describing the opposition met while approaching Canton in mid-December.

> The ships are surrounded by boats filled chiefly by women who pick up orange peel and offal, and everything that is thrown overboard. One of the gunboats got ashore yesterday, within a stone's throw of the town of Canton, and the officer had the coolness to call on a crowd of Chinese who were on the quay, to pull her off, which they at once did! Fancy having to fight such a people!

The expedition sailed north to the Gulf of Chihli (Zhili). Elgin took the Taku forts in May 1858 and occupied Tiensin (Tianjin). There, instead of pushing on to Peking, where he might have dictated terms, he stopped and negotiated a treaty. He didn't ask for any material guarantees apart from money payments, and by the time he returned to London he found the Chinese had backtracked when it came to ratifying the treaties. At Tiensin, Chinese villagers had come to the river's edge to greet the foreigners as conquerors, shouting 'Hail, O King! Be thou our Emperor. Come thou and reign over us.' Elgin, having seen the Chinese, with 'no notion of directing their firearms' and 'without tactics and discipline', said that he would 'venture to say that twenty-four determined men, with revolvers and a sufficient number of cartridges, might walk through China from one end to the other'. But as soon as the superior firepower was no longer levelled at their heads, the northern mandarins were quite capable to going back on their promises and regarding the British with contempt, barbarians in the face of the superior Chinese civilization.

By the time this was realized, the Chinese had strengthened their forces and the French, Americans and Russians were all clamouring to get a slice of the action. In the first attempt to retake the Taku forts, the British were forced to retreat to the water, having lost 89 dead and 345 wounded in a humiliating defeat. Karl Marx, then London correspondent of the *New York Daily Tribune*, scorned the way the affair was handled, saying the debate about responsibility 'evaporated in grotesque compliments showered . . . on the head of Admiral [Sir James] Hope for having so gloriously buried the British forces in the mud'. The mood of the people and press in Britain was for tough action to teach the 'perfidious hordes' of China a lesson. But there was a new government at home, with Lord John Russell as Foreign Secretary and Gladstone as Chancellor of the Exchequer, both lukewarm about strong action. But gradually opinion hardened.

Elgin came back, and an expeditionary force of 11,000 British and Indian troops plus a French army of 7,000 had moved up to Shanghai from Hong Kong by May 1860. The Chinese rejected an ultimatum. The British and French forces got to Tiensin, but were halted when China prevaricated over peace negotiations leading to the Treaty of Tiensin. Henry Parkes, Consul at Canton, had gone to negotiate under a flag of truce, but was arrested and taken as a prisoner to Peking. The British joined the French in plundering Peking's Summer Palace outside the city walls. China itself was going through turmoil, racked by internal rebellion. For a long time there had been growing nationalist sentiments against the Manchu Ching rulers. The

Triad societies were one focus of this resentment. A more powerful one came through the nation-wide Taiping rebellion, in which a poor school-teacher, Hung Hsiu-chuan, embraced a form of Christianity and rallied people to revolution in the names of God and Christ. In 1851 he inaugurated his own state which he named 'The Taiping Heavenly Kingdom', calling for war against landlords and feudalism. In three years, his forces grew from 10,000 to a million, and he set up a government in Nanking, the southern capital. In spite of squabbling among themselves the Taipings occupied large parts of China and were a threat to the Ching rulers. Then a 'peace party' within the government camp had the bright idea of yielding to the foreigners in the hope of enlisting their help against the Taipings. It carried the day. It regarded the foreigners as the lesser of two evils. They were described as 'injuries of the limbs', while the Taipings were 'a disease of the vitals'. The Chinese rulers now sought support from the British and French to combat the internal disease, and by the mid 1860s were successful, though at a price. So Elgin and his procession triumphantly entered Peking on 24 October and the Convention of Peking brought at last the ratification of the Treaty of Tiensin.

There were two other consequences of note. Elgin was so moved by the poor treatment and unhealthy conditions of British prisoners that his 'sense of duty' forced him to avenge it. Several prisoners, including a Frenchman and a Sikh, had died in prison, with maggots eating into their flesh. Captured coolies had been buried up to their necks and left for dogs to eat. The British envoy decided on the destruction of the Summer Palace. The palace, or Yuan Ming Yuan, the Garden of Perfection and Light, had a number of buildings in Italian baroque style designed by Jesuit missionary priests. Its sacking was one of the blackest contributions that the European brought to China; showers of burnt embers fell all over Peking. The other development was a new clause in the Peking Convention that had not been in the Treaty of Tiensin. This added the tip of the Kowloon peninsula to Hong Kong's territory. The revised terms stated that 'with a view to the maintenance of law and order in and about the harbour of Hong Kong [the Kowloon peninsula] be ceded to Her Majesty the Queen of Great Britain and Ireland, her heirs and successors, to have and to hold as a Dependency of Her Britannic Majesty's Colony of Hong Kong.'

The first significant reference to the importance of the Kowloon peninsula had come in March 1858, four months before the Tiensin Treaty was agreed. Captain W. K. Hall of HMS *Calcutta* argued that the peninsula would provide much-needed sea-front space for commercial buildings and barracks. In addition, the occupation of Kowloon would remove the danger to ships anchored during the typhoon close to Tsim Sha Tsui, which was noted for the presence of Chinese brigands. It was Britain's second bite of China – or rather more of a nibble, since the area of the peninsula was a mere 3.5 square miles.

By the last years of the century Hong Kong was already becoming crowded. Demands for an extension of its territory became an important preoccupation during the last decade of the century. It was not that the overcrowded and insanitary conditions of the ordinary local Chinese people played any leading role in the discussions; the harsh international facts of life were the spur. The real campaign for new territory began in 1894 and was sparked by the Sino-Japanese war. Sir William Robinson, then Governor, remarked that the Chinese government and empire were 'rotten weeds on which to rely'. He claimed: 'I desire to point out most forcibly that an adjustment and an extension of the boundaries of this colony is peremptorily necessary and that the position of Hong Kong, the "Gibraltar of the East" is by no means so secure as it is supposed to be.'

Indeed, reading the various dispatches and minutes to and from the Colonial Office, it seems that London had no clear long- or even medium-term plans. For a while, expansion of the Hong Kong boundary seemed to be becoming a live issue as the Japanese expanded their naval power, Russia built a far eastern fleet and France had a big garrison in Indo-China. But the Earl of Salisbury, the Prime Minister of the day, had other things on his mind. Sir Richard Burton, the explorer, is reported to have dismissed Salisbury thus: 'he was, in reality, a very nice old lady'. The issue was shelved for the moment. Not much later, however, Germany, Russia and France all began to make demands on China and effectively forced Salisbury to reconsider. Japan's victory in the war of 1894–5 had demonstrated China's weakness and also encouraged new claims and new claimants to portions of China's territory; they included Russia from the north, looking for an ice-free port as the terminus of the Trans-Siberian Railway; France from the south, through Indo-China; Germany, seeking a foothold on the coast; and the US and Belgium anxious not to miss out. Britain was already well entrenched in China and therefore sought to preserve its presence while preventing dismemberment of the Chinese Empire.

Talks between Britain and China began on 2 April 1898, when the Minister in Peking, Sir Claude MacDonald, informed Chinese ministers that Hong Kong wanted its boundaries extended. Yet again the impression comes through clearly that the talks proceeded in a haphazard way. MacDonald himself was badly supplied with documents and maps and believed that Hong Kong's territorial demands were excessive. G. E. Morrison, *The Times* correspondent in Peking at that time, wrote that MacDonald had many detractors. 'He was attacked as imperfectly educated . . . weak, flip and garrulous . . . the type of military officer rolled out a mile at a time and then lopped off in six foot lengths.' The Chinese government dug its heels in, refusing to cede territory, and promised only a lease. Sir Arthur Balfour, Salisbury's nephew and Foreign Secretary, told MacDonald to accept 'a lease without fixed period terminable only by mutual agreement', but two days later (such was the casual way business was done, and such were the fears of triggering off other powers' demands) he allowed MacDonald to accept the ninety-nine-year lease that provided the basis for Hong Kong's extension. The Chinese seemed to accept immediately the principle of further extensions of Hong Kong's territory, so the negotiations centred around the details. The final treaty, known as the Convention of Peking of 1898 (more fully 'Convention Respecting an Extension of the Hong Kong Territory, June 9, 1898'), was signed in early June 1898. It reserved Chinese jurisdiction inside the Walled City of Kowloon. (This was later removed by a controversial British Order-in-Council.) It gave a pledge that Hong Kong would take all precautions to prevent the leased territory being used for smuggling to China or activity detrimental to China, but allowed Britain a further 365.5 square miles of territory.

The *Hong Kong Weekly Press* jubilantly proclaimed that the extension was 'another wedge of civilization driven into Kwang-tung [Guangdong]'. The document setting forth the terms of the Convention declared in its preamble: 'it has for many years past been recognized that an extension of Hong Kong territory is necessary for the proper defence and protection of the Colony . . .' The lease was to begin on 1 July 1898 and expire on 30 June 1997. Curiously, the question of a rent, surely the natural consequence of taking a lease, was raised only once, by the Chinese Delimitation Commissioner Wong Tsun-shin. Hong Kong's Colonial Secretary James Haldane Stewart Lockhart replied: 'I do not know. That is a question that cannot be settled by me. Is any rent paid for [Kiaochow] by the German government or for Port Arthur by the Russian government? I think China may rest satisfied that Great Britain animated by feelings of friendship will deal as fairly with China in this matter as any other Power.' No rent was paid by France, Germany or Russia for their leaseholds, and MacDonald commented, 'doubtless they [Chinese officials] are afraid of being denounced for selling their country'.

With the acquisition of the New Territories Hong Kong's present-day boundaries were complete. Peter Fleming has summed up the nineteenth-century developments with a hardly subdued imperialist cheer. 'The foreigners', he wrote in *The Siege at Peking*,

> came to China to trade; the motive may not have been lofty, but it was natural and legitimate. When the Chinese refused to let them trade, the foreigners could hardly be expected to understand, let alone to sympathize with, the reasons for this refusal. They were in hard fact very silly reasons, based on a conception of the world which was self-centred, obsolete and doomed, and they were normally explained – if at all – in a gratuitously offensive manner . . . It was inevitable that the Powers would come, with selfish aims, to China. It was inevitable that they would be prepared to use force to further those aims. What, as we look back down on history, does not seem wholly inevitable is that China's rulers should have immured the country for so long in a cocoon of childish bigotry that her first important encounters with younger civilizations were bound to end in tears.

The more modern and educated Chinese began to appreciate some of the benefits that the British had brought to their coast. Hong Kong won the praise of Sun Yat-sen, leader of the Chinese revolution that overthrew the Manchus in 1911. He had been banned from Hong Kong in 1896 as a troublemaker, but in an address to the Hong Kong University congregation in 1923 he said: 'Afterwards I saw the outside world and I began to wonder how it was that foreigners, that Englishmen, could do such things as they had done, for example, with the barren rock of Hong Kong.'

With this background, it might be thought that Hong Kong offered the only safe modern haven on the China coast and was ripe for developing as a modern metropolis. Upheavals in China certainly provided an increasing population, which reached 500,000 in 1916. Hong Kong University was opened in September 1912 and would be a powerful aid to modernization. Yet in Hong Kong tradition was still powerful. The rise to power of Sun led in China to a wholesale cutting of 'queues', the pigtails previously worn by Chinese men. But even in nineteenth-century British Hong Kong, the local Chinese had maintained the traditions of China, and a person like Edinburgh University-educated Dr Ho Kai, who no longer wore a queue, was an exception. The cutting of the queue might be seen as symbolic of a readiness to embrace and consider wider ideas. But Hong Kong failed to rise to its opportunity. The opening of China proper to international trade and investment meant that Hong Kong was by-passed. Sir Henry Norman, MP, in *The People and Politics of the Far East* (London, T. Fisher Unwin, 1907) quoted a woman who enlightened him on the difference between Shanghai and Hong Kong: '"In Shanghai," she explained, "everyone is equal. In Hong Kong, everyone is not equal. There are those of us who call at Government House, and those who do not."' In a newspaper column, 'Veronica', in the *Hong Kong Weekly* in 1907, commented on the attributes needed in a marriage partner: 'Has she her aspirates under control? Most of the women here have. Does she use crested notepaper? Most of the women do here. Is she connected with the Peerage? Most of the women here are. Has she private means? That is the most important point of all.' This was frivolous, especially as most of the Hong Kong Europeans would not have made the top drawer at home. They were mostly from the professional classes and very often the families of younger sons.

Hong Kong exhibited all sorts of social distinctions and gradations, such as only the snobby British at their worst can devise. Paul Gillingham in his book *At the Peak: Hong Kong between the wars* (Macmillan, Hong Kong, 1983) captures the mood beautifully. He writes that:

> To those who lived in the colony there were clearly defined social strata. One's place was fixed according to race, nationality, position, accent and education. The Peak was a visible manifestation of class and position. On its upper reaches lived the taipans of the great hongs, their staff and leading civil servants. Only one Eurasian lived there and he was probably the richest man in the colony. Other rich Chinese of the comprador class had spacious homes in the

> mid-levels . . . the better-off Japanese who in the early 20s had earned some degree of acceptance by the British in Hong Kong, having defeated imperial Russia and joined the Allies in the war, had encroached as far as Macdonnell Road.

Former Hong Kong civil servant Austin Coates claims in his book *Mountain of Light* (Heinemann, 1977) that there were stepping stones to social prominence between Macdonnell Road in mid-levels and May Road, which marked the start of the Peak:

> In the lower part [lived] Portuguese, Jews, Armenians and Parsis. In the upper part – dreadful, but one had to concede it – 'dirty continentals', of whom the French were the most vigorous at nest-building and social mountaineering. In what was socially the most triumphant of all their Asiatic aggressions, the French very nearly reached May Road. The French consul-general's fine old house shows to this day the point at which they were held; to avenge the loss of Calais, as it were. [The house has now been demolished.] From May Road upward to heaven was the exclusive preserve of those who gloried in the name of Britain.

Between the British and the local Chinese population there was a huge gulf. Perhaps the British and the Chinese were well matched. The Chinese believed in the Middle Kingdom and the superiority of their race above all things under heaven. The British similarly isolated themselves and lived in their own superior world. One of the most enlightened governors of Hong Kong, Sir Cecil Clementi (1925–30), worried that:

> my acquaintance with Hong Kong and with things Chinese now extends over a quarter of a century and nothing has been a cause to me of more anxiety throughout that period

> than the fact that the Chinese and European communities of Hong Kong, although in daily contact with each other, nevertheless move in different worlds, neither having any real comprehension of the mode of life or ways of thought of the other. This is a most regrettable misunderstanding which retards the social, moral, intellectual and even the commercial and material progress of the colony.

By the late 1930s the lifestyles of the ordinary Chinese were still a long way below those of the British, the privileged race. According to a housing report of 1935, 'the Chinese peasant works long hours for a scanty wage and gets practically no holidays'. A government administration report four years later declared that 'it must be admitted that the majority of the colony's working class exists under deplorable conditions at rates of pay which can hardly be regarded as a "living wage". For example, one contractor employing several hundred coolies, and being asked what the sick rate was, said there was none, as all sick coolies were dismissed.'

Whereas the British on the Peak lived in airy luxury, living conditions for the Chinese were poor and dingy. What would be a servant's room on the Peak would be subdivided many times into tiny airless cubicles for the ordinary Chinese. Most people couldn't afford electricity or even gas or coal, so that cooking would be done by burning wood in containers; there was little ventilation, so rooms were thick with soot and grime. Rubbish bins were always full to overflowing, offering ready opportunities for rats, cockroaches and dogs. Out in the New Territories people often lived in home-made hutchments, similar to those seen today on the edges of Calcutta or in the poorest areas of Bangladesh.

With all this snobbery and pretension Hong Kong fell behind Shanghai, which became China's *international* city. Lord Kadoorie, who lived in both cities at various times before the war, puts Hong Kong into perspective and cuts it down to size at the same time. 'Shanghai was international with people who had an international outlook. Hong Kong was very British. Who were the British? They were small shopkeepers in their mentality. It was a nice quiet little place.' Damning its 'snobby and provincial' atmosphere, he remembers: 'If Shanghai was London then Hong Kong was Hastings.' Kadoorie says that the best aspect of Hong Kong was the harbour. 'The harbourmaster thought he was the king.' But Shanghai port was busier because of the flow of industrial produce coming down the Yangtse river to be shipped from Shanghai. Hong Kong had some industries, remembers Kadoorie, but they were small and insignificant compared to those of Shanghai (conversation with the author).

The war shattered Hong Kong's complacency and the four years after the Japanese attack on 8 December 1941 were the grimmest the colony has seen. G. B. Endacott opens his *Hong Kong Eclipse* (Oxford University Press, 1978) by stating that 'The Japanese struck Hong Kong without warning on 8 a.m. on the morning of 8 December 1941. Pearl Harbor, the Philippines and Malaya were simultaneously attacked in a four-pronged blitzkrieg against the Western Powers, aimed at realizing Japan's openly-avowed ambition to control East and South East Asia.' But the attack should not have come as a surprise. The Japanese had already taken much of China, causing refugees to swell the population of Hong Kong. By March 1941 there were more than 1.4 million people in Hong Kong, with about another 200,000 in the New Territories, giving a total population of 1.65 million, compared with just under 1 million in December 1937. David MacDougall (who became Colonial Secretary immediately after the war) recalls that troublesome Chinese in the colony before the war were threatened with ejection to China. 'There they would have to face Japanese border guards who were very tough and known to extract teeth for the gold in them' (conversation with the author).

In Hong Kong itself the Japanese were openly spying under the noses of the naive colonial authorities. One of the most popular characters was Mr Yamashita, barber in the Hong

Kong Hotel; the day after Hong Kong surrendered he turned up in Japanese uniform and became the first commandant of Stanley Internment Camp. Another famous Japanese was Miss Takamura, who advertised her services as an 'electric and hand massage expert' in the *South China Morning Post* and passed information on to Colonel Suzuki, head of Japanese Intelligence in Hong Kong, supposedly seconded from the Imperial Army to learn English. He had a big network of informers including some Chinese Triad members who had worked for the British military. When a British intelligence officer discovered that Suzuki had already collected many details on the Hong Kong defences, it was three months before the decision was made in Hong Kong to expel him. But then London stepped in and refused to do anything that might upset Japan, pointing out that the two countries were not at war. Indeed, it is doubtful whether any army was ever better informed about an enemy than the Japanese were about Hong Kong. Japanese officers were able to cross the border carrying detailed maps of Hong Kong's battle dispositions. It was also clear in the days before the attack that the Japanese were actively preparing for invasion. Yet when the attack came Hong Kong was badly prepared and the colony's British population paid dearly for their aloofness from the Chinese.

Novelist Ernest Hemingway visited both Hong Kong and a war zone of the Sino-Japanese struggle in 1941 and got a good idea of the attitudes of British and Chinese towards each other. Hemingway, who had had plenty of rice wine, told a Chinese general what the British thought of the Chinese: 'Johnny's alright and a very good fellow and all that. But he's absolutely hopeless on the offensive you know . . . we can't count on Johnny.' The general asked who Johnny was. 'John Chinaman,' came the reply. 'Very interesting,' responded the general; 'let me tell you a Chinese story. Do you know why the British staff officer wears a single glass in his eye?' Hemingway said he didn't. 'He wears a single glass in his eye so that he will not see more than he can understand.'

It took the Japanese only a matter of days to roll up Hong Kong. The surrender came on Christmas Day 1941. The Japanese were not true to their cartoon images: it had been assumed that they were inflexible and lacked imagination and that their equipment was inferior to that of the British. The contrary proved to be the case. Ching's 'Bird's Eye View' column in the *South China Morning Post* on 10 December captured some of the feeling: 'Trouble about fighting the Japanese is that the blighters don't seem to have tiffin [lunch].' It took only four days before the British troops, their defence lines broken through, had to be evacuated to Hong Kong island. The immediate aftermath of the British surrender was an orgy of Japanese looting, including raping and killing of nurses and civilians. The *Hong Kong News*, the newspaper which the Japanese set up, crowed in an editorial: 'the vaunted supermen of the white race have melted like butter. In 18 days of conflict it was all over, a horrible muddle of inefficiency and helplessness which bequeathed a miserable aftermath.' The Japanese collected considerable booty. According to Endacott, a Filipino businessman estimated that 2.5 million tons of freight worth US$250 million were shipped back to Japan from Hong Kong.

Several thousand prisoners of war were transported to Japan as virtual slave labour; others were put to work locally. Some daring escapes from the prison camps were helped by the British Army Aid Group underground resistance network and some local sympathizers. But this was a dangerous business for anyone caught. Civilian prisoners had a short time at liberty before they were rounded up and taken to an internment camp in Stanley. All the 2,500 interned civilians suffered physical and mental deterioration. One woman, Dorothy Jenner, summed up the experience: 'when I went into Stanley Camp in January 1941 I had black hair, I weighed about ten and a half stone. When I came out almost four years later my hair was dead white and I weighed less than six stone. I was weakened and disoriented and once in town I hadn't a clue where to go or what to do.' Eric Himsworth, who was among those interned, remembers how strong personalities and some prominent members of the community disintegrated, while some less significant people bore their detention more stoically. Several prominent people, including the head of the Hong Kong Bank, Sir Vandeleur Grayburn, died in captivity because of malnourishment and ill-treatment. Another banker, C. F. Hyde, was executed by the Japanese because he was suspected of being in communication with the enemy via the underground.

G. A. Leiper, a Chartered Bank officer, wrote that:

> when liberation came in August 1945 they were few internees who had not sold everything of value which they possessed, even to gold fillings in teeth in order to purchase the one thing that really mattered – food. Engagement and even wedding rings had been sold, and one of the many unusual activities which were carried on in the camp was the manufacture of substitute wedding rings from the rims of cupronickel twenty cent coins.

The local Chinese also had a tough time. The Japanese regarded conquered Hong Kong as theirs, and complained about the apathy of the local Chinese. After September 1943 they effectively drove most of the people out. From a refugee-swollen peak of more than 5 million, the Hong Kong population had dropped to under 600,000 by August 1945.

When the Japanese surrendered, there was a question over who should rule Hong Kong. Chiang Kai-shek, the Kuomintang (Nationalist) leader, would have liked to take Hong Kong over on behalf of China. He was supported by President Franklin D. Roosevelt of the USA, who believed that clause 3 of the Atlantic Charter of March 1943 – urging the liberation of all people – applied as much to British colonies as to those of Germany and Japan. According to R. E. Sherwood in *The White House Papers of Harry L. Hopkins* (1948), Roosevelt 'once or twice urged the British to give up Hong Kong as a gesture of good will'. At the Yalta talks, in February 1945, Roosevelt sought Soviet help in the Pacific, and to achieve this offered concessions at the expense of both Japan and China. To balance this and to keep China on his side, he argued that Britain should give up Hong Kong. Churchill, not privy to these US–Soviet discussions, later 'exploded' when he heard that attempts were being made behind his back to take Britain's colonies away. Chiang Kai-shek also argued that in January 1943 Washington and London had each made a treaty with China renouncing all concessions, settlements and special privileges attached to the treaty port system.

Yet in spite of all this the British moved quickly to regain control of the colony. Thanks to Colonial Secretary Franklin Gimson, who had taken up his post literally the day before the Japanese had attacked and had been interned, a provisional administration was set up. The British flag was raised on 18 August 1945. Gimson was quickly sworn in as, as he put it, 'virtually acting Governor of Hong Kong' by Chief Justice Sir Athol MacGregor, on 29 August. The following day the British fleet, under the command of Rear-Admiral Cecil Harcourt, entered the harbour via the Lei Yue Mun gap. Bob Clark, an Australian correspondent on board, reported:

> On the rocks, a coolie whistled shrilly. It was like an obscenity in that stillness. Then we were in Victoria Harbour and still there was no movement. Sunken Japanese shipping lay half submerged all over the harbour. Even on shore there seemed to be little sign of activity. There was not a launch or a sampan moving on the water. A few Chinese, not more than about 50, stood on the waterfront opposite the Peninsula Hotel watching. We walked into our berth in Kowloon and tied up. The Chinese clapped and cheered. It was a watery reception and made practically no impression on the oppressive silence. It was like entering a near dead city. An American civilian came running on to the jetty. He threw out his arms. Tears were streaming down his face and he was crying 'Thank God you've come at last. We've had four years of hell. I tell you,

the bastards have given us hell.' (Quoted in *Captive Years: The Occupation of Hong Kong, 1941–1945*, by Alan Birch and Martin Cole, Heinemann, 1982)

Eric Himsworth remembers being released from Stanley camp and climbing up to the hills to look down on the harbour before Harcourt's fleet sailed in. 'It was empty. Not a sign of movement or life, just as the harbour must have looked when the people first came over the hills from Kowloon to make a settlement in Hong Kong.' Banker Leiper also tells how the newly released internees 'gazed in awestruck silence at the roadway overgrown with vegetation, and at the ruins of houses, several of which had almost vanished in jungle encroachment. Then one of them spoke: "We'll have to start almost from the beginning again, just as they did 100 years ago."'

The formal surrender was fixed for 12 September 1945, but postponed after protests from Chiang against the intention of the British to receive the surrender in Hong Kong, as the colony lay within the Chinese war-zone. In the end the ceremony took place in Government House on Sunday 16 September, when Harcourt received the Japanese surrender on behalf of Britain and China.

Then there was the task of putting Hong Kong on its feet. All those in the colony at the time speak of the desolation which had overtaken Hong Kong, particularly in the last years of the war when the Japanese were being defeated and had too many preoccupations even to make sure that the colony was ticking over properly. David MacDougall quickly arrived in Hong Kong with the title of Chief Civil Affairs Officer and the rank of Brigadier. 'When I was last in the army I was only a private soldier,' MacDougall recalled. 'It was quite a jump to go from private to brigadier in one go.' MacDougall had served in Hong Kong from 1929 until the day of the British surrender and then had escaped bravely. He became Colonial Secretary when the military administration was dismantled and Governor Sir Mark Young returned after a period of rest and recuperation in the UK.

The people of Hong Kong might rejoice that they were liberated, but that didn't bring them food. On top of that, every aspect of Hong Kong needed rebuilding. The shortage of materials and men was exacerbated because the rest of the world was also just beginning to emerge from war, and supplies were short everywhere. Eric Himsworth was put in charge of exports and imports when he arrived back in Hong Kong after recuperation, and recalls that 'Our intention was to hand the economy back to private enterprise as quickly as possible. It's not the job of the government to run the economy, only to set the general framework of law and guidelines.' But it took time before foreign exchange controls on imports could be lifted. An estimated 80 per cent of the population suffered from malnutrition. During the military administration at least 22,000 totally destitute people a day had to be fed free of charge from government rice kitchens. The problem of food supplies began to increase as the population rose, reaching a million by the end of 1945 and growing by 100,000 a month. MacDougall recalls that it was a massive military exercise simply to make sure that sufficient food and other supplies reached Hong Kong: officials went to Indo-China for coal, to Canton for rice and vegetables, to Borneo for wood, to India for cotton and to Australia for building supplies. Lord Kadoorie and MacDougall both remember the effort to get power-generating equipment from the UK, which had its own problems of post-war reconstruction.

But the speed of the economic recovery surprised everyone. By 1946 trade was already half of the pre-war levels in volume terms and more than double in dollar terms. Total trade was worth HK$2.7 billion in 1947, almost HK$3.7 billion in 1948 and HK$5.1 billion in 1949. The then Colonial Secretary David MacDougall pays great tribute to the role of the chief manager of the Hongkong Bank, Arthur (later Sir Arthur) Morse, a Northern Irishman. The bank itself had to struggle to find its feet. (During the war its head office had been transferred to London by Order-in-Council of 13 January 1943 retroactive to 15 December 1941. It was restored to Hong Kong by Order-in-Council of 15 May 1946.) Morse understood the plight of the industrialists struggling to get their businesses going and went out of his way to help. He was particularly far-sighted in making advances for capital equipment and raw materials, often with no security at all except the goodwill of the factory-owners. Of course, he was helped by the bank's knowledge of businessmen in Hong Kong and Shanghai in pre-war years. His generous attitude later brought good business for the bank, as it established the trust of the rapidly growing industrialists; but at the time Morse was often taking risks. When the banker retired in 1953 Hong Kong's Governor paid him tribute, saying: 'He did things which from the purely banking point of view could hardly be justified, but which certainly could from the point of view of the colony as a whole.'

One of the old vestiges of privilege which MacDougall scrapped immediately after the war was the Peak District Reservation Ordinance of 1904, which restricted residence on the Peak to Europeans. After the war many of the old colonial characters who saw themselves as superior to the Chinese had died or did not return. So there was a slightly more relaxed atmosphere between the races, though the masses of the Chinese still tended very much to keep themselves to themselves.

The new era had most unpromising beginnings – in the shape of hundreds of thousands of refugees flooding down from war-torn China. Many of them were desperate and in fear and poverty; others were unhappy with the new Communist political regime, but had managed to escape with some of their wealth plus a great deal of experience and know-how in the running of industrial ventures.

The Kuomintang regime of Chiang Kai-shek had crumbled quickly. The Nationalists fled to Taiwan, and by 1 October 1949 Mao's Communist forces had captured enough of China to be able to declare the creation of the People's Republic from Tian'anmen Gate. An immediate fear in Hong Kong was that the communists might march on across the border and 'liberate' Hong Kong too. Roy Munden, then a young British

Army subaltern and later to become executive director of the Hongkong Bank, remembers the reinforced British garrison in the New Territories. Serving in the area known as Robin's Nest, commanding a good view of the border, he and other soldiers wondered aloud how the Communist guerrilla troops could be persuaded to stop at the border. After all, it was open country, and few Chinese recognized the 'unequal treaties' that had given Hong Kong to Britain. It might be too tempting for a new regime in China to put right the old colonial wrongs; or it might simply be difficult to stop the raggle-taggle guerrillas marching into Hong Kong. After all, thousands of refugees had already crossed. But such fears were unrealized: the Communist troops maintained strict discipline and stayed on their side of the border.

The end of the physical threat of Chinese occupation did not end the worries of the hard-pressed Hong Kong administration. The sheer numbers of people coming across, and the rapid rise of the population (which reached 2.5 million by 1951) continued to pose enormous problems of feeding, sheltering and clothing. Then the Korean war broke out and the Western countries under the United Nations flag imposed embargoes on trade with China – and this apparently threatened Hong Kong's economic foundations. But in fact this proved to be Hong Kong's great opportunity. For some time there were enormous sums of money to be made in trading with China illegally. In those turbulent times, those who were smart and lucky saw great opportunities; they may not have become millionaires overnight, but some were Hong Kong dollar billionaires before the conflict was over. China richly rewarded those who successfully defied the trade embargoes.

In the Hong Kong of those days there were a small number of people rich enough to tear down a whole hilltop to build themselves their own private castle; there were also the multitudes huddled together, grateful for only a shadow of shelter like a tin sheet or tarpaulin. There were the wealthy who would take tea in the Peninsula Hotel; and there were those starving, begging for a few grains of rice from the polished tables of the rich. There were the few who didn't have to work, other than to let their money make more money; there were the hungry masses clamouring for any job that would give them a dollar or so to buy those few grains of rice to stay alive. Han Suyin in her novel *A Many Splendoured Thing* (Jonathan Cape, 1952) piled the words and phrases on top of each other in a higgledy-piggledy way to describe the teeming and varied life in Hong Kong, as the colony started its adventurous road from being a small town to becoming the international city it is today.

> O sea-wet rock thronged, thronged and swarming with hunger and misery and wealth and want and abundance and waste, vice and purity and corruption and law and justice and privilege, charities and private property and Monopoly and Big Business and rackets and tuberculosis and beauty and horror; window of democracy Hongkong, haven of Shanghai racketeers and American missionaries and Chinese professors and international businessmen and out-of-job Kuomintang generals and Peking prostitutes and London marriageable girls and Mainland opium addicts; refuge of refugees and political exiles, end-of-the-road to so many rejects of the New World and relics of the Old fusty order, Grand Hotel of men at a loose end and men on the make and men with nowhere else to go; outpost of Empire Hong Kong, excrescence off China with two million four hundred thousand Chinese, communists and Nationalists and nothing-ists and so many many sitters-on-the-fence; deep-roaring, bustling eternal market Hong Kong; where life and love and souls and blood and all things made and grown under the sun are bought and sold and smuggled and squandered, spring is come home to you.

From precisely this unpromising jumbled-up beginning emerged the modern metropolis of Hong Kong.

6 Kindly but Colonial Paternalism

The dirtiest word in Hong Kong is not a four-letter one. It has six letters: C-O-L-O-N-Y. It has been banished from Hong Kong banknotes since 1985. Government officials have done their best to remove all traces of it from schoolbooks. They prefer the more neutral, less politically and emotionally laden expression 'territory' to describe Hong Kong. Yet it is hard to get away from the reality that Hong Kong is a colony and remains a very *colonial* place.

From the point of view of administration and – dare anyone mention another dirty word, this time one of eight letters, P-O-L-I-T-I-C-S – Hong Kong is cast in the colonial mould of the 1930s. The London-appointed Governor, a former high-flying Whitehall mandarin – just like his chums and colleagues back in the Foreign and Commonwealth Office – is very much the king pin in the colony. He has a knighthood, and is a Knight Commander of the Order of St Michael and St George, allowing him the letters KCMG after his name which, as all Whitehall knows, stands for 'Kindly Call Me God'. He is Commander-in-Chief of the British forces in the colony. He works through an executive council (Exco), which has resemblances to a cabinet, and a legislative council (Legco), the law-making body. But he presides over both bodies, appoints ten of the fourteen members of Exco (the others are ex-officio leading officials), chooses twenty-seven of the fifty-seven members of Legco (and another three are ex-officio), and has to sign any bill passed by Legco before it becomes law. There are no political parties and most of the members of the two councils are trusted pillars of society.

Over the years gubernatorial style has changed. Fading photographs in the archives show old governors who were aloof, remote, almost vice-regal figures weighed down by the braid on their uniforms and ostrich-feather hats. Today's Governor goes about in more modest style, dressed in a lounge suit, and in the hot and humid summer months in a bush suit. He looks uncomfortable, not to say embarrassed, when for ceremonial occasions he has to put on the fancy colonial suit with the funny feathered hat. The personality of the Governor has also changed. Until the 1970s Hong Kong was the preserve of the old British colonial service. In 1971 the big change was made. For the first time the new Hong Kong Governor was chosen not from the ranks of the colonial service but from among career diplomats of the FCO. Sir (Crawford) Murray MacLehose had been an ambassador first in Saigon and then in Copenhagen, but he wasn't a top-rank man, such as occupy the plum jobs of ambassador in Washington, Paris, Bonn or Brussels. Posted to Hong Kong in charge of one of the world's greatest cities, he hadn't run anything bigger than a middle-sized British Embassy. He quickly spent a few months learning the ropes of big British city governments such as Manchester, so that he wasn't totally unacquainted with the problems he would meet. He did know Hong Kong, having previously served as political adviser to the government.

In personality terms, MacLehose was a huge success. His commanding physical presence, from a height of well over six feet, gave him a good start. But 'Big Mac', as he quickly became known among the kinder wags in the Hong Kong government (he was also known as 'Jock the sock', among other less flattering names) didn't hide himself away in Government House or stay aloof and visible only on ceremonial occasions. He was quick to make public tours of his new territory. The bush suit became his trademark in tropical summer. MacLehose, like some practical member of the royal family, or indeed like a good politician, went on walkabouts of workaday Hong Kong, shaking hands and talking to ordinary local Chinese, as he tried to discover what made Hong Kong tick and what the government should be doing to remedy the grave social deficiencies. He finally retired as Governor in 1982 after a record eleven years, and was ennobled as Lord MacLehose of Beoch. This was the first time that a governor had been raised to the peerage for his work in Hong Kong, though other governors had become lords for their work elsewhere (for example, Frederick Lugard, Governor of Hong Kong from 1907 to 1911, and later Governor of Nigeria).

MacLehose's successor, Sir Edward Youde, was also a career Foreign Office man, but a very different personality. A former Ambassador to Peking, who was Chief Clerk and the number two civil servant in the Foreign Office, Youde had not served in Hong Kong, but he spoke Mandarin fluently and read Chinese with ease. In 1949 he had received the award of Member of the Most Distinguished Order of the British Empire (MBE), when as Third Secretary in China he had negotiated with the new Communist Chinese authorities for the release of the British frigate HMS *Amethyst*, trapped and under Chinese fire in the Yangtse river. Youde was physically small and slight, and had been educated at London University, unlike the decidedly patrician Oxford-educated MacLehose (who had been to Eton and then Balliol College).

Youde's quiet personality led critics to make snide remarks to the effect that no one noticed when the Governor walked into a room. But Youde fought hard for Hong Kong interests in the talks with China, though his room for manœuvre was limited by the British government's position. In late 1986 Youde died suddenly in his sleep in the British Embassy in Peking. His body was returned to Hong Kong for the funeral and cremation. Large crowds of ordinary Hong Kong Chinese lined up to pay their last respects, a tribute to a man who lacked personal colour but had done his best for the colony in the most difficult circumstances.

Another Foreign Office man took over. David Wilson was only fifty-two, of Scottish stock, a man who had served as political adviser and then been in charge of Hong Kong in Whitehall. He was knighted hurriedly before taking up the governor's job. The new man was regarded as ambitious and capable, qualities masked by the consummate smoothness of a practised diplomat and the retiring exterior of a scholar. Wilson, also Oxford-educated (Keble College), had left the Foreign Office for six years to do a Ph.D. and to edit the *China Quarterly*, a scholarly publication. In addition he is a keen mountain climber, and some years before his appointment had accompanied Chris Bonington on his expedition to climb the Himalayan Mount Kongur from the Chinese side. He speaks and reads Mandarin fluently, but not Cantonese in spite of his four years in Hong Kong as political adviser.

If some of the colonial trappings and pomp have been abolished, the colonial reality remains. In larger erstwhile British colonies, such as India, the powers of the governor, governor-general or viceroy were long ago diluted by the coming of local elections and self-rule. Indians enjoyed a considerable degree of autonomy years before the Second World War. But in Hong Kong it was 1985 before limited elections were held for seats on the colony's legislative council, commonly known as Legco. Prior to this the only Hong Kong-wide elections were for district boards, bodies which, officials admitted, had influence over the siting of bus-stops and post-boxes, but few other powers. Essentially, as Norman Miners, senior lecturer in the Department of Political Science at Hong Kong University pointed out in late 1984, 'for the past eighty-eight years, the institutions of the central government in Hong Kong have remained substantially unchanged. The last significant development in the direction of self-government and democratic representation took place in 1896 when two unofficials [that is, not officials or civil servants] were admitted to membership of the executive council.' Miners conceded that since that time the size of both executive and legislative councils had increased – and indeed non-civil servant members outnumber officials on both councils. But, argued Miners, 'the structure of government and the relationships between the Governor, the executive council, the legislative council and the civil service, have not been altered'.

After the limited legislative council elections, the majority on the council overwhelmingly consists of local Hong Kong Chinese. But the Governor's powers remain virtually untrammelled. The elected members are still a minority on the council, and in any case the governor doesn't have to heed any of his advisory bodies. He is appointed by the British sovereign and derives his authority from Letters Patent passed under the Great Seal of the United Kingdom. He has to observe instructions given by Whitehall, but he can override the wishes of the majority on Legco or indeed of the executive council. Supporters of the British colonial system say this doesn't mean that Hong Kong ignores the wishes of the local population. Indeed, according to Sir Philip Haddon-Cave, Hong Kong's Chief Secretary until he retired in 1985, the abiding principle of British colonial government remains the famous Devonshire Declaration of 1922 (named after the Duke of Devonshire, then Secretary of State for the Colonies): 'the fundamental principle on which His Majesty's Government's colonial policy is based is that the interests of the local people are paramount'. But Haddon-Cave quotes his favourite colonial Governor as adding: 'and I'm the best judge of where their interests lie'. The former official had himself claimed paternalistically that Hong Kong practised government by consultation, consent and consensus, although 'public opinion cannot be considered the only determinant of government policy: public interest must be considered too.'

In pre-independence India the viceroy had to contend with a stream of instructions from London, but in the late twentieth century Hong Kong has been largely allowed to go its own sweet way. The outstanding instance of London insisting on its views, against the wishes of Hong Kong inhabitants, concerns capital punishment. In 1973 Britain intervened to reprieve a convicted murderer, whose execution had been approved by the Governor. Most local Chinese support the death penalty, and capital punishment remains on the statute book, but all recent Hong Kong death sentences have been commuted to life imprisonment. A former senior Hong Kong government secretary did complain that Whitehall had tried to interfere in the colony in the 1970s by urging increased social spending and 'socialist policies'. He also suggested that Governor MacLehose was sent with specific instructions to increase spending on housing and social amenities. (Maclehose denies that in increasing spending he was obeying instructions.)

Norman Miners (in *The Government and Politics of Hong Kong*, fourth edition, Oxford University Press, 1986) quotes Lord Goronwy-Roberts, Minister of State at the British Foreign Office during the 1970s, as saying that though the British Labour government 'exercised progressive and necessary pressures' on the Hong Kong government, it drew the line about giving formal instructions. 'I certainly pressed Hong Kong for a more progressive system of taxation,' said Goronwy-Roberts to Miners in an interview,

> but I could not have imposed it. The paramountcy of the British government is normally only exercised in matters of foreign affairs and security. Where internal policy has security implications, such as the possibility of riots and civil disorder, the ministers might be obliged to take action. But matters would have to go far down the road before a minister would insist on his views on a matter of taxation policy.

Later, in 1987, the London government refused to intervene to stop the 'False News' clause in the Public Order (Amendment) Ordinance. This section threatened a two-year jail sentence and HK$100,000 fine for anyone who published false news likely to cause alarm to the public or a 'section thereof' or disturb public order. The law itself alarmed Hong Kong newspapers, who claimed its loose definitions left them vulnerable to lawsuits. One British lawyer MP lobbied by angry Hong Kong journalists commented, 'If we had this, the first people I would prosecute would be the weather forecasters; they spread false news all the time which alarms sections of the public.' But junior Foreign Office Minister Timothy Renton told journalist Jim Biddulph: 'Britain does not interfere in the internal affairs of Hong Kong' (Quoted in the *Correspondent*, Hong Kong, February 1989). The law was later repealed.

Indeed, Hong Kong's biggest complaint against Britain is that it has been left to fight for itself, often against British interests. This was true in countless textile negotiations, in which British millowners pressed for restrictions against Hong Kong.

Hong Kong's whole history of government reveals slow and grudging progress towards allowing non-officials or local Chinese a role, let alone the governing role: not until 1880 was the first Chinese appointed to Legco and then only on a temporary basis to fill the place occupied by a European away from Hong Kong; not until 1896 were the first non-civil servants appointed to the executive council; and not until 1926 was a Chinese, Sir Shouson Chow, made a member of Exco. As late as the mid-1960s, the legislative council was balanced equally between officials and unofficials, and as late as 1980 expatriate British were still in the majority on the executive council. The most common complaint, heard throughout Hong Kong's history and even to the present day, is that members of the two councils are in no way 'representative' or even understand the feelings of the ordinary people of Hong Kong. In the 1970s Governor MacLehose appointed a leavening of newcomers who were not business tycoons nor lawyers, nor other high-income professionals like bankers. Two of MacLehose's appointments were the Reverend Joyce Bennett, teacher of the Church Missionary Society, and a Jesuit priest, Father Patrick McGovern. McGovern confessed that he felt an odd man out beside some of his colleagues, especially 'when I parked my motor scooter outside Government House alongside the Rolls-Royces and Mercedes'. Governor Youde further extended Legco's membership by appointing younger people, including a primary school-teacher.

The biggest step forward was the expansion of Legco by election in 1985. After the fanfare of publicity the scope of the new measures proved hardly breathtaking. The executive council was not touched. Legco was expanded by twenty-four elected members (raised to twenty-six in 1988). However, in the newly revamped council of September 1985, the elected members formed only 40 per cent of the total membership of Legco. And by world standards the new Hong Kong electoral process was timid indeed. All the members were indirectly elected. The franchise was far from universal. Half the elected members were chosen by nine 'functional constituencies' and the other half came from twelve electoral colleges comprising members of the lower councils.

Creation of functional constituencies caused controversy. Three constituencies, 'commercial', 'industrial' and 'labour', were given two members each, while the other six, 'financial', 'social services', 'medical', 'teaching', 'legal', and finally 'engineering, architectural, surveying and planning' returned one each. In some functional constituencies, for example legal and teaching, the vote has been given to the individual, whereas in others the company has the vote. In the financial constituency, only the licensed banks (141 at the time, by 1989 165) are allowed to vote, with one vote apiece. Finance companies, stockbrokers, gold dealers and other pillars of the financial community do not figure at all. On the whole, Professor Peter Harris of the University of Hong Kong described the newcomers to Legco as 'middle class and middle-minded'. This, he said, was what the authorities wanted, not people who might 'rock the boat'. Norman Miners was more acid in his comments, claiming that 'The arguments now used to recommend functional constituencies recall the case made by defenders of the unreformed British Parliament before the Reform Bill of 1832, to the effect that Parliament should represent all the significant interests in the country, and that the rotten boroughs played an essential part in achieving this.' Miners continued that 'since then, however, it has come to be accepted that the only proper basis for a democratic assembly is "one man, one vote"'. There was a great deal of arbitrariness in choosing which interests should have functional constituencies. Miners said scathingly:

> One may ask why the medical constituency only consists of doctors and does not include nurses . . . [in the 1988 election nurses were given a constituency] Why not a constituency for the Indian community or for the disabled, or for the sanitary workers and garbagemen? The choice of interests seems designed to ensure that at least eight of the representatives from the functional constituencies will voice the views of the upper strata of society and only three, or possibly four, will speak for the poor (two from the trades unions, one social worker and perhaps one teacher). (Paper to a Hong Kong University seminar, December 1984)

Whitehall's hand can be seen in the failure to move away from cosy colonialism. As early as 1946 Governor Sir Mark Young put forward a plan to extend the franchise, initially allowing elections to the urban council, a local council covering the urban areas. But it was dropped because, it was claimed, the Chinese were not interested in elections or politics since they were too busy making money. When the Communists achieved power across the border, an additional reason cited against elections was that it might upset China or – worse still – bring the Communist Party into Hong Kong elections. For the next thirty-five years the arguments against elections swung to and fro between the claims that Peking would not like elections, that Hong Kong Chinese were not interested in politics or elections, as evidenced by low turn-outs of 20 to 30 per cent where elections were held for local councils, and that the existing system worked well. Defending the old system, former Chief Secretary Haddon-Cave argued that Hong Kong's consensus government was more democratic than many so-called democracies in which a 'one man, one vote' system of government obtained. 'We have no tyranny of the parliamentary majority,' he declared proudly.

But in fact democracy hardly had a chance. Until 1981 the franchise was highly restricted, to voters who fell into one of twenty-three categories by education, tax-paying or membership of professional bodies, and the urban council was the only body for which elections were held. It had limited powers over public health, recreation and culture. No wonder that only 440,000 people were estimated eligible to vote and only 35,000 bothered to register. Since then a whole panoply of nineteen district boards, an urban council and a regional council (covering the New Territories) has been set up. The franchise has been extended to all adults resident for seven years or more in Hong Kong. But even in 1989 all lower councils had a large number of appointed members. Only the limited district boards had an elected majority. It was a vicious circle. A budding politician was given little encouragement and the rich and influential did not need politics or democracy in order to exercise power. A Chinese university teacher of politics, Joseph Cheng, noted: 'You won't get people like Sir Y. K. Pao or Li Ka-shing out on the hustings because they feel that if they need something done, all they have to do is call up someone in the government or fly to Peking and talk to Deng Xiaoping.'

There were renewed demands for full democratic elections after the joint declaration in 1984, giving Hong Kong back to China in 1997. But the steadying hand of Whitehall was felt urging Hong Kong not to rush to something that Peking would not like. (See chapter 13.)

But whatever its virtues Hong Kong's colonial system also has a number of flaws. Senior government officials admit that they are in effect both civil servants and ministers in Hong Kong's government. A vigorous and vociferous public opinion may prevent the government from flying completely in the face of the popular mood, but this is a negative protection. There is no safeguard to ensure that the government's policies are in line with popular feelings or enjoy the careful forethought that a political party forced to face the electorate and win a mandate must expend. True, mandates are vague and the 'tyranny of the majority' in modern parliamentary democracies can be cruel. But policies can change sharply in Hong Kong according to who is governor and how strong he is; and whether he has commanding personalities as chief secretary and financial secretary. In the early 1970s immediately after MacLehose became Governor Hong Kong's spending on social services rose sharply. Sir John Cowperthwaite, Financial Secretary from 1961 to 1971, had fiercely resisted social spending, believing in the absolutely minimum role of government. Even after the Cultural Revolution-inspired 1967 riots he steadfastly kept spending down, scathingly rejecting the idea that 'the people of Hong Kong have to be given a reward, like children, for being good last year, and bribed, like children, into being good next year'.

Governor Sir David Trench (1964–71) also declared that 'Hong Kong's generally *laissez-faire* economic policies have always been based on considered decisions, not mere paralysis of mind and will'. Considered, maybe, but not publicly debated nor put to any popular assessment. The power of these two men may be seen in the fact that in 1970–71 spending on social welfare was HK$40 million; by 1985–6 it had risen to HK$2,534 million. The government was piling up problems for itself by soaring government spending – which reached 21 per cent of gross domestic product – and by overdependence on land sales as a source of government revenue. 'Philip (Haddon-Cave) just let things go to his head', recalls a finance official criticizing his former boss, who was Financial Secretary from 1971 to 1981. 'Revenues from land sales were booming and he just spent, spent, spent. There was no one with authority to check him.'

By the end of MacLehose's rule his administration was looking ragged. It was an open secret that Chief Secretary Sir Jack Cater and MacLehose himself had their differences. The harmony was not helped because MacLehose 'was a reacher-downer', remembers a Hong Kong government secretary. 'Increasingly it was difficult for Sir Jack Cater. He was supposed to be the managing director running day-to-day operations, but MacLehose's constant interventions made it difficult to do the job smoothly.' One token of MacLehose's autocratic temperament was that he insisted on using a special red-ribbon typewriter for his own instructions, while other lesser officials used normal black ribbons. And, the Governor didn't sign or initial his internal messages – 'he used to put just a big capital letter 'M' at the foot of his messages', says an aide who worked closely with him.

MacLehose's successor Sir Edward Youde was nothing like as flamboyant. He discontinued the practice of special red messages that set the Governor apart from ordinary officials. He didn't 'reach down', but preferred to work through a smooth-running government machine. A senior officer who travelled with both governors contrasted their styles:

> Let's say that while on walkabout inspecting a housing estate or district board, the governor spots a pile of festering rubbish or very poor housing. MacLehose would immediately wade in, wave his arms and say 'Why is this like that? Get something done about it immediately.' Youde on the other hand would not create a fuss but would promise to look into the matter and set the government machine in motion to discover the underlying cause and hope to clear up the mess, prevent it from happening again.

Legco and Exco members reported that Youde had a much more intellectual approach. 'He let everyone have his or her say, weighed the facts and then reached a decision', remembers an Exco member, adding: 'once he'd made up his mind, he was very difficult to deflect'. But neither governor's policies or attitudes were put into the crucible of popular test.

The most telling criticism of the Hong Kong government system is that it is still a 'colonial' system, based on the principle that the rulers know best. This is not to suggest that officials are busy feathering their own nests. On the contrary, most officials are assiduous in putting Hong Kong's interests first, even if it means quarrelling with London. The complaints are not that they are mendacious, but that they are limited in their talents and the proposals they make are not subject to the popular scrutiny that would take place in a proper parliamentary democracy. It is paternalism of a kindly sort. Formal sessions of Legco tend to consist of the reading of set speeches. There is little of the 'cut and thrust' of debate as at Westminster or in other flourishing parliamentary systems. The general sleepy atmosphere of Legco has been fostered by the government's desire to avoid adversarial politics. Most disputes are argued out beforehand behind closed doors, so that most of the speeches in the chamber itself are 'for the record'. But Chief Secretary Sir David Ford 'hotly' disputed the view that Legco was relatively powerless. He told *Asiaweek* (21 June 1987) that:

> Legco has a great deal of authority. Firstly, it can review and pass any piece of legislation proposed by the government. Point 2, it can refuse to vote any money that the government wishes to spend on any project – and every bit of policy involves the expenditure of money. That is a great deal of authority. And councillors can turn down a total budget from the government as well as any specific item.

In practice, however, until recently Legco has been a tame body. Yet its members are jealous of their special rights and privileges – so much so that when these were expressed in a special bill in the mid-1980s, a well-known lawyer, David Birnbaum, wrote that members of Exco and Legco were 'perceived as a chorus of yes-men out of tune with the true needs of the people of Hong Kong'. He added: 'Question: What do you call a rubber stamp with a machine gun? Answer: A Umelco member [unofficial member of Exco or Legco].'

On a few occasions recently Legco has forced the government to change its policy. Most notably in 1984 the legislative council voted against proposals to raise taxi licence charges and fares approved by the executive council. But this hardly reflected credit on the appointed members. The measures seemed to have been accepted, but then a taxi strike and ensuing violence in the street made the Legco members change their minds – under duress, effectively.

The limited democracy, through indirect Legco elections, was by 1989 having an impact. A senior official remarked: 'Legco members are getting sharper, more critical. Unfortunately, they are also getting involved in details, which should not be their business. For example, they want a say in not only whether to buy a computer for a department, but which brand of computer should be bought.' He pointed out that this detailed supervision opened the door to corruption.

Another area in which Hong Kong is still strongly 'colonial' is at senior levels of the civil service. The question of 'localization' – meaning giving jobs to Hong Kong Chinese as opposed to expatriates – is a touchy one. When Hong Kong Chief Secretary Haddon-Cave was taxed about it in 1985, he responded that more than 95 per cent of the civil service posts were localized. This was true, but he was counting all posts, down to lowly clerks. At the very top, the civil service was still heavily biased in the mid-1980s towards expatriates. At the end of 1984 fewer than a third of the secretary-level posts were held by Chinese, and at the level immediately below, locals held only 14 per cent of the administrative posts. Thereafter, there has been a rush to ensure that good Chinese administrators are promoted to the highest posts – but this policy has brought its own criticisms.

What is true for the mainstream civil service is even more true for more sensitive posts like senior police positions. In mid-1986 the ratio of senior police officers (those of superintendent and above) was 70 per cent expatriates to 30 per cent local Chinese. It had been deliberate policy to leave the control of the 25,000-strong police force responsible for law and order firmly in British hands, because of fears of Communist infiltration of the police. At best local Chinese might make up half of the more than 400 senior police officers by 1997.

All this means that Hong Kong in the late twentieth century is less prepared to cast off colonialism and accept the pitfalls of independence than most other erstwhile British colonies. And Hong Kong is not being offered independence. Instead it will face a unique autonomous status within the confines of the world's biggest state with a ruthless Communist Party in charge. An official who had seen the sun set on various parts of the British empire was in Hong Kong and China in 1985 to watch the mutual self-congratulation over the agreement. His judgement: 'These people in Hong Kong are so naïve and immature. They have spent so much time making money that they have no idea of the devious way of politics. The hardened Communists will run rings round them.' No wonder that the thoughtful commentators fear that Hong Kong will get rid of one set of colonial rulers simply by swapping them for another set – the Peking colonialists.

7 The Hong Kong Dragon Catches up with the West

In the space of a few weeks in mid-1989 views about the prospects and potential of Hong Kong's economy changed dramatically. Until May of that year the economy went from strength to strength. Companies were squealing about the shortage of labour and pleading with the government to permit 'imports' of workers. Manufacturers rejoiced over new-found ties with factories across the border in China allowing them to farm out some of their production at up to a fifth of Hong Kong labour costs. Financial Secretary Sir Piers Jacobs (although he was only knighted in the Queen's birthday honours of June 1989) was looking forward to slower growth – a mere (by Hong Kong standards) 6 per cent – to relieve the pressures on inflation. Then came the Tian'anmen Square protests and massacre and Hong Kong began to realize that there were liabilities involved in the growing ties with China. Being too dependent on its big brother and soon-to-be ruler could be uncomfortable if China's economy faltered or changed course. And there was a real possibility that the Peking crackdown would produce not just a a bleeding from a brain drain of scared mobile managers and entrepreneurs, but a wholesale haemorrhage of talent from Hong Kong. On the other hand there were also optimists who predicted another Hong Kong boom as only the colony knows how to boom, with entrepreneurs making their last attempts to make as much money as possible while the going remained good. This would be in the classic Hong Kong tradition.

The Secret of Success?

It is frequently claimed that in Hong Kong it is possible to register a business in the morning, open the factory or office by lunchtime and be making good profits by the evening of the same day. It is difficult to find actual live businessmen prepared to boast that it is that easy to make profits – probably they are all too busy making money to take the time off to talk about it.

Hong Kong, more than any other place in the world, is dedicated to the pursuit of making money, more money and still more money. Stories are told about the frustration of managers unavoidably held up attending to little chores like burying a father or getting married, watching rivals leap on the next aircraft to snap up a business order. The proof of Hong Kong's success is plain to see. The territory desperately teeming with refugees in the late 1940s and 1950s, the city whose inhabitants are still largely refugees or the children of refugees, peasant duck farmers and other assorted riff-raff, has made it. Hong Kong has conquered most imaginable misfortunes, and today stands poised to overtake the United Kingdom and most of the rest of Europe in terms of per capita annual income.

The tiny territory that's a mere dot on any physical map even of Asia, 'a flea hanging on to the rear of China', as one cynic called it, is one of the world's biggest economic and trading powers. Total gross domestic product,the sum of the value of goods and services produced in Hong Kong, has risen by twenty times in twenty years, from US$2.5 billion in 1967 to US$55 billion in 1988. Total exports of goods and services in 1988 were US$75 billion. That alone puts Hong Kong into the top twelve exporters in the world. Most of the rest are western industrialized countries. In per capita terms the achievements are all the more remarkable. Tiny Hong Kong, with fewer than six million people, is producing more exports than China itself, which has 180 times as many people: it exports four times as much as India with 130 times as many people. Hong Kong exports goods worth about US$12,750 per person per year, about five times the exports of the average Briton, six times those of the average Japanese, and more than ten times those of the average US citizen. Yet in the rest of the world there is still a tendency to describe Hong Kong in sometimes exotic, often quaint, and usually demeaning terms. If you believe US Congressmen complaining about the flood of Hong Kong exports reaching their country and swamping and destroying US home-grown industries you would imagine a giant sweatshop built on cheap labour turning out shoddy goods for the rest of the world. No one who has actually seen Hong Kong and its industries or met its industrialists would insult them by taking them so lightly.

In any case Hong Kong today is much more diversified than a mere manufacturing centre. Manufacturing is still important and accounts for about 22 per cent of total gross domestic product. It also employs almost 900,000 people, the largest chunk – about 34 per cent – of the labour force. But these days Hong Kong is also a big financial centre involved in round-the-clock trading; has a strong service sector catering for tourists and business conferences, especially for people who want to see new ideas and a dynamic marketplace; and has an important communications role, keeping the Asia-Pacific region in touch with the rest of the world by means of air and shipping services and telecommunications.

Hong Kong differs from most of the rest of the world in the lightness of the government's economic controls. Officials reject claims that Hong Kong is a *laissez-faire* territory, or that it disregards international rules and regulations. Many such charges were true twenty or thirty years ago, when a freebooting Hong Kong at the painful start of its economic miracle flouted international labour conventions and ignored pollution, and its employers were happy to exploit a steady supply of cheap refugee workers streaming in from China. Today things have changed, though there is a lot of painful catching up still to do, especially in regard to the infrastructure and the environment. Hong Kong is now a signatory to most international labour conventions. The government Environmental Protection

Department, run and staffed by a single man in 1977, had grown to more than 800 employees by 1988 (though pollution curbs are still too lax). In the mid to late 1980s the government stepped in, admittedly only after a series of scandals, to tighten up banking regulations and to clean up the securities market (see chapter 8). Officials take pride in the government's role in housing: it has built flats for more than 2.8 million people or half the total population.

At one point in the early 1980s government services were expanding so quickly that it looked as if the government alone would soon account for almost 25 per cent of national income. Such rapid expansion outpaced the growth of revenues and coincided with a double slump brought about by a world economic downturn and by political uncertainty. The government budget went into deficit. That taught the authorities a sharp lesson; expenditure was cut back sharply. By the mid-1980s the government share of national income had been reduced to about 17 per cent. What the government has tried to do is to create the infrastructure in which business can flourish, make its own decisions and its own mistakes and enjoy the fruits of its labours. Hong Kong is not a tax haven in the classic sense of allowing people to evade taxes. The colony learnt long before President Ronald Reagan and Mrs Margaret Thatcher came to power that the best way to ensure that people pay their taxes is to keep rates low. This does not take away from workers and businessmen the incentive to work hard, since most of their earnings remain their own.

In 1986 the then governor, Sir Edward Youde, went to the United States to make major presentations to businessmen. There he was able to boast the following successes, and to explain the reasons why Hong Kong is a good place to invest:

> The territory has almost no natural resources. Its economy has been built by its greatest natural asset, its people. Yet today it can claim these achievements:
>
> - Asia's leading financial centre and the third in the world after New York and London.

- Asia's largest gold trading centre.
- World's largest exporter of garments, toys and plastic products.
- World's largest exporter in volume of watches, clocks and radios.
- 18th among the world's trading nations [now about 12th].
- 20th among the world's exporters of domestic manufactures.
- World's third busiest container port after Rotterdam and New York [Today the busiest container port in the world].
- World's biggest single air cargo terminal.
- Highest living standard in Asia outside Japan.
- World's largest public housing programme.
- World's third largest diamond trading centre after New York and Antwerp.

Hong Kong has the kind of economy which is familiar to American businessmen and with which they can feel at home personally and in their business activities. It is open and market oriented. The government seeks to intervene only when prudent regulation and the good name of Hong Kong require. But it also seeks to ensure the provision of an efficient business environment and supporting infrastructure. This includes good communications, an efficient port and airport, a stable currency linked to the US dollar and free from exchange controls, low tax [see below] and an established legal and judicial system. Hong Kong has a well understood law of contract, based on the same principles as the United States. The business community at home and abroad has confidence in it. In addition Hong Kong is now establishing an international arbitration centre, the first of its kind in East Asia. The centre will enhance the standing of Hong Kong as a regional business centre.

Hong Kong's corporate and personal taxation is among the lowest in the industrial world, providing incentives for workers to work and entrepreneurs to invest.

- 18.5 per cent corporation profits tax [now 16.5 per cent].
- 17 per cent on others like partnerships [now 15 per cent].
- 17 per cent salaries tax [now 15 per cent].

There are no interest rate taxes on foreign and local currency deposits. There is no exchange control or restriction on remittance of capital or profits overseas. (Document prepared for Governor's visit to USA.)

An intelligent, versatile and above all hard-working labour force has also helped stimulate rapid economic growth. The number of days lost through strikes is small. Hong Kong's educational system, topped by two universities with a third on the drawing board, is intended to ensure continuously improving skills and flexibility in the labour force, and a good knowledge of modern industrial and economic life. Several thousand Hong Kong students each year also gain foreign university and professional qualifications. Chinese families place great faith in the value of education and there is always a clamour for places.

The government itself is stable, not threatened by unsettling things like political parties or elections. The civil service is efficient and honest, shiningly so by the standards of many other Asian countries. It wasn't always so. Until the mid-1970s the police force in particular was riddled with corruption. A former senior official, Sir Jack Cater, claimed that corruption was like a runaway bus: the choice for an individual civil servant was whether to stand in the way and be run over, or jump on the bus. The setting up of the Independent Commission Against Corruption in 1974 (first headed by Cater) helped to curb the excesses.

Starting a business in Hong Kong is still easy and almost totally free from the red tape that entangles business in other countries. It's a simple matter to pay the small annual fee and levy to begin operation. Other rules governing companies are straightforward. In Hong Kong, customs formalities are kept to a minimum. Import and export licences are required in certain areas, since Hong Kong has to comply with international obligations and make provisions for health, safety and security, but government spokesmen stress that things are done speedily. 'If licences are required, the trade department normally issues them within two clear working days from the date of receipt of a textile licence application and one clear working day in the case of a non-textile licence application,' says an official. The government doesn't believe that it is its job to tell companies which industries they should try to get involved in.

For all its progress Hong Kong remains a highly vulnerable place; some economists claim that its very success comes from its vulnerability. A territory that is not featherbedded by controls or restricted by onerous taxes has to face the full force of the external climate. Since 90 per cent of manufacturing output is exported, this means that Hong Kong's economic conditions swing with the world economy, and particularly with the economic climate in the USA and Europe, its two biggest markets. When the West is doing well, the super-competitive Hong Kong industries are able to grow rapidly, and real economic growth of 10 or 12 per cent a year is not uncommon; but when the world economic winds are chill, Hong Kong really shivers. There have been good examples recently. Boom times in the late 1970s and early 1980s brought a misplaced overconfidence that, as noted above, affected the government as well as the private sector. Property prices soared sky-high, and the government embarked on a spending spree that was backed by the speculative prices it was getting for its land sales, and couldn't be sustained. The world economic downturn coincided with Hong Kong's political soul-searching over the prospects of a Chinese takeover. Property prices plummeted and the government budget ran into deficit. Growth fell sharply and in 1985 was negative.

Former big business tycoon John Bremridge took over as Financial Secretary in the middle of 1981. The florid and flamboyant Bremridge realized the seriousness of the situation and took measures to put the house in order. He imposed new taxes, including raising the airport departure tax to a huge HK$100, introduced taxes on perfumes, cosmetics and soft drinks, and cut government spending plans sharply. By the time he handed over in 1986 the government budget was again showing a modest surplus. By 1987 and 1988 the economic turnaround was complete and a HK$10 billion surplus was rung up in 1987 and an even bigger one of HK$15 billion in 1989. Bremridge's successor, Piers Jacobs, was nearly as different a character as one could imagine. Whereas Bremridge came from the private sector, Jacobs is a civil servant through and through, a lawyer who did twenty-four years in government service before taking the Financial Secretary's job; whereas Bremridge was abrasive, and often rude, Jacobs is polite and thrives on consensus; whereas Bremridge flourished in the limelight, Jacobs runs away from publicity; whereas Bremridge loved to pull out the well-chosen word, Jacobs generally utters commonplaces; perhaps not unexpectedly for someone who rose to the top financial job through the post of Registrar-General and Secretary for Economic Services. Faced with buoyant fiscal revenues in his very first budget, Jacobs had a choice of increasing government spending, cutting taxes or increasing fiscal reserves. Typically he opted for a 'prudent mixture' of all three. Charged that his budget was bland and boring, Jacobs responded: 'I sincerely hope that I shall not produce anything exciting. That is not what Hong Kong wants.'

In the face of contrary pressures, Jacobs clung firmly to the pegging of the local currency against the US dollar at a rate of HK$7.80 to one US dollar. This had been introduced in October 1983 by Bremridge when political uncertainty had sent the Hong Kong dollar tumbling in world currency markets, reaching 9.55 against the US dollar one panic-stricken September Saturday morning. Pegging of the dollar gave a steady currency and meant that interest rates would have to take the strain. In the late 1980s when the US dollar itself tumbled against all other major currencies, it meant that the Hong Kong dollar weakened, except against the US dollar. Hong Kong exports thus remained extremely competitive on world markets. Exports grew by more than 35 per cent in the single year 1987, and the economy roared ahead by 11 per cent each year in 1986 and 1987. This was a faster rate than any other country in the world except South Korea. The rates took the government by surprise, and Financial Secretary Jacobs had to revise his forecast upward. In 1987 he was expecting 6.2 per cent growth, but the economy grew at a huge 13.6 per cent. The ever-prudent Jacobs cautioned that 'volatility and uncertanty continue to be facts of our economic life', and predicted much lower growth rates in the wake of the 1987 stock market crash. Real growth in 1988 was about 8 per cent, and some economists warned that without labour imports Hong Kong would only be able to grow at 5.5 per cent a year or would pay a heavy price in inflation.

Flexible economic development and bowing to changing world currents are assisted by the fact that trade unions are not well entrenched in Hong Kong, and there are no statutory minimum wages. Of the 2.8 million workers (1.75 million men and just over 1 million women) fewer than 400,000 belong to trade unions. The unions mainly cover the civil service, construction, textiles, plastics, metalworking and community and social services employees. There is a basic political split between pro-Peking and pro-Taiwan unions, and workers generally are fragmented into 458 separate trade unions, many of which are squabbling and compete for members. There isn't a single union, for example, for all workers in the restaurant and food business: there's one calling itself the Bird's Nest Soup Workers Union, another the Dried Bean Stick Trade Workers, another the Pork Stall Workers Chi-Ping General Guild. There is another union for Roast Pig Workers, yet another for Roast and Dried Meat Workers, not to speak of separate unions for Chinese and Western Food Workers, the Eating Establishment Employees, Hakka Food Establishment Workers, Café Employees, Eating Shop Workers, European Hotel and Restaurant Workers, Restaurant and Café Workers, Tea House Industrial Association and even Western Style Catering Trade Workers.

Supporters of the Hong Kong system say that there is a tradition of give and take in the territory: when economic times are tough, employers will not lay workers off, but will instead cut working hours; in boom times, workers get the benefits of higher wages and overtime. Some credibility is given to this argument by the fact that when the economy picked up in the mid-to late 1980s, wage rates were rising at about 15 per cent a year, much higher than the rate of inflation. However, in the 1960s and 1970s employers had been helped by the steady inflow of population from China. The labour force rose from 1.9 million in 1976 to 2.5 million in 1983. In the 1980–84 period, labour costs in Hong Kong fell by 17 per cent. The real test of the flexibility of the system will come in the early 1990s when labour is scarce and new workers are unavailable.

By 1988, reported the Financial Secretary, unemployment was a record low 1.3 per cent, virtually negligible. The government was under pressure to allow foreigners in, since there was a shortage of 100,000 workers in construction, hotels and tourism, retail and manufacturing alone. Industrialists in many sectors began to look at subcontracting part of their work across the border to China, where labour is more plentiful. Literally thousands of Chinese factories employing almost 2 million workers were involved in subcontracting work for Hong Kong establishments by the late 1980s. This, noted Governor David Wilson, was twice as many manufacturing workers as in Hong Kong itself. Hong Kong's boom could be seen spilling out over the Chinese countryside as far as Canton.

Wage rates in Hong Kong reflect the labour shortage. Basic unskilled workers were earning HK$4,000 a month (US$512) by the late 1980s and some factories were having to offer a HK$3,000 bonus to anyone staying three months. Skilled workers could earn HK$6,000 and ordinary secretaries started at HK$6,000 to 8,000. These wage rates were obviously still below western rates, but above those of poorer Asian developing countries like Bangladesh or Sri Lanka, where workers may get between US$1 and $2 a day.

Manufacturing

In terms of output Hong Kong industries have moved well beyond the cheap – and by implication nasty – ranges of goods. By the mid-1980s Hong Kong officials boasted that the colony was producing computers and computer systems, audio-visual equipment, facsimile machines, microwave and infra-red burglar alarms, precision engineering products, sophisticated office equipment, AC/DC motors and a whole range of modern household goods. Every month the Hong Kong Trade Development Council, a government body supported by a levy of 0.25 per cent on export bills of lading, puts out a richly illustrated 550-page catalogue chock-a-block with details of Hong Kong-made goods. It amounts to a cornucopia of goods; every type and style of clothing, both underwear and outerwear; jewellery; sports goods; hardware; and toys and games of all sorts, including trinkets and knick-knacks; electrical goods. In one edition a Hong Kong breakthrough was claimed, with production of successful 'instant image' video telephones. Another advertised telephones that don't need the caller to hold the handset. There are pages galore of watches and calculators, including liquid-filled and transparent calculators and a watch that 'took 30 million years to make' (because it is made from marble). There was a whole assortment of goods, including watches, jewellery and even candles, all dressed up or disguised as toys.

Textiles and clothing still take pride of place in Hong Kong's manufacturing sector. Largely because of Hong Kong's example, the production of textiles is now acknowledged as the best start-up step for a developing country trying to industrialize. Textiles and clothing alone employ almost 40 per cent of Hong Kong's workers involved in manufacturing, and also provide more than 35 per cent of domestic exports. But Hong Kong has moved worlds away from countries that are taking their first painful steps to being a textile-maker. The colony's spinning sector operates almost half a million spindles and has some of the most modern mills in the world. The weaving sector produces 700 million square metres of fabrics each year. There's also a significant knitting sector, producing both for direct export and for the local industry.

Design and manufacturing are usually assisted by computers, which reduce wastage and improve precision and quality control. The output of Hong Kong's textile factories is highly varied. But some garments from Hong Kong are now near the top end of the market, the kind of goods that would sell well in leading department stores – including Harrods of London and Saks of New York's Fifth Avenue – throughout the West. The quality road is the one that Hong Kong's manufacturers have been forced to take, because of years and years of quota and other restrictions in the world's clothing industries. When western countries started to place curbs on the amount of goods imported from Hong Kong, the obvious solution was to raise the quality and the price-tag on the garment to keep profits rising.

By the 1970s, Hong Kong clothes manufacturers were supplying a large proportion of the clothing displayed in European mail-order catalogues, notably German ones. At the same time Hong Kong factories were winning orders to produce garments for big department stores that would sell under the store's own brand names. One Hong Kong manufacturer, Mohan Bhagwandas Murjani of Murjani Industries, had the bright idea of buying the rights to glamorous or household names in the West. The company made its big breakthrough with the 'Gloria Vanderbilt' label of fashion jeans in 1978. These glitzy figure-hugging designer jeans sold for four times the price of Levi's. From sales of US$30 million in 1976, Murjani leapt ahead to $500 million in 1983, with profits being big enough for Murjani himself to shift base to New York and splash out on his next daring venture. He bought the franchise for making clothing products under the Coca-Cola label. The clothes, from spectacles through tee-shirts to high fashion, were launched in the US in 1985, and sales reached US$250 million within eighteen months. Murjani's major manufacturing and buying operations are still in Hong Kong, but the Coca-Cola clothes are made under licence by producers in the Far East, Europe and the USA. Murjani's itself makes only 15 to 20 per cent of its products because, Murjani says, 'when you use your own factory you end up trying to market what you are producing. We are marketing what the consumer needs'. But he paid tribute to Hong Kong producers, asserting: 'As long as you are in the upmarket category, Hong Kong still offers the best value and quality'. (Quoted in *South China Morning Post*, 28 June 1985).

Hong Kong has also begun to attract its own fashion designers, who make upmarket clothes under their own labels. Some of these are expatriates; others are young Hong Kong designers who have been educated in Hong Kong and show considerable flair. They include Diane Freis, Jenny Lewis, Judy Mann, Ragence Lam, Eddie Lau and William Tang, all of whose clothes command a premium on the international fashion market. All in all, says Ira Kaye, managing director of Lark International, Hong Kong garment manufacturers are now in the upper 30 per cent of the price range for clothing on sale in the United States. In terms of the variety of garments produced, Hong Kong has also shown initiative and imagination. In the mid-1980s a number of manufacturers began to produce a new and profitable line in the sportswear department – fashion clothing for the ski-slopes. This was a field completely foreign to subtropical Hong Kong, but a successful breakthrough.

Some of the young designers have been enviably successful. Lam was named one of Britain's best designers in the mid-1970s by *Cosmopolitan* magazine and by *The Times* newspaper. The slight, boyish Lam returned to Hong Kong in the late 1970s, and says he now looks to China for inspiration. 'We are the first of a new generation of designers in Hong Kong and as such are having to break new ground. Hong Kong is emerging as an important fashion centre for the Chinese market. China will look to us for direction. So now is the time to consolidate and then strike out when the time is right.' In 1984 Lam produced what was called 'a punk-accessoried version of the cheongsam' and 'a brick-red sash-tied top which looks something like casual wear for a Tang dynasty space invader' (*Asiaweek*, 21–28 December 1984). Lam said: 'I think my customers, both men and women, must be self-confident, the kind of people who want comfortable but not conventional clothes.'

Eddie Lau also draws on China for ideas, not least because in 1983 he was sponsored by China Arts and Crafts, the Communist-owned department store, and designed the Kai collection for them. 'They wanted their own Chinese designer, who understands their silk fabrics and how to make the best of them,' said Lau. Diane Freis was so successful in her designing that she encountered imitations. In the mid-1980s she took advertisements in London's *Sunday Times* to warn against copies of her clothes bearing almost exact replica labels. Development of young designers' talents has been encouraged by the Institute of Textile and Clothing at Hong Kong Polytechnic, which offers a Bachelor of Arts degree in textiles and clothing marketing and a professional diploma course in fashion and clothing technology. Each year the college puts on a highly regarded fashion graduation presentation, in which students display clothes they have designed and made themelves. Some of the college lecturers believe that local design 'is as good as Japan and much better than in the United States'.

The garment business is still a tough one. Quota restrictions are a problem for many manufacturers. Indeed in Hong Kong there is actually a secondary market in the sale of quotas! Some leading garment-makers annually spend HK$10 million or more buying quotas. Restrictions by the USA which enforced stringent rules on the local content of textile products caused hardship in the early 1980s. The manufacturers had been shifting some of the simpler knitting work in producing panels for sweaters across the border to China, where labour was more plentiful and cheaper. The USA decided that sweaters with such panels couldn't be counted as Hong Kong-made (even though American labelling requirements meant that they had to be labelled 'made in Hong Kong'). But ingenious Hong Kong manufacturers were only rebuffed for a year or so, during which time they increased investment in the most sophisticated automated computer-controlled knitting machinery.

There is acute awareness in Hong Kong of the immense political strength of the textile lobby abroad, especially in the US – 'it's almost as powerful as the gun lobby', says one Hong Kong manufacturer. Tom Chan, deputy managing director of Crocodile Garments, said: 'You can lose your shirt in this business.' Crocodile, whose medium-priced garments bear a crocodile logo, has gradually gone upmarket, but in the mid-1980s found that not all its customers even in rich European countries could keep pace with its progress. 'We have upgraded our market and become more designer-oriented,' said Chan, but this meant that we 'can no longer compete, particularly when buyers want high volumes at cheap prices with less emphasis on fashion and quality'. He cited one particular large European chain-store which refused to follow Crocodile upmarket and went instead to South Korea for clothing.

Along with the move to higher quality, Hong Kong textile and clothing factories have intensified their search for new markets, preferably ones that don't have quota restrictions. After years of apparently closed doors, some manufacturers have begun to make some headway selling to Japan. Finally, Hong Kong manufacturers have been looking at setting up plants abroad, especially in places where there is a local Chinese community. Novel Enterprise, one of the leading Hong Kong knitters, has established a factory in Mauritius (besides others in Macao and in Shandong, Shanghai and Heilongjiang in China). From this Mauritius base it gets preferential entry to the European Community countries since the Indian Ocean island country is a signatory of the Lomé Convention. Like many of Hong Kong's textile industrialists, Novel's founder, K. P. Chao, came from Shanghai in 1949. At that stage he realized that no one was making knitwear, but since 'people were wearing more casual clothes after the Second World War, there was a great demand for comfortable knitwear, especially in the US and Europe. I didn't have much capital during the 1950s, but I managed to operate a small factory, and its first overseas shipment was delivered to the UK in 1959.' From these small beginnings Chao's Novel Enterprises has grown to a multi-million-dollar business, one of whose main product lines is Polo-brand jumpers. Other textile companies are looking at setting up plants in Ireland and in Italy. With bases there they would not face quota restrictions either in Europe or in the USA. But Hong Kong companies have hesitated, as one manufacturer says smilingly, 'because we can't guarantee the quality of the labour in those countries'. Even so, critics say that at the lower end Hong Kong's textile industry still looks scruffy, with a profusion of small subcontracting factories that need to improve their quality.

After textiles and clothing, the next biggest sector of Hong Kong's manufacturing is electronics, accounting for 18 per cent of domestic exports and employing about 12 per cent of the workforce in manufacturing. There are almost 1,500 electronics factories, employing more than 100,000 people. Unlike textiles, dominated by Shanghai migrants, the electronics industry exhibits a blend of local and overseas involvement. The industry has moved rapidly from the original work of simple assembly of basic transistor radios to manufacture of diversified high-quality products. Government propaganda cites an impressive list, mentioning

> 'cassette recorders, hi-fi systems, television sets, wire and cordless telephones with built-in memories and automatic dialling functions, telecommunications equipment, microcomputers, computer memory systems, Winchester and floppy disk drives, read/write magnetic heads, computer printers, switching power supplies, computer-aided design and testing equipment, multi-layer printed circuit boards, electronic modules, liquid crystal displays, quartz crystals and semi-conductor devices including integrated circuit

wafers (e.g. microprocessors, RAM/ROM memory and logic chips).'

Put like that it sounds extremely sophisticated. In reality, Hong Kong's electronics industry is still on the simple side by world standards, and most realistic industry analysts admit that it will ever be so. There are several reasons for this. One is the small size of the companies. Unlike Singapore, which relies heavily on multinational investment, Hong Kong benefits from its mix of multinationals and domestic electronics companies. This saves the industry from being at the mercy of foreigners who might get up and leave whenever labour costs become too high or the political climate changes. But the small size of many concerns means that research and development, which is the key to the real high-tech game, is limited in Hong Kong.

K. Y. Yeung, then Hong Kong's Director of Industry, pointed out that Hong Kong is disadvantaged compared to bigger places like Korea and Taiwan. 'We haven't got the research and development because we haven't got defence, aerospace, capital intensive industries.' This view is echoed by manufacturers who suggest that intensive spending on research and development wouldn't in any case fit in with Hong Kong's place in the world market. Dennis Ting, chairman of the Federation of Hong Kong Industries, commented that 'as manufacturers, we would develop whatever the market would accept rather than have anybody tell us what to do'. The same view was put more bluntly by Tommy Zau, whose Electronic Devices makes transistors. For research and development, he says, 'you need a lot of doctors sitting there doing nothing. We cannot afford it. We don't have the facilities and we don't have the education.' Zau says that what Hong Kong offers is 'improvement of products'.

During the economic boom of the early 1980s, some Hong Kong supporters lost sight of this hard fact of life. A number of electronics companies enlivened a local stock market previously dominated by banks and property concerns. Wilder-eyed newspapers began to speak of the electronics miracle in Hong Kong.

Gold Peak Industries, one of the companies listed on the stock market during the 1980s, has chosen to look for joint ventures with multinational companies. It is making car radios with Philips in China and has teamed up with Shinwa of Japan to make cassette mechanisms. Gold Peak sees nothing wrong with subcontracting and using cheap labour in China, and says that without it, Hong Kong's down-market electronic concerns would have been driven out of existence. Specialists in the Industry Department say that Hong Kong still needs to upgrade its efficiency. The note of gloom – or realism – was sounded in spite of an electronics mini-boom during the mid- and late 1980s. But realists respond that the apparent good times were supported more by the highly competitive Hong Kong dollar than by advances in the industry. Victor Lo, managing director of Gold Peak, commented: 'Our growth is not market growth. It's purely a shift of workload from one place to another.'

The next biggest industry is plastics, with about 10 per cent each of domestic exports and employment in manufacturing. This may seem surprising, as it is not an obvious export subject, but plastics sustained the early manufacturing export drive and have continued to develop new exports, especially toys. Many of the injection and extrusion machines used in the industry are made locally and much of the production involves high quality toys. But government reports in the mid-1980s suggested that the industry is facing serious problems. According to these, quality control is 'generally poor' and given no priority, and industrial design capabilities are 'very weak at best'. A report from the Industry Department summed up: 'While the industry does not face an emergency, it faces serious problems in maintaining its share of world markets, never mind catching up with changes in the pattern of demand.'

Toys account for two-thirds of the plastics factories' production, whose other goods include handbags, packaging products, plastic clothes and tiles. Yet again the official report pointed to Hong Kong's trading advantages in the marketplace. 'Hong Kong's advantages are on the commercial side – relatively low prices, short lead times, reliability of supply and delivery, and responsive manufacturers ... The disadvantages are mainly technical – a narrow range of product capabilities, inadequate emphasis on quality, inability to make precise mouldings, and minimal research and development.' The report warned that there was danger that some industrial users of plastics, notably toy-makers, might outpace the abilities of the plastic-makers. In particular, the international market increasingly demands that toys be made to higher safety standards and be creative in design. There is still plenty of opportunity for the plastic-makers to grow, especially in household goods markets (so far dominated by Japanese and European manufacturers), and in the sports and motor car fields. But all of these areas require greater attention to quality and product development, the Industry Department report warned. It also criticized the Hong Kong plastics manufacturers for tending to invest 'for quick returns, rather than long-term development'.

Hong Kong is not the biggest toy-maker in the world, but it is the world's leading exporter of toys. From Kowloon to the New Territories almost 2,200 toy factories are strung out, employing more than 50,000 people. In this industry there's more diversity than in almost any other. At one end of the scale, there's a handful of large companies, such as Universal Matchbox, a concern with sales of more than US$250 million and a listing on the New York Stock Exchange; Universal Matchbox took over the Lesney Group of Britain, on the verge of bankruptcy in the early 1980s. Other big groups are Kader Industries, Applied Electronics, and Playmates Holdings. But only ten of the toy-makers employ more than 500 people. The vast bulk of the factories have fewer than 20 workers each. Subcontracting work is the name of the game. This is Hong Kong's *laissez-faire* at its vigorous best, producing as cheaply as possible, quick and reliable in meeting delivery dates, and able to switch rapidly from one product to another with the changing demands of the market. In this business there's an advantage in being small and flexible. Indeed, the bigger a company gets, the more problems it may face. With the single exception of Playmates, the big companies depend on contract work for US giants. Kader gained fame as the biggest maker of Cabbage Patch dolls for Coleco in the USA. At one time the 'Cabbage Patch Kids' accounted for more than 50 per cent of Kader's output. Similarly, Applied Electronics turns out electronic toys for companies like Fisher Price and Mattel.

Kader and the other bigger toy-makers have had to shift increasingly to subcontracting their work across the border to China. Dennis Ting of Kader says that he has several factories on the mainland. Applied Electronics has only 350 of its total workforce of 6,000 in Hong Kong. Lorries carrying almost obscene-looking spare parts for dolls, from bare heads to empty staring eyes, travel the roads between China's neighbouring Guangdong province and Hong Kong. The important jobs of final construction and quality control have to be carried out in Hong Kong, since Chinese standards are not high enough. But 'If you don't have a Chinese plant, you are finished', said Raymond Hung of Applied Electronics (quoted in *Far Eastern Economic Review*, 17 December 1987). 'There would be no way that I could get 6,500 workers in Hong Kong, or expand to 400,000 square feet. In China, it cost us HK$24 million. If we did the same thing in Hong Kong, it would have cost HK$150 million.'

Playmates Holdings, almost alone of Hong Kong toy manufacturers, tried to buck the trend, with mixed results. It decided to make and market its own dolls. It won a local stock market listing in the mid-1980s. As a reward for its courage in going it alone and marketing dolls under the 'Playmate' label, it was shunned by most stockbrokers and regarded as a risky investment, even when the economy was booming. Playmates tried to amalgamate traditional toy-making with electronics. Its star turn was 'Cricket', a chatterbox doll launched in the USA for Christmas 1986. It was a huge success and quickly became the seventh most popular toy in the US. However, the company soon discovered that success is full of perils: 70 per cent of the company's sales rested on a single product. Playmates could not afford to stand still, so devised a playmate for Cricket, a freckled boy doll called Corkie. An attempt to produce a more sophisticated talking doll called Jill and selling at US$100 fell flat and was abandoned.

Another problem for Playmates was that more than 80 per cent of its turnover was concentrated in the US. The company began to look at the Japanese market and tried to develop Cricket as a conversation-piece for Japanese children learning another language. A revised version of the doll came complete with conversation tapes, useful for Japanese children learning English. In 1988 Playmates announced another coup and developed a 10-line doll with an unpromising name – 'Teenage Mutant Ninja Turtle'. According to toy experts the turtles stole the show at exhibitions in New York and Germany. They are based on a successful US comic-book story in which four pet turtles slip down a sewer, are dosed with a gas and turn into 'tortoise-shelled teenagers with all of the obsessions of adolescents but none of the skin problems'. They then became expert in Ninja and determined to fight evil forces – and slumping toy sales. 'Hong Kong is exactly the right place to make weird out-of-this world creatures,' says a toy industry expert. In the Great Christmas Toy Battle in the US in 1988 the Ninja Turtles came second to a Japanese video-game system.

But in December 1988 Playmates announced that it was no longer viable to make toys in Hong Kong, and so it would be switching its production to China. Joint managing director Paul Kwan Yuen-chiu cited Hong Kong's labour shortage and soaring land costs as the reasons for the move. He also acknowledged that attempts to develop high-technology, high-price toys for the USA had cost the company too much money, and said it would be switching back to more traditional low-cost products.

The perils of dependence on the USA and on bigger companies were demonstrated with a vengeance at Christmas 1987. Christmas is traditionally the merry-making season for toymakers, and 1987 should have been a year of celebration, with toy exports hitting a record US$1.5 billion. Instead, a number of Hong Kong toy-makers recorded substantial losses. The reason was that Worlds of Wonder, the US toy giant, went into the red, filed for reorganization under Chapter 11 of the Bankruptcy Code, and told Hong Kong suppliers it was unable to pay the US$40 million it owed them. Hong Kong makers producing Teddy Ruxpin, a talking bear, and Laser Tag Pistols, were badly affected. They included Kader Industrial, Applied Electronics, General Electronics and Universal Appliances. Bill Blaauw, chief executive of Meco Development (Hong Kong) and a toy industry expert, comprehensively criticized US business methods, claiming that 'The US method is so screwed up – with retailers demanding massive payments up front before toys are sold – that doing business in the US is like betting at the Jockey Club.' This was Hong Kong's best market. The problem for toy-makers is that consumers in the mass markets are demanding ever-more-sophisticated trinkets, but at the same time are more and more faddish and lose interest more quickly. The so-called 'Cabbage Patch Kids' were a best-seller for three years and took a large part of Kader's production. But by 1987 interest had faded and Kader was still owed money. In spite of filing for bankruptcy, Worlds of Wonder was trying to recover by producing a US$150 high-tech race car set using technology derived from missile guidance systems. It seemed an expensive gamble. With the toy giants demanding extended credit from the actual makers, Hong Kong concerns face an increasingly tough time.

Watches and clocks are yet another important area for exports and employment in Hong Kong, also cashing in on the colony's ability to manufacture quickly and cheaply in response to market shifts. Hong Kong is the world's biggest watch-producer in volume terms and second biggest in value to Switzerland, having surpassed Japan in 1987. In the same year watches overtook toys as an earner, with exports worth HK$13.4 billion. In the 1980s watches, like textiles, fell foul of quota restrictions, France in particular being quick to apply protectionist policies.

The way round this for one local manufacturer was to set up a plant inside the European Community and thus avoid the quotas. Shing Cheong Electronics chose Ireland, a move which proved profitable, thanks to special tax breaks and depreciation allowances. But there was a price to pay: labour costs in Ireland are about 2.5 times greater than in Hong Kong, and workers are also less cooperative and less flexible, not anxious to do overtime since it might push them into a higher tax bracket. No company, however, could afford to stand still and hope the quotas would go away. In early 1989 the American watchmaker Timex Corp., which had plants in the Philippines and Thailand, was pressing Congress to allow duty-free entry status to watches produced in those countries. If such concessions were granted, then Hong Kong watchmakers would have to consider moving out of their home base to other countries offering a better competitive edge.

Hong Kong's manufacturing sector as a whole has recovered with the world boom. In the early 1980s it looked as if manufacturing would drop below 20 per cent of GDP. But the sector remains vulnerable, especially to rivalry from neighbouring countries that have bigger domestic markets and thus have a cushion to support research and development. In 1989 Hong Kong, along with South Korea, Singapore and Taiwan, was considered a rich country and lost benefits under the Generalized Scheme of Preferences; it remains vulnerable to competition from poorer countries that still qualify under the scheme. South Korea and Taiwan have both made big strides towards getting into true high-tech, while Hong Kong manufacturing remains essentially based on super-smart assembly lines. Another worry is that really smart operators have moved from manufacturing to property and finance, seeking bigger and quicker profits. And a wholesale shift of manufacturing to China would be worrying. As one of Hong Kong's Chinese industrialists puts it: 'Young people pooh-pooh the ideals of hard work and patience that stood their elders in good stead. They want quick results, and would rather mortgage their assets in property speculation where they believe that they can get rich quick.' Sometimes there is a shady aspect to such deals. Hong Kong does have some industrial market-leaders. Johnson Electric Industrial, for example, is one of the leading makers of electric motors in the world. (Its rival is Japanese.) Johnson's product line is diversified and its motors are used in power tools, food mixers, video recorders and cars, including Mercedes. The motors are so good that some of its customers, the German Robert Bosch group for example, gave up making their own motors. But even the capable manufacturers like Johnson, showing a return of about 25 per cent on sales, are not glamour stocks in the eyes of the get-rich-quick punters on the stock market. Johnson has never been a liquid stock.

Outside the textile and garments fields Hong Kong manufacturers have frequently found themselves in deep waters when they have tried to venture beyond the assembly-line operations they know best. Elek and Eltek was much praised for its production of computer components, and so decided to go into making finished products. The company had good assembly-line experience but found itself in trouble because it lacked marketing skills.

The complaint that the colony is weak in high technology has long been a major talking-point. S. K. Chan, executive director of the Hong Kong Productivity Council, in mid-1987 urged that manufacturers must switch to technology-intensive and technology-differentiated manufacture as Hong Kong loses its comparative advantage in labour-intensive production. One of the main problems holding this back is the short-sightedness of management. Companies are geared to risk-avoidance and fast pay-back. A study by the Productivity Council found that there was little commitment in Hong Kong to longer-term staff training or to marketing. The small size of Hong Kong companies is also a handicap, since improved technology is often very expensive. By the late 1980s venture capitalists had arrived in Hong Kong, but they were more interested in low-tech schemes, such as backing retail clothing franchises or schemes of cooperation between Hong Kong and Chinese concerns, rather than the high-tech schemes that have caught attention internationally. Their view is that, given the smallness of the domestic market, Hong Kong companies can so easily make a wrong decision costing millions of dollars. 'We've regretted past investments in high-technology,' said one venture capitalist. 'We've learned a lot about why we shouldn't be investing in that field.' The government has several times pledged to encourage high-technology industry, but is naturally shy of setting itself up as a decision-maker rather than letting entrepreneurs and the marketplace decide. There are plenty of possible ways forward, including increasing the money paid to the Productivity Council; setting aside land in the industrial estates for high-tech companies; and building a third hundred-hectare industrial estate at Junk Bay, close to the site of Hong Kong's third university, dedicated to science and technology, due to take its first students in 1991. The two existing estates are almost fully let and have a mixture of factories involved in food manufacturing, chemicals, electronics and brewing. In contemplating aiding high technology the government is moving away from the idea that Adam Smith's 'invisible hand' will guide correct economic decisions; but it is following rivals in South Korea and Taiwan which have promoted high-tech.

One important factor contributing to Hong Kong's exporting success is the container terminal at Kwai Chung. In 1987 this became the largest container port in the world, and was still straining against capacity limitations. Unlike at other ports, the containers are not strewn out over hectares and hectares of land, stacked one or two high. Because of pressure of space at Kwai Chung the boxes are piled four and five high. This means Hong Kong has about four times the number of containers per unit of land that Rotterdam has, and seven times the density of the New York container port. Even so, in 1987 the Hong Kong port moved almost 3.5 million twenty-foot equivalent units (TEUs) of containers, up by 25 per cent, from 2.8 million in 1986, to overtake Rotterdam (with about 2.9 million units).

Hong Kong does not have the fastest turnaround time in the world. It takes thirteen hours to load or unload a container ship (whereas Singapore can do it in about seven). Moreover, congestion has meant that some ships have had to wait up to ninety hours for a berth or have been forced to unload away from the container port. There is little romance about modern container unloading of ships, nothing of the exotic smells coming from mysteriously shaped packages pulled from a vessel's hold as happened years ago in Joseph Conrad's novels of Asia. The containers are standard sized boxes moved like giant Lego-parts by robot cranes and shifted and balanced on to box-like ships by impersonal computers. Almost half of Hong Kong's cargo was containerized by the late 1980s and all the prospects are for continued growth.

The re-emergence of the entrepôt trade and strengthening links with China mean that China accounts for 80 per cent of re-exports, and re-exports by 1988 had surpassed domestic exports in value.

Officials complained that they were taken by surprise by the rapid expansion of business in the late 1980s as the container traffic continued to grow and gobble up new capacity. Advertisements – like the one from Li Ka-shing's Hutchison Whampoa Group which owns one of the big container operations – explain Hong Kong's appeal, proclaiming: 'From Fujian [China] to Felixstowe [UK] via Kwai Chung.' The very efficiency of the port, in spite of the high stack of boxes, means that it pays some neighbouring countries, notably China, to trans-ship through Kwai Chung. The port operates round-the-clock all year round, except for the three days of Chinese New Year holidays, when it is closed.

In May 1988 the first berth of the sixth terminal became operational and tenders opened for building a seventh. When this is completed in 1993, Kwai Chung's capacity will be 4.2 million TEUs. Plans are also being made for eighth and ninth terminals, but officials have waited to see whether the years of surge in 1986 and 1987 continue. As the container berths are privately owned, owners are leery of being caught with spare (that is unprofitable) capacity.

Hong Kong remains a favourite location for business with Asia-wide interests. Its top flight communications put it on a par with Singapore and give it an edge over Tokyo. The ready availability of English-speaking staff again places it well ahead of Tokyo, though probably below Singapore. But Hong Kong is superior to all of them when it comes to doing *business*. Singapore Chinese and foreign businessmen living in Singapore have to be careful not to say or do anything that might offend a government highly sensitive to criticism. Hong Kong businessmen haven't had that worry. 'We frequently get official Singapore delegations here, asking what is the secret of Hong Kong's success in some area or other,' says an amused senior official. 'I tell them they're part of the explanation. If it weren't for the government role in the economy, Singapore businessmen might be more entrepreneurial. It's not something that a government can do, *make* people into businessmen.' Yet in the last few years there's been a large rise in the number of companies, especially financial concerns, moving to Tokyo; some of them have shifted their Asian headquarters or important parts of it from Hong Kong to Japan. The rise of Tokyo to be the world's biggest stock market, the financial power of Japan and that country's emergence as second only to the US in overall economic strength, have all helped this shift. But Japan is still very much preoccupied with the problems of Japan, is expensive and bureaucratic, and companies setting up there face a heavy tax burden. Hong Kong, because of its flexibility and the dedication to making money, remains the best centre for doing business in the region. And there's still the dream of the continued opening up and modernization of China on its very doorstep.

Services

Hong Kong's dynamic economy has shown great growth not only in manufacturing but also in services. The financial sector has expanded and is an important contributor in its own right, notwithstanding a whole range of problems (see chapter 8). Other services have also grown, including property and tourism, a major contributor to the economy. Hong Kong's property market has tended to move in boom and bust cycles. After the slump of the mid-1980s some experts thought that property would never recover. But even by 1986 things were beginning to pick up and by 1987 another boom seemed to be on the way in spite of completion of many new tower blocks in the central area. Hongkong Land originally seemed to have over-extended itself with its expensive purchase of the Exchange Square site. It was competing against itself, encouraging tenants to move to Exchange Square who could only come from The Landmark or Connaught Centre (later renamed Jardine House). or one of the Land Company's other properties. But by 1988 all three towers of Exchange Square were full, as were other Land properties. Rents in Central District topped HK$50 a square foot per month, and the Central business district began to spill over both eastwards into Wanchai and into Western. By 1989, reported property consultants Richard Ellis, Hong Kong was vying with London, as the world's second most expensive city for prime central office space. Tokyo was in the lead at US$1,680 per square metre a year, followed by London, US$1,129 but Hong Kong, at almost US$1,113 per square metre, was well ahead of New York, at US$482.

Only in 1989 did development of new hotels catch up with tourist growth. During the mid-1980s it was hard to get a room in the peak months of October and November. By 1989 Hong Kong had 6 million visitors, but hotel capacity had jumped to more than 30,000 rooms. The very best of Hong Kong hotels are obsequiously good. Some businessmen complain that they try too hard. The old favourite, the Peninsula, built in 1928 and now Hong Kong's oldest hotel, was rumoured to be ripe for demolition. The Kadoorie family which owns it had, after all, pulled down another old favourite, the Repulse Bay Hotel. The Peninsula has only 210 gracious rooms on seven floors. Other hotels even in height-restricted Kowloon run to seventeen storeys. But instead of knocking the hotel down, the Peninsula announced plans to add two seventeen-storey towers to the existing structure and thus more than double its capacity to 425 rooms. The central old façade of the Peninsula, and its gracious lobby where the rich and famous go to have tea (just as they have done for fifty years, since long before the Mandarin Oriental and the Regent hotels were ever dreamed of), will remain.

The Big Names

Few things ever stand still in Hong Kong, and that applies to people too. The dynamism of the economy has been marked by the emergence of new business names and by the crashing of some of the old favourites. By the 1980s, the domination of the old *hongs*, as the British-owned and -managed all-embracing trading houses were known, had come under challenge and the British had lost out to newer more ambitious local Chinese businessmen. Jardine Matheson and Co., the Swire Group, Hutchison Whampoa, and of course the Hongkong Bank, all remain famous names on the Stock Exchange. Up-and-coming young Chinese enterpreneurs showed a skill in money-making and an energy lacking in some of the born-to-rule laid-back British. Several of the British-established *hongs* flourish under new (Chinese) management. The Chinese challenge was underlined when Li Ka-shing took over Hutchison Whampoa and when Sir Yue-Kong Pao swallowed first Hongkong and Kowloon Wharf and Godown Co., and then Wheelock Marden. Jardines and its associate, Hongkong Land, survived under British management, but had many nervous times. The Hongkong Bank was protected by the clause in its articles enshrined as a special Hong Kong law, not allowing any single shareholder more than 1 per cent of the stock. No Chinese executive in the bank was within reach of the board even in 1990. Many analysts regard Swire (carefully controlled from

London by the family) as the strongest and best managed of the British *hongs*. But its Cathay Pacific airline found it politic and advantageous to seek a Chinese shareholder: the Peking-run China International Trust and Investment Company now owns 12.5 per cent of the airline.

Hong Kong's cosmopolitan character is enhanced by other rich and famous business names. They include the Kadoories, 'who came down from Baghdad on camels and now go about in Rolls-Royces'. Lord Kadoorie, Hong Kong's first peer, is a few months older than Hong Kong's New Territories, and as of 1988 was still actively involved in a variety of businesses including China Light and Power (supplier of electricity to Kowloon and the New Territories) and the Hongkong and Shanghai Hotels, owners of the Peninsula. In 1987 and 1988 the Kadoories almost lost control of the hotel group to Chinese predators. The Harilela family of Indian origin retains tight control of its businesses, including ownership of the Golden Mile Holiday Inn and a stake in the Harbour View Holiday Inn. The Harilelas made a fortune in textiles and tailoring but shifted to real estate, including hotels, in the late 1960s when tourism was depressed.

But in spite of this diversity of businessmen's origins it is the local Chinese who today dominate the Hong Kong business scene. Among the well-known Chinese families of Hong Kong the 1980s saw something of a shakeout. There's an old Chinese saying: 'Great fortunes have no third generation', a variation on the English expression 'Clogs to clogs in three generations.' Hong Kong Chinese wealth has several roots. There are some families like the Lis, the Kans and the Fungs, all founders of Bank of East Asia, who arrived in Hong Kong several generations ago. The Chinese Communist Revolution saw the arrival of new potential entrepreneurs including Yue-Kong Pao and many Shanghai businessmen. Some came with money made in Shanghai. Others had extensive business experience, and were able to borrow money to form the backbone of the Hong Kong textile industry. Other rich men have made their own way up from poverty. They include Li Ka-shing and also Stanley Ho, owner of the Macao gambling casino as well as hotels and ferry services. Ho knows about the ups and downs of business. His grandfather, Ho Fook, was the brother of Jardine's legendary comprador Sir Robert Ho-tung. 'They had Hong Kong wrapped up,' recalls Ho. But then Ho's father and uncles squandered the wealth in stock market speculation. Stanley Ho arrived in Macao, aged nineteen, 'with two dollars and by the time I was 23, I'd made my first million'. It was war-time and Portuguese-controlled Macao was an ideal place for making money.

> 'In Macao during the war you could make a million in a week. You could sell anyone anything,' Stanley Ho recalled. 'A tin of cigarettes would cost $100. People paid it. They didn't know when the war would be over. Macao was bombed only once – by the Americans and I made money off that because they bombed the government petrol reserves. I was selling gasoline and immediately raised the price. You had to do business in the morning. I knew how to test whether the kerosene was watered down or not and I'd stick my gauge into each tank very fast, make my deals, pay cash – always cash – and get out. That way you avoided trouble.'

Later, Ho made vast sums of money during the Korean war selling chemicals and metals, and many political observers say that it was Chinese gratitude for his trading during the war that led to his winning the Macao gambling franchise. Ho commented: 'Although I'm in this business of luck, there is very little luck in success. You must suffer for it. You must be able to fight for it, to accept challenges. That is how the new rich people in this town who started from scratch have made their money. The old families are on the run.'

So it proved in the mid-1980s for an important clutch of distinguished names. For the Fungs, Chaos, Kwoks and Tung families, the old saying was an unhappy reminder. Sir Kenneth Ping-fan Fung was one of the pillars of the Hong Kong community, a gentleman, steward of the Royal Hong Kong Jockey Club, Justice of the Peace, knighted by the Queen, member of the exclusive Bohemian Club in the USA, director of many companies, active on the committees of a myriad charities, friend of the great and good, and head of the family business Fung Ping Fan and Co., a trading house dealing in everything from spirits to stereos. The Fung family's connections with Hong Kong date back to the early years of this century, when Sir Kenneth's father Fung Ping-shan left China to escape from the corruption during the last years of the Qing dynasty. He moved to Hong Kong and was one of the founders of the Bank of East Asia. Kenneth Fung was one of three sons of Fung Ping-shan's two concubines (his wife died early). Unfortunately by 1986 it was revealed that the seventy-five-year-old Kenneth Fung's businesses were saddled with HK$300 million of debts that the company couldn't pay off. He ruefully told an interviewer: 'All of my sons went to Harvard. They must have learned something.' The group had thrown off its conservatism and gone chasing after splashy new business ventures. One of them was a roaring success. Son Cyril helped to bring McDonald's to Hong Kong, making its distinctive red and yellow signs and long-lunchtime queues a familiar sight all over the territory. But not all ventures were as successful. 'We had too many irons in the fire,' said Fung, who returned to the active management role that he had previously left to his sons.

Two other families feeling the pinch were the Chaos and the Tungs, both of them involved in shipping. Unlike Y. K. Pao they were caught when the world shipping market turned down. The Chaos' firm, Wah Kwong and Co., owed US$850 million. The sale of the family jade and porcelain collection raised US$10 million to help pay off the debts – 'a token of our sincerity', according to Frank S. B. Chao, the president of Hong Kong's third largest shipping fleet. Frank Chao and his brothers took over a fleet started by their father T. Y. Chao, a Shanghai lawyer who had fled to Hong Kong in 1949. A younger brother, Cecil, was one of the delights of the Hong Kong gossip columnists, not least because he drove a Rolls-Royce with the number-plate '4', a homonym of the Cantonese word for 'death'. Wah Kwong's fleet was smaller than that of the Tung group – and the Tung group's debts were also bigger, a staggering US$2.6 billion.

The Tungs' fleet was also built up by a famous father, C. Y., a shipowner who had backed Chiang Kai-shek and then fled to Hong Kong and Taiwan in the face of the Communist victory. C. Y. Tung had bought the original Queen Elizabeth liner and converted it into floating Seawise University (a pun on his name), but it caught fire and rolled over in Hong Kong harbour in 1972. The rescues of the two shipping companies were complicated by the number of creditors, 40 in the case of Wah Kwong and 200 in the Tungs'. Ironically, given their history as escapees from China, C. Y. Tung's son and successor C. H. Tung turned to Henry Y. T. Fok, a rich Hong Kong businessman with close links with China. Fok made an initial deal for a US$120 million emergency loan with the Communist-owned China Ocean Shipping Co. The deal was a sign of a new era, giving China a chance of learning about shipping or of building bridges to Taiwan.

Another leading Hong Kong trading family was the Kwoks, owners of the Wing On group, including the famous department store of that name in pre-war Shanghai – the store is still there, renamed the Number 1 Department Store, on Nanjing Road. Wing On department stores in Hong Kong formed only one part of a group that included hotels, real estate, and the Wing On Bank. Troubles occurred when Albert Kwok, son of the original founder, was discovered to have diverted US$10 million in bank funds for his personal use. This only emerged when the bank lost US$36 million, more than total shareholders' funds, and the government was called in to take it over. Albert Kwok, safely dead of cancer when the discovery was made, was a useful scapegoat, a heavy-drinking, gambling man who was reputedly prepared to bet US$25,000 on a single horse race. But other members of the family had also benefited from insider loans. Prominent family members included Philip Kwok, former chairman of the group, a district board member and pillar of society, who was from time to time seen accompanying the Duke of Edinburgh on World Wildlife Fund activities. The Kwoks and the Fungs were part of the loyal breed sometimes called 'the Queen's Chinese'. Keen social critics in Hong Kong say that its *laissez-faire* system makes it easy for fraud to flourish. This has been seen most notoriously in the financial sector (see chapter 8), but it is equally a complaint about the conduct of general business life. The lack of exchange controls, the fact that there is no central bank or watchdog, the absence of penalties for insider trading (legislation against insider trading was enacted in 1989), the skimpy requirements for disclosure of corporate information, have all made it easy for unscrupulous Chinese businessmen (who tend to be secretive anyway) to get away with practices that in the West would be considered borderline or illegal.

Other families have sprung up to take the place of the old ruling classes. The dream of Horatio Alger, of leaping from rags to riches in a lifetime, comes to life in modern Hong Kong. The mega-rich, like Li Ka-shing and Sir Yue-Kong Pao (see chapter 9), are legends. But there are plenty of others in the ordinary multi-millionaire class. Some people have become prominent in both business and politics, including Dame Lydia Dunn, a career businesswoman and director of the Swire Group, who is the senior member of the executive council (the nearest Hong Kong has to a cabinet) and chairman of the Hong Kong Trade Department Council. Some of her colleagues in government councils, like Allen Lee Peng-fei and Stephen Cheong Kam-chuen, also have extensive business interests; another leading figure on both the executive and legislative councils, Maria Tam Wai-chu, is also a lawyer. But these prominent personalities are not in the league of the really super-rich. Some newcomers are. Joseph Lau, who, with his wife Theresa, launched Evergo

Industrial Enterprises, a maker of ceiling fans, has won a reputation for challenging the establishment. He made a big profit in 1987 in just failing to gain control of the Hongkong and Shanghai Hotels from the Kadoories. This was only one of his daring and profitable trading activities. Critics accused him of being a 'green mail' specialist, that is, buying big stakes in companies to frighten them into buying the shares back at a higher price. Lau's Evergo got a stock market listing in the early 1980s, at a time when industrial companies were a (short-lived) fad, attractive in a market sated with property companies. He made a useful profit in unloading some of his shares at that time. Over the next few years other establishment figures also felt the Laus' presence, sometimes through midnight telephone calls telling them that a deal had been made involving their company's stock. From very small beginnings Lau, forty in 1990, has become one of the most talked-about, if not liked, Hong Kong entrepreneurs. But even high-fliers can stumble. Evergo and two associated companies reported huge losses in the stock market crash of October 1987, though Lau claimed that his flagship was still financially sound and looking for new opportunities.

Among others coming up, Vincent Lo Hong-shui comes from a well-off and well-connected family. But he broke away to start his own construction company under the Shui On name. Within a few years he was winning important construction contracts in Hong Kong and trying to win a reputation for reliability as well as for reasonable cost. He also emerged as a keen budding politician, keeping in tune with China's line, and spoken of as one of a handful of possible candidates for the job of first chief executive of Hong Kong under Chinese sovereignty.

More controversial is Gordon Wu, regarded by some people as 'Hong Kong's visionary developer'. Wu, the seventh of nine children, started Hopewell Holdings and erected Hong Kong's tallest building (before the Bank of China was finished), the sixty-six-storey Hopewell Centre. More controversially, Wu has mammoth dreams for linking Hong Kong physically more closely with southern China. In 1987 he unveiled a huge HK$25 billion scheme to create an artificial island east of Lantau as a site for a new international airport and for industrial and residential development on the southern shore of an enlarged deep-water harbour. All of this would be linked to another pet project of his, the HK$8 billion Guangdong super-highway to connect Hong Kong with Canton.

Wu's admirers describe him as the man of the future and (forgetting Li Ka-shing) as Hong Kong's first Cantonese billionaire; his detractors claim he is a man of talk rather than action who is trying to cosy up to China. His road project was proving slow in building, but that didn't stop Wu from having fresh ambitious dreams. He announced plans in 1988 and 1989 for a massive new 2,400-room hotel in Wanchai that at ninety storeys would tower over even the Bank of China. His ambitions provoked a humorous footnote in the 'Lai See' column of the *South China Morning Post* of 5 December 1988, wishing him a happy fifty-fourth birthday and noting that Wu 'continues to shake the foundations with his seemingly endless plans for things wider, larger and taller'. The Princeton-educated Wu works from a cluttered office with commanding views of the Central District to the sound of classical, frequently baroque, music. His involvement with China began some years ago when he was responsible for putting together the consortium to build Canton's China Hotel, a joint venture in which several Hong Kong property barons including Li Ka-shing were partners. Wu denies that he is over-ambitious. He claims he learnt a lesson during the Hang Seng Bank crisis of 1965.

> A week after the bank run, I stood in front of the then chief accountant at the Hongkong Bank. He gave me a cash loan of HK$3 million, which saved the company. From that, I learned never to overspend. People think I have too many ambitions, but I'm ultraconservative. I do my sums, my analysis. But you also have to tackle problems. There must be the will to get things done. (Quoted in Cathay Pacific *Discovery* magazine, March 1987.)

Unfortunately, Wu was an early casualty of the Chinese crackdown. His plans to raise HK$3.8 billion through a stock-market offering, the colony's biggest, were scrapped when the market fell.

Prospects for the Future

With 1997 drawing increasingly close, Hong Kong's dynamic prosperity does come under threat from several directions, even apart from the tricky political equation with China. Free trade is Hong Kong's very lifeblood – yet many already industrialized countries have resorted to protectionist policies. In 1987 and 1988 the so-called Asian dragons (Korea, Singapore and Taiwan along with Hong Kong) were lumped together and attacked frequently for denying access to US goods. Lydia Dunn, chairman of the Hong Kong Trade Development Council, had a ready answer. 'We practise total free trade. We impose no barriers on people who want to do business with us. Anybody who wants to sell to Hong Kong, can sell to Hong Kong. We have a declared non-interventionist policy on the part of the government.' The then Governor Sir Edward Youde told Japanese business leaders in the Keidanren (the federation of economic organizations) in 1986 that:

> We practise free trade and open our markets to all. There are no tariff or nontariff barriers to imports into Hong Kong. Nor are there any barriers of institutional prejudice. We buy the best product available at the best available price wherever we can find it. A Japanese company is leading a consortium in constructing our second road–rail cross-harbour tunnel. Our power engines use both British and Japanese turbines. An Australian consortium is constructing a light rail system in one of our new towns. Canadian marine authorities, in association with our own Marine Department, are developing a new traffic management system for our harbour. Our Auxiliary Air Force flies

> French helicopters, and Cathay Pacific flies a fleet of US-manufactured aircraft around the world. I could name many more such examples.
>
> Competition in Hong Kong is free and fair. We do not provide our industries with subsidies. They must remain competitive in world markets in order to survive. We too have our declining industries, but we have to let market forces settle their fate. This is because we must adapt and reinvest our limited resources in the most profitable areas in order to achieve economic expansion.

South Korea and Taiwan could more correctly have been the target for angry Congressmen, but very often all four dragons get lumped together by an undiscriminating US legislature. Governor Sir David Wilson also had to draw attention to the dangers of 'creeping bilateralism' in world trade, effectively protectionist barriers likely to hurt Hong Kong exports. Wilson warned in 1988: 'There is an increasing tendency throughout the world to form, or consider forming, trading blocs and free trade associations. Sadly, these tend to share one common tendency – that is, they secure preferential treatment for their participants to the exclusion of third parties.'

It wasn't just the USA that was being tough. In December 1988, Hong Kong got 'a nasty shock' when the European Commission imposed duties of up to 59.3 per cent on Hong Kong videotapes and cassettes, claiming that manufacturers were guilty of 'dumping', that is exporting the goods at loss-making prices in an attempt to undercut European domestic producers. Hitherto, it had been assumed that producers in small, open Hong Kong without the cushion of a domestic market could not be guilty of dumping, as they would go bust. The Commission was about to begin an inquiry into small-screen colour television sets, photograph albums, denim cloth and audio tapes. Hong Kong officials were unhappy about the ruling, but so were some respected British economists who questioned the basis of the findings, especially since the figures used were confidential. The economists said that the EC investigations appeared to be biased in favour of a positive finding of dumping, and procedures were being used as an instrument of commercial industrial policy rather than of simple prevention of unfair trade. Peter Montagnon, trade editor of the *Financial Times*, commented that: 'It is becoming easier for any European company facing a competitive market to find a willing ally in the bureaucratic parlours of the Berlaymont (European Commission headquarters).' (*Financial Times*, 10 January 1989). John Chan, Hong Kong's Trade Secretary, warned that the charges on video cassettes could price Hong Kong out of the market.

Officials of the American executive branch also put pressure on Hong Kong, urging that the territory should revalue its dollar, linked since 1983 to the US unit at HK$7.80 to one US dollar. The influential Paris-based Organization of Economic Cooperation and Development also added its voice, claiming that Hong Kong had built up a large balance of payments current account surplus. Some Hong Kong-based economists expressed agreement with these calls, especially when interest rates, supposed to take the strain of the pegged currency, fell lower and lower. In 1988 the Hong Kong Association of Banks announced plans to impose negative interest rates – that is, penalties would be imposed on large deposits. This was a sure sign, said the proponents of revaluation, that the currency should be floated or repegged, at, say, HK$7 to the US unit, or perhaps linked to a basket of currencies. A rise in inflation also prompted calls for revaluation to keep import prices under control. Financial Secretary Jacobs resisted the demands steadfastly.

The Hong Kong Financial Secretary was in a difficult position: if he allowed himself to be pushed once to change the parity, he would risk putting the currency back at the mercy of volatile political winds. Pegging the currency to a basket of currencies would be more attractive, but would undermine the interest-rate arbitrage. With a basket of currencies as a peg, there would be no clue what the interest rate should be.

One important trade issue at least was solved early. Before the agreement with China over Hong Kong's future, the territory had been represented in trade negotiations by the UK. The British trade representatives had been assisted by Hong Kong government officials based in British embassies in key commercial cities like Geneva (home of the United Nations' Conference on Trade and Development) and Brussels (headquarters of the European Economic Community). Not everyone was satisfied with the job the British had done. One typical complaint was that Hong Kong had frequently been sacrificed to British interests, notably in textile negotiations. With the impending transfer of sovereignty over Hong Kong to China, many Hong Kong officials were afraid that they might now be sacrificed to China's interests. These fears were party answered when Hong Kong was given its own independent membership of the General Agreement on Tariffs and Trade (GATT) as the ninety-first contracting party in April 1986. Contracting parties to the GATT account for more than 80 per cent of world trade. By joining the trade club Hong Kong thus had some measure of protection against protectionist moves. It was also seen as a measure of goodwill that Peking had allowed the move when China was not a GATT member.

As Hong Kong moves into the 1990s, its economic strengths and weaknesses are clear enough. Entrepreneurial initiative, a hard-working refugee labour force, a government that has stood back even at the expense of tolerating abuses, have all served the territory well in the past. But by the late 1980s, the labour shortage was beginning to bite. Even with concealed Chinese bureaucratic and administrative costs, and poorer quality work, the attraction of shifting to China was obvious.

At first the Hong Kong government steadfastly refused to allow any large-scale labour immigration to alleviate the shortages. In November 1988 Financial Secretary Jacobs called upon Hong Kong industrialists to move towards greater automation. But he also reiterated government reluctance to get involved, stating that the government 'can throw billions of dollars at the problem and intervene in the affairs of the industry – that is very expensive and I am not sure if that is always productive. The Hong Kong way, frankly, is to let the industrialists and businessmen make their own decisions.' Squeals about labour shortages and pleas for help were increasingly heard from industrialists and businessmen. The Mandarin Oriental Hotel group devised a special share scheme to try to keep staff, while some retail concerns spoke of employing Vietnamese refugees. Later the government relented and was prepared to consider limited immigration of workers on contract. In absolute terms there was probably no shortage. All over Hong Kong there were at least several regiments of odd-job men, hawkers, fruit sellers, glorified rag-and-bone men, dealers in flotsam and jetsam, all underemployed, pushing and heaving barrows, carts, stalls, through the traffic jams or playing hide-and-seek to prevent the authorities confiscating their unlicensed goods. In the Central business and banking district, in the very shadow of the swanky plate-glass towers, there were rows of elderly shoe-shine boys whose customers were often bright young international bankers and stockbrokers about to spend the equivalent of a month's wages for the shoe-shine men on a single lunch. These casual workers have been by-passed by the industrial and economic revolution which has swept Hong Kong in less than a generation; no one has yet found a way of incorporating them into the mainstream economy.

The United States remained Hong Kong's biggest market for domestic exports, though with a reducing share. By the late 1980s the USA accounted for only 22 per cent of Hong Kong's total exports (though still a high and valuable 37 per cent of domestic exports – the difference is made up of re-exports), a significant fall. Both the growth of re-exports and the diminishing share of the USA were caused by the growth of trade with China. Trade with Japan has grown and Hong Kong exporters made inroads into the difficult Japanese market.

The government was maintaining considerable and comfortable budget surpluses, but Financial Secretary Jacobs was aware of the thin tax-base. Only one in five of the economically active population pays tax, and 3 per cent of the working population contributes three-quarters of the total salaries tax. Jacobs himself admitted favouring a sales tax imposed at wholesale level as the best way of spreading the tax net. With a small wholesale tax he claimed he would be able to do away completely with salaries tax. But there were many economists and bureaucrats advising against plunging into new taxation which could prove complicated to administer. A former head of the Inland Revenue had said he would be happy to see a value-added tax – but only after he had retired from government, since it was so complicated to administer!

The Financial Secretary's wish to consider new taxation when the government budget was in surplus to the tune of more than HK$10 billion a year might seem odd, but reflected the realization that the embarrassment of riches could prove temporary. By the late 1980s people at last began to see that Hong Kong's economic miracle had been achieved at the cost of considerable deterioration of the environment. By 1989 it was routine for popular beaches to display notices stating that they were unsafe for swimming because of pollution. The celebrated Tolo Harbour had become infamous, and Jacobs joked that 'someone had been seen swimming in Tolo Harbour and survived – but only for a short while'. Some environmentalists claim that the harbour can never be restored to a safe condition. The bill for bringing Hong Kong's drainage and sewage systems up to late twentieth-century standards was reckoned to come to HK$12 billion alone. And there was a long list of other infrastructure improvement schemes planned including road-building, water supplies and land reclamation. The total bill came to HK$100 billion. One government secretary commented that the rush of activity to improve the basic infrastructure reminded him of traditional British colonies 'just before they become independent when the government realizes that the services fall short of those required for a modern independent state'. The government was going ahead with these infrastructure schemes in a programme extending to the next century. The healthy budget should cover the bills, but Jacobs and his successors have to be careful not to push government spending faster than the overall economic growth. The HK$100 billion did not include the cost of a new airport, a hefty HK$50 to 60 billion tag on its own. In downtown Kowloon on a typical afternoon, there are traffic jams as far as the eye can see, adding to the pall of smoke from the cramped factories and caged apartments squatting together cheek by jowl. From time to a time a jet aircraft roars into Kai Tak airport, and the whole place seems to vibrate and tremble under its wings. Even if these basic problems are tackled effectively, the worries about 1997 will not go away. This was true even in 1986 when the economy was racing full-speed ahead and when foreign investors enthused over the advantages that Hong Kong offered over other places. 'It's more flexible than Europe,' enthused a young European director of a financial concern. 'People say, "Yes, let's try it," rather than "No, we won't take a risk", that you hear in Europe. It's more international than Tokyo or Peking. And my goodness the Hong Kong Chinese are still hungry to get ahead.' Japan has been joining China in pouring in investment: Japanese concerns have 60 per cent of the land allocated to foreign investors in the industrial estates, or 30 per cent of the total leased land, as of mid-1987. Of the eleven new manufacturing units set up in the first half of 1987, ten were Japanese. But clearly not all the Hong Kong Chinese share the foreigners' faith. The evidence always has been that China's political prerogatives will carry more weight than Hong Kong's prosperity when it comes to a crunch, and this view has been tragically reinforced by the crushing of the pro-democracy protests in China in the late spring of 1989. But how the Hong Kong Chinese perceive China is also important.

Even before the Chinese action, there were more than enough signs of worries among the up-and-coming Hong Kong Chinese middle classes. The Hong Kong Management Association started a scheme to try to lure back departing Chinese executives. 'We are losing too many well-trained middle-level Chinese staff,' said Jimmy McGregor, then director of the Hong Kong General Chamber of Commerce. Some US multinationals reported that they were losing 25 per cent of their managers and said that if the exodus continued they would have to consider pulling out of Hong Kong. Another unusual sign of the unease was a sharp rise in dishonesty – by employees cheating their bosses to make enough money to emigrate. 'People who have been perfectly honest for years are seizing opportunities for making fast bucks to buy their way into Australia or Canada,' one international lawyer based in Hong Kong commented. One trick was for managers to organize clandestine making of counterfeit goods such as jeans or video tapes in their employers' factories in China and then ship the goods for sale for their own benefit. Abuses were getting so serious that some companies were taking out 'fidelity' insurance to guard against being cheated by their workers.

But the Chinese crackdown added a whole new dimension to Hong Kong's economic prospects. The growing number of companies with factories in China began to wonder if they had made a mistake. According to some estimates, by the end of 1988 more than 90 per cent of Hong Kong companies in garments, toys and electronic goods had at least some of their production done across the border in Guangdong. New border crossing points were being built for the articulated lorries clogging the roads between Hong Kong and China. On the busiest day in 1988 about 12,000 lorries crossed at Man Kam To. Long tailbacks were common. In 1988 alone Hong Kong concerns invested US$1.8 billion in Guangdong. The manufacturing connections between Hong Kong and China became so strong that some companies, including toymaker Playmates Holdings, had planned to close their Hong Kong manufacturing entirely, to switch to China. Some economists warned that the colony's manufacturing industry would see a sharp and dangerously vulnerable decline if trends continued. So China's upheaval prompted some overdue re-thinking. In the medium term Hong Kong may not be too badly affected provided that southern

China's infrastructure is maintained and communications and transport keep flowing across the land border. But Hong Kong's growing domestic trade with China will decline if growth in the People's Republic falls.

The turmoil offered object lessons for manufacturers not to put all their eggs in a single basket, no matter how attractive it looks, and to be aware of political factors. Businessmen were quick to set off to look again at Taiwan, the Philippines and other places in south-east Asia as well as re-examining Hong Kong. Victor Lo, managing director of Gold Peak Industries (Holdings), said: 'We'll have to hedge our political risks.' Stephen Codron, marketing director of Shenzhen-based China Bicycles Co., a joint venture of Chinese, Hong Kong and US interests, said in mid-1989: 'The problem isn't our new production line. That is working very well. But our foreign customers are unwilling to place orders in China.' Other Hong Kong manufacturers with plants in China echoed these comments.

And Hong Kong's middle-class managers were even more determined to get their foreign passports. Money in the twentieth century world is the most liquid asset, generally able to travel across frontiers without difficulty. But what economies need are the middle managers to make the money work. Without them Hong Kong would be sunk.

8 GLOBAL FINANCIAL CENTRE WITH A SMALL-TOWN MENTALITY

A BANNER headline screaming across seven columns of the front page of the *South China Morning Post* in October 1988 told an important part of the recent history of Hong Kong's financial system and provided clues about the future. 'Local brokers claim victory,' it reported; then, in slightly smaller type, 'International firms shut out of line-up for new stock exchange'. The news story gave the results of elections for the colony's freshly reformed and cleaned-up stock market. These were clearly a victory for small-town Hong Kong. Yet during the 1970s and 1980s, Hong Kong used to boast that it was the third biggest international financial centre in the world – 'after London and New York', officials and bankers claimed, confidently indicating that they were playing right at the top of the financial super-league. But a series of scandals rocked first banking and then the stock market in the mid- and late 1980s, exposing the smug hollowness of the boast.

Hong Kong's reputation as an *International* centre had suffered further heavy damage during and after the October 1987 Wall Street stock market crash. Not only did market values in Hong Kong fall (as they did right round the world), but the authorities shut down the exchange for four days, the only market in the world to be completely closed. Later the former chairman of the exchange and a number of key executives were charged with corruption. After all this sceptics and particularly some of the really big international players claimed that the Hong Kong stock market was neither serious nor to be trusted, but was a 'Mickey Mouse' gambling operation for the favoured few. With time ticking away to the Chinese takeover, Hong Kong has not got long to make up its mind what role it wants for its financial system, 'international' or 'home-town'.

Most of the indicators suggest it will be too much of an effort for the territory to play a truly world role and the events of 1989 in China can only limit it further. As the financial world moves towards the twenty-first century, the old Hong Kong boast has increasingly been drained of substance. Tokyo has effectively taken over as the third leg in twenty-four-hour global financial trading, along with London and New York. In the twenty-first century world of big international trading, starring huge banks and financial conglomerates, Hong Kong seems an increasingly modest place, flawed equally by its own inadequacies and the fact that in 1997 it will become part of China.

The 1970s: Hong Kong Arrives on the World Map

Hong Kong's emergence as a financial centre on the world map dates back to the 1970s and owes much to the freedom with which banks and other financial institutions could come and go. Even in the late 1970s, when there was a moratorium on granting of new full bank licences, foreign banks could freely set up offices in Hong Kong, not allowed to do banking business proper but permitted to do financial business through deposit-taking companies.

Global financial markets were in their infancy in the 1970s. Banks active in New York, the biggest financial centre in the world, and London, the heart of the growing Euromarkets, needed an Asian centre to complete their round-the-clock operations. Hong Kong offered the ideal location. It was easy in every way to set up an office. Freedom from foreign exchange controls and an absence of the bothersome restrictions, rules, regulations and the mountains of paper that other countries demanded made it more attractive than virtually anywhere else. International communications were also excellent, both physical communications by air and sea and telecommunications by telephone, telex, facsimile and other modern methods. Cable and Wireless, originally an offshoot of the British Post Office and later privatized, made Hong Kong an important telecommunications centre, and offered communications facilities that were both better and cheaper than anywhere else in Asia.

Another advantage of Hong Kong was the use of the English language and of the English common law legal system. Unlike, say, Japan, Hong Kong offered a sizeable pool of local people used to speaking and reading in English. And if there weren't enough people already speaking English, the local Cantonese are practical people and quick to learn (unlike the Japanese, who study English at school for years but tend to retain it as a 'book' language, often untainted by practical application).

When restrictions on full bank licences were removed in 1981, new banks came flooding into Hong Kong. By 1989 165 banks had licences. Virtually all the world's very biggest banks were operating in the territory. Altogether these banks had almost 1,400 branches, or a bank branch for every 4,000 inhabitants, including children. In addition, there were more than 130 representative offices of foreign banks. Other financial institutions proliferated, including almost 40 licensed deposit-taking companies (equivalent to merchant or investment banks), nearly 250 registered deposit-taking companies, more than 800 stockbrokers and more than 400 licensed money-lenders. No matter that there clearly wasn't enough business in the domestic banking market for all of these institutions: Hong Kong was seen – and saw itself – as a regional and international centre. The late 1970s and early 1980s were the heyday of international lending. At first banks doled out what was later called 'plain vanilla' syndicated loans to countries like the Philippines, Indonesia, Korea, Malaysia and even Australia and New Zealand. Sometimes these were loans for particular projects like a steel mill or a new port complex. At other times the money was just a general loan to help prop up an ailing balance of payments. Later the lending business got more complicated, and loans became more and more exotic, with new instruments like swaps and floating rate notes and ever more complicated packages being offered.

Hong Kong thrived on this. Leading international banks like Citibank, Bank of America, Banque Nationale de Paris, Lloyds and Barclays all opened Hong Kong offices and were filled with bright young men and women cutting their teeth on devising complicated new deals for the international syndicated loan markets. Critics carped that the Hong Kong merchant bankers were not in the same intellectual or inventive league as those in London: but it was a good place for a young person to prove him or herself and win a reputation, before moving on to head office in London or New York or Paris, a jump ahead of peers who had stayed at home. In those days few people had heard of Japan as an international centre, so Tokyo was no rival. Japan was a closed society, preoccupied with its own economic problems and not ready to open its doors to the rest of the world. There were foreign banks in Japan, but they were few in number and they were still trying to build up their own branch banking business and to make connections with corporate Japan.

The exciting and hectic activity in the international financial markets spawned ever-new activities and created jobs. International lending attracted lawyers to work on the loan documents. Respected law firms such as Coudert Bros., Paul Weiss Rifkind Wharton, Garrison, Johnson Stokes and Master, Slaughter and May, Herbert Smith, and Baker and McKenzie were all prominent. The giant accounting firms were also quick to open offices.

Hong Kong's growing role as a regional financial centre attracted new waves of people, for example in the fund management business. Leading British and indeed American fund managers set up offices in Hong Kong, from which they could handle pension and other accounts, using the city as a base for investing funds in markets throughout the Far East. Insurance companies also set up regional offices covering Hong Kong and its neighbours. The boom in the Hong Kong stock market in the late

1970s and early 1980s that saw local companies like Hutchison Whampoa, Hong Kong Land Co., Cheung Kong and China Light and Power Co., gain increasing international recognition only added to the excitement of the place.

Singapore was the only rival at this time, and Singapore's more controlled environment gave Hong Kong important advantages. The impression in Hong Kong was that Singapore was always lagging behind, and had to create artificial markets, often using special tax concessions as bait. 'Singapore had a manual of how to set up a financial centre and followed it slavishly,' charged a foreign banker based in Hong Kong. 'The rule book said that a discount market was important, so Singapore set up a discount market. Then Singapore was lagging behind Hong Kong in loan syndication so it offered special tax holidays for banks doing international loan syndications from Singapore. Next there were tax concessions for international fund managers. Hong Kong has never offered special favours to force the pace.' In Hong Kong business grows naturally – according to the demands of the marketplace. The existence of local, sometimes exotic, markets didn't detract from Hong Kong's international standing, but merely added exciting flavours. Hong Kong became the Far Eastern centre for the international gold market, with the local quotations starting each global financial day. At the same time the local Chinese Gold and Silver Exchange Society had its own bullion market quoting prices in local dollars per tael, an old Chinese measurement roughly equivalent in Hong Kong to 1.2 Troy ounces (525 grams). (The tael's weight varies from about 1 ounce to 2.5 ounces in different places.)

Hong Kong in the late 1970s had not one, but four, stock exchanges. The oldest was the Hong Kong Stock Exchange, founded in 1891. But the Hong Kong exchange had been surpassed in terms of business volumes, if not in terms of prestige, by the Far East Stock Exchange, formed in the mid-1960s by a disgruntled group of stockbrokers who resented the monopoly of the oldest exchange. Some of the Hong Kong stock exchanges opened their doors to foreign brokers and also welcomed the listing of foreign stocks on their exchanges, thus adding to the international atmosphere of the place.

Indeed the hectic daily activity on the stock exchanges symbolized the warm greeting which the local Hong Kong people gave to financial activity. At busy times the floors of the exchange, especially of the busiest Far East Exchange, were like a rugby scrummage in perpetual motion, as brokers rushed to place their orders on the huge blackboard on which prices were written. Away from the market floor interest was just as keen. Throughout the city, banks and other financial institutions have found it worth their while to display boards giving the latest quotation of the Hang Seng index and also the prices of leading individual stocks. There is always a crowd clustered around these boards. The average stock-watchers in Hong Kong are not limited to the normal 'city gents'. All manner of people show a close interest in the market, including gold-toothed amahs, clad in traditional Chinese pyjama costume. To budding Hong Kong entrepreneurs, and indeed to the general populace of a refugee city anxious for upward mobility, flourishing financial markets are an important ingredient of business success – just as are the ordinary street markets where haggling over fresh produce is an accepted part of daily life.

Crises and Scandals Hit the Markets

In 1982 and 1983 Hong Kong's reputation as an international financial centre suffered a series of serious blows. It wasn't coincidental that the damage was done as the territory ran into crises, political as well as economic. The political background was the opening of negotiations over Hong Kong's future. Economically, the colony's trade, its life-blood, contracted as recession hit the main western markets buying Hong Kong goods. These economic and political factors together led to the bursting of the local property market bubble. Banks were squeezed as individuals and businesses couldn't meet loan schedules. Often the property that had been put up as security for loans had plummeted in value, sometimes to a half or a third of its previously assessed value. More damaging, as banks got into trouble, were revelations of gross imprudence in extending loans, and indeed of fraud and illegality in some of the lending practices of the banks and finance companies.

The most dramatic demonstration of the tangled and murky financial affairs going on in Hong Kong opened in a quiet, though sinister way. In July 1983, police made an unexpected find in a secluded banana grove in Hong Kong's New Territories: a strangled body with a bathrobe cord from a leading hotel around its neck. With that discovery, police launched the year's forty-seventh murder hunt, and also began to unravel ever more complicated twists and turns in Hong Kong's – and at that time probably the world's – biggest financial scandal. The murder victim was Jalil Ibrahim, assistant general manager of Bumiputra Malaysia Finance (BMF), a deposit-taking company that was one of a distinguished string of lenders to the mysterious Carrian Group of companies. At that time merchant bankers were trying to put together a rescue package to save Carrian. The murder hunt led the police to open BMF's filing cabinets. These showed that the scandal went deeper and darker than anyone had supposed. BMF's lending to Carrian was much larger than previously imagined. In fact there was a whole separate set of books for Carrian loans. Jalil's misfortune was that he had opposed a US$4 million loan to Carrian, peanuts in terms of BMF's total lending to Carrian. The murder discovery was also the death-knell for the Carrian Group; it owed too much money. When it finally went down it had debts of about HK$10 billion (US$1.3 billion).

Some of the biggest and most glamorous names in international banking were involved in lending to Carrian, including the Hongkong and Shanghai Banking Corporation group, and the local offshoots of Bank Bumiputra Malaysia, Barclays Bank, WestDeutsche Landesbank Girozentrale, Bankers Trust, Banque Paribas and the China-registered Bank of Communications. Altogether about sixty banks had lent money and the biggest of them was Bumiputra Malaysia Finance (BMF), with HK$4.6 billion – more than the paid-up capital of the parent bank.

One curious aspect of the case was that Bank Bumiputra was set up specifically to help the *bumiputras* (the Malay word literally means 'sons of the soil', therefore effectively the indigenous Malays who economically lagged behind the Chinese in that country). Yet the bank's wholly owned Hong Kong offspring had lent vast sums to little-known Chinese companies based hundreds of miles away across the South China Sea in Hong Kong. 'It seems a denial of the very purpose for which Bank Bumi was set up,' a prominent Malay politician commented bitterly. Even after subsequent court hearings and inquiries the Malaysian authorities were slow to probe deeply. No wonder! Some of the hearings revealed allegations that Malaysians involved in encouraging BMF loans to Carrian included prominent politicians and leading members of the cabinet. Here was dynamic proof that Hong Kong was a useful place for foreigners to do business. In order to make domestic political capital many Malaysian politicians were publicly scathing about the loose business climate in Hong Kong. Yet it had suited them to take advantage of this laxness.

If any novelist put together the outlines of the Carrian plot that surfaced in the court hearings he would probably be told that his tale was too far-fetched to be believed. The group revolved around George Tan Soon-Gin, chairman of the empire when it went into liquidation. For a while he was the golden boy of Hong Kong, sought and known by the lions of the land. He went to the races with Michael (later Sir Michael) Sandberg, chairman of the Hongkong Bank from 1977 till 1986, and sat in Sandberg's box. (Sandberg later tried to create distance between himself and Tan, saying that he had 'many people' visit his box at the races.) John Bremridge, then chairman of John Swire and Sons (HK) recalled that Sandberg had introduced him to Tan. Bremridge, cautious, was not convinced that Tan was the genius that people claimed. But he was in a minority. Tan did business with Hongkong Land Co., and the Land company's managing director sang his praises. In a massive deal of August 1981 Carrian and the Land company were linked in the purchase of the site of the old wing of the Miramar Hotel on Kowloon's 'golden mile' for HK$2.8 billion (at that time worth about US$500 million), then a world record for a single building. Carrian had 55 per cent and Land 25 per cent of the deal, later a casualty of Carrian's collapse.

Tan cultivated the image of someone special who had arrived to take Hong Kong by storm. Only guests with special badges were allowed by guards into his locked inner sanctum. His office dripped with wealth, from the valuable oil paintings hung like wallpaper on the wood-panelled walls to the thick-pile oriental carpets. A few bankers, notably local ones resenting a parvenu, criticized the office as a tasteless clutter. 'It was as if he had bought a job lot from Nieman Marcus' furniture department and hadn't the faintest idea of how to arrange it', one critic said scathingly. 'It was Hong Kong baroque with the taste of a used car salesman,' claimed another. The Carrian chief had cultivated little quirks like refusing to be photographed by the press. 'I don't want to give assistance to potential kidnappers,' he declared in a lordly way. He also said he was not going to leave Hong Kong for several years because the *fung shui* (Chinese spirits) were against it. Later it turned out that there was a more prosaic reason why he had not left Hong Kong, but the excuse of *fung shui* helped to build George Tan's image. He was a restless will o' the wisp. This author recalls an interview in late 1981. On one side of the table was a phalanx of senior expatriate executives, all grave and nodding deferentially to Tan. His fellow director and right-hand-man Bentley Ho giggled a lot. Tan himself kept darting from the room, returning to spray around grand plans like a supercharged geyser, but not stopping to explain why or how he would be able to accomplish them.

Tan was certainly ambitious. He first made his mark in

property and attracted big headlines in January 1980 when Carrian bought Gammon House, a thirty-nine-storey block in central Hong Kong from the Hongkong Land Company for HK$998 million, a deal that gave Land a 40 per cent profit on the price it had paid only a year before. Only months later, in September of the same year, Carrian announced it was reselling Gammon House to another group, Bylamson and Associates, in a deal that 'attributes a value of HK$1.68 billion' to the building. With this deal Tan became Hong Kong's property whiz-kid. (Ironically, the great coup on which his reputation was built was never completed as Bylamson could not come up with the full amount, and Carrian had to sell the building floor by floor. Bank of America bought several floors for US$124 million and the building was renamed Bank of America Tower. The exact profit, or loss, on the deal was never disclosed.)

Tan didn't want to stop at property development. Carrian bought a majority share of Grand Marine Holdings shipping group, then Hong Kong's fourth largest fleet; a 53 per cent interest in China Underwriters Life and General Insurance Company; 27 per cent of Union Bank of Hong Kong. It moved into consumer retailing, energy resources, hotels, fast food and restaurants, bought 400 taxis, 200 coaches and 56 hire cars, and ran several travel agencies. Tan raised his sights beyond Hong Kong, and spread Carrian's wings across the Pacific ocean to the USA. He bought an office building in Oakland, California, 14 per cent of Oakland's Hyatt Regency Hotel, land in Los Angeles and Florida, and 80 per cent of a Texas oil exploration partnership.

Tan even took Carrian to Japan, with a 21 per cent stake in Nikkatsu, a quoted film company producing low budget 'roman porn' (romantic pornography) films and with an interest in hotels, a night club and an art gallery. He went into a joint venture with a New Zealand property group and outlined a plan to build a hotel in China. He floated a scheme to become Hong Kong's second airline operator (after Cathay Pacific), with Boeing 747 jets flying to Europe and the USA. Tan declared with a flourish that he wanted to be involved in every aspect of life 'from the cradle to the grave'.

Carrian's fame was such that in November 1981 London stockbrokers Vickers da Costa (later taken over by Citicorp, owners of the biggest US bank) put out a special review which turned into a virtual paean of praise for Carrian Investments, the publicly quoted arm of the group. Thousands of copies were printed. It would probably have been the year's best-seller, but it was proudly given away free.

There was always an air of mystery about Carrian and Tan. He had a positive genius for spawning new companies with exotic names that could only have been invented in Hong Kong, including Born Rich, Ample Gain, Extradollars, Extragold, Extraluck Investments, Extramoney, Extrawin, Smartmoney, Beat the Bush, Outwit. There was rumoured to be big money behind the group. Some analysts claimed that more than US$1 billion was waiting to be poured in from outside Hong Kong as the company found profitable investments. One set of rumours speculated that the Marcos family in the Philippines was backing Carrian. Another that there were rich Chinese in Indonesia, or the ruling Soeharto family in Indonesia, or East Malaysian rich timber interests. The concentration of Carrian on the tourist trade fanned such stories, since tourism offered an easy way of laundering money and escaping Malaysian controls. There were whispers that 'golden triangle' drug funds might be involved. For a while it seemed as if nothing could stop the high-flying Carrian.

Declared after-tax profits in 1981 were HK$626 million on turnover of HK$1.5 billion. In the first half of 1982 profits were HK$270 million on HK$839 million turnover. But in late 1982 the Hong Kong property market tumbled in the middle of political uncertainty – and Carrian's problems began. In October the company announced that it had 'short-term liquidity problems', withdrew an interim dividend and planned to issue HK$500 million's worth of preference shares to raise money. The Hongkong Bank agreed to underwrite half of the issue (which was subsequently cancelled), adding that it would not be doing so unless satisfied about the question of Carrian's ownership. The rescue attempt dragged on for almost a year and looked as if it might be successful – until the implications of Jalil Ibrahim's murder began to sink in. Initially Carrian only wanted relief of HK$700 million, but as the police did their work, the debts grew and grew. Access to the BMF files showed another set of books, another set of loans and a whole world of deals which bankers and others putting together the rescue package never knew existed. Even after they had realized they had been conned, a small group of bankers claimed that in other times and with better luck George Tan might have become a man who built an empire of solid rock. 'If the property market hadn't collapsed, if other things hadn't turned sour . . .' suggested one. They were making excuses for their own failures. His empire was a skyscraper of paper: bankers were lending money to him on the strength of their own loans.

One matter of particular concern was that bankers had been hoodwinked into suspending their normal prudential checks and controls. In addition, there were hints that some bankers were sweetened by generous gifts. Company spending included multi-million-dollar purchases of jewellery, curiously not an area in which Carrian had interests. Tan is reported to have described such purchases as from the 'tea-money'. Certainly, routine bank credit checks should have unearthed the fact that George Tan had a record as an undischarged bankrupt from Singapore going back to 1974. The sum (which Tan said was S$33,000) was paid off in 1980 after Carrian companies had started. At least one Hong Kong bank knew of this as early as 1982. 'We were tipped off by someone who obviously had an axe to grind against Tan,' remembers a bank official. 'We weren't absolutely sure since the Singapore legal papers don't use Chinese characters and the transliteration of Tan's name into English sometimes differs. But a bank with the reputation and resources of the Hongkong Bank should have been able to check and should have been cautioned.'

This man's bank did lend money to George Tan, and the banker pleads the excuse that his institution was blinded by the large sums of money that Tan was wielding and by the obvious backing he was getting from the Hongkong Bank. 'I had my own objections. Things didn't quite smell right, but I was told that the Hongkong Bank was backing him and he was moving in a big way', the banker says. The Hongkong Bank chairman at the time, Sandberg, after the collapse of Carrion scoffed at reports that the Hongkong Bank had lent US$400 million to the group: 'It's a good deal less than half that figure,' Sandberg said, pointing out that the majority of loans were secured and the bank quickly made provisions against the losses. Sandberg added: 'We certainly took an exposure which we'd rather not have had, but we would like to sleep well at night and we make provisions prudently and conservatively.' He made a dig at other banks' heavy lending exposures in Latin America and Eastern Europe, saying 'I'm glad that we don't have the exposure that some banks have on sovereign risk lending.'

Tan continued to write his name in the various record books even after his business empire finally collapsed. There was mystery about his birthplace and birthdate. When creditor bankers and government officials were asked, several said Sibu in Sarawak, Malaysia; others said Sabah; Brunei; Singapore; or Amoy (Xiamen) in China. Tan himself told reporters in early 1983 that he was born in 1938 in Sibu. But his Singapore passport – which had expired in 1974 – gave his date of birth as 10 December 1933 and his birthplace as China. Singapore's Home Ministry revoked his citizenship in March 1984. But Tan had more than one iron in the nationality fire: when he surrendered his travel documents to Hong Kong police, he also handed over Paraguayan and Tongan passports. Tan was also shown to have overstayed his welcome in Hong Kong by a matter of eleven years – since he had entered in June 1972 on a three-month visit permit, never renewed. When the case went to trial Tan's bail was set at a record of HK$50 million (US$6.4 million), plus two sureties of HK$1 million each. The bail money had to be paid in advance in cash.

In May 1987 the prosecution finished its case, more than a year after the trial started. The court then went *in camera* while Tan's lawyers claimed there was no case to answer. In September 1987, after hearings lasting 281 days spread over nineteen months, Justice Dennis Barker decided that there was no case for George Tan and five co-defendants to answer. He ordered the seven-member jury to return a verdict of not guilty, without their ever having to consider the merits of the case. This judgement itself caused a furore. The judge declared that the indictment of conspiracy to mislead shareholders and creditors by falsifying certain financial transactions and company accounts was 'bad' for reasons of 'duplicity' – meaning that multiple charges had been brought in the prosecution case, whereas the indictment allowed only one. Other lawyers criticized the judge's verdict, and the Court of Appeal criticized the judge and said he had erred: 'He should not have gone on to direct the jury to return verdicts of not guilty.' But the Appeal Court had no power to set aside the judgement or order a retrial.

A stinging rebuke was delivered in the *Hong Kong Law Journal* by its editor Henry Litton. He claimed that the judge had made blunders that 'no first-year law student should have made'. He claimed that the trial had been 'bizarre and irrational'. The consensus was that the Hong Kong legal system and the operations of the Attorney General's department had earned disgrace by the failure of the prosecution. Yet for the Carrian chief George Tan it was not the end of the matter, as he had to face other corruption charges.

The editor of the *Far Eastern Economic Review*, Derek Davies, later declared:

> Hong Kong has for many years been fighting a losing battle with its international image among business and investment circles as a Tom Tiddler's Ground for sharp operators, the smart money boys who chase the big, quick bucks with scant or no regard for business ethics or the interests of shareholders.

Codes have been promulgated and legislation passed in attempts to regulate the securities and banking industries. But, it would seem, to little avail. Even after the lessons which should have been learned from the collapse of the Carrian empire in 1983, the world has been treated to the spectacle of a succession of massive failures and impudent scams in Hong Kong. (*Far Eastern Economic Review*, 24 September 1987.)

Bremridge Bails out the Banks

The Carrian affair offered an object lesson in the freewheeling business and banking ways of Hong Kong. A lot of supposedly experienced bankers got their fingers burned, and world-renowned institutions had to make heavy loan loss provisions; but no Hong Kong bank went broke as a result of Carrian (though Bank Bumiputra in Malaysia had to be bailed out). In the five years after the Carrian fiasco, several banks effectively did go bust and had to be rescued. Indeed by the middle of the decade financial secretary Sir John Bremridge, a former big business tycoon in charge of what boasted of being the world's most successful *laissez-faire* economy, was taking over commercial banks as if he were some Communist commissar or third world military muscleman. When Bremridge became Financial Secretary in mid-1981 the government didn't own a single bank. In 1983 Bremridge took control of Hang Lung Bank. By the end of 1986 the government had orchestrated rescue operations for seven banks, some of which it took over itself, and others it prompted bigger banks to rescue. It wasn't that Bremridge or the Hong Kong authorities liked taking over banks. The Financial Secretary at one time joked, 'You want to own a bank? I'll sell one of them to you for only a dollar – provided you take responsibility for their debts.' That was the catch. All of the Hong Kong government's banking empire was picked up as a result of last-ditch rescue or clean-up operations.

On the international financial scene, the bank failures hardly created many ripples. But they were not small as far as the government – or the taxpayers – of Hong Kong were concerned. In the space of a few years, probably HK$5 billion had to be provided as the cost of bailing out the banks. (The government has refused to make the figures public.) Of more lasting importance, some of the banks collapsed because of incompetent management, or even criminal actions, that the local authorities had not been able to pick up through their regular checks. These failures thus reflected on the competence of the Hong Kong government itself. Before he left Hong Kong in 1986, Bremridge enacted new tougher banking regulations, though some of the tough measures were held by some unhappy bankers to threaten Hong Kong's attractiveness as an open international city. Japanese banks in particular complained about new stiff capital ratios.

The first of the banks to fall, the Hang Lung, cost the government about HK$1 billion. As the police and banking authorities pursued their investigations, it became clear that the bank failure wasn't the result merely of imprudent management, still less of bad luck that the property market had collapsed and the political atmosphere had been poisoned by uncertainties over Hong Kong's future. Police probes revealed complex webs of fraud. Executives of Hang Lung Bank and Dollar Credit and Financing, the biggest of several deposit-taking companies that had also collapsed, were involved in a vast illegal cheque-kiting scheme. The total sums involved in the cheques were US$21 billion, huge by international standards. This was a bigger scam for example than the one in which US investment bank E. F. Hutton and Co. in 1985 admitted illegally writing $4 billion in overdraft cheques. In Hutton's case the cheques were written against uncleared deposits in an attempt to improve the company's cash flow. But in the Hong Kong scandal, bad cheques were used to cover bad cheques, so that the perpetrators enjoyed hundreds of millions of dollars in interest-free funds for their personal use.

Worse was to follow. In June 1985 the government moved in

smartly to take over Overseas Trust Bank (OTB), on the brink of bankruptcy. On the day of the collapse of 'the bank you can trust' Patrick Chang Chen Tsong, a director and son of the founder, was picked up at Hong Kong's airport carrying a suitcase filled with cash, diamonds and securities, together worth US$1.5 million. Showing desperate audacity he had interrupted a crisis meeting with Banking Commissioner Robert Fell to try to arrange a flight out of Hong Kong. Overseas Trust Bank had assets of more than HK$10 billion and on that basis was the fourth biggest of the thirty-five banks registered in Hong Kong. Soon afterwards, Hong Kong Industrial and Commercial Bank, OTB's 63-per cent-owned subsidiary, was also taken under the government's wing. Investigations revealed that OTB had been in trouble since February 1982 when it was caught by a cheque-kiting scam. Chang's father Chang Ming Thien (who then had a month to live) decided against reporting the US$66.8 million bad cheques. The bank contrived to show profits over the next three years by virtue of an elaborate scheme creating 'dummy loans' to conceal the losses. These fictitious loans were booked under nominee names in the bank's foreign branches to stop the Hong Kong bank examiners from getting too suspicious. When Chang pleaded guilty to charges of conspiring to defraud shareholders, depositors and creditors of OTB, his lawyer, Martin Lee Chu-ming, said on his behalf: 'Mr Chang had been trying to salvage a collapsing business empire . . . living under constant fear that there would be a run on his bank.' By June 1985 when Chang agreed to declare the bank insolvent, OTB had more than HK$2 billion in doubtful debts.

At the end of 1985 another small concern, Wing On Bank, with assets of HK$2.5 billion, was rescued by the Hang Seng Bank, part of the Hongkong Bank group. In early 1986, agreement was reached for a Chinese company, China International Trust and Investment Corp (Citic) to take 90 per cent of Ka Wah Bank, with assets of HK$5.5 billion. These rescues were not painless to the government or taxpayer. Even when the government wasn't involved directly, as with Wing On and Ka

Wah, it had to promise to hand over the bank more or less 'clean' to the rescuers, that is, without bad loans. Two more banks also needed a helping hand. In March 1986 the government passed a credit line to Union Bank of Hong Kong and handed the management over to Jardine Fleming, a merchant bank. The government sponsored a takeover of Union Bank by a joint venture dominated by China Merchant Steam Navigation Co., a Chinese state concern. Finally, in September 1986 the government took control (but not ownership) of Hong Nin, a small family-owned Chinese bank. The bank was later bought by the First Pacific group.

A feature linking the number of fallen banks was common business connections, not just in Hong Kong but over South-east Asia, notably Malaysia, Singapore and to a lesser extent, Indonesia. Overseas Trust Bank, for example, was a small part of a complex and secretive business and banking empire founded by the Malaysian Chang Ming Thien, who died in March 1982. The empire expanded to North America, Australia and South-east Asia and spanned hotels, shipping, paper and flour-milling interests as well as the bank.

OTB wasn't the only bank that Chang founded; among others was United Malayan Banking Corp, one of the big three banks in Malaysia. He later sold his stake in UMBC to Multi-Purpose Holdings, the investment arm of the leading political party, the Malaysian Chinese Association, then controlled by businessman politician Tan Koon Swan. Among other banks at one time controlled by Chang, or by close friends or associates, were Hang Lung Bank and Ka Wah Bank. Keeping tabs on exactly where the tentacles of Chang's empire extended is difficult enough; knowing exactly how Chang pulled the strings is impossible. When he was Financial Secretary, Bremridge tried to track the business links and dealings involving Overseas Trust Bank. His staff produced a chart a square metre in area with Overseas Trust Bank at the centre. The Financial Secretary summed it up as 'a group of octopuses having an orgy'. Among the businesses that the Hong Kong authorities picked up along with the bank was a brothel in Macao. Bremridge claimed he felt great distaste at having to take over a bank with what he said was 'a management that deliberately set out on a series of absolutely disgraceful criminal actions' (in a speech to the legislative council, June 1985). But he regarded the takeover as the lesser of two evils – in spite of a HK$2 billion price tag for the taxpayer. The takeover exposed the dilemma of the authorities. They were constantly fearful that if a large bank like OTB was allowed to go under, it might bring about the collapse of a number of vulnerable smaller banks. If this didn't happen directly, then it could easily do so by indirect means, as depositors became afraid to put money in smaller banks. Hong Kong thrives on rumours. A small incident illustrates the dangers. A rather long queue at a bus stop was trying to seek some shelter from the driving rain. The wall they were huddled against was that of one of the medium-sized Chinese banks. Immediately a rumour was sparked that there was a run on the bank and the people in the bus queue were depositors trying to get their money out.

The authorities' action in saving Overseas Trust Bank, a bank with a management that wasn't incompetent but fraudulent, could give hope to other banks that the government would always come to their rescue. Lawyer Martin Lee, by then a member of the legislative council, complained after Wing On Bank had been saved that the Exchange Fund intended to support the Hong Kong dollar was turning into a 'guarantee fund' to prop up ailing banks. But Financial Secretary Bremridge claimed that 'we have to deal with fires as they occur and we use the appropriate means to put them out at minimum possible cost before the fire can spread'. The then Banking Commissioner Robert Fell said, 'we can't just let a bank collapse'.

The Hongkong Bank and the Rest

Scandals were an expensive embarrassment for the government. But there were general problems too, notably the failure of the banking supervisors to keep track of what was going on in a fast-changing world. Throughout the late 1970s and 1980s the Hong Kong financial authorities devised schemes or regulations to tidy up one area of the market, only to find that they caused unwanted repercussions elsewhere. The task was compounded by the peculiar nature of the Hong Kong banking scene and its unequal blend of one giant local bank, many aggressive international competitive ones and a host of minnow-sized operations. The biggest bank and very much the local star is the Hongkong and Shanghai Banking Corporation, with its 61-per-cent-owned subsidiary, the Hang Seng Bank. The two together have almost 400 branches and are traditionally reckoned to account for up to half the local Hong Kong dollar deposit base. (There are no public official figures.) A growing rival to the Hongkong Bank is the Communist Bank of China group, embracing thirteen sister banks and a network of more than 240 offices. Another long-established bank, older than the Hongkong Bank, is Standard Chartered Bank (originally called the Chartered Bank of India, China and Australasia). Other large banks operating in Hong Kong include most of the international giants. Some like Citibank (with almost thirty offices) have hopes of challenging the big Hong Kong banks for a large slice of the local retail banking market. Other internationally known names like Barclays and Banque Nationale de Paris have retreated from retail ambitions, but retain a number of branches throughout the territory to allow them to compete for wholesale and trade business. But the international giants have posed fewer problems. They are supervised in their own countries and the majority of them have only limited ambitions for the local market; they came to Hong Kong in the 1970s and 1980s to take advantage of the colony's role as a financial centre, especially for offshore business. Japanese banks, facing tight regulations at home, flooded into Hong Kong in the late 1970s and early 1980s to make the most of the looser Hong Kong rules and its international position. Just how active the Japanese had been was revealed in 1986 when the Commissioner of Banking pulled back part of the veil of secrecy surrounding banking statistics. These showed an almost staggering growth in the operations of Japanese.

By the end of 1986 the Japanese banks and financial institutions had built an asset base of HK$980.5 billion, up from HK$560.4 billion the year before. It wasn't merely the growth, but the fact that this was more than 45 per cent of the total assets of all financial institutions in Hong Kong. Equally noticeable was that the deposit base of the Japanese institutions was very narrow and had declined from HK$68.5 billion to HK$54.4 billion, only 9.7 per cent of total deposits. Other banks maintained a more careful ratio between deposits and assets. By comparison US banks together had assets of HK$199 billion and deposits of HK$62.8 billion. European banks had assets of HK$370 billion and deposits of HK$99 billion. Mainland Chinese banks had HK$155.5 billion in assets and HK$101.8 billion in deposits. The Banking Commissioner declined to provide any figures that might identify the share of the dominant Hongkong Bank group.

The largest among the locally registered banks, apart from the Hongkong Bank and the Hang Seng, is Bank of East Asia, with more than fifty offices and an assets base of almost HK$25 billion at the end of 1988. (This may seem impressive, but it is less than 3 per cent of the assets of the giant Hongkong Bank group.) This bank is itself a giant compared to the smaller local banks. A few of them have total assets of only a few hundred million local dollars. Even these are not the smallest banks: Hong Kong has three unincorporated banks limited to taking deposits from the public of a maximum of merely HK$2 million. They are so small and insignificant that when asked about them the Banking Commissioner couldn't remember their names. (They are Chan Man Cheong Finance Co., Lee Shing and and Ming Tai Finance Co.)

Over the last few years many local Chinese banks have been seeking a bigger stronger partner. 'In the present environment it seems increasingly difficult for a small bank without a big brother connection to see where it is going,' commented William Purves, who took over from Michael Sandberg as chairman of the Hongkong Bank, underlining the importance of strong well-capitalized banks. By 1987 only a handful of the smaller banks hadn't found a partner. But it wasn't easy for any of them. The most logical solution would have been for groups of smaller Chinese banks to combine, but this was made difficult because very often the banks represented different clan or group interests or even families that couldn't get on with each other. Even within the Bank of East Asia, there had been family quarrels. That bank had been founded by ten local Chinese families. Over the years some families dropped out and rivalries grew among those remaining in the bank. The Kans, one of the founding families, had supplied the chief manager, as the chief executive is still called, during the 1970s. But by the 1980s the Kans didn't get on with the Lis, a difficult situation since David Li Kwok-po was then the chief executive. In the end, the Li family solved the situation, raising its stake to just over 50 per cent by buying out shares from the other families. Bank of East Asia is large by local standards, has a reputation for sound and prudent banking, and is publicly listed on the stock exchange. But that bank also has two important minority shareholders in Société Général and Bank of China's China Development Institute.

The solution for many of the smaller banks was to take a big brother from abroad. A few did it by choice; others sought help only when they had got into difficulties. As examples, Bangkok Bank and Tokai Bank each took shares in Commercial Bank of Hong Kong; Standard Chartered bought 13 per cent of Wing Lung Bank; Irving Trust controls 51 per cent of Wing Hang Bank.

A clutch of Japanese banks found useful opportunities to extend their Hong Kong interests by buying a stake in a local bank: Fuji Bank took 55 per cent of Kwong On Bank, Dai-ichi Kangyo Bank bought 95 per cent of Chekiang First Bank; and Mitsubishi Bank took 25 per cent of Liu Chong Hing Bank. In

1988 the parent of Dah Sing Bank, which had bought Hongkong Industrial and Commercial Bank, sold a 22 per cent stake to Mitsui Trust and Banking Co. For others of course, finding a big brother was more painful, as Ka Wah, Wing On and Union Bank discovered.

Many banks, particularly the smaller family-dominated Chinese banks, did little to lessen their vulnerability until it was too late. A number of factors together conspired to bring about the financial crises that occurred in the early 1980s. The financial world of the 1970s changed rapidly, becoming truly international rather than being a series of markets constrained by national boundaries. Hong Kong as an *international* city was given an important supporting role as bankers and their funds jumped over mere national boundaries. The Hong Kong authorities recognized what was happening and welcomed its importance to the increasing sophistication and development of the city; but they were slow in devising policies that would welcome new financial developments while restraining the excesses. To prevent Hong Kong being over-banked while avoiding turning away new financial institutions altogether, the authorities created a new institution, the deposit-taking company (DTC). A DTC could be set up with a minimum of fuss through a simple registration process and offered banks an opportunity to be active in international lending and merchant or investment banking without the bother of a full bank licence. Capital needs, reporting and other requirements were minimal. But in allowing the creation of DTCs the Hong Kong authorities were short-sighted. The procedures were oversimple; the controls the authorities had were negligible. In the heady days of the late 1970s everything seemed to be going right for Hong Kong; political doubts were cast aside, and the party was in full swing; everyone seemed to be making money and Hong Kong could live forever.

But registration as a DTC could cover a multitude of sins and sinners. The DTC became the popular flavour of the month and almost 350 concerns registered themselves. At one end of the scale were simple money-lenders; at the other extreme were international banks that couldn't get full bank licences. Hong Kong had trouble with both. The financial climate was aggressive and competitive, and to get business, institutions had to offer the best possible rate. The licensed banks had one hand tied behind their backs because of the government-enforced interest rate agreement. Financial Secretary of the time Sir Philip Haddon-Cave declared that with a local dollar floating freely (not anchored to the US dollar as it became after the panic of October 1983) the only control the authorities had over the money supply was through direction of interest rates. The government effectively told the banks what interest rates they could pay to depositors. This offered a measure of protection to the smaller Chinese banks – but also meant they did nothing to improve their competitiveness and remained small and liable to trouble when the good times ended. But the interest rate agreement didn't cover non-banks. DTCs could attract funds by offering higher rates than the banks, so some banks with full licences simply set up a DTC to circumvent the interest-rate restrictions. Controls about the minimum size of deposits that the DTCs could handle didn't pose a problem: in freewheeling Hong Kong deposits from several sources could be bundled as if they were one. At the smaller end, some doubtful institutions were running bucket-shop operations and gambling with depositors' money.

The Crash: A Failure of Regulation

It was all a merry-go-round of money providing an exciting ride for everyone – until the crash came. When Hong Kong's economy and politics turned sour at the same time many people found that their prudential controls hadn't been working properly and they were exposed. The authorities were not in a good position to police things because they didn't have the information or the policing skills for a complicated market. Nor, in the case of the DTCs, did they have the power to demand action.

The crises of the early 1980s posed damaging questions for government financial regulators. Until Robert Fell was appointed to succeed Colin Martin as Banking Commissioner in 1984, the Hong Kong authorities hadn't pursued the 'hands-on' policy that marked, say, Singapore's banking regime. They didn't have the trained manpower or the resources to do it. Compounding the problems for investigators was the Chinese way of doing business. Chinese families tend to be close-knit, somewhat secretive and resentful of outsiders. Management is kept within family hands. Sons are expected to follow their fathers into the bank. This is all right when one talented generation follows another, but it begins to falter when a son doesn't have the inclination or the competence to follow in his father's footsteps. It can also break down if there are several brothers, each with sons vying for predominance.

Bank management isn't the only worrying aspect of tight family control and resentment of outsiders. In addition, many of the families that ultimately came to grief had a special proprietorial attitude towards the money put into their banks. Deposits were taken from the public and then often freely lent to support businesses of the family or friends. The practice among Chinese families of closing a business deal merely with a handshake and without proper documentation simply added to the blurring of the lines between family and public funds. The Overseas Trust Bank empire was a case in point. After Chang Ming Thien's death in 1982 it was found that many loans had been made to friends and business colleagues without formal documentation. The details were known only to Chang himself. One of the most trenchant critics both of the families and of the government for its failure criticized the system in these terms:

> What is the point of controlling a bank if you cannot lend the depositors' money to your friends or relatives? This philosophy of banking as an aspect of family loyalty and *guanxi* [connections] seems to be given a boost by none other than the Hong Kong government. Some details of

> the deals by which the government's Exchange Fund will be used to preserve some family interests in the reconstructed equity of two effectively bust banks, Ka Wah and Wing On, respectively controlled hitherto by the Low and Kwok families, indicate that the authorities see little wrong with the way in which these banks made huge and apparently irrecoverable loans to family members or business associates which appear to be in breach of existing rules limiting exposure to related parties to 25 per cent of net worth. (Philip Bowring, in *Far Eastern Economic Review*, 29 May 1986)

Bowring is referring to the fact that in the case of Wing On, a 'substantial proportion' of the bank's exceptional provisions of HK$311 million for 1985 related to loans to the late deputy chairman and chief manager of the bank, Albert Kwok. Another loan, for HK$45 million, was made to the company of which Albert Kwok and brother bank chairman Philip Kwok were directors. In addition, the Kwoks, having failed to repay their debts to the bank, called on minority shareholders in other Wing On family-controlled companies to subscribe to rights issues to shore up the position of the rest of the group. In the case of Ka Wah, the Low brothers, who previously controlled 40 per cent of the bank, had their shares written down to one-twentieth of their previous value – better than nothing. The Chinese concern Citic got the bank for a bargain price, thanks to the government agreeing that the Exchange Fund would cover the bad debts, some of which were to companies in Malaysia with which the Lows had links, including some associated with disgraced Malaysian politician Tan Koon Swan.

The case of Ka Wah also showed the way in which a bank already under suspicion was allowed to continue its contentious lending right up to the moment when the government finally blew the whistle. Investigations by Cheah Cheng Hye of the *Asian Wall Street Journal* showed that bland government assurances that Ka Wah got into trouble through circumstances beyond its control were incorrect. Secretary for Monetary Affairs Douglas Blye in mid-1985 described rumours about the bank as 'completely unfounded'. But Cheah concluded, after a study of documents in Hong Kong, Malaysia, Singapore and Taiwan, that 'Ka Wah collapsed precisely because of mismanagement – deliberate mismanagement at that. A consistent pattern of abuse over many years emerges. From the late 1970s until the bank's collapse at the end of 1985, Ka Wah, a medium-sized local bank, was systematically ripped off by its own directors and executives' (*Asian Wall Street Journal*, 5 and 6 January 1987).

Union Bank provides another example of the failure of the Hong Kong authorities to keep up with the freewheeling activities of some of the colony's bankers. When US authorities arrested Oen Yin-choy, founder and chairman of Union Bank, in California in 1985, a few new facts about him came to light. Among them: that Oen had another name for use in Indonesia – James Semaun – and that he also controlled two other banks, United City Bank in Indonesia and Trans National Bank in California. The Hong Kong banking authorities didn't begin to unravel the Indonesian activities until the bank ran into trouble in 1985 and its books revealed that Indonesian lending made up more than half the portfolio and that many loans were in default while others were fictitious. The problems at Ka Wah and at Union Bank emerged after the new stricter regime was in place.

Even after Fell came and senior government officials recognized the dangers and beefed up the resources available to the regulators, there were still grumbles that officials were not paid enough to attract people of the right calibre. With salaries in the banking sector exploding skywards, it wasn't easy to see why a talented youth should be interested in becoming a bank regulator. One report in the mid-1980s said that a stockbroking analyst moved company and was given a signing-on fee of HK$3 million and a salary of HK$2 million (US$250,000) a year. At this time the Chief Secretary, the senior official in the government, was earning only HK$750,000 a year and middle-ranking bank regulators were getting about HK$300,000 a year. Equally important, until Financial Secretary Bremridge put Fell into the job with a specific mandate to clean up the system, Hong Kong's banking commissioners had limited experience. One senior foreign banker noted that until Fell's appointment 'the banking commission conceived its job as checking a bank's books to see whether the sums added up correctly. They didn't ask questions about what sums were involved, or probe into the loans.' A middle-ranking official in the Banking Commission itself added, 'Colin Martin took a strictly bureaucratic 9 to 5 view of his job.' Fell was different. Formerly chief executive of the London Stock Exchange, and before that a British civil servant who had served at home and abroad, he originally went to Hong Kong as Commissioner of Securities, and was immediately plunged into unravelling the complexities of the Carrian affair – which gave him an insight into the devious highways and byways of Chinese finance. Bremridge laid down the policy that 'protection of depositors is the most important factor', and with Fell's appointment it became more effective. Inspectors of the Banking Commission were encouraged to go beyond the books to ask leading questions, to check loans or directorships that might be linked, to examine the quality of loans and ask whether proper provisions had been made for bad debts. Officials also claimed they were encouraged to put pressure on banks if there were doubts. 'We are now saying that if an action is against the spirit of the regulations, something should be done,' commented Richard Farrant, a Bank of England official seconded as adviser to Fell (in a 1986 interview). 'We are insisting on prudent provisions' for bad debts, he added; 'we are much more confident today', an admission that before Fell arrived the Commission staff were demoralized and sought to avoid taking any decisive action.

As another indication of the new 'hands on' policy, David Nendick, Secretary for Monetary Affairs, also seconded from the Bank of England, emphasized 'the need for bank supervisors not only to have the powers, but to use them'. Banking officials must ask questions about management of risk and quality of management. But officials were circumspect about whether the new policy – if it had been implemented earlier – would have prevented any of the scandals. No one believes that the government could have stopped the Carrian affair, as that went beyond banking irregularities and into share manipulation and playing with accounts of companies. But more penetrating bank supervision might have impelled big international banks to ask prudent questions before doling out large sums of money. As to OTB, the party line expressed by Bremridge and lower officials was that 'fraud is very difficult to detect, especially where highly placed people are set on a particular course'. But one ranking official added a rider: 'we might have prevented it from spreading so far and might have asked the awkward questions earlier'.

Monetary Secretary Nendick cautioned that:

> an incompetent banker does not need to resort to fraud to lose money. I see a remarkable similarity between what happened in Hong Kong in the early 1980s and London in the mid-1970s. There was a property boom carried on the back of an enormous increase in bank lending which saw disregard of the cardinal principles of banking: (1) Is the asset you are creating going to repay the loan or service the interest payments?; and (2) Beware that what goes up can come down, and your security may not be as much as you thought, if it ever was (interview with the author).

He added the advice for bank supervisors that it is important to ask awkward questions early, or an action can become self-sustaining.

Tougher Banking Rules

New tougher banking regulations are an integral part of the current active government approach. Previously, in an attempt to sort out and classify the multiplicity of financial institutions, Financial Secretary Haddon-Cave had created a special category of deposit-taking companies that are licensed, not merely registered, in effect merchant or investment banks. Subsequently the authorities moved to strengthen both the capital and supervision of the registered DTCs and by 1986 their number had fallen by both voluntary and forced revocation to about a hundred fewer than at their peak. In September 1986 a new Banking Act came into force. Its rules set capital adequacy ratios for banks and DTCs; strengthened liquidity ratios; gave new powers to the Banking Commissioner and Financial Secretary to ensure efficiency and integrity of bank managements; placed limits on loans to a single borrower; tightened up on loans to directors; and imposed obligations on bank auditors if they come across irregularities. Other clauses demanded that the government approve bank directors and changes of 10 per cent or more in any bank voting shares.

Not everyone was satisfied by the new rules. David Li of the Bank of East Asia, backed by some other leading Chinese bankers and by the Bank of China, called for the setting up of an official discount window (a device through which banks in temporary liquidity difficulties could get help from the government), a demand resisted by the Financial Secretary and even more fiercely by the Hongkong Bank. Li and the Bank of China argued that a discount window would avoid smaller banks having to go cap in hand to the Hongkong Bank as the territory's quasi-central bank and lender of last resort. When he was Financial Secretary Bremridge had argued that a formal discount window was not necessary: 'none of us knows what a discount window means in a place like Hong Kong where there is no central bank and, more important, no government debt'. He also claimed that 'all the bits are in place' for a bank experiencing temporary liquidity difficulties to receive prompt assistance. Generally, in the authorities' view, the terms under which larger banks assist smaller banks are reasonable, and if a bigger bank did try to impose unreasonable terms, or if for some reason the larger banks were unable or unwilling to assist in a particular instance, Bremridge said 'it is always open to an individual institution to discuss the matter with the Secretary for Monetary Affairs. If the matter still cannot be satisfactorily resolved, I would be prepared to consider assistance by the Exchange Fund.'

But the then Financial Secretary also warned the legislative council that he was talking about:

> circumstances in which a bank, through no fault of its own, experiences temporary shortages of liquidity. No one must assume that the authorities will rescue a bank or its shareholders from the consequences of stupidity, mismanagement or fraud. Our interest is in the protection of depositors and the integrity of the system. It should be obvious that public money cannot be entrusted to incompetent and fraudulent managers.

He also stressed that there were limits to what the government should be expected to do.

> I do not see it as government's task to make a market in particular financial assets in order that banks can then regard those assets as truly liquid. Banks should have due regard for the intrinsic liquidity of assets which they propose to acquire. This means that *they* should assure that proper, broadly based, secondary markets develop alongside the primary markets when new debt instruments are introduced. If this does not happen the primary markets will sooner or later cease to provide a worthwhile source of finance to those seeking capital.

Secretary for Monetary Affairs Nendick has had practical experience of running lender-of-last-resort facilities. Immediately before going to Hong Kong he was deputy head of the banking department of the Bank of England. He expressed little sympathy with the complaints of Hong Kong bankers that the big banks sometimes charged penal rates. In Hong Kong, he pointed out, banks know what their overnight positions will be – which is not always the case in the UK – yet at the Bank of England he was sometimes charging banks up to 35 per cent interest for the privilege of using the discount window. For Hong Kong, the option of a full-fledged central bank is a particularly tricky one, not least because it might infringe on the terms of the Sino-British agreement on Hong Kong's future after 1997. The People's Bank of China, China's central bank, might object to the notion of a central bank in Hong Kong, seeing it as a rival institution. Peter Wrangham, director and general manager of the Hongkong Bank and at various times chairman of the Hong Kong Association of Banks, also expressed scepticism about the need for a discount organization, pointing to the costs and problems of organizations. 'Presumably, it would have a staff and keep them employed. It would have to charge a commitment fee. One of the problems of Hong Kong is that there is always a glut or famine. If you only used it during the famine, the discount would be high, as the discount house would have to secure itself . . . There are numerous practical problems with a discount window. On the other hand, the present system has worked.'

But in mid-1988 the Hong Kong government did move a step closer towards setting up the facilities that would normally be located in a central bank, without such costs. In essence, the move made the Exchange Fund (which holds the government's inner reserves), rather than the Hongkong Bank, the ultimate provider of liquidity to the interbank market. 'The changes give the Hongkong Bank greater freedom to pursue its commercial interests in case these are in conflict with its responsibilities acting in the market as our agent,' said a government spokesman (quoted in the *Financial Times*, 18 July 1988). 'They will help us to control interest rates, and will make it easier to control the link rate with the US dollar.'

Under the new deal, the Hongkong Bank maintains a Hong

Kong dollar account with the Exchange Fund and tries to keep the account's balance equal to the net clearing balance in the local banking system. The Hongkong Bank acts as clearer for all banks in the territory. The bank is charged interest on any shortfall below the equilibrium point. If a client wants to borrow a large sum in Hong Kong dollars, it will borrow from elsewhere to keep its Exchange Fund balance in equilibrium.

There are other opponents of the stricter regime. Some bankers object on the grounds that the new law is too tough and goes against the grain of an attitude that has laid emphasis on lightness rather than heavy-handed rules. Japanese banks and deposit-taking companies were upset about new capital adequacy ratios that set an absolute statutory minimum of 5 per cent and lay down up to 8 per cent for banks and 10 per cent for deposit-taking companies. The reason for the protest was obvious enough – self-interest. The Japanese banks' huge assets are carried on a narrow deposit base. Of the twenty-three Japanese institutions in Hong Kong at the end of 1985, only three would have been able to comply with a 5 per cent ratio; the average for the Japanese institutions was about 3 per cent. Managers of Japanese banks in Hong Kong said that if the capital adequacy provisions were enforced in 1986, between them Japanese banks and DTCs would need to bring in between US$30 and $50 million in fresh capital. The Japanese pleaded for special treatment on the grounds that the new regulations mixed up domestic and international demands; for banks operating primarily in international markets, the Japanese said, the ratios could be relaxed. Some local bankers supported the Japanese claim for special treatment. David Li of the Bank of East Asia suggested that a new concept of 'offshore bank' or 'limited bank' could be created to allow the Japanese to continue their essentially offshore business without bringing in large sums of new capital and without endangering the policing of the more tightly controlled local market. In his final year as Financial Secretary Bremridge bluntly dismissed the Japanese special pleading, saying 'We've got to tell them to get stuffed in a polite way' (interview with the author). He said he was against creating special considerations that would allow the Japanese any privileges they had been refused in London, New York or in their own country. This point was echoed by Wrangham of the Hongkong Bank, who expressed 'doubts whether there will be concessions in New York or London, so why should Hong Kong be different?' Monetary Secretary Nendick also expressed the need to ensure that banks in Hong Kong were not given favours they couldn't get at home. 'The one thing we don't want is banks arbitraging between different supervisory authorities.' By 1988, when the ratios came into force, banking authorities had agreed on common international standards.

Crisis and Scandal in the Stock Market

Hardly had most of the banking problems been sorted out than Hong Kong's stock market reeled under even bigger disasters. 'Black Monday', 19 October 1987, on Wall Street caused gloomy reverberations right round the world, and nowhere more so than in Hong Kong. Until shortly before the Wall Street crash the Hong Kong market had been one of the world's star performers. The Hang Seng index had reached a record high of almost 3,950 early in the month. In Hong Kong itself on 19 October the index had fallen by 420 points before Wall Street had opened.

Watching the plummeting of the New York exchange in the early hours of 20 October local time, Hong Kong's stock exchange chairman, Ronald Li Fook-shiu foresaw the Hang Seng index dropping by another 800 points or so in a single day. He telephoned the Financial Secretary Piers Jacobs before dawn to inform him that he was closing the exchange for the rest of the week, four trading days. The worry wasn't just about the stock market itself. A slump in the Hang Seng index would have presented traders on the futures exchange with liabilities of more than HK$3 billion – whereas the guarantee fund for the exchange had a puny HK$22 million in its coffers. During the days when the stock exchange was closed, the Hong Kong authorities, the stock exchange and their bankers and financial advisers put together a HK$2 billion 'lifeboat' package to avert disaster, later doubled to HK$4 billion. The Bank of China joined the support scheme. Robert Fell, who had only two months before retired as the colony's Commissioner of Banking, was appointed chief executive of the stock exchange.

When the market reopened the prophets of doom were justified. The Hang Seng index plummeted a record 1,120.70 points or 33 per cent on the first day. A roast pig was brought on to the stock exchange, almost a gesture of despair, traditionally used by Chinese when other appeals to the gods have failed. Altogether HK$1.8 billion of the futures lifeboat funds were used.

After the dust had settled, many questions remained about the operations of the Hong Kong markets. The futures exchange was in the firing line. The Hang Seng stock-index futures contract before Black Monday had been one of the world's most heavily traded, even though the stock market itself at its peak was worth only US$80 billion. Outstanding short positions against physical holdings of stock were between HK$5 and 6 billion, considerably higher than the HK$22.5 million in the capital and reserves of the futures guarantee corporation. Margin requirements were ludicrously low – for a HK$180,000 contract, only HK$15,000 had to be put up – so that the futures market resembled a casino. The financial rescue package was criticized, not least by financial institutions more or less dragooned into contributing to the lifeboat even though they may hardly have used the exchange. Among the most active players on the futures market were big financial institutions, including subsidiaries of the Hongkong Bank. Some critics contended that such bodies ought to be able to take care of themselves, and that if any financial aid was provided it should be based on the Hang Seng index itself. David Li, of the Bank of East Asia and a nephew of stock exchange chairman Ronald Li Fook-shiu, claimed that the rush to provide a bailout was evidence that the

Hongkong Bank is the most powerful player in Hong Kong, to which even the government defers.

There was criticism of the panic closing of the exchange. Some bankers and brokers conceded that it was probably inevitable to shut down the exchange, but questioned the wisdom of announcing in advance a four-day closure. Of more lasting concern were large questions about the whole organization of the Hong Kong markets.

In December 1987 the futures exchange, bolstered by new officials, announced sweeping reforms in an attempt to rebuild confidence. The exchange promised closer supervision, better monitoring of margin requirements and limits on the number of open positions a member could hold, depending on his or her capitalization. It also demanded more information about speculators and higher capitalization for members who want maximum trading freedom. The reforms were announced in advance of a general review of Hong Kong's securities industry being carried out by Ian Hay Davison, formerly chief executive of Lloyd's of London.

The end of the first chapter in the Hong Kong stock market collapse came in early January 1988, when officials of Hong Kong's Independent Commission Against Corruption (ICAC) went to Ronald Li's house at 6 a.m. one Saturday and arrested him 'in connection with inquiries into the operation of the stock exchange'. They released him on bail of HK$10 million after questioning him for ten hours. Charges were not brought until mid-January, when Li appeared in court accused of accepting an unlawful advantage from the local subsidiary of Japanese construction giants Kumagai Gumi. He was charged under the prevention of bribery ordinance with accepting an advantage – namely a beneficial interest in 1.1 million Kumagai Gumi (Hong Kong) shares without lawful authority or reasonable excuse. The Hong Kong offshoot of the Japanese construction group was one of the most successful of thirty-two companies floated on the Hong Kong exchange in 1987. Its offer of 67 million shares was oversubscribed by more than 200 times. The shares were issued at HK$2.50 each, but immediately began trading at HK$4.50, an instant windfall profit for the lucky holders.

Ronald Li, aged fifty-eight in 1987, was the flamboyant king-pin of the Hong Kong exchange. Some Hong Kong commentators described him as the third richest man in Hong Kong, with a personal fortune reputedly worth HK$14 billion. He had come to prominence in the local market during the late 1960s when he was one of a group of brokers dissatisfied with what they considered the fuddy-duddy traditional attitude of the old-established Hong Kong Stock Exchange. Li and his partners broke away and set up the Far East Stock Exchange, which became the liveliest of the four Hong Kong exchanges. He then played a key role in merging the four exchanges in 1986 into the unified Stock Exchange of Hong Kong. This meant getting agreement among more than 900 constantly bickering broker members of the exchanges, more than 600 of whom were active. In place of the rugby scrums, Hong Kong went high-tech with one of the world's most modern computer-run trading floors. Earlier in 1987 Li had caused eyebrows to be raised when he announced a proposal to float Club Volvo, claimed to be the world's largest 'girlie' nightclub (see chapter 3). Li owned under 10 per cent of the club and defended the move to apply for a market listing, declaring that 'the stock exchange is like a department store; we sell all kinds of merchandise'.

By early October 1987 Li seemed to have made an international reputation for himself. He visited the New York market as part of a Hong Kong road show. There he was celebrated in fine style by the New York industry, and declared confidently, 'we are now a stock exchange of international standing and therefore we are trying to make our stocks international'. Li loved the limelight and rode to the top helped by his quick and ready tongue. He had a reputation for unabashedly loving making money. When his only daughter was married, she caused a stir with a gown decorated with diamonds; Li himself played a supporting role with a dinner jacket sporting large diamonds for buttons.

Ronald Li walked a tightrope between his undoubted international ambitions and his very close-knit bunch of supporters. All the time that Li was boasting of Hong Kong's international prowess, there were no foreign brokers on the stock exchange committee. This was true even though by the time of the boom foreigners accounted for 70 per cent of the stock market turnover. About seventy-four of the biggest brokers account for half the stock exchange's daily trading, but Li still pandered to the gallery of local, mostly very parochial, brokers. The stock exchange itself was described by the *Asian Wall Street Journal* as 'run on the style of a family business. Its chairman answers to a board dominated by Mr Li's supporters. Its clubhouse pays rent to a company controlled by his family. It hands out legal work to a firm co-founded by one of his two sons' (27–8 November 1987). Li quickly retaliated against the charges of the big foreign institutions, claiming that 'white faces' were trying to bully the local brokers as part of their campaign to have a larger say in making of stock market decisions. His quick temper was displayed for world television cameras in October 1987 when a reporter questioned the legality of the stock exchange closure. Li slammed his fist down and demanded an apology. 'This is slanderous,' he shouted. 'What is your name, and I want my solicitor to take this down. I am going to sue you for this. You said I have acted against the law and I have committed nothing against the law – you have gone too far. If you don't retract right now you are going to get a lawsuit right now,' and with television cameras whirring Li leapt to his feet, repeating 'Charge him – take him to the police station.'

Robert Fell, the new chief executive of the stock exchange, tried to do his best at damage limitation. He said that 'any stock market in the world depends on three elements. It depends on the fact that it has professional members able to deal easily and confidently with each other; they must be able to settle those deals; and, that the listings must be of the quality that has been described [in the prospectus offering the shares]' (speech to the Foreign Correspondents' Club, Hong Kong, 12 November 1987). He claimed that the mess in Hong Kong had been exaggerated:

> When I was in London I went to the London stock exchange and talked with the brokers who were interested in this market. And the story I got was that there were cheques bouncing all over Hong Kong and there was this disruption in the market because people weren't trusting each other at all. So the first job I did here was to get a grip on these bouncing cheques, and of course, I found that there was more emotion than real truth in the stories.

Fell claimed that only about thirty cheques totalling 'no more than HK$5 million' had bounced. He pointed out that the stock exchange had come a long way in a short time. Before the amalgamation of the stock exchanges, only individual brokers were allowed to join, with individual seats. A corporate member or partnership was illegal, not just by the rules of the stock exchange, but by law. By the time of the crash there were seventy-one corporate members of the exchange. But because of the principle of one man, one vote prevailed and there was no weighting to allow corporate membership on the stock exchange committee. Fell asked whether the exchange should move from democracy to something that wasn't democracy.

New Securities Rules

Another associated issue came up in the aftermath of the crash. Fell's deputy Susan Selwyn, seconded from London, announced that she was in favour of criminal penalties against insider dealings. But a majority of the stock exchange committee was against making insider trading a criminal offence. In 1989 a bill was introduced to penalize insider trading, but as a *civil*, not a criminal offence. Offenders will be disqualified from running companies and face fines. Underlying all the problems was a basic dilemma: to institutionalize and internationalize the Hong Kong corporate and stock exchange scene with proper voices for the big international players and criminal penalties for offences would make Hong Kong internationally respectable; but it would go against the very local spirit that had built up the local exchange and economy in the first place.

When his four-hundred-page report was published in June 1988, Ian Hay Davison had little mercy on the pretenders who ranked Hong Kong as an international market. His judgement on the stock exchange was particularly damaging: 'An inside group treated the exchange as a private club rather than a public utility for the general benefit of members, investors and issuers. Its executive staff is ineffective, lacking adequate knowledge and experience to cope with the evolving and expanding securities industry, and insufficiently independent of the governing committee.' In another tough and demanding turn of phrase, Hay Davison claimed about the securities industry in Hong Kong: 'This place is absolutely stuffed with vested interests, and they can't be allowed free play.' As for the securities commission that was supposed to police the stock exchange, Hay Davison claimed it showed 'an absence of direction' and played a 'passive and reactive role'. This wasn't helped by a shortage of funds: 'repeated pleas for additional resources to cope with the rapidly developing markets had often been delayed or rejected by government'. Revenue from stamp duty on share transactions had steadily grown to HK$1.44 billion in 1987, but the annual budget of the Commissioner's office was only HK$13.4 million. The stock and futures markets were prone to manipulation by insiders. Hay Davison reported that 'Ten families controlled companies representing 54 per cent of the stock market's capitalization' in March 1988.

Hay Davison's report suggested a large number of reforms, among them:

- A complete revision of the constitution of both the stock exchange and the futures exchange to allow representation on the council for corporate and lay members as well as for individual brokers.
- A professional, independent executive for both exchanges.
- Replacement of the existing twenty-four-hour settlement system for equity dealings with a three-day settlement, and establishment of a computerized central clearing system.
- A better management system and a properly established guarantee for the futures exchange.
- A new statutory regulatory body which should be independent of the government, be funded by the market and have extensive reserve powers to back up any system of 'self-regulation'.

The report made it clear that the authorities, as well as the stock exchange itself, were at fault. The inefficiencies and inadequacies, as well as some of the more obvious manipulations of the system, should have been easily spotted and dealt with before. The *Asian Wall Street Journal* reported on 1 June 1988 that on her first day as deputy chief executive of the stock exchange at the start of 1988 Susan Selwyn asked the staff who looked after the exchange's money. She was told there was no accounts department, nor any system of financial records. Ronald Li and chief executive Jeffrey Sun paid the bills and left scraps of paper for records. 'The money wasn't misappropriated,' Selwyn told the newspaper; 'it was all out there somewhere, millions and millions sloshing around.' Some Hong Kong officials took a perverse pride in some of the antiquated parts of the system, for example share settlement. Hundreds of messengers can be seen going from one office to another by motor-cycle, bicycle and on foot, carrying bags, suitcases and even laundry baskets stuffed to the brim with share certificates. In one of the busiest offices, an officer sits simply signing his name all day long, marking the transfer of share certificates; on a busy day he signs 16,000 times. The share certificates take a complicated journey from the seller to the buyer's broker to the client or to the share depositary, often with a separate cheque for each leg of the journey.

The government accepted most of the Hay Davison recommendations and set in train a reform process. By the end of 1988 Ronald Li, Jeffrey Sun Hon-kuen and six other stock exchange officials, including Li's successor as chairman Charles Sin Cho-chiu, had been charged by the ICAC under bribery provisions. Li faced thirteen charges and the others between eight and ten each. All except one were on the listing committee before the stock market crash. The charges related to acceptance of preferential allotments of shares in return for approving company flotations. In August 1989 the Kumagai Gumi charge against Lee was dropped 'for technical reasons', but other charges' remained.

Before the fresh elections for the reconstituted stock exchange could be held in October 1988, the government vetted the list of candidates. It appointed a new independent chairman of the exchange, Sir Quo-Wei Lee, chairman of the Hang Seng Bank, and a new chief executive, thirty-six-year-old Shanghai-born Francis Yuen. Lee sat on Hong Kong's executive council until 1989, and is one of the most respected bankers in the territory. Yuen took a considerable salary cut when he left Citicorp, Scrimgeour Vickers in Hong Kong for the HK$2.5-million-a-year job. He said he originally rejected the offer. 'I said "no" unless there were substantial reforms because the chief executive's job was pretty useless – he just headed the administration, and the staff were related to the committee members and were loyal to them. Now the problem of the committees will be sorted out by the new council, so staff problems will also be sorted out' (interview with *Financial Times*, 19 October 1988).

Yuen said that Chinese-style 'family connections' would be discouraged. 'Our idea is to make it a more professionally run exchange, turning from an entrepreneurial management style to more professionalism. This means getting job responsibilities of key employees defined for the first time, sorting out conflicts of interest, developing relationships with the Securities Commission to avoid duplication, and strengthening staff in the listing department.' Yuen pointed to his strengths: his Hong Kong upbringing, US university education and international broking experience in Hong Kong. He thought that he could 'talk in their own way to the small brokers'. He explained that many of these were 'sole traders, one-man shops and stockbrokers who cannot speak English and may even be illiterate'. He gave credit to Ronald Li for 'his contribution in popularizing the stock-market', but he optimistically declared that the days of Li were past. 'I believe in historical forces – once you've gone on you can't come back. Hong Kong has gone beyond the stage of entrepreneurs running the exchange.'

Before and after the new stock exchange team took over in October 1988, moves were made to tighten the rules and see that they were adhered to. Companies were banned from issuing controversial 'B' shares (which would have higher voting rights than ordinary shares); a tightening of listing rules involving higher minimum market capitalization was promised. Planning was begun for a modernized computer-based clearing and settlement system.

However, elections for the new committee showed the strength of resistance to the idea of a fully international Hong Kong stock market. To try to achieve a balanced committee, elected seats were divided into three categories: four for individual members, four for corporate members and eight for either individual or corporate. Six other members were appointed from outside the industry. Only one non-Chinese was elected, Alan Smith, managing director of Jardine Fleming, and only one representative of an international brokerage house, John Seto of Wardley Thompson, a Hong Kong Chinese. Brokers from big international brokerages like Barclays de Zoete Wedd, Hoare Govett and County Natwest all failed to win seats. Chao Shing-On, chairman of Chung Mao Securities and of the Po

Sang Bank, both part of the Bank of China group, was elected. Some brokers cautioned against seeing the result as a rebuff to the international financial institutions, and the idea of Hong Kong as an international centre. But, in addition, the four brokers chosen for the individual seats had all been members of the previous council.

There have been some exciting new financial developments in the colony. In the mid-1980s the Hong Kong local capital market began to take off. New issues were being made at the rate of one a week and for a while Hong Kong pioneered some interesting experiments. In the space of eighteen months the market bounded, in the words of one banker, 'from being a sleepy bazaar to the fastest growing financial market in Asia'. Borrowers discovered commercial paper (CP) and certificates of deposit (CDs), both means of obtaining money more cheaply than through conventional bank loans. But in 1987 there was a slowdown. There are severe limits to what can be done in Hong Kong alone. In the local capital market there was a shortage of borrowers with prime names and a lack of a secondary market. Initially banks bought most of the paper and put it into their own vaults so that little secondary trading was done. Shortage of institutional investors is an important drawback in the secondary market. The fact that the government has virtually no tradeable debt also inhibited the growth of the Hong Kong capital market. The 1984 issue of HK$1 billion of government bonds to cover the unexpected budget deficit matured in 1989. Hong Kong officials, including a somewhat reluctant Financial Secretary Jacobs, considered the idea of introducing government paper, either short-term bills, or long-term bonds linked to specific projects, such as a new international airport. In 1989 Jacobs gave the go-ahead for the introduction of Exchange Fund bills which will allow the government to play a more sophisticated and active role in the interbank market. In addition, they will give a boost to a capital market limited to the CP and CDs with an occasional treat of floating rate notes and corporate bonds. Monetary Secretary Nendick saw the

Exchange Fund bills accumulating over a thirteen-week period to HK$5 billion.

Another attempt by the government to open up Hong Kong's system internationally attracted bitter local opposition. The government decided in 1988 to allow foreign law firms to hire local solicitors. Supporters of the move claimed it would enhance Hong Kong's reputation as a financial and commercial centre as well as leading to improved services and lower legal fees. Acting Solicitor-General Stuart Cotsen described the change as a response to the developing needs of Hong Kong as a sophisticated international commercial centre. Besides improving the legal service, it would encourage multinational companies to invest in Hong Kong and help local lawyers gain first-hand experience of big international commercial transactions. But the move was bitterly opposed by the Hong Kong Law Society, the professional body for local solicitors. Local lawyers claimed the scheme would undermine the independence of the local legal profession and lead to its domination by big foreign firms.

But the biggest resistance of all was saved for the attempt to draft a new tough securities law, setting up a watchdog with sharp teeth to guard the industry. The main author was Robert Owen, a former British government official and chairman of Lloyds Merchant Bank, headhunted for the job of chairman of the Securities and Futures Commission. Originally Owen wanted far-reaching powers, allowing his investigators to march into business premises without a search warrant; to take away the right to silence from people questioned; and to use any statements obtained as evidence in criminal proceedings against them. After howls of disapproval from the local financial community, which claimed that the Securities Commission would have more powers than the ICAC, Owen compromised and by his account included 'a lot of checks and balances'. The regulators now need a magistrate's warrant to enter premises, but there are provisions to prevent documents from 'disappearing' while the warrant is being served. The new law removes the right to silence of a person questioned, but concedes that any information he or she provides cannot be used in criminal proceedings. Owen pointed out that the revised measures meant that Hong Kong was a step behind the UK in investigations of securities dealings. The stock exchange also protested about the Commission's budget of HK$140 million a year for a staff of 225 people, particularly because the budget would be funded through a levy on stock exchange dealings.

Critics attacked the sweeping powers of punishment given to the Commission, and complained that it was doing jobs best left to other bodies. The new SFC has four functions: the listing and licensing of concerns engaged in the securities business, of which there were about 7,000 by 1989; supervising listed companies and policing of listing requirements; supervising the stock and futures exchanges; and investigation and prosecution of offences in the securities business. In some other countries, the critics argued, the second task is that of the stock exchange rather than the Commission, and it doesn't need a whole commission to check whether the head of the stock exchange is doing his job properly. Another complaint concerned the powers of investigation and prosecution. Originally, Owen's idea was that the SFC should be judge, jury and appeal court rolled into one; but, after protests, an appeals body was set up. Other critics questioned whether the commission was the right body to do the prosecution and whether its powers shouldn't be left with the police, by strengthening the commercial crimes branch of the police force.

There was also the fear, pointed out by Philip Bowring, editor of the *Far Eastern Economic Review*, that very authoritarian powers were being given to the Commission – with possibly frightening implications for authoritarianism after 1997 when China is running Hong Kong – which might not in fact be used until then, thanks to politics, bureaucracy, cynicism and naïvety. Bowring wrote: 'Result: history might repeat itself, with the government making lots of noise and spending lots of money but leaving market abuses unchecked and most of the bigger crooks at large.' A cartoon in the *Far Eastern Economic Review*

(3 November 1988) showed a huge field-gun marked SFC, but with the caption 'Don't worry – no one knows how to fire it.'

The fact that chief executive Yuen was placed at the head of the stock exchange by a colonial Hong Kong government but has to deal with a stock exchange committee regarded as philosophically close to Ronald Li will prove a major test for him. The view of traditional brokers – expressed and repeated by new chairman Sir Q. W. Lee – was that self-regulation should first be given a chance. Immediately after the elections Lee declared: 'The stock exchange ought to be a self-regulating body. The securities and futures commission will oversee us.' Yuen added: 'To maintain the stock exchange as a self regulating body is the priority job of the new council.' The original draft of the Bill setting up the SFC promised to promote the development of 'efficient and orderly conduct' of Hong Kong's markets, to 'secure the integrity of the participants' and to protect the investing public. After pressure an amendment was added requiring the Commission to promote the concept of self-regulation.

In introducing the Bill, Financial Secretary Jacobs said: 'our aim is to ensure that Hong Kong fully measures up to the standards required of major international financial centres, so that we attract the international investing community'. Asked whether more dirt was going to be uncovered, he responded, 'We have already done a lot of cleaning up in the last month and I would not expect to find much more dirt – but maybe one or two cobwebs.' Jacobs's ambitions for Hong Kong were large. They were echoed by former chief executive Robert Fell, who saw a much wider role for Hong Kong linking all the Pacific rim economies in a 'true Pacific securities market' with common listing, dealing and settlement. 'We are well placed in Hong Kong to harness technology to economics in the expansion of the utility of our market. Taking confidence from the success of our own market and our newly developed economic links, we should be beginning the political task of working with the other exchanges, not to form a unification, but to establish with them an inter-related market which is certainly within our grasp.' But

Fell's confidence ignored how small and really restricted the local stock market is – in spite of its international reputation. Hong Kong's market capitalization is a tiny fraction of that of Tokyo, and indeed lower than that of any other world market apart from Seoul and Singapore. With fewer than 300 quoted companies, that gives less variety than any other world market apart from Milan. Property firms make up a quarter of the value of all shares. There are just twelve foreign stocks quoted on the exchange. International fund managers who do invest in the Hong Kong market typically place only a small fraction of their funds there, maybe 1 or 2 per cent. New York, London, Frankfurt, Paris are all bigger, more diversified, more attractive and more liquid markets. Seoul and Taipei are up-and-coming stock markets, potentially bigger than Hong Kong simply because their own populations and economies are bigger. And the biggest stock market of all is only three to four hours' flying time from Hong Kong: Tokyo today accounts for about 40 per cent of total major world stock market capitalization on its own.

The Rise and Rise of Tokyo

The biggest change that occurred in the 1980s was the rise and rise of Tokyo, both in banking and in broking.

In spite of Hong Kong's superiority when it comes to doing business, the weight of money in Japan is beginning to tell. When bankers talk of round-the-clock global trading in equities or in government securities, they are talking of Tokyo as the third leg (with New York and London) in the twenty-four-hour trading sytem. Tokyo is horrendously expensive for foreign banks, and the Japanese still maintain an insular if not racist attitude towards foreigners. But Robert Binney, senior vice president of Chase Manhattan Bank and its general manager in Tokyo until 1988, commented: 'Hong Kong is becoming a backwater financially compared to Tokyo. This is where all the action is.' Sir Piers Jacobs, who took over from Sir John Bremridge as Financial Secretary in 1986, derided the claim of being the world's number 3 as 'ridiculous – it is probably based on the number of financial institutions in Hong Kong.' The best that the colony can expect is to be a satellite of Tokyo. Yusuke Kashiwagi, chairman of the Bank of Tokyo, supports this idea. In September 1986 he predicted: 'The growth of the Tokyo financial market will enhance Hong Kong and Singapore. They will become important satellites of the Tokyo market' – as Frankfurt and Paris are of London, he suggested.

The reasons for the rise and rise of Tokyo are obvious enough. Thanks to its growing surpluses on the trade and current accounts, Japan is the largest provider of capital to the rest of the world. The United States has slumped and by 1986 was the world's biggest net debtor, far more heavily in debt than Brazil or Mexico or any Latin American country.

Japan is emerging as effective banker to the world. The figures are big. In 1986 Japan took over from the United Kingdom as the world's largest creditor nation, with a net balance a little over $120 billion. By the end of the century, forecasts the influential Japan Economic Research Center, the net Japanese balance with the rest of the world will be US$3,000 billion – that's if Japanese exclusiveness does not invite political action to curb the surpluses. By the 1990s interest income from the capital exports should make the current account surplus self-sustaining. Perversely, the best hope of a smaller surplus will be if Japan continues to lose money investing in US Treasury bonds. The vastness of these sums explains Japan's rise. It may not be a popular place from which to do business, but it is essential for financial institutions to be close to the source of capital flows. By the mid-1980s Japan's financial muscle was beginning to make itself felt. The big Japanese broker, Nomura Securities Company, became the world's most profitable financial institution. In auctions of US Treasury bonds, Japanese institutional investors were taking up to 40 per cent. Without Japanese buyers US interest rates would probably have to be raised by several percentage points and markets frequently fluttered on rumours that the Japanese might be staying out of the next auction. Tokyo became an important partner with New York in trading the US instruments, with London also doing some business to maintain the twenty-four-hour trading clock. The growth of US debt and of Japanese capital exports encouraged the role of Tokyo as the third leg in the global financial system. So did trends towards growing securitization of financial instruments and away from heavy bank lending to developing countries. Syndicated lending at the start of the 1980s accounted for almost 80 per cent of merchant banking business in Hong Kong; by the middle of the decade it was only 10 per cent.

Hong Kong super-optimists say that Japan hasn't yet developed the international understanding that is Hong Kong's great advantage. Moreover, Asia is a big continent. Let Tokyo strengthen its position as the global financial centre; and Hong Kong will serve the rest of the region with its 2.5 billion people, half of mankind. Superficially, this is an attractive proposition: after all Japanese banks are already in Hong Kong and have built up their assets, so they must find the colony profitable. But the establishment in 1986 of an offshore financial centre in Tokyo itself meant that Japanese banks were increasingly doing offshore activities at home. Japan will come to accept that it has to play an international role. The idea of Hong Kong as a centre for other Asian countries' financial activities is appealing, but runs counter to the nationalist desires of those countries to keep business for themselves. It also ignores the fact that – unlike say the UK with its international financial powerhouse in the City of London – Hong Kong's domestic base is tiny. The Asian countries are at vastly different levels of development. In all, it's hard to see Hong Kong as the capital market for India or Indonesia.

That still leaves China as a source of promising financial activity. China's international borrowings have greatly increased. But since Deng Xiaoping became China's strongman, heralding a new era, an opening to the world and a rapid increase in China's economic development, bankers have learned from hard experience that the promised China boom is like the pot of gold at the other end of the rainbow. Profits from China business are slow and hard-won and won't pay the rent on their own. China itself has spoken warmly of the importance of continuing to promote Hong Kong as a financial centre. One of the best signs, say the optimists, is that the Chinese banks themselves have greatly expanded their Hong Kong activities. Growth of the Bank of China and its sister banks has been among the fastest of all. Between 1985 and 1987 the banks' assets and deposits were rising at about 30 per cent a year. By the late 1980s the Communist banks together had about 20 per cent of the bank deposits in Hong Kong, enough to mount a stiff challenge to the domination of the Hongkong Bank. The entry of Citic (purchasing Ka Wah) and the China Merchant Steam Navigation Co. (Union Bank) surely shows a desire on the part of China to make Hong Kong work and to profit from it. The super-optimists see the Hong Kong stock market boosted by listing of Chinese companies such as Citic and China Merchants. But there have been some hard experiences along the way. Chinese banks (admittedly along with others) were overcommitted to Hong Kong property when the market turned down. Their financial support for companies which ran into financial difficulties taught them that capitalism isn't an easy road. The 1987 stock market crash also caught many of the mainland Chinese concerns in Hong Kong unawares.

It is as well not to be carried away by the dream of China. Not everyone in China wants to see Hong Kong as the financial centre for the whole country. Leaders in Shanghai remember the glorious days when Shanghai was the centre of China; there are officials in Peking who think that the capital should rule the roost; there are even officials in South China who think the financial capital of the south should be Guangdong (Canton), not Hong Kong. To all of these Chinese officials, Hong Kong is the intruder. If a flourishing centre adds jobs and revenues why should Hong Kong benefit? Why not China?

There's always something self-seeking about China's attitude to Hong Kong. This was the clear undertone of comments made in 1985 by Jiang Wengui, vice-chairman of the Bank of China and the man responsible for the success of the bank and its sisters in the colony. Jiang approved of Hong Kong's international role, saying 'If Hong Kong can keep its position as an international financial centre, this will be a benefit to the economic development of the Asia Pacific region, to Hong Kong's economic ties with the various countries of the region and with western countries and to the economic construction of China.'

In the same article he also suggested that something should be done to make the secondary market in bonds, commercial paper and certificates of deposit more attractive in Hong Kong. This comment was immediately seen as a suggestion that China wants to put more of its own debt paper into Hong Kong. Earlier in the year Jiang had also pointedly suggested that Hong Kong banks awash with liquidity should club together to make syndicated loans available to China. 'What they seem to be saying is that Hong Kong should be an important international centre – but for China's benefit', warns a Hong Kong official. 'But if Hong Kong is setting itself up for China's benefit that could spell the end of its international role.' It will require brave Hong Kong officials indeed to keep this in mind and be prepared to resist China.

After 1997 Hong Kong will be under the sway of a Communist regime, whatever the fine promises of the agreement with Britain. This will undoubtedly involve an element of political risk in investments in Hong Kong. As a sceptical Hong Kong economist wrote in 1987, 'who would keep a trust account in Belgrade or Budapest so long as Zurich is available? This is the bottom line of international financial life.' The question that remains is whether the Bank of China's headquarters in Hong Kong is a monument to China's acceptance of the old freewheeling ways, or whether it is a Trojan horse for a different kind of era. In the aftermath of Tian'anmen Square young Hong Kong

Chinese financial managers increasingly decided that not only could they not risk their savings in a Communist-ruled Hong Kong, but they did not want to be around themselves either.

9 CAPTAINS OF FINANCE AND BUSINESS

Jardine Matheson: *The Princely Hong*

If any one person or company embodies the spirit of Hong Kong, Jardine Matheson, the so-called 'princely *hong*' has the best boast to that claim. (The *hongs* are old-established trading companies.) Indeed, not only is the company ten years older than Hong Kong, but one of its founders, William Jardine, was principally responsible for the foundation of the colony. From 1830 to 1840 he was active both on the China coast in forcing open trade with China and back home in Britain, where he persistently urged British Foreign Secretary Lord Palmerston and Parliament to teach China a lesson. Later Jardines came to represent the epitome of British business in Hong Kong, and was the model for James Clavell's blockbuster novels, *Taipan* and *Noble House*. (The company is today normally familiarly called Jardines.)

Even today a casual visitor might imagine that Jardines still controls Hong Kong. It seems to have a finger in every business pie. Immediately on arrival at Kai Tak airport, visitors encounter Hong Kong Air Terminal Services, 50 per cent Jardines-owned, responsible for offloading them and their baggage from the aircraft. The car to the hotel may well be a Mercedes distributed by Zung Fu Company, 75 per cent of which belongs to Jardines. A visitor may go to the Mandarin Oriental Hotel, reckoned to be one of the top five hotels in the world; or if he or she is less well heeled, to the Excelsior; both are in Jardines' empire. If on financial business, the visitor is bound to come across Jardine Fleming, a leading merchant bank and stock-broker, a joint venture between Jardines and Robert Fleming and Co. of London. If he or she goes shopping, whatever the price-range she or he can't miss buying something distributed by Jardines: its products range from luxury goods by Dior and Dunhill, through Canon cameras to White Label Scotch and Hennessy cognac, down to a myriad of mundane items on sale at 300 retail outlets belonging to the Dairy Farm group.

The visitor wanting a Chinese meal may go to a Maxim's restaurant, also part of the empire. If a late snack is required Jardines has the franchise for Pizza Huts and for 250 7–Eleven stores open twenty-four hours a day. Whether admiring the pace of development or cursing the noise and dust kicked up by the bulldozers and constantly clashing pile-drivers constructing an ever-new Hong Kong, the chances are that the visitor will be looking at a project by Gammon, Jardines' joint-venture construction associate. Even if he or she merely wants a casual stroll in central Hong Kong, it's hard to get off Jardines territory. Many of the buildings in the central area are owned by the Hongkong Land Co. These include the twin-tower Landmark, the Mandarin, Jardines' own fifty-storey Jardine House headquarters (formerly called Connaught Centre) and Exchange Square, one of the smartest new buildings in Hong Kong that is turning into the territory's financial centre, housing the new stock exchange and hosts of banks and financial institutions. Altogether it is estimated that the Land company owns central Hong Kong property worth more than US$3 billion. When the time comes to go home, Jardines will see that the visitor goes safely on his way. If travelling on British Airways, Air France, Air India or on China's national airline, his or her airport arrangements will be handled by Jardine Airways (which has no airline of its own). Having checked in and cleared immigration, a 50 per cent Jardines venture is responsible for the security clearance before the passenger reaches the final departure gate.

All this is impressive evidence that Jardines is a big player in the modern colony. But times have been pretty tough recently. The real financial muscle in Hong Kong no longer belongs to the British tycoons but to local Chinese who are friends of China. Jardines had to spend most of the 1980s fighting for its very existence against Chinese predators. Symbolic of the changing times was Jardines' decision in 1984 to transfer its registered headquarters from Hong Kong to the Caribbean island of Bermuda. Bermuda is still a British possession and the move summed up the distrust which the oldest of old colonial concerns felt about Hong Kong being ruled by China. It wanted to stay safely British, subject to British law, not trusting the Chinese. The announcement rocked the local stock market. Simon Keswick, then Jardines' chairman and architect of the move to Bermuda, denied that Jardines was pulling out of Hong Kong and China. After all, it would be difficult, given the Land Company's big property empire right in the heart of Hong Kong. Subsequently, in 1987, Jardines put through a major corporate restructuring to strengthen its hold over the rest of the empire while keeping the greatest flexibility. In 1988 there was more scrambling to ward off the Chinese threat to the big Land Company.

Of Jardines' close involvement not just in the history, but in the actual creation of Hong Kong, there is no doubt. Its colonial past was remembered in the 150th anniversary year of its foundation in 1982. As part of the celebrations the company asked local Hong Kong Chinese what they thought of its revamped company logo, representing a thistle, a reminder of the Scottish origins of the two founders, William Jardine and James Matheson. A number of Chinese responded that they thought the logo represented the opium poppy. As described in chapter 2, opium was at the centre of Jardines' existence for many of its formative years.

One of the contributors to *The Thistle and the Jade* (the coffee-table book commemorating the first 150 years of the company) noted,

> It was the opium war that began the forcing of China's door; it was the forcing of China's door that permitted Jardine, Matheson and Co. to become what it has become. A China permanently shut to western enterprise, if such a thing is imaginable, would have reduced the 150th birthday of our firm to the simple celebration of a rather small thing that had nevertheless managed to hang on for rather a long time.

William Jardine, 'the iron-headed old rat' as the Chinese called him, and James Matheson were both from Scottish families. Jardine left Scotland in 1802 when he was eighteen to join the East Indiaman *Brunswick* as surgeon's mate. Promotion gave him an allowance of 'privilege space' to ship cargo on his own account, or to sublet to others, and this activity taught him about Far East trade. He apparently learned quickly, since in 1817 he left the East India Company's service and applied to become a 'free merchant'. He was reputedly a tough, shrewd character, as evidenced by the story of the single chair (his own) in his office. His partner James Matheson was of Highland stock and founded the first English language news sheet in China, the *Canton Register*. The partnership of the two men was actually the last in a series of businesses which, notes Jardines' historian Alan Reid, 'changed names as often as the partners came and went . . . The changes start to look like intricate to-ing and fro-ing of some Scottish reel, except that departing partners left the dance altogether, some claimed by success, some by bankruptcy and some by the little cemeteries at Whampoa and Macao.'

Jardine Matheson was actually founded at Canton in 1832, and in some ways it is surprising that the name has persisted. Neither man had a child and by the early 1840s neither was active in Hong Kong or China. Jardine died in 1843, and Matheson departed early for the UK, where he became an MP.

1. The view from the top: Bank of China seventy-two-storey skyscraper towers over the Hongkong Bank's headquarters and myriad other booming palaces of commerce and finance.

2. Governor Sir David Wilson.

3. Financial Secretary Sir Piers Jacobs.

4. Government House, spick and span, but a superior dolls' house compared to the skyscrapers around.

5. At Yau Ma Tei an ancient sampan operator ferries passengers to the boats moored in the typhoon shelter.

6. The peace of Lantau's village of Tai O contrasts with . . .

7. Bustling overcrowded Kowloon.

8. Trade: Sam the tailor at work in his Tsim Sha Tsui shop (see Chapter 2).

9. And Finance: the Hongkong Bank and Bank of China skyscrapers straddle Lower Albert Road, where the main government offices are situated.

10. Tranquil Po Lin Buddhist monastery on Lantau.

11. (*Above left*) A tiny girl learns from her grandmother how to play with fortune-telling sticks at Wong Tai Sin Taoist temple. The god reputedly gives horse-racing tips and cures illnesses.

12. (*Above right*) An old woman in traditional black pyjama costume makes offerings at a temple on Hong Kong dedicated to Sui Tsing Paak and Tin Hau.

13. From the outside the Walled City might be just any other part of seedy overcrowded Kowloon.

14. But inside, the Walled City is a fetid rabbit-warren. Local factories are important suppliers to the cocktail circuit in luxury hotels. A man makes buns. (See Chapter 11.)

15. Old and new on Hong Kong: a tram passes the Legislative Council building, with the Mandarin Oriental Hotel, Jardine House and Exchange Square in the background.

16. Hong Kong is full of entrepreneurs: a fisherman sells his catch on the seashore.

17. (*Left*) The sharp knife-like edges of I. M. Pei's new Bank of China building tower over Hong Kong's Legislative Council building (formerly the Supreme Court).

18. (*Right*) The lion guardian of the Hongkong Bank headquarters holds no terror for local Chinese.

19. In Hong Kong anything goes – magazines showing Chairman Mao Zedong and other Communist leaders are placed alongside scantily clad girlie covers.

20. China's special economic zone, Shenzhen, displays towering progress, but most of the investment money comes from Hong Kong.

21. Vietnamese refugee children wonder when they'll ever be free.

22. A Hong Kong Chinese in his cardboard-box home adjoining the General Post Office.

23. A Cathay Pacific Airways' TriStar about to land skims over Kowloon almost close enough to pick up the family washing.

24. Varieties of housing: housing on Diamond Hill consists of hugger mugger shanties, with new housing blocks in the background.

25. A man takes his birds for a walk.

26. Mother, with child carried traditional-style, goes to market.

27. Diamond Hill child has to do the family washing under an open tap.

28. Isabelita Santos, a Filipina amah – of whom there are 40,000 in Hong Kong – with blond expatriate boy, Fearghas Hilton.

29. New housing blocks behind a rickety junk house at Yau Ma Tei.

The names 'Jardine' and 'Matheson' slowly disappeared from the company executive roll, and the last Jardine left the Hong Kong company board more than sixty years ago. But it remains a 'family' concern. Even today members of the Keswick family, which has supplied two of the last three *taipans* (Hong Kong local slang meaning approximately 'big boss') of Jardine Matheson, boast that they are direct descendants of a sister of the founding Jardine.

With foundations built on the opium trade, Jardines avoided the pitfalls that sent many of the other trading agencies that were for a brief while household names skidding into bankruptcy. The greater part of the company's business was in China itself; but in smug little colonial Hong Kong the company gained strength as well as no small reputation for arrogance, to which the daily 'Noon-Day Gun' still testifies. The recoil-mounted three-pound Hotchkiss built in Portsmouth in 1901 is fired from a site in front of the Excelsior Hotel.

But by the late twentieth century, Jardine Matheson had become the subject of power plays, both internal and external. The battles surrounding the company provided living examples that truth is often stranger than fiction. However, unlike the heroes of epic novels, Jardines real-life executives proved all too human, struggling and fallible. As we have already seen, Hong Kong's business community has changed rapidly since the Second World War. No longer do British pedigree or a good public school education count in a colony where money increasingly makes things move. And in the money games of the twentieth century, rising Chinese self-made billionaires have proved more adept on their own turf than the traditional and often complacent colonialists. In the early 1980s lively questions were being asked about whether Jardines would survive at all, or would be picked up and picked over by one of the newly rich Chinese entrepreneurs.

The first public blows showing the obviously changed Hong Kong business scene were struck in 1980, when Jardines had to yield control of the Hongkong and Kowloon Wharf and Godown

Company. This company, commonly known as 'Wharf', and the Hongkong Land Company had both been founded, in 1886 and 1889 respectively, by Sir Catchick Paul Chater and Jardines' partners. The princely *hong* had apparently been lulled into a false sense of security by a clause in the articles of the Wharf company allowing it to provide the chairman. Over the years Jardines' shareholding had fallen below 5 per cent. To its surprise, Chinese shipping billionaire Sir Yue-Kong Pao had bought a 17 per cent stake in Wharf in 1978, and subsequently increased it to 30 per cent. Dramatically, over a weekend in June 1980, the old *hong* and the rich Chinese newcomer were locked in a takeover play that excited banner headlines in the British as well as the Hong Kong press. In the end, the princely *hong* had to surrender the Wharf company. Pao put together a HK$2.2 billion financial package over a weekend to take his holding to 49 per cent. Jardines had the final humiliation of convening a special meeting of shareholders to change the articles of association and yield the Wharf chair to Pao.

Jardine Fleming, Jardines' merchant bankers, did manage a pleasant parting shot in the form of a HK$2 billion payoff for selling the Hongkong Land Company's 20 per cent holding in Wharf. This was achieved in spite of specific instructions from Pao not to buy from Land. His own advisers, Wardley, the Hongkong Bank group's merchant banking arm, made the mistake. John Boyer, chairman of the merchant bank (and deputy chairman of the bank itself), agreed over the weekend at home on the telephone to take 10 per cent, not suspecting who the seller was. David Newbigging, then Jardines and Land chairman, says that another 10 per cent was offloaded in the market; 'we thought that the offer price was too fancy and it was better to take his money than raise our bid.'

That was only the first stage in the poker game. Pundits predicted that the next target for the marauding *nouveaux riches* Chinese would be either Jardines itself or more likely its associate Hongkong Land. Newbigging himself played the role of worthy *taipan* when in late October 1980, in a man-to-man session at

Jardines' forty-eighth-floor headquarters in the Connaught Centre (as it was then called), he persuaded Chinese property baron Li Ka-shing to sell his 25 million shares in Jardines, 10 per cent of the equity. The fear was that Li might try to get Land through his Jardine stake. The next stage came in early November, when Newbigging and Jardine Fleming masterminded a deal giving the two associates 40 per cent crossholdings in each other. The culmination of the masterstroke was the purchase by Jardines of 80 million shares and share equivalents in Hongkong Land through open market operations on Monday 3 November 1980 at HK$30 per share. To accomplish this, Jardines put together credit lines totalling HK$4 billion in a single weekend, and was ready to swoop come the opening bell on the Hong Kong stock market. Company executives patted themselves on the back. The then finance director William Downey claimed that it was a reflection of the company's excellent standing that it could put together such a support package over a weekend. Chairman Newbigging remembered: 'Security was extremely tight, and I don't think anyone expected it to happen that Monday morning. In fact, quite the opposite: people were expecting someone to bid for Jardines.' With the interlocking 40 per cent holdings Jardines and Land were regarded as invulnerable to any but the richest and most determined bidder. But there was a price to pay: repaying the money spent on the purchase. Many business analysts regarded it as a pyrrhic victory. In 1981 the interest cost of Jardines' investment in Hongkong Land was HK$620 million, whereas the company's contribution to Jardines' profits was HK$494 million.

In addition, Hongkong Land, previously regarded as a cash cow because of its rich property income from prime central Hong Kong buildings, had chosen the market peak as the occasion on which to splash out on a series of controversial investments. When the property market began to tumble and interest rates remained high, the servicing costs of the debts became enormous. The battleground now changed; an equally fascinating struggle took place inside the Jardines camp.

It was a bitter struggle. The previously ruling Keswick family clearly regarded it as treason that its throne had been usurped by David Newbigging. Newbigging supporters boasted that he was a professional manager who would modernize and eliminate once and for all the British public-school colonial image. Newbigging too was a Jardine man, but only one generation deep. His father had been a director of the company before the war and might have become *taipan* had not his health been damaged by war-time imprisonment by the Japanese. Newbigging had his handicaps. He was a prickly character. Simon Murray (a colourful personality who had served in the French Foreign Legion, and wrote a book about it, before becoming a senior Jardine executive and then quitting because he hadn't been made a director by the time he was forty) recalls meetings that 'Newb' chaired. 'He would go round the table at the "morning prayer" meetings. If the person two before you had no contribution to make, then you began to get worried. If the immediately previous person said nothing then you knew you *had* to speak, but not for too long. Anything above 30 seconds Newb regarded as long-winded and you risked being cut off.' Murray regarded Newbigging as 'a funny guy. In a one-to-one conversation he could be charm itself. But in a group he was on his dignity and could not bear to be contradicted or challenged.' Company insiders praised Newbigging for tidying up Jardines' empire after an orgy of takeovers in the years when Henry Keswick was chairman. But his prickliness led some friends to describe him as a good chief of staff rather than an effective chairman.

In the eyes of the Keswicks, one of Newbigging's main crimes was that he'd lost control of the Wharf company. Newbigging himself claimed that it wasn't his fault; that the holdings had been run down before he was in charge. 'When I first became aware of the significance of these things,' he shrugged, 'we were down at 5 per cent and then got a bit less.' Asked why the holdings were reduced, he responded, 'Don't ask me. It was before my time. I suppose it must have been a conscious decision. You don't just sit and let it happen when it is a major associate and when, by the articles of association, Jardines has to provide the chairman.' But the Keswick family was clearly unhappy. Other sources within the group said that in the late 1970s (while Newbigging was chairman) executives at Jardine Fleming had produced a plan to protect all three companies, Jardines, Land and Wharf, but it was not taken up.

Henry Keswick, Newbigging's predecessor, sat brooding in London where he'd gone hoping, family friends said, to get into politics. But all his money, his business experience gathered from Jardines (where he had become chairman at the age of thirty-four), and his boyish charm failed when it came to getting a safe Conservative seat at Westminster. He bought the *Spectator* magazine and later sold it. He had time on his hands and, turing his attention back to Hong Kong, wanted to place his younger brother Simon in what the Keswicks regarded as the traditonal family seat, the chairmanship of Jardines. There were disputes about the size of the Keswick family holding. Some analysts claimed it was as little as 6 per cent. Henry Keswick said in late 1982, just before he made his move against Newbigging, that the holding was 'more than 10 but less than 20'. But the Keswicks clearly had many friends in the City of London, and some of those were strong institutional shareholders in Jardines.

The first public indication of the in-fighting between the Keswicks and Newbigging surfaced in 1979, when it was declared that the board had 'unanimously' endorsed Newbigging as chairman for at least five years. 'Whoever heard of a big public company making such a statement in support of the chairman,' Simon Keswick later scoffed (in an interview with this author). In fact the quarrelling had begun in 1977, only two years after Newbigging had taken over.

The Keswicks really got their chance in the early 1980s when Hongkong Land, Jardines' 'Siamese twin' after the crossholdings, went on a spending spree. Newbigging was also chairman of Land, which bought controlling holdings in two utility companies, Hongkong Electric Holdings and Hong Kong Telephone Company, made joint ventures with the controversial Carrian group, and paid a massive HK$4.7 billion for the site on which Exchange Square was later built. Even at the time it seemed like delusions of grandeur; coming at the time of property price collapse it left Land vulnerable. From being cash rich, with virtually no debt, the Land Company rapidly found itself with rapidly growing debts.

Thanks to the crossholdings and equity accounting, the already heavily indebted Jardines was doubly indebted, carrying HK$14 billion of debts on shareholders' funds of less than half that. With interest rates at record highs, 'the reality was that the companies could not service the debt', claimed Simon Keswick, adding that 'at one time we did think that the only way of getting rid of David Newbigging might be in going bust' (interview with this author). In the end it was nothing quite as dramatic. After a showdown, and a reportedly handsome pay-off, Newbigging stepped down as chairman in 1984, but left Simon Keswick to run the company on a day-to-day basis from mid-1983. In 1984 Simon Keswick took over what was seen as the family inheritance, the fifth Keswick to be chairman.

Simon Keswick's first step was to transfer the registration of the company to Bermuda. The next step was to bring the debts under control. 'We bet the ranch at the wrong time,' said Brian Powers (*Financial Times*, 16 February 1987), an American lawyer who was brought on to the Jardines board to be responsible for the group's strategy. Powers came from a New York investment bank. David Davies, a Briton who'd also had a career in investment banking and in property, was brought in to bring Land under control. Chairman Keswick dismantled much of the group superstructure, reducing the number of executives on the top floor of the Connaught Centre from twenty-two to five. Managers of individual companies were left to run them without too much hindrance from group headquarters. Some assets were sold off under virtual distress conditions. The Hongkong Electric stake was sold to Li Ka-shing and that in Hong Kong Telephone to Cable and Wireless. The company was helped by economic and stock market recoveries and by falling interest rates, which reduced the debt burden.

The final stages of the Keswicks' masterplan for restructuring of Jardines' empire were revealed in late 1986 and early 1987, and brought a falling out with David Davies, who resigned and later went to London to head Britain's Hill Samuel merchant bank. Davies objected to the selling off of Land concerns. The first step came with the flotation of Hongkong Land's 100-per-cent-owned Dairy Farm Company, which ran profitable supermarkets and other retailing activities. Dairy Farm was sold to shareholders of Land by means of a rights issue. In 1987 the rest of the scheme was put into place. Another Hongkong Land activity, the Mandarin Oriental Hotels group, owners and managers of the successful hotel of the same name in Hong Kong and other top-ranking luxury hotels in Asia and round the world, was spun off as a separate company.

Thus there were three operating companies within the former Hongkong Land group, namely Hongkong Land itself, now a pure property player, the Mandarin Hotels and Dairy Farm. There were four operating companies if Jardines is included, through its operating arm Jardines Securities. Jardines Securities was renamed Jardine Strategic Holdings. The complicated cross-ownerships designed to protect both Jardines and the Land group from a hostile takeover were then revamped.

In the 1986/87 reorganization, Jardine Matheson Holdings (the Bermuda-registered company) took a 49 per cent stake in Jardine Strategic Holdings, which itself owned 26 per cent of Jardine Matheson Holdings. The two Jardine companies also held big stakes in the three Land companies that were thought effective to ensure their control of the now split-up Land group. Jardine Strategic Holdings had 35 per cent in Mandarin Oriental Hotels, 27 per cent in Dairy Farm and 15 per cent in Hongkong Land, while Jardine Matheson Holdings owned another 9 per cent of Dairy Farm and 11 per cent of Hongkong Land. All of the companies were newly incorporated in

Bermuda. Simon Keswick declared that new corporate arrangements 'will soon be seen by the business schools like Harvard as a textbook restructuring exercise'.

At management level Keswick tried to create a super-level of strategic planners and thinkers, to leave operating executives free to get on with the day-to-day business without having to worry about such matters as whether the company should be expanding or run down, or even sold. Alongside corporate restructuring, Keswick's advisers devised plans for capital restructuring, to create a new class of shares, called 'B' shares, and to introduce leveraged voting rights. The 'B' shares would be in the ratio of four 'B' shares for every existing ordinary share, with a value of only 10 per cent of the ordinary shares, but with the same voting rights. In effect, this offered the Keswick family the chance of raising its holding to 28 per cent (assuming it had previously owned 10 per cent) by converting its 'A' shares without spending any money. Alternatively, it could raise its stake to 35 per cent for just over HK$250 million or to 50.1 per cent by paying HK$1.87 billion for 'B' shares. This would ensure complete control of a group then enjoying market capitalization of HK$10 billion. The whole scheme was done carefully, step by step to forestall the possibility of a predator pouncing before the arrangements could be completed.

For several weeks the situation seemed set fair. Jardines believed it had got approval from the authorities for the capital restructuring. But then in early 1987 several other companies tried to jump in and there was a spate of proposed issues of new categories of 'B' shares. The Hong Kong stock exchange suspended all plans for such special share issues, including Jardines', amid accusations that such 'B' shares were 'unfair'. Simon Keswick responded that many international companies had categories of shares:

> Some of the most magnificent and renowned companies have them. General Motors has several classes of shares and Japan is riddled with companies that have A, B and C

shares. There has been a lot of talk that it is unfair to have two classes of shares, but the issue was to be put to shareholders. Should the regulators have a greater influence than shareholders? If a company depends heavily on good will, different categories of shares may be important to protect it from takeover bids.

Even before Simon Keswick handed over the reins and went back to London in mid-1988, his textbook reorganization was found wanting, and Jardines' holding of the Land company had to be shored up. In May it was announced that Jardines had spent HK$1.83 billion (US$234.6 million) in buying an 8 per cent stake in the Land company from a consortium of local businessmen. The most prominent figure in the consortium was none other than Li Ka-shing, again pursuing his long-cherished dream of adding Land to his empire, to make him Hong Kong's undisputed property king. Others in the group were two local property developers, Cheng Yu-tong of New World Development and Lee Shau-kee of Henderson Land, plus the Peking-based China International Trust and Investment Corporation (Citic).

The deal also contained a promise by Li and his Chinese partners that they would keep their hands off the five Jardine-controlled companies for at least seven years. Agreement marked the culmination of a nervous six months in which the Hong Kong stock market had echoed with speculation that a group was planning a takeover of the Land company. Li and his partners had begun buying Land shares in October 1987 just before the stock market crash. The share price peaked at HK$11.70, at which time Li discussed buying Jardines' stake for HK$16.50 a share, and was rebuffed. Then the price of Land stock had plummeted to HK$7 a share as the market fell headlong. The deal with Li Ka-shing was struck at about HK$8.95 a share, just above market prices, but leaving the Chinese consortium with considerable losses. Keswick commented: 'Once and for all, people will accept that Jardines is here to stay in Hong Kong.'

As a result of the frustrated takeover attempt, Jardines raised its stakes in each of the associated companies, realizing that the previous levels, unassisted by a special category of 'B' shares, were insufficient. Jardine Matheson Holdings increased to 55 per cent its holding in Jardine Strategic Holdings, and the latter also increased its stake in the holding company to 32 per cent. Jardines' stakes in each of the other associates were also raised, in the Land company to 32 per cent, in Mandarin Oriental to 43 per cent and in Dairy Farm to 45 per cent.

Alongside Simon Keswick at the negotiating table with Li was Brian Powers, then thirty-eight years old, who took over from Keswick in mid-1988 as chairman and became the first American *taipan* of the princely *hong*. Powers said of the deal with Li, 'we quite frankly hadn't found anything better to invest in than the stock of our own companies'. It was a revealing statement. Powers had first met Simon Keswick when handling the sale of the Jardines' sugar estates in Hawaii – an acquisition that dated back to the expansionary period before Newbigging took over. After the 1987 restructuring Powers was made managing director of Jardines and chairman of Land, and his first move was to make a deal for a 20 per cent stake in the New York securities house Bear Sterns. This was done on the eve of the great Wall Street crash at the very top of the market. Jardines later invoked an escape clause to pull out of the deal. A lawsuit was started, disputing the cancellation. Analysts were puzzled about the planned acquisition, since the street-wise and Jewish-dominated firm didn't seem to fit well with the very *British* Jardine Fleming. Cynics simply commented that Jardines was living up to its reputation by buying at the top of the market. Powers himself lasted only five months as *taipan*. He resigned and went to the USA at the end of 1988 reportedly because of his wife's illness, though there were rumours of a falling-out with the Keswicks. He was succeeded by Nigel Rich, an accountant by training, seen as 'sound' and enjoying a friendly relationship with Simon Keswick. The Keswicks retained the chairmanship, though in a non-executive role from London. In 1989 Henry Keswick took over as Jardines' chairman from his brother Simon.

When Keswick departed for London he left behind a company with sharply reduced debts. Critical stock market analysts noted however that the debts were held by the companies at the top of the pyramid, while the cash was being made by those at the bottom of the structure. This, they claimed, meant that the shareholder value was locked in rather than unlocked as the supporters of the restructuring had claimed. More seriously, the Jardine group had ultimately done little more than protect its historical holdings – over a period when other Hong Kong (Chinese) companies had gone from strength to strength. Simon Keswick's determination to reduce debts had seen the Land company reduced to a Hong Kong property concern when a few years before it had been the biggest foreign corporate investor in Australia and had been the powerful driving force behind Jardines itself. David Davies' scheme would have allowed Land to retain its diversity and flexibility to raise capital and continue on an expansionary path. In 1989 Jardines announced plans to form a new company, Jardine Pacific, incorporated in Bermuda but based in Hong Kong, to embrace the group's Asia-Pacific trading and service businesses. With revenues of HK$10 billion Jardine Pacific will be set up between Jardine Matheson and Co. and the holding company.

The question about the company's ability to make good business profits is still open. Twenty years ago Chinese rivals like Li Ka-shing and Yue-Kong Pao would have been regarded as upstarts; today they are uncrowned kings of the Hong Kong business world. Even among expatriate companies Jardines no longer holds undisputed sway. Many analysts regard the Swire group as better balanced and better, more prudently managed. Swires is effectively controlled by the family from London, with the help of 'A' and 'B' shares, but Hong Kong managers are left without drama to run the local businesses. Swires' airline, Cathay Pacific Airways, grew from being a small regional carrier to one of the top twenty airlines in the world in size; in terms of quality of its service it regularly comes in the top five in surveys. Other Swire businesses included property, which weathered the Hong Kong slump without the traumas of Hongkong Land, and a series of retail and trading interests such as the franchise for bottling Coca-Cola in Hong Kong, major shares in aircraft engineering and airport operations.

Questions also remain about Jardines' commitment to Hong Kong. The new group structure, with its top level of management above the daily fray, would permit the super-executives to control the company from anywhere. Registration in a (still) British colony might afford some protection against future capricious rules, but the predominance of physical assets in Hong Kong could be a weakness if a regime was determinedly hostile. So is this the approaching end of an era? Simon Keswick decisively says 'No.' But his ambition is nevertheless to diversify, so that 50 per cent of the group's interests are in Hong Kong and 50 per cent worldwide (compared with a 70:30 bias to Hong Kong throughout the 1980s). (In fact even this aim has been difficult to realize. Dairy Farm in 1987 bought 25 per cent of the British Kwik Save discount retailer, but it was specifically a non-controlling stake. Efforts to develop insurance and financial services have not proved world-beaters.) Keswick defends Jardines against accusers who claim that the group is no longer a force in Hong Kong. 'Our combined stockmarket capitalization is more than 12 per cent of the total market. That makes us a major force in this town.'

Foreigners could sympathize with the company and family desire to reduce its exposure to Hong Kong in the face of a Communist takeover of the colony. After all, the Keswicks had the experience of the Communist takeover of China itself. But in some ways the flight of Jardines to incorporate in Bermuda symbolized the plight of the old colonial regime in Hong Kong. If the very first company and virtual founder of British Hong Kong was going, what hope was there for Hong Kong as it had been known?

The Hongkong and Shanghai Banking Corporation: A Very British Bank

There is an old saying that four people effectively run Hong Kong: the Governor, the chairman of Jardine Matheson, the chairman of the Hongkong and Shanghai Banking Corporation and the chairman of the Royal Hong Kong Jockey Club. The real question is their order of importance. Immediately before and after Hong Kong's establishment as a British colony, Jardines was the most important player – thanks particularly to William Jardine's key role in creating Hong Kong. From the end of the Second World War until the 1980s there's no doubt that the chairman of the Hongkong Bank was the most important single person in the life of the colony. For good measure, Michael Sandberg (knighted in 1986), chairman from 1977 to 1986, was also chairman of the Jockey Club in his final years in Hong Kong.

By the late 1980s the old order was changing. A new and more powerful name should be added to the list of traditional movers and shapers of Hong Kong, that of the local director of Xinhua, the New China News Agency (see chapters 12 and 13 for the changing political scene). All four traditional rulers are under pressure, and none more so than the chairman of the bank. The bank has grown internationally, just as Hong Kong has, so the chairman has to decide whether to spread the bank's wings and turn it into a fully fledged international institution with its headquarters in an international banking centre, or to stay in Hong Kong under Chinese Communist tutelage. The choice is hedged with far-reaching political as well as financial implications.

The bank was not the first to be established in Hong Kong. Indeed its foundation in 1865, when Hong Kong was itself in its early twenties, marks it out as a relative latecomer to the colony. Between the two world wars its head office was in Hong Kong, but its main operations and most profitable business came out of

Shanghai, China's business capital. During the Second World War the bank's head office was transferred by Order-in-Council to London. But immediately after the war it established a dominant grip on the banking and business life of the fledgling international city of Hong Kong. In the late 1980s it was the biggest bank in Hong Kong. Guesstimates of its strength ran from 40 to a full 60 per cent of total deposits. It has branches on almost every important street corner, more than 400 of them in all, if other group companies are counted. It has a sophisticated network of electronic banking facilities including hundreds of automated teller machines (ATMs). Most important of all, the Hongkong Bank dominates financial business throughout the city, serving all types of customer from small and medium-sized entrepreneurs to big business magnates like property billionaire Li Ka-shing, deputy chairman of the bank. Internationally, the bank has spread its wings and by the mid-1980s the majority of its assets were located outside Hong Kong.

The bank certainly has its critics, many of them in Hong Kong and some within the bank itself. The senior director of an old-established Hong Kong Chinese concern says he banks with Citibank 'because it's more modern and understands modern management', and with one of the Chinese Communist banks 'frankly, for political reasons'. 'The Hongkong Bank management has not moved with the times,' he charges, claiming that 'its managers are still largely old traditionals brought up in minor English public schools, taught to play rugby, who can be relied on to keep their hands out of the tills and away from other women's skirts. Hongkong Bank managers are so solid that they don't know about modern developments in banking such as interest rate swaps or floating rate notes.' Chairman of the bank William Purves responds with a rounded single-syllable five-letter expletive, indicating that he thinks the charge is nonsense.

Though Purves makes light of them, echoes of these criticisms can be heard within the bank. One of the younger brighter managers puts the issue bluntly like this:

There is a shortage of talent among the older managers. With exceptions like Purves himself, most of the men in their late 40s and early 50s are not terribly bright. They are honest, but unimaginative, the ideal kind of manager for a colonial Kota Kinabalu or Kuching where nothing much moved, except commodity trade. They are certainly not bankers with an international cast of mind. On the other hand, there are a lot of younger managers, now reaching their late 30s, and who are bright, ambitious and internationally minded. It's a management problem of how to deal with the old timers, whether to let them serve out their time and disappoint the young and hungry ones, or to bypass them – which might mean lower morale among those reaching retirement age.

This executive is also critical of the bank's total operations:

Though our assets are diversified, Hong Kong is by far our biggest profit centre. We're also strong in Malaysia and Singapore, but that's also a colonial inheritance that's slipping away from us as the local governments encourage local banks. We've some strength in India and we're reasonably strong in the Middle East. But we're weak in Japan, where we were the oldest *bank*, let alone foreign bank. We are weak in Europe. Most of all, we are weak in putting the strong bits together to create new strength. With 1997 coming we are vulnerable in Hong Kong, but where else would we make such profits *and* enjoy low tax rates.

But it is as well not to get carried away by the 'colonial' jibe. Many of the charges against the Hongkong Bank are unfair and untrue. The Hongkong Bank *has* moved with the times. Immediately after the war, the then chief manager (as the chief executive was called), Ulsterman Sir Arthur Morse, played a major role in building Hong Kong manufacturing business. As was described in chapter 5, he was prepared to lend money on virtually no security to refugee Chinese who were budding industrialists. Sometimes he made loans because their families and credentials were known to the bank in pre-war Shanghai; or sometimes because he trusted their faces and ideas. It was risky business, but it paid off, for Hong Kong and for the bank, not least in the abiding loyalty of small and medium-sized Chinese businesses even today.

The bank's size and strength are impressive. Its assets in 1987 topped the US$100 billion mark, putting the Hongkong Bank among the world's top thirty banks in terms of assets, in the top 12 in terms of capitalization, and in the top twenty in declared profit rankings. Banks in Hong Kong do not have to declare all their profits, and the Hongkong Bank has secret hidden reserves which may now total HK$30 billion (US$3.8 billion).

Of its more than 1,000 offices worldwide, a good slice are in Hong Kong. But there are almost 350 in the USA, more than 150 in the Middle East, 44 in Malaysia, 32 in the UK, 28 in India, 26 in Singapore, 18 in Australia, 9 in Japan and 7 each in China and West Germany. Altogether the bank operates in 55 countries. Financial concerns within the group include the Hang Seng Bank, Hong Kong's second biggest bank, Marine Midland Bank of the US, the British Bank of the Middle East, and stockbrokers and investment bank James Capel. To overcome its weakness in Europe, new chairman Purves in 1987 agreed a deal with Midland Bank of the United Kingdom whereby the Hongkong Bank took a 14.9 per cent share in the Midland. Under the arrangement, the Midland became the Hongkong Bank's flag-carrier in most parts of Europe, while the Hongkong Bank took over as Midland's standard-bearer in large parts of Asia and in Canada.

The individual responsible for developing the Hongkong Bank as an *international* institution was former chairman Michael Sandberg. When he took over in 1977, the bank already owned the Mercantile Bank (bought in 1959 and sold to Citibank in 1984 when all but the name and the Bangkok branch had been incorporated within the Hongkong Bank) and the British Bank of the Middle East (bought in 1960). Both of these had colonial roots, like the Hongkong Bank itself. Sandberg, who joined the bank in 1949 without a university education straight after military service, had a world, not a colonial vision and firmly pulled the bank onto an international stage. His biggest coup was the purchase of 51 per cent of Marine Midland Bank of New York, for US$314 million in 1980. He didn't stop there, but led the bank to buy Antony Gibbs, the London merchant bank, and James Capel and Company.

There are criticisms of Sandberg. He left the bank without a strong European banking arm. It was also weak in each of the world's big financial centres, London, New York and Tokyo. Marine Midland is a New York state bank, not strong in the city. He made a bid for Royal Bank of Scotland, an attempt which was effectively killed by the opposition of the Bank of England and particularly of its Governor Gordon (now Lord) Richardson. Ironically, Prime Minister Margaret Thatcher let it be known later that she didn't share Richardson's opposition. The British regulators considered the Hongkong Bank 'foreign' – odd indeed when it is established in a British colony where senior regulators include seconded Bank of England executives and when the Hongkong Bank senior management are almost quintessentially British. Some senior people within the bank blame Sandberg personally on the grounds that 'it's said that Richardson had a personal score to settle with Sandberg; if that's the case, it was pointless tackling him head on and we should have countered with some plan to neutralize his opposition'.

Sandberg's entrepreneurial spirit – 'He was more of a trader than a banker,' commented a colleague – was also blamed for leading the Hongkong Bank to fuel the property boom in Hong Kong in the early 1980s and in particular to foster the rise of George Tan, head of the Carrian group (see chapter 8) which collapsed with debts of almost US$1.3 billion. Sandberg defended himself by responding that stories about the bank's exposure to Carrian were greatly exaggerated. Actual exposure was less than US$200 million and much of that was secured against property. Ironically, the part of the bank group most damaged by lending to Tan was its merchant banking arm, Wardley. Wardley men regarded themselves as a cut above the ordinary, solid, unimaginative, staid Hongkong Bank executives; Wardley men were fast-moving, fast-living merchant bankers who understood modern developments like floating rate notes and interest rate swaps – but they were hoodwinked. Purves, who became chairman of Wardley before taking over the bank itself, had to take clean-up action. 'Not to put too fine a point upon it, he put the boot in quite a bit,' says a Wardley executive.

Sandberg did – as he proudly pointed out – leave the bank with a strong balance sheet. In sharp contrast to the big US commercial banks, heavily exposed in indebted Latin American countries, the Hongkong Bank has virtually no outstanding risky sovereign lending to Latin America or Eastern Europe. (Admittedly at least partly because its geographical location and its ties with China haven't encouraged it to lend heavily to either area.)

The most public and controversial symbol of Sandberg's reign in the Hongkong Bank is the new headquarters, fifty-two storeys of steel, aluminium and glass designed by British architect Norman Foster. It is one of the most modern buildings in the world, and so it ought to be at the price. 'It's got Sandberg's mark all over it,' notes a middle-ranking manager in the headquarters, 'glittering, arrogant and hang the cost.' The building is topped by the bank's laser-lit logo. Executives are sticking to the claim that the cost was a mere HK$5 billion. But an insider closely associated with the building commented that 'the $5 billion figure is not quite a lie, if you take it as the bare construction costs. But if you add in the financing costs over five years and decorating the building I would put the figure in at the HK$8–9 billion range. That of course is without land costs, as the land already belongs to the bank.' The Bank of China's new building just across the road, a full twenty storeys higher, was estimated to cost HK$2 billion, of which half is the price of the land. The new Hongkong Bank headquarters defies an easy description. Even architectural specialists have had a hard time, calling it variously 'a stainless steel ladder', 'a Chinese lantern', 'a megolith of super technology', 'like an English cathedral', 'a film set for the main block of San Quentin jail', 'the eighth wonder of the world', 'of surpassing ugliness, somewhat in the style of a modern chemical works'. The architecture correspondent of *The Times* of London, Charles Knevitt, suggested that he was still baffled when he wrote that the building 'is a meeting of technical sophistication of the west with the somewhat inscrutable mysticism and superstition one associates with the east'.

The bank scoured the world for materials fit for its palace. The prefabricated kit of parts came from more than 100 subcontractors in 80 countries. Most of the 30,000 metric tons of steel came from the UK; its 'jigsaw puzzle cladding' consisting of 'thousands of aluminium curtain wall panels, almost all different in shape and size' came from St Louis in the US; the circular door to the bank's vault, weighing 50 tons ('so beautifully balanced that it can be moved with one finger' enthused the Sandberg bank's PR department), came from France; lavatories pre-fitted down to the ashtray and toilet-roll holders came from Japan; the document transportation system was tailor-made in Germany; the maintenance cranes came from Arnhem in the Netherlands. Originally Foster had wanted the building finished in red or green with chevron-shaped crossbeams. The bankers were appalled, but so too were the *fung shui* men (geomancers) inevitably consulted in Hong Kong. In the end a banker-like grey and silver finish was chosen, with the paint supplied by the company that makes the paint for Porsche motor cars.

Strangely, many staff complain about the light and airy atmosphere inside the building. 'It's like living in a glass zoo cage,' commented one senior executive. But most of them are blasé about the cost. 'We have a fine building. What does it cost? – A few years' profits, but it's put us on the world architectural map' is the typical view. Yet some executives jokingly refer to the building as 'Sandberg's folly'.

In spite of the achievements, it's still a legitimate question to ask whether the bank can maintain its position on the world banking map. There are two issues: can the Hongkong Bank build on its good foundation and become a truly *international* bank; and can it maintain its dominance in Hong Kong, a Chinese city, when it comes under Chinese rule?

The man who took at the helm in 1986, Purves, is almost the antithesis of his predecessor. Where Sandberg is small, Purves is tall; where Sandberg loved the limelight, Purves is shy; where Sandberg was a delegator, Purves is very much a hands-on manager; where Sandberg was good at smooth-talking and charming people, Purves will be blunt and to the point. 'Sandberg was far too political and I got the blame for sorting out some of his messes,' Purves is reported to have told friends. A rival banker in Hong Kong, who doesn't want to be identified, sums up the difference between Purves and his predecessor:

> Sandberg was very much a popular figure, a merchant banker and deal-maker by temperament. He'd still be smiling at you and you at him, even as the knife slid into your back and the blood was dripping between your shoulder blades. But Willie Purves is very much a traditional hard-nosed commercial banker. He's direct and to the point. If he got a knife out for you, you know it. He shows you it.

In many ways the new chairman conforms to the archetype of a Hong Kong colonial banker criticized by the Chinese executive. He is Scottish, though a grammar-school boy rather than a public school product, and a keen former rugby player. He first showed his mettle during the Korean war when as a nineteen-year-old conscripted second lieutenant in the British forces serving with the United Nations he won the Distinguished Service Order, Britain's second highest award for gallantry. Some soldiers felt that he deserved the Victoria Cross, the highest decoration for his action, but under the rules action has to be witnessed and recommended by another officer before a VC can be won. Purves is modest about his gallantry, perhaps because it was won fighting the Chinese, the bank's particular friends and allies. He originally started his banking career with the National Bank of Scotland, but shifted to the Hongkong Bank soon after his return from Korea.

Inside the bank the new chairman enjoys a first-rate reputation. 'He's not an easy man to get on with,' admits an executive in his thirties, who nevertheless confesses to being 'a tremendous fan' of Purves. 'He's very strict, yet very fair. If you go in to see him you better have something worthwhile to say and say it, or hold your tongue. If you've made a good point, he'll accept it; if you try to waffle he has little patience.' Officials in the bank public relations department say that Purves reads voraciously and gets copies of every single telex sent out of or coming into the bank. On occasions, too, he shows he's reading almost every line by commenting on the felicitousness or otherwise of a message. A junior manager, a man who wouldn't normally have dealt directly with a board member, let alone the chairman, emphasizes that Purves is very much a 'hands-on' chairman: 'I had just come back from an extended visit to one of the smaller countries in which we operate. The chairman called me in and gave me a grilling. All his questions were tough and right on the ball. It was a testing fifteen minutes. Then he relaxed and began to talk about rugby.'

Another, more senior, manager adds to the praise, declaring: 'Purves is just the man the bank needs, tough, hardnosed, absolutely clean, the man to get a grip on our problems.' Purves defends himself against criticism of his 'hands-on' role: 'We operate in 55 countries. I have to keep my antenna up on political developments in all of them.' He told the *Asian Wall Street Journal* (7 May 1987): 'If there's a bad egg somewhere in the bank, I want to know about it too. This is a big bank. If the chairman doesn't stay informed, he gets his head chopped off.' The experiences of the Carrian scandal, in which Purves advanced his career by doing much of the cleaning up, reinforced these attitudes. Yet there must be doubts about how long one man, however energetic, can survive working an eighteen-hour day. And even if he can physically cope, can his judgement stand the pace?

The new chairman moved quickly to overcome the most obvious of his problems. In his first year in office, in a US$800 million buyout, he took over the 49 per cent of Marine Midland that the Hongkong Bank didn't already own and paid £380 million for a 14.9 per cent investment in Britain's Midland Bank, a stake that most bank analysts believe presages a full partnership soon. Both deals were Purves's personal handiwork.

Purves's own explanation for the Marine Midland deal is that 'We wanted to avoid conflicts of interest in deciding which bits of business went where. And since we were responsible for 100 per cent of Marine Midland and if they had got into any trouble, we would have been responsible for getting them out of trouble, we decided that we wanted for the 100 per cent responsibility to have 100 per cent of the return' (personal interview, March 1988). Originally, in July 1987, the Hongkong Bank had offered US$70 a share for the Marine Midland minorities, but it was forced by mid-September to raise this to $83 a share. Purves shrugs that if he had foreseen October's 'Black Monday' on Wall Street (when share prices collapsed) the deal could probably have been wrapped up more cheaply. Some analysts claim they are puzzled that a hard-nosed chairman paid a premium to net asset value for the Marine Midland shares when, if the worst had come to the worst and the US subsidiary had got into trouble, the Hongkong Bank would have been presented with the tab, but at a discount, not at a premium. Purves does admit that there were disagreements over Marine Midland's provisions for third world debt. The Hongkong Bank, virtually free of third world debts, was uncomfortable with its subsidiary's exposure. Purves said: 'We had been talking to our colleagues in Marine about making greater provisions during 1985 and 1986, but their own external accountants and their own regulators thought they were adequately reserved. Minority shareholders would have been unhappy if their own auditor's recommendations hadn't been followed.' The bank made more than HK$2 billion of new provisions for Marine's third world debt, and in consequence in 1987 the Hongkong Bank had to pick up the full tab for its subsidiary's loss.

With barriers to inter-state banking in the US crumbling, Hongkong Bank executives believe that Marine Midland is well placed to capture business in the prosperous north-east of the country. The bank has been shorn of its international business and lacks strength in New York city, but the view in Hong Kong is that 'upstate banking is much more profitable than in the overcrowded city'. With Marine Midland, the Hongkong Bank is the largest foreign bank in the USA. Hongkong Bank executives won't say so openly, but another reason for wanting 100 per cent of the action was to tighten management and achieve better returns. Marine Midland's average return on equity in the 1980–86 period was 10.4 per cent, below the average of 13.8 per cent for US money-centre banks and 12.7 per cent for regionals.

The partnership with Midland was a much bolder stroke, the answer, most analysts immediately assumed, to the bank's twin prayers, giving it a European presence and an alternative home after 1997 if China-run Hong Kong proves too uncomfortable. The partnership was very much the product of two Washington sessions between the two chairmen, Purves and Sir Kit McMahon of Midland, during 1987's International Monetary Fund–World Bank meetings. The 14.9 per cent stake was just below the critical 15 per cent above which Bank of England permission would have been required. The Hongkong Bank promised not to alter its stake for three years without the permission of the Midland board. 'It gives the Midland a big capital injection and a breathing space to put the bank together,' says a middle-ranking Hong Kong executive. 'But three years of the standstill agreement isn't long and would leave the Midland as our prisoner if we wanted to move in.' The partnership also gives the British authorities time to get used to the idea of an expanded and permanent link.

Senior executives at both banks deny that any long-term plans have been set in concrete. Purves says sharply that speculation about a full takeover of Midland 'is in danger of being entirely media driven'. He adds: 'The Midland Bank had a need; I had a need. Midland had been approached by one or two strange investors, including an advertising agency [Saatchi and Saatchi].' The idea of an ad agency calling the shots at a major international bank clearly appals Purves as much as it did the Bank of England. The partnership, avers Purves, 'gives the Midland capital and a chance to get people like Saatchi and Saatchi off its back'. For the Hongkong Bank, the attraction is the opportunity of riding into Europe on the Midland's back.

The Hongkong Bank chairman adds that the Bank of England was told of the prospective partnership. 'I didn't ask the governor for permission; I didn't need to,' recalls Purves. 'If he had expressed any doubts about it, I'd probably have scratched my head.' Both banks have gone to work with a will, closing offices almost as if they were already just one bank. The Hongkong Bank closed its branches in Hamburg (on the eve of its centenary there), Frankfurt (where it will retain a 'representative' office), Dublin, Paris, Amsterdam and the highly profitable niches of Madrid and Switzerland. The Midland similarly shut its branches in large parts of Asia, including profitable Seoul (though not Tokyo), and Canada. Purves justifies the closures by saying that the affected branches are 'relatively small, too small to be making any impact on the marketplace'. He questions 'whether it is worth having people and capital tied up in such farflung places' suggesting that corporate customers are better served not by having a series of outposts on the world map, but by having a partner bank that can offer a strong presence and quality services.

In spite of Purves's vigorous protests, later in 1988 there were two other straws in the wind indicating that the Hongkong Bank was actively contemplating closer ties to the Midland.

Peter Wrangham, general manager responsible for Hong Kong business operations, a main board director and a friend of Purves, was transferred to London in November to head the bank's European operations. There was speculation in Hong Kong that closer ties with the Midland Bank would be Wrangham's prime responsibility. Then, in an interview, Purves conceded that 'Kit McMahon says there might be merit in a merger. I don't disagree with him' (the *Guardian*, 6 November 1988). He added that the relationship 'looks like an engagement, but courtships don't always lead to marriage'. But Purves sniffed at the idea of moving from Hong Kong. 'This may prove to be one of the great places in the world to be based. It's rather nice to be the only truly international bank in Asia outside Japan. There are many international banks in London. I don't necessarily want to be one of them.'

But in its home base the end of the British colonial regime offers a string of difficult challenges to the Hongkong Bank. It certainly faces criticism for not being 'Chinese' enough. Not until after the Second World War did the Hongkong Bank employ its first Chinese executive. From the early days it used a Chinese comprador, the unique go-between or interpreter used for dealings between the Chinese and Europeans. Bank clerks were traditionally Portuguese or Eurasians and senior officers were expatriates, almost all from Britain. Even in the late 1980s the colonial inheritance lingers. The top executives are all expatriates, and the highest-ranking Chinese hasn't yet reached general manager level, let alone the board.

There are Chinese on the board, but they are all non-executives, Hong Kong business stars. One of them, Li Ka-shing, is non-executive deputy chairman. Former chairman Sandberg was instrumental in appointing a Chinese to the nominal number two job, with Sir Yue-Kong Pao in the place before Li. Non-executive directors grumble that they have a largely decorative function. For example, they don't normally see essential papers until thirty minutes before meetings.

Purves, however, has no doubts about the bank's Hong Kong

Chinese credentials: 'We are an international, multinational bank with a strong home base and a majority of Chinese shareholders,' he says, disclosing that 'more than 60 per cent of the bank's shareholders, who number 166,600, are Chinese' (interview with this author, 1988). He says confidently: 'there is no competition that we fear', and predicts that if anything the Hongkong Bank will *increase* its market share in Hong Kong. He acknowledges that the bank was slow to encourage its Chinese staff, but says that now 'it is the policy of the bank to bring on Chinese executives at a faster rate and to encourage them to move to the highest positions in the bank'. This policy was begun, he says, before 1997 became an issue. Purves readily admits it is a problem that 'the really bright well-educated Chinese prefers to go into his own business'. In addition, the demands of an *international* bank, that a young executive may have to go almost overnight to Riyadh or Djibouti or Timbucktoo, may prove troublesome to the family-oriented Chinese. The bank's rule is that its international staff must be prepared to move at twenty-four hours' notice, and Purves himself has won a reputation for shifting young executives who catch his eye to challenging locations (and not always to salubrious places or spots conducive to a settled family life). He comments that 'when a young Chinese gets to thirty and has family responsibilities, he sometimes says "bye bye" as he wants to put his family first'.

In its Hong Kong base, the bank faces a strong challenge from the Communist banks. The Bank of China and its associates have grown rapidly. Purves gives the Chinese some important points: 'In the last few years the thirteen sister banks have become more westernized as bankers. They used to do no marketing, and now they're doing it.' For example Nanyang Commercial Bank in October 1985 took space in international newspapers to advertise its MasterCard; the name embossed on the card in the ad was Bu Ming, the same as that of the then chairman of the Bank of China. In particular the Chinese banks have been active in offering housing finance. Purves recalls, for example, that in the early 1980s, when new housing blocks were going up in Hong Kong, 'the Chinese banks and Nanyang in particular were very quick and had a man with his table set up outside the block, offering home mortgages to the purchasers'.

But nobody seriously believes that the Bank of China group is yet in a position to challenge the Hongkong Bank commercially. It is difficult to judge, since only four of the sister banks are incorporated and therefore produce annual reports in Hong Kong. But these four have usually produced rates of return on capital a long way below those recorded by the Hongkong Bank. The picture is obscured because banks in Hong Kong publish minimalist accounts. Bankers who deal with the Communist banks also claim that they are often slow to reach decisions and refer back to Peking matters that any other bank would decide on the spot. But the battle isn't only a commercial one. It involves politics too. As one banker who knows China well puts it, 'Peking believes strongly that if you are ethnic Chinese, you belong to it, full stop. That gives the Bank of China great scope for making inroads.'

Purves himself bravely says that 'we see the Bank of China as a banking competitor and not a political competitor'. Ever competitive, he also boasts that the Hongkong Bank has carried its skills to China and is by far the biggest foreign bank in China. But Hong Kong is a small place and some people – like the executives of Hong Kong Chinese firms – are already hedging their bets. Businessmen are opening accounts with the Communist banks because it is politic to do so. When pressed, Purves concedes: 'The Hong Kong Chinese are great believers in having a foot in every camp.' The Hong Kong government also found it politic to invite the Bank of China along with the Hongkong Bank to share the credit for the lifeline it threw to Ka Wah Bank in 1985. A government official claims the action was 'the politically prudent thing' to do. The Hongkong Bank itself bowed to the new winds in 1986 when it chose the Bank of China as its partner in bidding for the financing for the construction of the new road and rail tunnel under Hong Kong harbour.

Former chairman Sir Michael Sandberg had an excellent reputation for hobnobbing with and charming the local Chinese. Purves, the tougher character with the blunt, sometimes sledge-hammer tongue, may find that the need to knock the bank into good shape conflicts with the need for diplomatic sweet talking skills.

Purves came back in early 1988 from his first visit to Peking as chairman of the bank, much reassured by what his Chinese hosts told him. No less a person than Li Peng, then Acting Prime Minister and later confirmed in that office, told him that China expected the Hongkong Bank to continue to play an important role as bank and quasi-central bank in Hong Kong even after China takes sovereignty. The bank chairman quoted the Chinese leader as making it 'clear that the Hongkong Bank has a very important role now and expects it to have an important role in the future, including post-1997. He recognized that the Hongkong Bank has more than just a banking role and sometimes has a quasi-central bank position in Hong Kong' (interview, March 1988).

But the 'business as usual' pledge still presents a problem for Purves. In essence, can the bank trust the honeyed words of the Chinese that the 1997 takeover makes no difference? On the other hand, can it afford to snub Peking by publicly diversifying away from its Hong Kong base? Among those expressing their distrust and 'voting with their feet' against China are many of the bank's own Chinese employees: in 1987 alone, more than 8 per cent of them left to migrate to what they saw as safer shores. And however hard chairman Purves may glare when the question is asked, the Hongkong Bank has a special duty to look ahead and to ask if it can risk leaving its headquarters in a city that will after 1997 owe its allegiance to a Communist state. Hong Kong is the last and biggest colonial bastion of the bank. It enjoys many entrenched privileges which make it the most profitable of the bank's operations. Although its assets have been diversified and most are outside Hong Kong, the colony remains the goldmine.

Hong Kong Bankers are sometimes touchingly politically naïve. Questioned about life for the bank after 1997 when China takes over Hong Kong, the bank's public relations manager George Cardona smilingly pulls out a copy of the Joint Declaration between China and Britain and asserts, as if there can be no further question, 'it's all in there'. The Joint Declaration promised that Hong Kong would be allowed to maintain its own autonomous capitalist system for at least fifty years after the takeover. He was speaking before the Peking massacre of 1989, but it was already clear that China's view of key words like 'democracy' and 'elections' was different from western definitions. The question which Cardona – and Li Peng – haven't answered is whether 'business as usual' (assuming that the agreement stands and Peking does not interfere) will allow the Hongkong Bank to bask for the next fifty years in all of its privileges, when Hong Kong has ceased to be a British colony. There are plenty of bankers who say that it shouldn't and it won't.

From its futuristic headquarters at 1 Queen's Road, Central, Hong Kong, the bank performs many of the functions that would be done elsewhere by a central bank or monetary authority. Hong Kong has neither. With the Standard Chartered Bank, the Hongkong Bank is the issuer of banknotes for the colony (the government issues coins plus the tiny Monopoly-style one-cent notes). The Hongkong Bank issues the lion's share of the banknotes – 83 per cent – a useful advert for itself, and a free one, since the government bears the expenses of the note issue. More important, the bank also runs the clearing system, is the main banker to the government and is the biggest recipient of public funds. Thanks to the interest rate agreement, the bank enjoys spreads (the difference between rates it pays on deposits and interest it charges on loans) of almost 5 per cent on its local business. 'It's one vast money-making machine,' says an experienced American banker who admits that he is envious.

The Hongkong Bank has also attracted the jealousy of some local banks. David K. P. Li, chief executive of the Bank of East

Asia, with only 3 per cent of the Hongkong Bank's assets, but the biggest of the local banks, has complained of the nexus between the bank and the government, in effect claiming that the government is at the beck and call of the bank. His grumble was echoed by the local Chinese Banks Association which in a July 1988 report complained that the Hongkong Bank's position was an 'unhealthy phenomenon' that 'inevitably gives rise to favouritism and conflict of interest'. As a profit-making bank, the report said, the Hongkong Bank should not be allowed to provide and manage the clearing house of the territory's banking system; it should be done by an exchange fund or a private-sector organization. Some market analysts claim that the bank was able to double its inner reserves by holding uncovered US dollar positions during the 1983 run on the local dollar. The report also warned that control by a socialist central bank (from Peking) would be harmful. The failure of the Hongkong Bank's bid to manage the new unified stock exchange's central clearing and depository system was a sign that winds of change are already blowing. In mid-1988 the Exchange Fund took over from the bank the role of ultimate provider of liquidity to the interbank market.

Most banking analysts in Hong Kong believe that the least that the post-1997 administration will do is make the Bank of China also a note-issuing bank and distribute more evenly some of the spoils of government business.

In these circumstances, when the Midland partnership was announced, it was natural to leap to the conclusion that a future Hongkong Bank–Midland merger offered the best future for both banks. A reverse takeover might not be possible, since the Hongkong Bank's articles don't permit any shareholder to own more than 1 per cent of the stock. But a full takeover of Midland – with the Bank of England insisting that the Hongkong Bank move its registration to London – could be the perfect answer. The Hongkong Bank, bolstered by its secret undeclared reserves, can afford Midland. The longer any decision is left, the more tricky and *political* it will be, since the bank is incorporated in Hong Kong with its own special ordinance, and legislation would be needed for a change.

Premier Li Peng's comments as reported by Purves throw an interesting but shadowy light on these speculations. Li had noted the link with the Midland and the full takeover of Marine Midland. Says Purves: 'He of course had no objection to these moves. They were commercial decisions. He did however hope that we would see the importance of our position in Hong Kong now and in the future. We reminded Li Peng that we have been an international bank from Day 1, and valued our position in Hong Kong.' Was there a threat behind Li's statement – that the bank shouldn't make any further moves away from Hong Kong? Purves wouldn't discuss the question further.

One interesting battle the Hongkong Bank thought it prudent to withdraw from came in 1985 over the first elections for the Hong Kong Legislative Council (see chapter 5). One seat was allocated to the 'financial community' and each bank had a single vote. It was natural to expect the Hongkong Bank to want its man on Legco. But David K. P. Li, chief executive of the Bank of East Asia, was also running. The Hongkong Bank, some of whose senior executives regard Li as an upstart, demanded (according to Li) that he should seek the chairman Sandberg's approval; if not, the bank would run its own candidate. But then the Bank of China took a hand, soliciting support for Li from the other banks. In the end the Hongkong Bank quietly sidled away from a contest and Li was elected unopposed.

After 1997 the Hongkong Bank (unless a Midland takeover changes the arrangements) will be a British colonial foundation in a Chinese city that has thrown off the British yoke; it will be a very capitalist, but yet Establishment organization in a city under the shadow of Communism. Surely, the battles are not going to get easier.

Li Ka-shing: From Rags to Riches

Of all the 'rags to riches' tales of Hong Kong entrepreneurs, the classic real-life fairy story is that of Li Ka-shing. He came as a virtual refugee to Hong Kong at the age of eleven, and by the 1980s he was probably the richest of the handful of mega-rich in Hong Kong. Not only was Li chairman of one of the oldest *hongs* (diversified trading companies), but he had a finger in almost all of the profitable pies in the territory. Companies he controlled accounted for almost 20 per cent of the local stock market capitalization – or about US$10 billion. But his fame went wider than this. Li had become almost part of the local folklore. His actions were watched carefully: and any statement from Li Ka-shing could on its own move the local stock market significantly.

After 1986 it looked for eighteen months as if he had retreated and was leaving big breath-taking deals to the new younger lions of the Hong Kong business scene. But in the October 1987 stock market crash some of them got their fingers burned and Li bounced back with a series of ambitious investment schemes both in Hong Kong and abroad. The total value of the Hong Kong investments alone was HK$27 billion (almost US$3.5 billion). Later, in November 1988, Li announced yet more plans, for a joint venture hotel in Singapore and huge development with China Resources Co. of almost a million square metres of residential space and 75,000 square metres of commercial property at Tin Shui Wai in the New Territories. Potentially this could be the biggest scheme of all, but – typical of Hong Kong – only bare details have been given, with no account of the costs.

How much Li is worth is a matter of conjecture. *Fortune* magazine in 1987 assessed his net worth at US$2.5 billion, making him the twenty-fifth richest person in the world. Like all Chinese businessmen Li owns both publicly quoted shares and private interests. Hong Kong's disclosure laws are not as strict as those in western countries, so even calculating the public side of the empire is a hit and miss business. But he's certainly in the same billionaire class as Sir Yue-Kong Pao, and is mega-rich even by world standards. He has come a long way since he first arrived in Hong Kong. Li Ka-shing was not one of the already experienced businessmen who migrated from Shanghai to Hong Kong after the Communists took over in China. He was born in Chiu Chow in Guangdong province in 1928, and came to the British colony at the age of eleven, just as the Japanese were busy extending their empire in China. He left school at thirteen to help support his family. His path to fame and fortune was along the difficult road of hard work and individual enterprise, helped along by a few timely slices of good luck.

Initially he became a salesman for, and later manager of, a toy factory. But in 1950 Li revealed the entrepreneurial instincts that lurk in the heart of many true Cantonese. He struck out on his own, setting up a company called Cheung Kong Enterprises. 'Cheung Kong' means 'long river', a reference to the Yangtse. The company started making plastic toys and household goods, with Li's savings of HK$50,000 as its capital. It was a modest enough beginning, and anyone from outside Hong Kong might be forgiven a little laugh. At the start Li worked hard, 'sixteen hours a day; seven days a week for the first twelve years', he recalled. Even great rivers start off as small mountain streams.

Li was also far-sighted enough to recognize the way that the world was changing. He chose to move into the then infant plastics industry, realizing that there were 'good prospects for substitution in areas where wood and metal had been dominant'. He was right. He was boosted by a general takeoff in Hong Kong's manufacturing sector at that time, so that the tiny territory was increasingly noticed by traders and buyers from industrialized countries.

In 1957 the Hong Kong plastics industry discovered how to make flowers that looked real. 'We knew plastic flowers were better than paper ones because you can wash them and they last forever,' said Li, explaining why he switched his resources into flower-making. He remained a flower-maker for ten years, before switching away because 'the technology was getting too easy to imitate'.

By 1958 Li was already a millionaire, and ready to move into property, the area in which he made his reputation. He got into property 'because I could see that the supply of land in Hong Kong was limited, whereas population was unlimited'. In addition, he spotted the emergence of smaller Chinese nuclear families, instead of the traditional three generations living under the same roof. His special secret was to realize that property could be traded like other commodities.

Li's great ability, which he demonstrated quietly during the 1960s, and showed off publicly in the 1970s and 1980s, was in being able to look at a building or even a site and calculate how much it was worth. Having done that, he had the ability to move swiftly to finalize deals. By the early 1970s, it was already clear that Li was a man of talent as far as property was concerned. By the late 1970s, his name was being mentioned in the same breath as that of Yue-Kong Pao, a Chinese businessman capable of taking on the old British *hongs* and beating them at their own game. The Hongkong Bank paid court to him, to ask to be his banker. That move occurred in the early 1970s when Li was operating from gloomy premises in Causeway Bay. 'We knew we'd got the account,' recalls William Purves, later chairman of the bank, 'because Li himself came down to the car to see us off'.

In 1979 the Hongkong Bank connection paid off for Li. The bank allowed him to buy 22 per cent of Hutchison Whampoa, an old-established *hong*, on the easiest of terms. This was effectively a controlling stake and it was the first time that a Chinese had taken control of one of the old British pillars of Hong Kong. Hutchison had begun life as a dockyard and shipping company in the mid-1860s. Under former chairman Sir Douglas Clague it had diversified, but then got into financial trouble. The Hongkong Bank took a 30 per cent controlling shareholding as part of the rescue operation. W. R. A. (Bill) Wyllie was brought in as effective company doctor to rescue the company. He was responsible for merging Hutchison with its former partly owned subsidiary, the Hongkong and Whampoa Dock Company. He got the old *hong* on its financial feet again – then Hongkong Bank chairman Michael Sandberg sold the bank's key stake (diluted to 22 per cent after the Whampoa deal) to Li.

It wasn't just the fact that Li was given the chance of buying the 22 per cent holding; the HK$639 million (then worth US$128 million) price and the terms of the deal made it too attractive to miss, and raised criticism that the bank had 'given Hutchison Whampoa away'. Wyllie, then the Hutchison chief executive, claimed that the 90 million shares had been sold at half their net asset value. In addition the Hongkong Bank offered Cheung Kong a deferred payment option, further reducing the real price. The bank replied that in selling the shares it was 'deliberately looking for a long-term and constructive holder.' Wyllie was naturally somewhat aggrieved, as he would have liked the chance of buying the Hutchison stake himself. Wyllie remembers now:

> Hutchison was sold far too cheaply. It was a steal. I think that the Hongkong Bank at that time took the view that Li Ka-shing was doing extraordinary things in the property market. Another factor was that China was going to open up. Being in bed with a powerful Chinese partner offered advantages. The bank was already in bed with Y. K. Pao. It certainly did not offer the deal around, for example to Jardines, Y. K. Pao or Swire. I would have loved the opportunity to buy the bank's Hutchison shares.

He nevertheless recognized that in business terms the purchase was a masterstroke. He wrote to Hutchison staff: 'His [Li's] acquisition of the bank's former shareholding was a brilliant move.' For the bank, the sale was profitable, and – Sandberg said – it had had no intention of retaining its stake indefinitely.

The Hutchison deal gave Li Ka-shing's empire added variety.

Cheung Kong by this time was bigger in market capitalization than Hutchison and in 1980 became the second company to post net profits of more than HK$1 billion. It was the third biggest property group, after the government and the Hongkong Land Company. Hutchison too had property interests, but was much more involved in management than in property trading, Cheung Kong's stock-in-trade. But Hutchison was also active in trading, quarrying, warehousing, cargo and container handling, engineering, retailing and making soft drinks. Hutchison was one of the big operators at Hong Kong's container port. It also owned the Park n' Shop chain of supermarkets, rivals of Jardine's Wellcome group, and the Watson's chemists and drugstore chain.

Towards the close of the 1970s and in the early 1980s, as described earlier, the Jardine Matheson management was afraid that Li might be tempted to try to gain possession either of Jardines or – more likely – go for Jardines as a way of getting control of Hongkong Land. (If he owned Land as well, Li would be Hong Kong's undisputed property king.) But no such bid was forthcoming from Li. His supporters claim that he has always shied away from making contested bids; he would prefer to make agreed deals.

As the 1980s moved on, however, Li, like other businessmen in Hong Kong, was caught by the slump in property and share prices. Profits from his enterprises fell and there was snide talk that special dividend payments were being made from Hutchison to prop up an ailing Cheung Kong. But by 1985 Li was back with a vengeance. On the evening of 21 January 1985, just after 6 p.m., Simon Keswick, chairman of Jardine Matheson, offered Li the chance of buying the 33.8 per cent share held by Hongkong Land in the Hongkong Electric Company, the utility concern that has the exclusive franchise for supplying electric power to Hong Kong island (see above). Li didn't require much time to think: a mere sixteen hours later Hong Kong's biggest-ever corporate deal had been agreed at HK$2.98 billion (US$372 million). Within two weeks the new controller of the utility company had reshuffled the board. He also sold Hutchison's 22.6 per cent stake in the Cross Harbour Tunnel property for HK$255 million. Executives close to Li explained that he doesn't like holding shares in companies that he can't control. Later he was able to sell 10 per cent of the Electric Company holding (for a nice sum of HK$1.1 billion), yet still keep control of the utility company.

The Electric purchase was the signal for a burst of new activity both at home and abroad for Li. He announced plans to spend the huge sum of HK$4 billion in developing the Whampoa Garden residential complex, on the Kowloon side of the harbour, a decision that was taken as a sign of Li's continuing faith in the profitable existence of Hong Kong (though Li will have got his return on his investment before 1997). In September 1986 it was revealed that Hutchison Whampoa had bought 4.99 per cent of Britain's Pearson Group, with industrial, banking and publishing enterprises. The Hong Kong concern said it wanted to discuss 'ways to increase this investment substantially which would lead to the creation of commercial links between the two groups'.

Hutchison's advisers suggested that it was looking for an enlarged holding, probably more than 20 per cent but less than the 29.9 per cent that would trigger a full takeover bid under UK rules. Given that Hutchison then owned 25 per cent of the Hong Kong newspaper group, the *South China Morning Post*, all sorts of exciting business link-ups were speculated on, especially in the field of newspapers and communications. In the end nothing came of potential tie-ups. The Pearson group was reluctant to get further involved, so Li sold his holding to an Italian concern (and it was later bought by American-naturalized Australian Rupert Murdoch. In Hong Kong too, Murdoch made an offer for the *Morning Post* and Hutchison pulled out of the Hong Kong newspaper.)

But this didn't stop Li's overseas ambitions. In 1986 he moved to buy a controlling stake in Canada's largest oil and gas concern, Husky Oil. Under the complicated deal worth about

HK$4 billion, interests associated with Li would hold a total stake of 57 per cent. Of this 43 per cent would go to Hutchison and Hongkong Electric, 9 per cent to Li's family and a further 5 per cent to Toronto-based Canadian Imperial Bank of Commerce.

The Husky purchase prompted a number of controversial questions. Chief among them was whether Li was moving away from Hong Kong. 'It is my private business, but I don't mind telling you,' Li told dogged reporters. 'I still carry a British Hong Kong passport and so does my wife – and I think that's good enough.' The purchase was also questioned by investment analysts, who pointed out that Li had jumped into a field in which he had no previous expertise. Li pointed out that after the Husky investment his group would hold only about 10 per cent of its assets outside Hong Kong. Simon Murray, the energetic former Jardines executive who was managing director of Hutchison Whampoa, said that as the group grew more assets would be held outside Hong Kong, perhaps up to 25 per cent. He saw this as a natural development of a company as it expanded.

Another major development came in 1987, when Li restructured his business empire. He set up a new company, Cavendish International, to hold all the non-electricity-related interests of Hongkong Electric. Some analysts said that the restructuring had been on the cards for some time but was triggered off by the feared presence of a predator who had built up a 20 per cent holding in Hongkong Electric, sufficient to challenge Li's domination. Li professed that he was relaxed about the Hongkong Electric share register, but the restructuring move would make him more relaxed still. Another reason for the restructuring is that Hongkong Electric Holdings, being a franchised utility, is subject to public scrutiny and political pressure. Profits on its electricity generation operations are regulated according to a government scheme of control. Profits from other ventures have sometimes proved politically sensitive. So the restructuring effectively left the Electric Company to produce electricity, allowing other operations to run separately and – it was hoped – with the political pressures removed.

Li himself said that a major reason for restructuring was to allow consumers to see that the Electric Company's profits arose from its functions as a utility and were not being used to fund other investments. Simon Murray, by now Hongkong Electric's chairman as well as managing director of Hutchison, added that 'It will make it easier for the consumer and the government to see what is happening.' The deal involved creation of Cavendish International Holdings as an intermediary holding company, plus the parking of most of the group's debt in a distant company, Hongkong Electric as shorn of its non-electricity interests. The Hong Kong takeovers committee exempted Hutchison from making a general offer for Cavendish when it raised its stake to more than 50 per cent, on the grounds that Hutchison already controlled Electric. This caused controversy because it broke a cardinal rule that all shareholders should be treated alike: Hutchison got control of Cavendish in a deal that was not priced by the market or offered to other shareholders. Later, Li tried to copy Jardine Matheson with a plan to issue 'B' shares for Cheung Kong and Hutchison that would carry more voting rights than ordinary shares. This was seen as an attempt to ensure control of the companies on the cheap. All schemes for 'B' shares were forbidden by the stock exchange after a spate of planned issues threatened collapse of the market.

Another side of Li's manner of business dealings came out in 1986 when he and other executives of his Cheung Kong group were censured for culpable insider dealing in connection with share trading in International City Holdings (ICH) in the first half of 1984. ICH was then a joint venture company, with Hongkong Electric, then controlled by Hongkong Land. The official inquiry, only the second in Hong Kong's history, took eighteen months to report. It concerned a property deal between ICH and Ever Bright Industrial Co., the Peking-linked group headed by Wang Guangying, the so-called 'red capitalist'. In January 1984 Wang had told reporters that Ever Bright had agreed to buy eight, then uncompleted, apartment blocks from ICH for HK$940 million (US$120 million). The news of the deal gave the depressed stock and property markets that were in the doldrums a big boost. It also lifted the ICH share price. Then, five months later, the two companies announced that the deal was not going through after all and cited a secret clause allowing Ever Bright to reclaim its deposit without penalty and indeed with interest on the money. The tribunal decided that the agreement itself had been made in good faith. The negotiations revealed in the tribunal's report showed something of the delicate business dealings between Hong Kong and Chinese interests. Li Ka-shing clearly thought he had to 'give face' to Wang by inserting the six-month option allowing Ever Bright to pull out of the deal at two days' notice. Li in fact frankly admitted to the tribunal that he became worried that the deal might make him beholden to China. He added that for 'political reasons' he didn't think that Wang would invoke the clause. So, he claimed, its existence had little bearing on the dealing in ICH shares done by Cheung Kong executives on all but two trading days before the sale was cancelled.

The tribunal took a different view. It cited the circular signed at Li's behest by all ICH directors, that the secret option should not be made public. In fact for good measure it pointed to Li's statements after the cancellation that he was not surprised that the deal had been called off. Altogether Li and another director C. W. Chow who actually did the dealings were found 'culpable to a high degree' of insider trading. Wang Guangying was criticized for allowing the 'true character of the negotiations, and then the transaction itself, to be misrepresented fundamentally to the Hong Kong public'. But he escaped censure. The censure meted out to Li and others is the most severe 'punishment' that the tribunal could provide.

Li appealed to the High Court against the verdict of the tribunal. His counsel challenged the findings as unfair, claiming that Cheung Kong itself hadn't been involved in the dealings, only Starpeace, a wholly owned subsidiary. Li lost and had planned a further appeal. But he decided not to continue after the High Court judge, though upholding the tribunal findings, stated that culpability in the context of insider dealing 'means no more than blameworthy' and 'need not be equated to a finding of dishonesty or fraud'. The curious fact about the tribunal inquiry was that it covered a very narrow issue, a sale of 55.6 million shares in ICH at an average price of 70 HK cents each. This was a very small number against the total 1 billion International City shares held by Cheung Kong. However, the tribunal hearings threw an interesting light on some of the wheelings and dealings that make up Hong Kong business.

Li hardly suffered because of the verdict against him. Indeed an international news agency report commented that 'securities dealers shuddering at the crackdown on insider trading in New York and London may wish they were in Hong Kong where offenders face nothing more onerous than public embarrassment'. Li remained in business and remained a non-executive deputy chairman of the Hongkong Bank, with hardly any indication that his business reputation or prestige had suffered.

Throughout 1986 and most of 1987 Li was quiet. But when he did move it was in a big way. In late 1987 he planned a huge HK$10 billion rights issue, the largest that Hong Kong had seen and an indicator that he was building a war-chest for new acquisitions. For other players on all other stock markets round the world late 1987 proved to be a singularly inauspicious time. But for Li and his four listed companies, which raised a net HK$6 billion, the timing couldn't have been better: the deadline allowing the underwriting banks and financial institutions to invoke *force majeure* clauses and pull out of the issues expired at 3 p.m. Hong Kong time on 19 October 1987. Just a few hours later Wall Street crashed, and with it stock markets round the world. Pressure was put on Li to cancel the issues. The then Commissioner of Securities appealed to him publicly and, according to some reports, Governor Sir David Wilson urged him privately to cancel. But Li insisted that the issue go ahead.

In the succeeding months he wasn't idle. Abroad, he led a

consortium that won the rights to develop the Vancouver Expo '87 site – 203 acres and a sixth of the downtown city – on such good terms that it later brought political controversy in British Columbia. The purchase price was C$320 million, yet the development was spoken of as a 'goldmine' likely to be worth C$2 billion. His Husky Oil was one of the front-runners bidding for Texaco Canada. At home in Hong Kong, in 1988 he launched a string of expansive developments: a HK$9 billion scheme for residential and commercial estates on Ap Lei Chau and Kwun Tong; a HK$6.8 billion deal for building the seventh terminal at Hong Kong's container port; plans to invest HK$3 billion in Hong Kong's cable television network, and another HK$6 billion if Li's Hutchison Whampoa won the right to operate the system; a HK$2 billion joint venture with the Kowloon and Canton Railway to redevelop accommodation for the railway's staff. Other projects were also in prospect. Among those most talked about were a share in the consortium to build the new international airport, property schemes on reclaimed land and satellite ventures to improve telecommunications in Asia, and boost Li's ambitions to be a big player in world telecommunications. A group led by Y.-K. Pao won the cable television contract. Hutchison insiders said that Li was showing new caution after the Tian'anmen Square massacre.

By late 1988, Li's complicated business interests centred around Cheung Kong, 34.9 per cent owned by him. Cheung Kong itself owned 39.7 per cent of the trading concern Hutchison Whampoa (in which Li himself held a further 0.27 per cent). It also owned Green Island Cement and half of CEF Capital, while Hutchison owned 61 per cent of the Cavendish group and 80 per cent of HIT, the biggest container operator at Kwai Chung. Altogether his empire embraced a host of property and trading concerns including the Hong Kong Hilton hotel, 39 per cent of the Hong Kong Sheraton hotel, plus a string of retail stores; electricity generation and distribution through Hongkong Electric (33.8 per cent owned) and Jiangsu power station in

China (40 per cent owned); oil with Husky Oil; telecommunications through telephone and paging systems plus a 23 per cent share in the Westar VI satellite; cement; shipping and dockyards; and an estimated 10 per cent holding in Canadian Imperial Bank of Commerce held personally by Li.

For all this, Li's reputation among stock market analysts is mixed. As a property trader in Hong Kong he is reckoned to have no real rival. His typical technique was to form a joint venture project to which his partner contributed the land. Then Li looked after planning, building, financing and marketing of mainly office blocks and pre-sold them. But not all his investment decisions have won the same high praise. He had been lucky to be presented with the initial stake in Hutchison and lucky to that Hongkong Land needed to sell its shares in the electric utility.

Li paid at the top of the market for a 4.9 per cent stake in Britain's Cable and Wireless (held by Hutchison and Cavendish). And he lost money, more than HK$200 million, in his frustrated 1987 attempt to get into Hongkong Land. Most analysts also calculate that he sold his newspaper shares too cheaply. In his US business dealings Li has had his fingers burned. At one time he owned 9.5 per cent of Kaiser Cement and made property forays into Texas. By 1988 he said he had written down his US property interests to a book value of $20 million. On the other hand, Li has done well in Canada, a much smaller country with a large Chinese population, mainly Hong Kong expatriates. He obviously feels at home there, and his elder son Victor is based in Vancouver and holds Canadian citizenship.

Inside Hong Kong Li is sometimes controversial, but obviously powerful. Some analysts worry that he is just too big for the market. On several occasions the authorities have granted Li special waivers of the rules. The latest one was after the 1987 stock market crash when he was allowed to hold more than 35 per cent of Cheung Kong and Cheung Kong to hold more than 35 per cent of Hutchison Whampoa without being forced to make a general offer, as the takeover rules decreed. Financial

Secretary Piers Jacobs told the Securities Commission to suspend the 35 per cent trigger. This was against the ruling of the takeovers committee. Li wasn't grateful, but attacked the government for not suspending the trigger rule unconditionally. Concern about Li being too powerful isn't an idle worry. One broker commented on his strong personality: 'If he has 20 per cent of a company, he thinks he owns it.' On the other hand he has plenty of supporters.

Simon Murray sings Li's praises: 'I've had a lot of bosses in my time – including myself – and I would rate Li Ka-shing the best. He's supportive when things are going a bit wrong and makes his feelings known when things have gone well.' Murray operates on the principle that he knows who is boss. 'He owns the railway line and I drive the trains,' says Murray. Then he switches metaphors to say that he regards Li Ka-shing as 'having the best ships in the Hong Kong business fleet'. Murray says that he and Li operate in a 'world with no surprises. Almost every day we have a conversation and there's an executive meeting once a fortnight.' The running of Hutchison is very different from Cheung Kong and other parts of Li's empire. The Hutchison team of executives are all westernized and mostly expatriate managers. Over at Cheung Kong, Li operates with a small group of mostly Chinese trusted colleagues.

By all accounts, Li is an energetic worker, 'able to cram 48 hours into one day', according to one senior executive. His greatest ability is to take decisions quickly, especially where Hong Kong is concerned. He knows the Hong Kong market and the value of its property – which is why sceptics claim he may come unstuck as he moves offshore. Again, according to Murray, '90 per cent of his business is talking. He doesn't like a lot of paper.' He's up early, often playing golf at 6 a.m. Though he leaves the office most days fairly promptly around 5 o'clock that doesn't mean he's stopped work for the day. Business meetings are liable to spill over into the evening, partly informally. To a westerner Li is a difficult man to know, not least because, although his English ability is reputed to be good, he often tries to hide it. He's choosy about being interviewed and the impression he gives is of a self-contained man who doesn't exactly welcome criticism with open arms.

His office collects articles about him, and in the early 1980s at least was marking passages regarded as unfriendly in bright green with appropriate comments beside them. The tycoon presents the image of a successful man, but a highly conservative one, who dresses neatly, in dark business suits which make his small figure appear even slighter. His wristwatch is a cheap quartz one, always set precisely eight minutes fast. This may be because he doesn't want to be late, but there's also special significance in that in Cantonese 'eight' is a lucky number, homonym for prosperity.

Former chief executive Wyllie also comments that Li likes to be the dominant player, the boss. Apart from the *South China Morning Post* and the Cross Harbour Tunnel Company (in both of which Li has now sold his shareholdings), 'K. S. Li's companies have either been subsidiaries or on the way there.' Wyllie describes Li as 'a first class bull market operator'. For Li, his life is his business. Though Wyllie cautions that Li 'has an ego that you couldn't jump over', he also adds that 'he has a superb reputation, that if he makes a promise he will keep it. I have never heard anyone say that K. S. Li made a promise and didn't keep it, never. That is what credibility is all about.'

The fascinating questions for the future concern Li's relations with China and whether he will manage to leave behind a successful business dynasty. Unlike the flamboyant Sir Yue-Kong Pao, who loves the political limelight, Li has always seemed to shy away from political involvement. On the other hand, he is a member of the Basic Law Drafting Committee, charged with devising a constitution for Hong Kong under Chinese sovereignty. And he's always enjoyed good relations with China. Indeed in the late 1970s when he was still building his awesome reputation as a businessman in his own right, some commentators saw him as 'China's man'. Opinions are somewhat different now, though he's retained his connections with his homeland and given HK$250 million to establish a university at Shantou, of which he was made chairman of the board in recognition of his endowment.

Simon Murray insists that the group has a flourishing business investment inside China as well as pursuing new ventures in the wider world. He puts great faith in the Husky investment: 'In the 1990s it will be an interesting company. It has excellent management, substantial cash flow and debts of only 10 per cent.' Low gearing, he says, is a mark of Li Ka-shing's business success. 'Husky has both downstream and upstream activities as well as good oil reserves. This balance protects the company at times of low oil prices as it can shut down and buy raw materials in the open market.' But Murray also concedes that not all the foreign ventures have been successful. 'We are still feeling our way and have been bashed now and again, though there is no trail of blood.'

The other unanswered question is whether Li's business will outlast him. Chinese business empires have traditionally encountered hard times as the dynastic founders have died, leaving behind a large empire that's too difficult to manage for the less talented second generation. Li has two sons in their twenties who've both enjoyed a high quality US education – such as he never had – attending Stanford University, 'but not the business school', says Murray pointedly; 'K. S. Li believes that the actual business is the best business school in the world.'

Sir Yue-Kong Pao: Friend of All the World

Asked how he had paid for one acquisition, the Hong Kong businessman smiled and joked lightly: 'Oh, I looked around the house, went along to the local pawnshop and sold a few things.' They must have been extraordinary and valuable knick-knacks, for this was Hong Kong shipping and property billionaire Sir Yue-Kong Pao, explaining how he had just bought a 14.9 per cent stake in Standard Chartered Bank at a cool cost of about £180 million (US$250 million). In the sort of way that ordinary people casually play with 'Monopoly' money, Pao plays with real millions. According to him the deal was all part of a single day's work in July 1986: arriving at London's Gatwick airport at 8 a.m., he bought 5 per cent of Standard Chartered in the morning, another 5 per cent in the afternoon and topped it all off in the evening with almost 5 per cent more just to make sure.

In doing the deal Pao helped rescue the old British colonial bank from the clutches of Lloyds Bank. (Pao and two other businessmen from the Asia-Pacific area, Singapore-based Malaysian hotelier Tan Sri Khoo Teck Puat and Australian Robert Holmes à Court, together bought more than 27 per cent of the bank, though they stressed that they were not acting in concert). For Pao himself it was a return to banking, the job in which he had started in his native (pre-Communist) Shanghai. He became the largest single shareholder and for a time deputy chairman of the bank. But it was hardly a wise investment. The shares cost Pao about 800 pence each. In June 1989 he sold his stake for a reported 495 pence a share, bringing him a loss of about £67 million on the deal.

Such forays brought accusations that Pao was a megalomaniac collector of businesses – 'just because they were there'. Nevertheless Pao deserves a place in the Hong Kong business legends because of the size of his fortune and the way his shipping empire has survived stormy vicissitudes. By 1990 he will be seventy-two and the main questions concern his health and whether the empire he so painstakingly built up can survive him.

At the height of his powers 'formidable' was the word most commonly used to describe him. He keeps a strict non-smoking, virtually teetotal, lifestyle. Every morning he rises at 5.30 and spends the first hour of his day 'every day wherever I am' skipping, jogging and swimming. His skipping rope became a legendary part of his baggage. Friends and rivals remember his ability to arrive fresh as a daisy after a flight halfway round the world, conclude a high-powered business deal, and hop on the next aircraft back again.

David K. P. Li, chief manager of the Bank of East Asia, was a colleague of Pao on the Basic Law Drafting Committee working out the constitution for Chinese rule in Hong Kong after 1997. Though Pao is twenty years older than him Li says: 'he has so much energy that I am envious'. Yoh Kurosawa, deputy president of Industrial Bank of Japan, adds that the only thing Pao doesn't do well is golf. 'He's too busy constantly asking questions about business, such as "what do you think is going to happen to the yen", to concentrate on the golf.' Pao's business interests today embrace shipping, property, hotels, industry, an airline and banking. He was an adviser to the Hongkong and Shanghai Banking Corporation until his August 1986 purchase of Standard Chartered shares, and is still an adviser to Chase Manhattan Bank and to the Industrial Bank of Japan. 'They never invite any foreigners as adviser, only me,' Pao boasts of his Japanese connection.

Pao steadfastly refuses to put a figure on his riches, though Hong Kong analysts in 1988 estimated them at between US$2 to $2.5 billion net of debts. It's not a bad empire for someone who fled to Hong Kong from war-torn Shanghai in 1949 and began to build a shipping fleet in 1955 at the age of thirty-seven, with the purchase for HK$2.2 million of a single 8,200-ton coal-burning vessel, the *Golden Alpha*. Pao recalls that his move into shipping was against the wishes of his father. 'My father was a property man and couldn't understand why I wanted to buy ships.' By the 1970s Pao was the biggest private shipowner in the world, with 200 vessels totalling 20 million deadweight tons (DWT). The marvel is that he still is the biggest shipowner, and still smiling about it. With other owners round the world sending SOS distress messages to their bankers, Pao sits on a fleet of seventy ships totalling almost 8 million DWT with no debts and with book value conservatively estimated at about $1 billion, less than their market value.

The pattern of Pao's shipping empire building was seen in the way he handled his first vessel. He soon put it out to 'time' charter, roughly a medium- to long-term lease, as opposed to the 'spot' or one-time charter. In 1956 at the time of the Suez Canal crisis this seemed shortsighted: there was more money to be made at spot rates, and Pao was derided as the raw new boy. But come 1957 and the slump in the shipping market Pao was the one laughing to the bank, making money from his time charter while the spot charterers were searching for business. Pao's was the banker's approach, eschewing risks, not that of a gambler or man out to make the fastest buck possible.

There were two bases for his shipping empire. He made *shikmuisen* deals with Japanese lines, effectively switchback arrangements under which Japanese yards built the ships, while Pao owned them and put them out to long-term charter with Japanese lines. Pao's Liberian registration and Hong Kong crews allowed him to offer more competitive rates than ships under a Japanese or British flag. His other supporter was the Hongkong Bank, which provided finance and owned up to 50 per cent of his shipping companies. In 1970 Pao became the first Chinese on the board of the Hongkong Bank, later rising to the non-executive position of deputy chairman.

Even today, Pao takes a keen interest in shipping and boasts that though he doesn't know where each vessel is at any given time, 'I can tell you which of my ships is making money and which is not.' Off the top of his head he can give an impressive shorthand summary of the state of the shipping market. By the late 1970s the largest private shipowner in the world began to think of expanding his empire on dry land. The move which made the expatriates of Hong Kong sit up and take notice was his audacious 1980 battle with the so-called 'princely *hong*', Jardine Matheson, for control of the old-established Hongkong and Kowloon Wharf and Godown Co. (later renamed Wharf Holdings).

The Wharf company had been a 'Jardines' company since its 1889 founding, but Jardines had let its shareholding slip. Pao had picked up 17 per cent of Wharf from fellow tycoon Li Ka-shing in 1978. Then in a flurry of activity over a June 1980 weekend Pao rushed back to Hong Kong from Paris and raised

HK$2.2 billion (then worth US$400 million) to take his stake to 49 per cent. Jardines retired gracefully, recognizing the power of Pao's money. He had spent HK$3.5 billion in all for a controlling stake that would repay a mere HK$80 million in dividends in the first year. The action gave Pao a huge land bank on the Kowloon side of Hong Kong harbour, plus control of the 'Star' Ferry Co., responsible for the ferry shuttle across Hong Kong harbour to Kowloon, and the Hongkong Tramways, running the trams on Hong Kong island. More significantly, it made him a considerable force in Hong Kong property and in the life of the territory generally. He thumbed his nose at the government Securities Commission. The Commission demanded that he make a full bid for Wharf. Pao and his advisers Wardley (the merchant bank arm of the Hongkong Bank) ignored it.

In 1985 Pao again showed his feistiness in battle when he took over Wheelock Marden and Co., the pauper among the old British *hongs*. This fight was triggered off when Singapore hotelier Khoo Teck Puat bought the shares of Wheelock chairman John Marden. Stunned by this, Pao negotiated and bought the larger holding of Wheelock board member John Cheung. After a bruising fight lasting several weeks, Khoo gave in to Pao and retired tens of millions of dollars richer. Control of Wheelock gave Pao the old-established department store Lane Crawford plus a host of property interests.

Although fleeing from the Communist turmoil – he says that what he was afraid of was the threat of civil war and the destruction of Shanghai – Pao never lost his ties with his native China. Before becoming a shipowner he and his father had traded in a small way with the new Communist China. After Deng Xiaoping came to power he began to turn to China for business, arranging for ships to be built in Chinese yards and being anxious to do something for his native Ningbo. He poured money back into Ningbo in the 1980s for both industrial and charitable purposes. Critics accuse him of cosying up and ingratiating himself with China precisely in the hope of earning business favours later. In the most notorious incident, when British Prime Minister Margaret Thatcher visited China in October 1982 (a momentous occasion that saw the start of talks about Hong Kong's future), Pao seemed to be everywhere, first by Chinese command, then by British command. British officials annoyedly complained that Pao wanted to get in on the talks. 'He behaved as if it was the Y. K. Pao benefit show, with Thatcher and Deng reduced to supporting roles,' chuntered a still aggrieved British official. Pao responds that he was acting as honest broker whose help was sought by both sides. He even claimed later to have helped keep the negotiations between Britain and China on track. 'I remember the 1984 summer when negotiations between the then British and Chinese governments were at a deadlock,' he told a *South China Morning Post* reporter (16 September 1985). 'By occasion I visited the UK and called on the British Prime Minister, and one of the British government's senior officials called asking me to elaborate to China two or three points between the British and the Chinese. So I said all right and flew back to Hong Kong with the message for China. So I solved this problem and the Chinese government were now prepared to further negotiate and compromise.' He later sent a paper fan to Foreign Secretary Sir Geoffrey Howe with a Chinese calligraphy message saying 'Where the shades of willows disappear, a bright flowering hamlet emerges.' A week later Chinese leader Zhou Nan gave Howe the identical message.

In general, Pao responds that he's precisely the opposite of self-seeking where China is concerned. 'This is my native country. I have no ambitions for myself. I don't go to Mr Deng Xiaoping saying 'I want to make $1 million or $10 million in China.' I would never ask. Anything I talk with him is from the view of the country people, from the view of the people of China.'

By the 1980s Pao was clearly a friend of China, a man who popped up to Peking for chats with Deng. The China connection led him into another venture, taking a controlling stake in a new Hong Kong-based airline, Hongkong Dragon Airlines. The airline had originally been set up with the backing of Bank of China money – until it was pointed out that Communist Chinese control would infringe Dragonair's claim to be a Hong Kong British airline. So in stepped Pao, leaving his seat on the board of Cathay Pacific Airways to do so.

By the late 1980s Pao had plenty of critics, both professional and personal. Alan Smith, managing director and chief executive of Jardine Fleming and Co., draws a distinction between Pao the shipowner, who has proved conservative, a long-range planner and someone who has read the market carefully, and Pao the property magnate and businessman who, he says, has frequently acted on impulse. In the case of the Wharf company he was reacting to Jardines; in Wheelock Marden to Khoo. Smith also questions whether Pao's investments have always paid off. For his Wharf shares he paid HK$105 each in 1980. Adjusted for splits and new issues, the share price only caught up six years later with the price he had paid. The yield was 2 or 3 per cent when, added Smith, 'interest rates almost reached 20 per cent. Of the purchase price, about HK$1 billion was borrowed when interest rates were 12 per cent, later rising to 18.' Pao himself admitted that he paid more for Wheelock than analysts thought it worth: 'they said that Wheelock was worth HK$6.80 a share and I paid more than HK$7. But I think it's worth it.'

Other critics claimed even more dismissively that Pao was becoming a collector on a grand scale, with just a hint that he may be a megalomaniac. He certainly devised some grand schemes. Dragonair, the tiny fledgling airline with, by 1988, two leased Boeing 737 jets, devised plans not only to fly all over Asia, but to spread its wings to Europe and even the USA. The airline's executives admitted that Houston was included in the destinations to which Dragonair was seeking permission to fly at the specific wish of Chairman Pao. Executives of Cathay Pacific, a much bigger and more experienced airline, with forty years' flying experience and (at that time) twenty widebodied aircraft, were amazed at the inclusion of Houston, a city with no obvious trade or economic or even tourist connections with Hong Kong.

Personally Pao is a difficult man to understand, and he sometimes seems a mass of contradictions. Besides being one of the world's richest men, he is also one of the best connected and he doesn't mind showing off some of his friends. A glimpse at his outer office quickly reveals his connections with the world's power brokers: there are several photographs of Pao with leaders of the world. At one time in the 1980s the two outer ones showed Pao alone with Japan's Prime Minister and with US President Ronald Reagan. Inside these were pictures of Pao chatting to British Prime Minister Margaret Thatcher as she uncomfortably tried to eat with chopsticks, and Pao sitting on a sofa gesticulating to chain-smoking Chinese strongman Deng Xiaoping. And the centrepiece was a picture of Pao talking to Britain's Queen Elizabeth II and to Ronald Reagan in a cosy threesome.

Pao-watchers say that he is very quick to note who is in or out of power, and that as soon as former Communist leader Hua Guofeng slipped from grace in China, he was also banished from among the pantheon of heroes. Pao reputedly hates going to parties or social gatherings, but people who attend them with him testify to his overwhelming charm. But it is not only the rich and famous with whom Pao is friendly. Visitors are made to feel comfortable and like long-lost friends – even when they have only known him for two minutes. But he is careful whom he sees. He doesn't waste his time hobnobbing with rivals and has something of a reputation as a loner in business. In dealing with ordinary people he has a chuckling earthiness. A merchant bank chief in Hong Kong also remembers 'Pao playing postman. We were going up in the lift of Connaught Centre [headquarters of Jardines and one of Hong Kong's tallest buildings] and the postman was with us. At every floor Pao held the lift doors and tossed the bundle of letters, joking away in Chinese. He was clearly loving every minute of it. I hated it because the lift was stopping at every floor for several minutes each time and I was in a hurry.' Pao's excess nervous energy led one friend years ago to describe him as 'a nervous wreck set to Chinese music'.

By the late 1980s Pao was preparing to hand over his empire, a tough task for someone who had been so actively involved. The difficulty was compounded by his determination to keep things in the family, even though he had no sons. The billionaire has four daughters, named in alphabetical order Anna, Bessie, Cissy and Doreen. Pao's aim was to draw his sons-in-law into the family business, and by 1989 all four of them were in the family camp and each had at least one parcel of business to look after. Pao remained chairman of the traditional privately held web of interests in the World-Wide Shipping Group, but he appointed son-in-law number one, Austrian-born lawyer Helmut Sohmen, as managing director of the complex holdings, to which he added Dragonair. Second son-in-law Peter Woo, formerly a banker with Chase Manhattan, was put in charge of the onshore and publicly quoted World International Holdings interests, including Wharf Holdings, Lane Crawford department stores, Wheelock International, the Marco Polo hotels and the US-based Omni hotel group, acquired in 1988 from Aer Lingus. Third son-in-law Japanese Shin Watari was made head of Tokyo insurance and general trading company Cornes. Finally in 1988 Pao persuaded fourth son-in-law Edgar Cheng, a doctor and cancer researcher in New York, to join the family group and take over the private portfolio, worth hundreds of millions of dollars.

The billionaire also insisted that his daughters should take an interest in the businesses. 'I told my daughters not to be so old-fashioned like their mother,' he told Dinah Lee of *Business Week* (10 October 1988). 'They should learn something about business and go to board meetings but have no power until they understand things much better.' In November 1988 his first and third daughters were given Pao's holding in Standard Chartered Bank, diluted to 10 per cent by a rights issue. Pao stepped down as deputy chairman and as a director of the British bank. The billionaire said he had learned lessons from other people's experiences: 'I have seen what happens to other families, everybody fighting. I thought it would be better to let each one manage something separately.' Critical stock market analysts said that Pao's departure could bring a needed new lease of life to the family businesses. One broker even said that the 'Brezhnev years' of arteriosclerosis had set in.

Jardine Fleming Securities estimated that share prices of the quoted companies were trading at a 32 per cent discount to their net asset values. Pao's handover strategy made sense, but a lot depends on the quality and business judgement of the sons-in-law, clearly all very different individuals. Cheng was a new and raw recruit with no financial experience. Watari, charged with the task of turning Cornes into an integrated trading company, was also largely unknown. Son-in-law Woo has a banker's caution, with so far no sign that he matches Pao's flair. Merchant bankers said he had been slow to seize business opportunities. There were questions too about whether he would stand up to Pao. The most interesting is Sohmen, who has demonstrated a tough streak and a preparedness to speak out. The Austrian was quick to attack the Hong Kong government and Cathay Pacific Airways in his attempt to secure new routes for Dragonair. He resisted Hyundai Heavy Industries' attempts to cancel contracts for three tankers when prices rose. He has also been prepared to attack Pao's idols in public. He declared roundly that the idea of Hong Kong as a special autonomous region of China was 'a wonderful concept to help Britain save face but not workable. Hong Kong cannot remain immune from the rest of China'. That is not what Pao's friend Deng Xiaoping claimed to profess. It suggested that at least parts of Pao's business could go through a tough unaccustomed realignment.

10 China's Takeover of Hong Kong

On 8 August 1988 a small but highly symbolic ceremony was held in an unfinished building close to the business heart of Hong Kong. More than a hundred guests put on plastic hard hats, crammed themselves into cage-like builders' lifts and were ferried creakily up and up. When more then 300 metres above ground the guests got out on to a rough concrete floor and watched as workmen shot home the final bolts, then hoisted a round steel girder above their heads and fastened it to the rest of the superstructure, to resounding loud cheers and the release of multi-coloured balloons. Guests took up red-ribboned gold shovels to put the final cement on to the floor to mark the 'topping out' of the building (completion of the superstructure). The chief guest then smashed open a huge barrel of sake with a splash, lit giant incense sticks and cut into one of three roasted pigs.

As Hong Kong ceremonies go it was pretty small, but from up there the view is spectacular: all Hong Kong laid out below like an overcrowded, grubby toytown. Government House, starkly white and spick and span, yet relaxed in a manicured green setting, stands out alone and aloof from the determined money-making hustle-bustle all around, a very superior doll's house. Elsewhere, each square millimetre of space, whether on land or sea, has some claimant. On land, skyscrapers grow like weeds, craning ever higher for some light and air, but they all look small, almost miniature, from this building. Among them, the steel and glass Hongkong Bank building is like a Meccano structure designed by a super-achieving child. Cars, trams, buses and lorries seem like buzzing busy insects.

This is not a model or toytown Hong Kong. It is the real thing, but looks tiny because of this high viewing platform. It is a fitting commentary on the approaching new order that this building, completed in 1989, looking down on the colonial British governor, the Hongkong Bank, Jardines, Hongkong Land and the whole host of nouveaux-riches is the new local office of the Communist Bank of China. This skyscraper, designed by I. M. Pei and Partners of New York, is seventy-two storeys high, a full twenty floors higher than anything else in Hong Kong's Central business district, 315 metres from the ground to the top floor and 370 metres high if the two chopstick-like posts atop the building are counted. It is the fifth biggest building in the world and the highest outside the USA. It gives Peking a new vantage point, holding, as it were, the whole of Hong Kong in its sights.

China formally takes sovereignty over Hong Kong only at midnight on 30 June/1 July 1997, yet that date is somewhat unreal. The occasion will no doubt be marked by considerable ceremony and pageantry as Britain's Union flag is hauled down for the last time, to be replaced by China's red banner with yellow stars; as the remaining British troops depart and soldiers of China's People's Liberation Army move in; as formal speeches are made to emphasize a new era, no doubt marked by much mutual congratulation about the historic day of handover and the momentous agreement which will allow Hong Kong to continue its freewheeling capitalist system while owing allegiance to a completely different set of rulers.

But all such pomp and circumstance is as important as drumbeats on the air – good for the record books and the morale of political leaders who like to bask in self-congratulation. The reality is that China's takeover of Hong Kong has been going on steadily for years. For at least a decade before the agreement between London and Peking, China played an important part in Hong Kong's life. Immediately after the agreement, Hong Kong saw further intrusion of Chinese money and influence. Many economists and businessmen expect that long before 1997 the real Chinese takeover will be virtually complete.

The important unanswered question is whether the Chinese takeover will really benefit Hong Kong, or will instead bring the death of the goose that lays China's golden eggs. Evidence so far points in different directions, but the balance tilts towards the view that China does not really understand how capitalism or Hong Kong works.

Interdependence

There's no doubt about China's active involvement in Hong Kong. Some commentators have even described the tiny colony and the vast mainland as Siamese twins. That may seem a ludicrous comparison, not least because the advantages might appear to be all on one side. China provides essential supplies of food and water to Hong Kong; the vast subcontinent of China hardly seems to need Hong Kong's help. Tiny, crowded Hong Kong can't possibly grow enough food for itself, and over the years its farming and fishing sectors have declined to nearly nothing. Hong Kong's own reservoirs don't provide enough water, especially when the monsoon rains are fickle. So every day the people of Hong Kong depend for their very existence on lorries ferrying pigs and other livestock and green vegetables across the border from China; as well as a continuous flow of water through the two pipelines from China through the New Territories to the thirsty urban areas of Hong Kong.

But China also gains. Sales of food and water provide a useful supplement to the country's earnings of hard currency. In the late 1970s when China's foreign earning power was low, and again in the mid-1980s when needed imports of capital goods had gobbled up reserves and threatened to turn China into a major debtor country, hard currency from Hong Kong kept

China's economy going. Sir John Bremridge, Hong Kong Financial Secretary 1981–6, made his famous boast that modern China had outdone the medieval alchemists' dreams and is turning cabbage into the equivalent of gold, Hong Kong dollars that are freely convertible into any currency in the world.

It is not just domestic Hong Kong consumers that China is supplying. Each year Hong Kong is visited by more than 5.5 million people, most of whom, say tourist officials, spend 65 per cent of their time – and a great deal of money – shopping. Among the goods they buy are silk, clothing, furs and jewellery as well as more exotic products like ginger, ginseng, and jade. Some of these goods are imported from Europe and the USA, but most of the exotic items and many of the most popular buys are from China itself. Chinese silk, for example, costs between US$5 and $20 a yard in Hong Kong shops. Some of the big department stores are actually run by Communist companies, such as China Arts and Crafts, and China Products. Their stores are veritable Ali Baba treasure caves of good things from China. Indeed they are far superior to any department store on the mainland. There, shop assistants are frequently found chewing gum or chatting blithely while potential customers try to attract their attention. Even when they succeed in this endeavour, the range of goods offered in China is much more limited than in Hong Kong and the prices are not lower. Hong Kong's secret is competition. Though the sales assistants in the Communist stores in Hong Kong do have a reputation for being surlier and taking longer to serve than those in free enterprise shops, they have to compete in an open market, so they are infinitely more attentive than their branches on the mainland itself.

Other contributions that Hong Kong makes to China come in the form of remittances and tourist traffic. Many Hong Kong families still have relatives living in the mainland to whom they send significant sums of money each year. In their regular visits, especially at the important Lunar New Year festival season, Hong Kong residents also contribute heavily to China's economy, carrying back both goods and money. In the few days before Chinese New Year, crowds snake back several hundred yards from the Hung Hom railway terminus of the Kowloon–Canton Railway; each person seems to be surrounded by more luggage than he or she can carry alone. Many foreign visitors to Hong Kong also take day trips into China just so that they can say that they have visited the great People's Republic, the most populous country on earth. They are also an important source of revenue for China itself.

An increasingly important part of China's earnings derive from goods sold to third countries, using Hong Kong as the entrepôt. In the early 1980s, trade using Hong Kong as the middle man also helped to prop up Hong Kong's ailing exports. By the end of the decade re-exports were worth more than domestic exports. Hong Kong has big advantages over China, especially in its superior shipping and export facilities. It's not just the fine natural harbour and deep water port, it's the facilities that have been built up along with this, including regular shipping schedules, quick customs clearance and a whole culture geared for trading that China lacks. Especially if the goods are from southern China, Hong Kong offers speedier and trouble-free port and customs clearance. Some ever-enterprising Hong Kong traders have even been able to show that it is quicker and more economical to use Hong Kong as a transshipment point for goods going from one part of China for sale in another part of that huge country.

Adding up the visible trade through Hong Kong produces substantial, multi-billion-dollar sums. By the late 1980s Hong Kong was China's biggest trading partner, accounting for about 25 per cent of China's exports. Japan sold about US$1 billion more goods to China, but only took in return half the value of Chinese goods bought by Hong Kong. On Hong Kong's side, China was its biggest supplier of imports, providing 25 per cent of total goods and 42 per cent of the colony's imported foodstuffs. China was also Hong Kong's second largest export market, though trailing a long way behind the USA. By 1988 total Hong Kong–China trade had topped US$30 billion. Of this

Hong Kong domestic exports to China were much the smallest part, worth US$4 billion. The vast bulk of the trade, almost 60 per cent, consisted of Chinese exports to Hong Kong. The rest was re-exports of goods shipped from elsewhere through Hong Kong to China.

But the visible earnings are not the full total. Economists haggle furiously over their estimates of exactly how much China earns from Hong Kong. The figures vary greatly, so that the only real consensus is that the sums are substantial. These consist of exports, remittances, and the earnings of Chinese companies in Hong Kong. Some experts have gone as far as to say that 50 per cent of China's annual foreign currency earnings are made in Hong Kong; more cautious economists choose a conservative 25 per cent. In the early 1980s the sums were billions of US dollars, perhaps as high as US$8 or 10 billion. By the late 1980s the totals probably reached US$25–30 billion. Gu Nianliang, the head of a Canton (Guangzhou)-based research centre admitted that 'Nobody knows for sure' how much China earns from Hong Kong. Different Chinese organizatons give different figures. Gu added that China was unsure 'which companies belong to us', and different companies had different ways of calculating their profits.

Hong Kong Investments in China

In the 1980s, as explained in the chapter on the economy, a new hybrid form of product developed out of Hong Kong–China cooperation. Hong Kong manufacturers began to find out that not only was domestic labour expensive, but for certain kinds of industries workers were just not available. But across the border in China there were plentiful supplies of much cheaper labour. Textile makers were quick to take advantage and contract out some of the simpler forms of work to companies over the border. Another disadvantage of Hong Kong is that there's very little room to build new factories. Few Hong Kong manufacturers can enjoy the large floor areas that they often need. By 1988 and 1989 some big manufacturers, especially of cheaper items like toys, were so badly squeezed by labour and land costs that they prepared to shift all manufacturing to China, despite skill problems there. Some leading economists describe the neighbouring province of Guangdong as 'Hong Kong's backyard', noting that, as Governor Sir David Wilson said, there are twice as many Communist Chinese as Hong Kong locals working in manufacturing for Hong Kong companies.

Indeed, without Hong Kong businessmen investing in China, the mainland's drive to attract foreign investment would look pretty sick. It is often very difficult to work out the mixture of sound commercial decision-making and mere sentiment for the homeland which has inspired some Hong Kong investment in China. Some Hong Kong businessmen have sought simply to do something for their motherland; others saw opportunities of profiting from the modernization of the most populous country on earth; yet others took timid toe-dipping investments, some of which were not profitable but offered a means of insurance, letting China know that they want to be on good terms with the Communist rulers (who will soon be their rulers too). Some attempts on the surface seem opportunistic if not frankly political. Hopewell Holding's Gordon Wu has devised several ambitious projects, the biggest of them being his super-highway to Canton. But stock market analysts have counted his political ties with China in his favour. He got a good report in an analysis by Alison Lutz of stockbrokers Barclays De Zoete Wedd. She admitted that he relied largely on political connections:

> Although Hopewell is underpinned by Hong Kong-based property assets, it interests many investors mainly because of the potential of its large-scale China projects. These are long term by nature, adding a degree of uncertainty to the pattern of future earnings, and will depend both upon the development of China's open door policy and on Hopewell's ability to capitalize on *guanxi* (connections). Hopewell has

> concentrated on the energy and transportation sectors, which are among China's top priorities for development and should continue to receive financial and administrative support even if other areas of the economy are damped down. Chief executive Gordon Wu's *guanxi* are among the most visible of those of any Hong Kong businessmen. He secured the intervention of Communist Party boss Zhao Ziyang in a labour dispute with Shenzhen authorities; he also sits on the Chinese People's Political Consultative Conference, a central government advisory body . . .

Other prominent businessmen have been keen to help China. The mega-rich like Li Ka-shing and Sir Yue-Kong Pao have given generous sums of money to charitable and economic projects. When Pao went back in the mid-1980s to his home town of Ningbo he was greeted in style, almost like a head of state, and attended by firework displays and crowds of cheering children. The counties of China bordering Hong Kong are much richer than the rest of China thanks to schools, hospitals and other facilities funded by rich men based in Hong Kong.

Hong Kong businessmen collectively are China's biggest investors. Altogether in the 1979–85 period, according to Chinese statistics, Hong Kong businessmen invested almost US$10 billion in China or 60 per cent of the total foreign investment, far ahead of Japan's US$1.7 billion or the US$1.4 billion provided by the USA. And the same sort of pattern has continued. In 1987 Hong Kong invested US$2.5 billion, or two-thirds of total foreign investment in China.

Typical investments are small, sometimes US$2 million or less, suitable for individual rich Hong Kong businessmen. The colony has advantages over other investors in China. The Japanese – and this has been noted in China – have been clever enough to put their energy largely into trading ventures, where there is an immediate pay-off, rather than into investments on plant which have a much longer and less certain reward. Americans, eager at first to get into the China market, have learned the hard way that setting up factories in China does not guarantee success. Wages are lower than in Hong Kong or in other parts of Asia, but productivity is also lower therefore so are profit margins. On top of this, there is political resistance to many of the work experiments that western industrialists want to introduce. Hong Kong factory owners sometimes boast that because they are Chinese they understand the Chinese mentality and can better persuade the Communists to agree to new working methods. Some of these Hong Kong businessmen of course, as noted above, were having second thoughts about their Chinese investments in the aftermath of the Peking massacre.

Another example of the growing Hong Kong–China nexus came in the mid-1980s when the head of Bank of China's operations in Hong Kong, Jiang Wengui, suggested that some of the funds with which Hong Kong was awash could be used to good advantage for China's own economic development. Some pro-China bankers in Hong Kong complained that the approach by Jiang, which was repeated more than once, was too heavy-handed for comfort.

What China Can Learn from Hong Kong

The *Hong Kong–Macau Economic Quarterly* published by the Bank of China predicted in October 1987 that Hong Kong would become increasingly important in raising capital for China. The magazine cited the increasing financial sophistication of Hong Kong and the close understanding between Hong Kong and mainland Chinese financial institutions. Loans arranged in Hong Kong for Chinese institutions grew by 33 per cent in 1987 and had topped HK$13 billion by April 1987. Xu Jiatun, Hong Kong director of Xinhua, also outlined Hong Kong's role in China's development. He took up Lord Kadoorie's point, saying 'Hong Kong plays a unique role in assisting the motherland in publicizing and pursuing its policy of openness. It can serve the motherland in obtaining the economic information of the world and absorbing the experiences of management, capital, technology and professionals.' Xu expanded on these hopes in 1988 when he spoke of China's ambitious plans for Hong Kong's role in developing its coastal areas. Hong Kong had the special advantage, he said, of immediate access to international information along with investment funds and technology.

Not all the flows of funds have been simply from Hong Kong to China. In 1986 and 1987 China's banking support was crucial in the propping up of two ailing shipping lines. Wah Kwong Shipping Group, owned by the Chao family, and the C. H. Tung Group were among Hong Kong's biggest business ventures. In the 1970s and early 1980s their and Yue-Kong Pao's fleets made Hong Kong one of the most important ship-owning centres in the world. But by the mid-1980s the bottom had dropped out of the market worldwide and there was too much shipping capacity. Pao read the signs and weathered the storms very well. But other shipowners were not so clever, especially Wah Kwong and Tung. Money from China was the catalyst that helped to bail them out at a time when other bankers would have let them sink. Even more important to Hong Kong as a whole was the way that China quickly joined in with help when the Hong Kong financial markets collapsed in October 1987. Xinhua director Xu hurriedly left the important meeting of the Chinese Communist Party conference in Peking and rushed back to Hong Kong. Xinhua's deputy director pledged cooperation: 'If the Hong Kong government needs our cooperation in addressing the problem, we shall make corresponding positive efforts, so long as they are within our capacity.' The Bank of China group provided a large chunk of the money used to support the futures market. Of course there was a good deal of self-interest in the move. Some analysts estimated that China-owned institutions held about 10 per cent of the Hong Kong stock market's total capitalization – about $8 billion – before the slide began on 19 October. 'Quite a few Chinese investors were burned very badly,' according to an anonymous Chinese source quoted in the *Asian Wall Street Journal* (30 October 1987). Xu of Xinhua played down the losses, claiming that they should be regarded as 'tuition fees' for learning the game of capitalism.

But Hong Kong offers China much more than dollars and cents. Hong Kong businessman Lord Kadoorie sees Hong Kong as China's great learning point and training school, where good Chinese communists can study capitalism and understand and benefit from it without tainting or corrupting their own systems. This was indeed happening rapidly, especially as China itself began to modernize. By the early to mid-1980s, China and its corporations were not only learning but were earning from Hong Kong. Old established companies like the Bank of China, China Merchants Steam Navigation Co. and China Resources became more active. New Chinese companies set up offices in the colony.

By the 1980s Hong Kong had begun to be increasingly important, not just as a window on to China as it had been during the dark days of Mao, but as a meeting place for the capitalist and Communist systems. American and other western corporations anxious to invest in China proper set up regional offices in Hong Kong through which to deal with China and even to set up investment deals in the mainland. Such corporations found Hong Kong a more congenial place to do business than Peking or Shanghai. Though Hong Kong is not cheap, at least business costs are competitive and not padded out by taxes and other charges imposed by Communist bureaucrats. In the British colony, also, the potential investor in China is more likely to meet Chinese who understand the way the capitalist system operates and will be aware that time means money. Trying to negotiate in China with Communist bureaucrats can prove an almost endless process, as meeting follows meeting indecisively; the western partners are never sure who is the most senior Chinese on the opposite side of the table to them.

Even Hong Kong Chinese, natural traders who know many of the typical Communist tricks and share common Chinese ancestry, find it tough going to deal with China. Proper documentation and well-established contacts of course help; but even so business deals involving China can prove nightmarish. One

Hong Kong trader commented: 'We live by our wits.' He told how he received a shipment of Taiwan-made zippers in Xiamen (Amoy), cleared them through customs and paid 85 per cent import tax, then loaded the consignment on to lorries for delivery to the Shanghai area. But these lorries were intercepted at a checkpoint organized by the State Administration for Industry and Commerce to prevent smuggling of goods. At first the trader was unworried, as the papers were in order, but when after a month the goods hadn't been released, he had to devise a solution. He believed that the Chinese state agency wouldn't be prepared to lose face by admitting that it had discovered no wrongdoing, so the Hong Kong trader made an accusation against himself that he had cheated customs by under-reporting the value of the shipment. 'Of course I didn't.' The tactic worked: he was fined Yuan 8,000, praised by the judge for cooperating, and got his goods back (incident reported in the *Asian Wall Street Journal*, 1 September 1986). In a country like China where there is no jury system and where penalties for business offences include heavy fines, jail sentences or even death, it's as well for a businessman to have friends to help him stay on the right side of the officials.

A more positive view of Hong Kong's supporting role for China's advances is put by Helmut Sohmen, an appointed member of Hong Kong's Legislative Council and a son-in-law of Sir Yue-Kong Pao. He calls the territory 'a gateway to China' and comments:

> Hong Kong is truly 'the handle on the teapot of China' in the pivotal role it already plays in helping China speed up its own progress.
>
> Hong Kong's proven ability to combine Western economic concepts and lifestyles with Oriental traditions of family cohesion and hard work, together with the stability of a proven legal system, the motivation provided by both the non-interventionist stance of government and a low tax base, and the absence of political confrontation so far, have

ensured the territory's success. There is no question that at the end of the twentieth century Hong Kong will still be the major gateway to China. It will be China's most important commercial metropolis, a regionally significant trading and transport centre and communications base, a location for both local and international investment supported by sophisticated financial markets and a fully developed range of professional services, and it will boast a highly trained and multi-lingual population. (The *Asian Wall Street Journal*, 12 May 1987).

Chinese Investments in Hong Kong

The most obvious sign of China's growing involvement in Hong Kong has been the proliferation of Chinese companies setting up offices. Chinese companies are not strangers to Hong Kong. The grandfather is China Merchants Steam Navigation. The company was founded as a mainland-owned concern way back in the 1870s. In those days it survived by making deals with shipping lines run by Jardine Matheson and Butterfield and Swire (now Swires). Under the unequal trading system, such British concerns dominated water transport even within China. China Merchants has thus had plenty of opportunity to learn about capitalist ways and is generally reckoned to be the smartest and most efficiently run of the mainland Chinese concerns operating in Hong Kong.

The Bank of China is another institution which originally opened its Hong Kong office long before the Communist revolution. The man charged with managing the first Hong Kong office was the father of New York-based American–Chinese architect I. M. Pei (who has designed the new Bank of China headquarters in the colony). The Bank of China simply switched allegiance from Kuomintang to the Communist side when the revolution took place in 1949.

Until the early 1980s it was reasonably easy to keep track of newcomers to Hong Kong from China and of their ventures.

Some local organizations recorded the names of companies and their ventures on a case-by-case, property-by-property, almost million-dollar-by-million-dollar basis. But then there was an explosive growth. By 1982 the magazine *Asiaweek* was recording that

> there are perhaps three hundred companies all wholly owned by China and run by cadres turned capitalists. Three years ago there was only a handful of organizations like the huge umbrella of China Resources. Some of the newcomers, Guangdong Enterprises or Tsim Lien Trading Co., for example – carry the formidable authority of an entire province. Others represent only a county, a small municipality, a commune, or even a single factory. Local businessmen call them 'briefcase companies' since they often rent no more than an office desk in an obliging Hong Kong firm eager for commissions. An established capitalist partner may stay in the forefront of every deal, leaving the Communist official working quietly behind the scenes.

By 1984 Wang Guangying, chairman of Peking-supported Ever Bright Industrial Co., claimed that China had invested about US$4 billion in various economic sectors ranging from transport and construction to property and finance. 'China needs Hong Kong to aid its modernization programmes . . . and Hong Kong is inseparable from China,' the newly arrived Wang said in an interview that year.

By 1985 Hong Kong's Trade Development Council gave a figure of HK$30 billion for China's investment in Hong Kong, citing banking, insurance, shipping, retailing, property and manufacturing. Its report saw Hong Kong serving as a uniquely convenient 'laboratory' for China's growing commercial operations – as well as offering a reservoir of skills and technical expertise to help China's modernization.

By 1987 further diversification had occurred: China's manufacturing investment in Hong Kong was gathering force and attracting attention – though it was still quite small as a share of total Chinese involvement. The Communist mainland was the third largest foreign investor in the manufacturing sector in Hong Kong, with almost HK$3 billion, or not quite 20 per cent of total foreign investment. It had long overtaken the UK (with about 7 per cent) and was running close behind Japan (21 per cent) and the USA (37 per cent). The figures can be treated with some caution as they don't include historic investments, though in China's case old investments would be small. Total overseas manufacturing investment in Hong Kong was given at just under HK$16 billion. 'Chinese investment is relatively recent,' the government's acting Director of Industry Tony Eason said. A government survey showed that China was involved in thirty-five manufacturing establishments employing more than 5,000 workers, including nearly 3,000 in nine electronics factories. Hongkong Bank's economist Vincent Cheng noted that Chinese investors preferred to buy existing companies, thus gaining the expertise that came with them: 'the ideal deal is to find a partner and inject cash into an existing company,' he said. Cheng added that manufacturing was still only a small part of China's total investment in Hong Kong.

Getting the total picture of Chinese involvement is more difficult. The Chinese authorities tried several times in the late 1980s to get a complete picture of mainland operations and offices in the colony, and had to retire baffled and defeated. The state-run China Resources Company (CRC) attempted in 1987 to compile a complete list and failed; some companies just refused to talk. According to a source quoted in the *Far Eastern Economic Review*, 'when the heads of those companies realized that someone from CRC was on the other end of the line, they simply slammed down the phone' (23 June 1988). Xinhua claimed it had no list of Chinese companies. US State Department and other sources identified more than 750 Chinese-run companies by name. They traced 54 companies under the wing of China Resources, 33 of China Merchants Steamship group, 20 of China Travel Service, and 49 in banking and finance. The

Chinese concerns in Hong Kong also include China Venturetech Investment Corporation, the country's only venture capital company. In 1988 it became a refugee from China's restrictive and immature financial markets. Altogether, bankers and brokers estimate there are somewhere between 1,000 and 3,000 Chinese mainland companies with offices in Hong Kong, though only about 500 are 'official'. China-watchers felt on surer ground in estimating total Chinese investment in Hong Kong; the consensus was about US$10 billion in 1988, a figure much higher than the US$6 billion invested by American concerns.

Probably the best known of all China's representatives in Hong Kong is the Bank of China. It hasn't been as long-established as China Merchants, the shipping group, but its physical location right in the centre of Hong Kong and the fact that it deals with money both help to ensure a respected presence.

In the 1960s and 1970s the Bank of China's physical presence, its huge building and its secretive behaviour guaranteed a place in folklore whatever its role was in fact. At least one popular spy story had the Communist orders and operations conducted from the Bank of China building. In the mid-1960s Central Hong Kong provided the bizarre sight of the Bank of China building sporting a huge picture of Mao and Maoist slogans while cricket was being played right in front of Mao's austere, no doubt disapproving eye. (The cricket club has since moved to Happy Valley and the ground has been turned into a largely concrete public park.)

Since those days China has also changed and the Bank of China has changed with it. In the early 1980s the bank and its thirteen sisters showed that they were quite ready to be competitive participants in Hong Kong's hyperactive banking scene. The banks organized an electronic network,' linking them all so that a customer of one could draw out money from any other. In mortgage finance, several of the sisters including Nanyang Commercial Bank were up and running even against the Hongkong Bank. 'We had to be up early in the morning to catch Nanyang,' recalled William Purves, chairman of the Hongkong Bank, paying his tribute to the fiercely competitive abilities of the Chinese bank. (See also chapter 9.) The Bank of China and its sisters participated in other new devices like credit cards. The parent bank set up a joint leasing company with a local concern, the Bank of East Asia, and a foreign partner, Société Générale of France. But several of the Chinese banks were badly caught and over-exposed when the property slump came. Not all bankers sing the praises of the Bank of China without qualifications. Most of them make nice diplomatic noises, but the rates of return achieved by the banks in the Communist alliance have proved well below those that other banks in Hong Kong enjoy. Nevertheless, the Chinese bankers were following a well-established and successful Japanese precedent of going for market-share as a key ingredient rather than looking for immediate profits. By the late 1980s it has succeeded and by common consent the Bank of China group accounted for about 25 per cent of local deposits. In mid-1989 the Bank of China took full control over six of its thirteen sister banks. A spokesman scotched speculation that the takeover presaged the bank's wish to be the colony's central bank. Chinese sources said it was for commercial reasons in the light of new international capital adequacy guidelines. The move would also discourage Chinese provinces, some of whom had wanted to buy a Hong Kong-based Communist bank to support their provincial development schemes.

China Resources is another well-known Chinese company in Hong Kong, also distinguished by its large building, a skyscraper on reclaimed land on the Wanchai waterfront of Hong Kong island. The close relationship between China Resources and the Chinese government is marked by the fact that the Ministry of Foreign Affairs has its local visa office in the China Resources building. Cynics also note that the building is a hive of activity for lorries unloading heavy western goods, with the implication that this is special 'diplomatic' traffic.

China Resources officials say an important part of their job is to help promote exports from the Chinese mainland. Tong Zhiguang, freshly appointed general manager of China Resources (Holdings) Co. in 1986, said frankly that the company's aim was to assist the mainland to raise both the quality and the quantity of its products. To this end, Tong said China Resources was considering setting up factories in Hong Kong. In late 1988 the company announced a giant scheme for a million square metres of housing and 75,000 square metres of commercial development in a joint venture with Li Ka-shing in the New Territories. Not everyone was happy with China Resources' efficiency. Indeed, one reason for the sending of so-called 'red capitalist' Wang Guangying to Hong Kong was – so Wang himself openly hinted – because of dissatisfaction in the Chinese politburo with China Resources. But by 1987 China Resources was widely reported to be all set for a new branch of business – banking. So keen was it to set up a bank that it had employed a local headhunting firm to find senior bank executives who might be suitable to run a bank that the company acquired. One target mentioned was Wing On Bank, controlled by the Hang Seng subsidiary of the Hongkong Bank ever since Wing On had had to be bailed out with government help.

If successful, China Resources would be the third Communist entity besides the Bank of China and its associates to have a banking operation in the city. China Merchants had acquired a dominant share in Union Bank and China International Trust and Investment Corporation had taken over Ka Wah Bank when that bank got into difficulties. Citic is very much a conglomerate and it is also run by an entrepreneurial man, Rong Yiren. Rong, said to be the richest man in China (a claim which he doesn't himself actively dispute), owes his fame and fortune to two rather contradictory elements. His family was one of the richest in pre-revolutionary Shanghai; the other factor is his friendship with Deng Xiaoping and senior Chinese leaders. In the Maoist days of the Cultural Revolution, Rong suffered an eclipse and ill-treatment at the hands of the Red Guards when he was held as a virtual prisoner. Founded in the late 1970s, Citic under Rong clearly sees Hong Kong as an important place in its business empire. By 1987 it had bought Ka Wah Bank plus a hotel and a majority stake in a housing project. In addition, it spent HK$2 billion buying a 12.5 per cent stake in Cathay Pacific Airways, the successful and highly profitable Hong Kong-based airline owned by the Swire Group. Deng Xiaoping himself had written the calligraphy for Citic's order of the day: 'Be boldly creative.' Rong himself called Citic 'a socialist conglomerate', but denied the label of 'capitalist'. He said: 'My view is very clear: the methods and approaches in capitalist management, if they can survive for so long, must have their merits. So we can use those parts which are beneficial to the development of our socialist economy – and, of course, discard the bad things . . . I think capitalism has failed in China. In the past I tried, but failed.' Rong's son Larry Yung was on the Cathay board and in charge of Citic's Hong Kong operations, further evidence that nepotism is alive and well in the People's Republic.

But the most talked about and most controversial of all the new Chinese investors coming to Hong Kong was so-called 'red capitalist' Wang Guangying. Wang too had suffered at the time of the Cultural Revolution. His sister was the widow of disgraced former Chinese president and erstwhile comrade of Mao, Liu Shaoqi. After being educated at Peking's Fu Jen (Roman Catholic-run) university, where he majored in chemistry, he founded one of China's first modern chemical factories in the city of Tianjin, where he later became deputy mayor.

He was never a party member, and during the Cultural Revolution he spent eight years in jail. Wang remembers 'a businessman can do the most in his fifties – I lost the prime of my life in prison'. He also recalls that 'I spent a lot of time watching the spiders spinning webs in one corner of my cell. Did you know it takes 14 days for a spider's eggs to hatch?' But he too had political connections that served him well. His most notable friend was Zhou Enlai, China's premier, who gave him the tag of 'red capitalist'. In 1983 and 1984 Wang prepared to take Hong Kong by storm. 'Fa Tsai' (*fat choy* in Cantonese), he grinned as he greeted people – meaning 'Get rich.' Certainly Wang arrived in a style that suggested that he had plenty of rich and influential backers. He moved into the whole 10,800 square feet of the thirty-ninth floor of the gold-curtainwalled Far East Finance Centre building, locally nicknamed The Amah's Tooth.

Wang became one of its most glittering occupants. He sported a flash Swiss wristwatch. He usually wore a comfortably rampled suit, and his crumpled gray cardigan, heavy frame and frequent, rather toothy, grin gave him an avuncular appearance. When an office opens in Hong Kong it is customary for friends to send wreaths of flowers, and when Wang opened the offices of Ever Bright Industrial Co. and Violight Industry Co., there were plenty of local tributes. But there were also large bouquets from China's Premier Zhao Ziyang, Vice Premiers Wan Li and Yao Yilin and State Councillors Gu Mu, Bo Yibo and Zhang Jingfu.

Clearly Wang wished it to be known that he operated at the very highest levels in China. A glimpse of his view of his stature was revealed in his explanation of how the companies came to be founded. Wang recalls how he came to Hong Kong in early 1983 'to meet old friends and to look at the business and financial setup'. In mid-February 1983, he said, he submitted a report to Premier Zhao and the Chinese state council that recommended establishing 'a comprehensive commercial company. They approved this the following day.' The day of the agreement was 22 February 'triple 2', said Wang through an interpreter, beaming broadly. 'It augurs well, as it is a lucky number according to Chinese tradition.' The official announcement was made on 1 April, and Wang was in business by the summer, after paying US$3 million for his office space. 'Wang has to have the highest-level backing in China,' remarked a senior Hong Kong banker; 'you just can't move that quickly without friends at the top.'

The establishment of Ever Bright, later renamed China Everbright Holdings Co., strongly suggested a Chinese commitment to exploiting the virtues of capitalism – but also revealed the weakness of the system in the fact that only a man with *guanxi* (the right connections) could possibly have succeeded in starting the company. Business contacts claim that Wang complained to Zhao that Chinese state agencies were lethargic, inefficient and too keen on protecting their own bureaucratic turf, although Wang himself, when asked, sidestepped and refused to give a direct answer to such suggestions. 'Chinese state agencies in Hong Kong alone can hardly keep up with the actual needs and growth of China's economy,' he said.

Initially, said Wang in an interview in 1984, 'I thought of setting up a comprehensive company doing business all over the world. This would be compatible with the future development of trade of China.' Marubeni, one of the big Japanese trading companies, was his model: 'It gives guidance to manufacturers in Japan on what products they should produce, and its foreign branches are in charge of selling these products.' Subsequently Premier Zhao himself modified the task. He ordered that Wang and his colleagues should serve the industrial and technological upgrading of China and concentrate on helping the 3,000 enterprises chosen for the forefront of the technical transformation. 'So I switched from modelling after Marubeni to C. Itoh, which is an industrial and trading company.'

Wang quickly showed that he was prepared to rub shoulders with all sorts of foreigners China itself isn't keen on, including those from such diverse places as Chile – where the government isn't exactly ideologically sympathetic to Peking – and Singapore, which has no diplomatic relations with China. Wang bought second-hand trucks from Chile for US$15.8 million, and looms from Singapore for US$3.5 million; on these two transactions alone, he says, 'I saved US$33 million for the state.' Wang was honest enough to say 'I have many connections' – deliberately contrasting his operation to typical Chinese factories.

'They have to file reports for level after level to get permission, whereas I can contact the relevant authorities directly and go to the factory manager and say, "There are looms available. Do you want them or not?" and take a prompt decision.'

But what about Hong Kong's future? 'Let's talk politics,' he suggested.

> At the moment, Hong Kong people are afraid that Chinese policies might be changed. Policies changed very much during the rule of the Gang of Four. What the Chinese government is doing now is to prevent such changes. One of the proofs is my presence here. Second, outsiders are afraid there may be another Cultural Revolution. I think that the one who is most afraid of another Cultural Revolution is myself, as during that period I was put into jail for eight years. As I see it, the government is taking every measure to prevent a recurrence.

Wang expressed confidence that 'there will be endless opportunities for doing business and making money in Hong Kong. There are more than sixty years to go [the remaining ones of the British lease plus the fifty years that China has promised of self rule for Hong Kong. 'If things are good, why should they not continue? I am fully confident I am now doing business and the next generation will be doing business.' In late May, before China's crackdown, Wang sent several dozen letters to senior Party and government figures in Peking urging support for the student pro-democracy protestors. Wang and disgraced Chinese leader Zhao Ziyang were friends.

A leading banker commented pithily, 'Wang travels too frequently to Beijing to be regarded as a truly independent operator. The impression is that he goes there to get his orders.' Some unkind critics see the company as a recruiting agency for the children of high party officials. (The fact that Wang himself put his daughter and son on the payroll underscores the value of connections.)

A senior Hong Kong bureaucrat added the view that 'buying trucks when the market is depressed is a smart move, but it is not a major step on the road to the white-hot technological advances that China needs'. Making a more substantial point, this official argued that 'Wang's establishment in Hong Kong is part of the great Chinese weakness. They cannot trust the outside world. Wang is safe because he is within party control and is not tainted by too many foreign contacts.' Furthermore, this bureaucrat suggested 'as a capitalist Wang is thirty years out of practice' – though Wang said he'd read *The One Minute Manager* and *The Third Wave* to bring himself up to date. 'Asking him, as a virtual one-man operation, to deliver the goods is expecting the performance of a magic wand. It's a great dream.'

Just how much of a dream it was quickly became clear. At first it had seemed that the burly 'red capitalist' was prepared to put his money where his mouth was and to back Hong Kong's development even in the teeth of market depression. A key example was his decision to spend US$120 million in January 1984 for eight as yet unfinished housing blocks that would create 1,100 flats. The local press treated the deal with banner headlines. Wang himself regarded the transaction rather dismissively as a little something China was prepared to do 'for the prosperity and stability' of Hong Kong. He several times denied rumours that he would pull out of the deals. But after five months of frantic searching for a buyer, Wang did pull out, and got his money back under a previously unpublished clause in the deal with Li Ka-shing and International City Holdings (see Chapter 9).

The deal received close attention and was treated to a 362-page official investigation to find out whether there was any insider trading involved. The report (published in April 1986) exonerated Wang, but exposed his complete lack of knowledge of the Hong Kong marketplace: 'He came to the property market with a complete lack of expertise, but he was an optimist,' the report stated, describing his optimism as 'genuine, albeit unfounded'. After the deal turned sour Wang was noticeably quieter than before. Not until 1988 did he speak out again. He told local reporters that 'Some people say I talk too much and do too little, so I'm doing more and talking less.' The tribunal summed up Wang's position 'at a time when the property market was stagnant, the stock market depressed, the political scene uncertain and the people of Hong Kong were awaiting anxiously the outcome of the Sino-British talks, he came on the scene as the prospective purchaser in what was heralded as a "HK$1 billion transaction". It is not surprising that the Hong Kong press fell upon him. He was the man of the moment.'

The efforts to find a buyer also revealed a lack of organization inside Wang's Ever Bright company. The person given the task of finding a buyer for the property was his daughter Wang Mi. The tribunal noted: 'Wang Mi deposed that although she was never specifically assigned to the City Garden transaction, she had taken responsibility for it as nobody else had done so.' According to her evidence the company was looking for 'a professional person in the property and development sector but at the time the person had not come to light in our company'.

Subsequently, Ever Bright has been busy. It formed lots of subsidiaries, made a joint venture agreement with Japanese construction giant Kumagai Gumi, went into furniture manufacturing, into the partnership to build Hong Kong's second cross-harbour tunnel, and became involved in transferring technology to China. But it has never achieved the heights that Wang dreamed of.

It wasn't the only time that China has shown its ignorance of the ways of Hong Kong business. At about the same time two other Peking-controlled companies paid HK$178 million for a controlling stake in Conic Investment Co., at that time regarded as Hong Kong's highest-flying electronics company. But Conic was in difficulties before China took its stake, and its founder and chairman later fled from Hong Kong, leaving the Chinese with red faces and heavy debts.

By the time that Citic bought Ka Wah Bank, the Peking Communists had clearly learnt one important lesson – not to be saddled with a loss-making venture. Citic cleverly and successfully argued that it shouldn't be responsible for the losses that Ka Wah had run up. The Chinese concern pushed its case so strongly that the Hong Kong government (and effectively the Hong Kong tax-payer) promised to pick up the tab for the bank's accumulated losses.

But Wang Guangying's venture with Li Ka-shing over the block of flats also neatly demonstrated another worrying aspect of Hong Kong–China relations. The insider trading inquiry showed how sensitive even the most capitalistic and entrepreneurial Hong Kong businessmen are towards their homeland, and how anxious not to upset Peking. Li was not prepared to risk flatly telling Wang that the project wasn't viable economically and he should clear off – nor on the other hand was he ready to let Wang be sufficiently grown-up and run the risks of his own mistakes. Li was very much concerned that a leading Peking-backed businessman shouldn't lose face. In a Hong Kong under effective Communist rule this could prove a pressure point that would damage Hong Kong's business environment.

But as the 1980s wore on an even more worrying aspect of Communist Chinese operations in Hong Kong became apparent – growing corruption. It became so bad that Peking itself noticed and sent economists to investigate. Wang Guangying spoke out, claiming that some Chinese had brought bad habits from China. They 'are very good at bickering among themselves, but totally inefficient in handling business deals with others', railed Wang in an interview with *Zhongguo Tongxun She* (quoted by BBC Monitoring Service SWB FE/0236, 22 August 1988). According to the report, Wang accused Chinese officials in Hong Kong:

> They were incompetent at their own jobs. Such people became jealous of others doing good business and ridiculed those who suffered losses. Such people went so far as to spread rumours, to slander others, to make reports on others' conduct to the higher authorities in a stealthy fashion and would not be satisfied until they saw the downfall of others. Consequently, many Chinese officials sent here would rather 'look on with folded arms' than do any practical work.

The complaint wasn't just that the Chinese firms were bad at business. Many of them had established offices in Hong Kong precisely to evade Chinese financial controls. By 1989 considerable sums of money, running to billions of Renminbi, were said to be making the round trip from China through Hong Kong and back to China in an evasion of foreign exchange and planning controls. If routed through Hong Kong, such investment money would qualify for tax-breaks as foreign investment. And not all the money found its way back to China. If goods were 'shadow-priced', that is priced artificially cheaply on being exported from China to Hong Kong, and then sold on at a higher price, the difference left money free to be spent for whatever purpose. Nepotism and corruption became by-words with which Hong Kong people described the Communist cadres. It was difficult to get a Hong Kong post without good *guanxi* – no wonder since there was lots of money to be made in Hong Kong. If unchecked, such practices could poison the whole business climate in the territory.

Even the approved, official Chinese concerns under Peking's wing publish accounts and information that are minimal by the poor standards of disclosure in Hong Kong. Chinese companies are thought to be more highly geared than most Hong Kong companies, but the information isn't public. Bankers have pointed out that although the Chinese banks have boasted of rapid growth in loans and advances, they have said little about their provisions against bad debts. By 1989 only two Chinese companies could be said to have Hong Kong stock market listings. Wah Shing Toys, floated in June 1988, is 37.5 per cent owned by Yue Xiu Enterprises, itself owned by Canton municipality. Tian Au China Investments is 60 per cent owned by China Resources, the Bank of China and Xinhua. Other Chinese concerns wouldn't be able to meet the requirements for proper reports and accounts.

China by 1988 was apparently making slow headway in its attempts to unravel the complexity of its interests in the British colony. A pro-China Hong Kong publication, *Wen Wei Po*, reported in November 1988 that 'with the exception of those companies within the jurisdiction of the central authorities, ministries and commissions, it [the Ministry of Foreign Relations and Trade] is completely in the dark concerning how many organs with Chinese capital of various categories at various levels exist in Hong Kong.' Critics quickly pointed out that although Peking had expressed public concern about corruption among Chinese concerns in Hong Kong, the colony's Independent Commission Against Corruption (ICAC), quick to probe into the police force and the Royal Hong Kong Jockey Club for wrongdoing, had not uncovered any evidence against Chinese companies. John Burns, a lecturer in political science at Hong Kong University, wrote in July that 'China's political muscle has also influenced the rule of law in the territory. Corruption among mainland companies appears to be so serious that it has come to the attention of the central authorities in Peking. Has the ICAC investigated these cases, and if not, why not?' The alternatives for the Hong Kong government were tricky: should it turn a blind eye or should it cooperate with China in investigations, as *Wen Wei Po* urged, thus potentially undermining Hong Kong's own independence?

On top of all the economic links are increasingly close political ties. China has steadily stepped up its political influence on the district boards and by mid-1987 pro-China members were in a majority on one board and formed about half of membership on another handful of the nineteen boards. Hard-headed political commentators said that China had absorbed the lessons of Lenin and would take over Hong Kong by stealth, gradually but inexorably tightening its grip through the economy, financial system and politics.

Other symbols at the topping-out of the Bank of China building did not go unnoticed in ever-super superstitious Hong Kong. The date, the eighth day of the eighth month of the year eighty-eight, was chosen with great care, billed as the luckiest day of the century (because the Cantonese word for 'eight', denotes 'prosperity'). What could be luckier than 8.8.88, especially in a year of the dragon, reputedly the most auspicious of the twelve-year Chinese cycle! No matter that traditional Chinese use a lunar calendar, but the lucky day was based on the western solar calendar. However, senior officials of the bank, perhaps demonstrating that good Communists do not believe in superstitious nonsense, stayed away from the topping-out, saying it was a matter for the construction company. The building was opened with fanfare in 1989. Worried Hong Kong *fung shui* men respond that the building will need all the luck it can get. They claim that the bank's shape, based on a series of interlocking triangles or pyramids, is unlucky,. The Chinese for pyramid, *kam che tap*, is similar to *kam tap*, Chinese for the urns that contain remains of the dead. In addition the bank has many sharp sides. You can't miss them gleaming razor-like in the sun. The *fung shui* men compare these sharp sides to daggers. One points at Hong Kong's legislative council building, another is directed at Government House, while others seem to point inwards towards the Bank of China building itself. There is also unhappiness about the two 'chopsticks' on top of the building, giving it extra height. No good Chinese, says a local *fung shui* expert, would ever place chopsticks upright. The Chinese always lay them flat. To put them upright resembles placing incense sticks, a memorial for the dead. They hope it won't happen to the Bank of China building, still less to Hong Kong itself.

11 Hong Kong in China: China in Hong Kong

THE growing ties between Hong Kong and China have led some commentators to say that the two territories are inseparable, even to call them Siamese twins. Until mid-1997 there is still the buffer of British administration separating Hong Kong from China proper. But on its borders with Hong Kong there is a special part of China that was set up as Peking's capitalist answer to the British colony. Superficially Shenzhen has gone from strength to strength, with mushrooming buildings and a rapidly growing economy. However, closer examination shows that it's not so easy for Communists to play at being capitalists. And if Shenzhen is a tiny corner of China in which capitalism prevails, then there's also a small corner of Hong Kong where the capitalist government's writ doesn't run. Jurisdiction over the Walled City has long been claimed by China. It is not the best advertisement for self-rule (nor even for the judgement of Peking officials).

Shenzhen: Brave New Hong Kong in China?

A tall wire fence tipped with ugly barbed-wire snarls stands about 3.5 metres high and snakes its way along the small river valley. Through the wire a city can be seen springing up. New buildings, many of them infant skyscrapers, burst from the ground daily, a rate of growth that would teach mushrooms about productivity. Sparkling new tower blocks of offices and flats stand smartly to attention, neat and uniform as soldiers on the parade ground. There is a sprawl of factories for electronics and other modern industries. There are hotels, one with a revolving restaurant offering views down to the sea and beyond. The fence is to keep intruders out. A determined and athletic man can get over its barbs in about 11 seconds. The record is believed to be 8.4 seconds. 'We timed him, and asked if he would do it again, so we could ratify the record,' jokes a soldier who caught the man. To reinforce security the fence is lit at night by searchlight, and equipped with sensing devices. If touched, they will set off a light on the monitoring board in a nearby control tower indicating the location of the intruders. Within seconds, a military patrol will be on its way. All through the night, whether during the sticky humid summer heat or the chilly misty winter, soldiers keep a watch, some of them with dogs. They have special hideouts as well as regular patrols, and are equipped with sophisticated nightsearching equipment able to peer into the blackness and spot intruders.

This *is* the boundary between capitalism and Communism, between Hong Kong and China. But the first unexpected fact is that the soldiers are on the capitalist side of the fence trying to prevent runaways from Communism from getting in. The second curious factor is that the towering new buildings are on the *Communist* side of the fence.

The town is Shenzhen (Shum Chum in Cantonese), showpiece Special Economic Zone (SEZ) of the People's Republic of China. Its rapidly growing modern buildings make the New Territories of Hong Kong look shabby by comparison. Indeed, a trip by helicopter through Hong Kong territory just south of the border, across the marshes, small fields, duck farms, vegetable small-holdings and roads congested with lorries carrying produce to and from Shenzhen, confirms this impression. A visit to the small town of Shau Tau Kok, where the border between Hong Kong and China actually runs down the main street, and where the small wharf abuts into Chinese waters, is revealing. The Hong Kong side has a patched-up look, whereas on the Chinese side there are many brand-new buildings. One explanation for the apparent poverty on the Hong Kong side of the boundary is that the colonial authorities have deliberately developed their new towns and industrial estates at a safe distance from the Chinese border. Indeed, Hong Kong land close to China is a 'closed area' for which special entry permits are needed. It is common – but strange – to see tourists on the Communist side pouring down the main street and being discouraged from taking souvenir snaps of the divided street by *British* police, while the colonial authorities maintain a strict 'no-go' policy, not letting non-residents wander down the street or even take pictures from a safe distance.

The new Special Economic Zones are important as an example of Peking's new look at capitalism and willingness to learn from it. And Shenzhen has been singled out as China's answer to Hong Kong. Perhaps, some political commentators suggest, it offers a glimpse of what Hong Kong will look like under a Chinese flag.

Shenzhen is both the biggest and the most developed of China's special economic zones. By 1985 China had opened four special zones and fourteen coastal cities to foreign investment. It is no accident that all the original SEZs are near Hong Kong or areas of traditionally strong overseas Chinese influence. In Guangdong province the zones are Shenzhen, Zhuhai (on the border with Macao) and Shantou, formerly known as Swatow; in Fujian province northeast of Guangdong is the Xiamen zone (the city used to be known as Amoy). In area, the Shenzhen zone is bigger than all the others put together. It totals more than 327 square kilometres, against the 15.16 square kilometres of Zhuhai and the 52.6 square kilometres of Shantou. Attached to the Shenzhen zone and technically inside it, though administered independently, is the 10.7 square kilometres Shekou industrial zone, situated at the tip of a small peninsula on the western side of Shenzhen. The Shekou zone is under the management of China Merchants Steam Navigation Company, a Chinese shipping conglomerate with its headquarters in Hong Kong, but reporting directly to the Ministry of Communications in Peking.

The idea behind the SEZs was to set up safe independent areas where China could experiment and learn about foreign investment, new technology and capitalist ways without corrupting the whole country. If the experiments failed, China's policies would not be at risk; if the experiments succeeded, China proper could adopt them. As a bonus the zones could provide employment and income opportunities. However, in national debates economists and leading Communist Party figures argued that this was of secondary significance. Sun Ru, director of the economic research section of the Guangdong Provincial Academy of Social Sciences, argued that 'an important question to ask about the special economic zones is: "How do they relate to national development?" They are small, particular zones; theirs is not a national policy but a regional and local policy that seeks to influence national development.'

In terms of physical changes, Shenzhen and other zones have transformed the landscape. If statistics issued by the Chinese authorities are to be believed, their growth has been even faster and more impressive than that of Hong Kong. Shenzhen in the early 1970s was a small agricultural and fishing area with only 30,000 people; as late as 1979 Shekou was 'a stretch of sandy beach and wide hills', according to Yuan Geng, vice-chairman of the China Merchants company. By 1989 the population of Shenzhen had expanded to about 800,000. Before Shenzhen was given its status as a special economic zone it had only 34 factories and fewer than 10 hotels, guesthouses and restaurants; by 1989 there were 1,200 factories and hundreds of hotels and restaurants. Altogether, more than 4,000 companies had been set up, 1,400 of them with the help of foreign funds. The zone was producing a vast assortment of goods and the municipal authorities were able to provide almost fairy-tale figures showing constant rapid economic progress. According to the mayor's office in late 1988, Shenzhen per capita income had increased by almost 28 per cent a year, and had grown from less than Yuan 500 in 1979 to almost Yuan 3,500 (US$950) by 1987. Total industrial output in 1987 was Yuan 5.76 billion and exports were worth Yuan 3 billion. Total industrial output and industrial output for export had risen by 94 times and 245 times since 1979. By the end of 1987, 3 million square metres of industrial factories and 1 million square metres of warehouses had been completed. The zone was producing electronics, textiles and garments, mechanical engineering products, sporting goods, chemicals, plastics, foods and beverages and building and printing materials. Electronics was the most important product accounting for more than 43 per cent of total industrial production. The range of electronics output was rapidly widening and in 1987 included radios, tape-recorders, telephones, fans, personal computers, mini-calculators and watches.

The 1,200 industrial enterprises employed nearly 150,000 people. Of Shenzhen's industrial concerns, 500 were exporting, producing 450 different commodities with a value of US$722 million in 1987, or 51 per cent of total exports. Foreign investment deals worth more than US$2 billion had been signed for industry, though less than 45 per cent of the money had actually been spent. More than 80 per cent of the contracts were with Hong Kong concerns and the next biggest investors were US and Japanese companies with 4 per cent each. Shenzhen's authorities predict continuing rapid progress and expect GNP per capita will be US$1,500 and export value per capita US$1,700 at the end of 1990. At that time, industrial output will exceed Yuan 10 billion and industrial exports US$1.5 billion.

Expressed like this, Shenzhen seems to have a short but booming history of unalloyed progress. The Chinese began early on to dream of the zone rivalling or surpassing Hong Kong. Among the prominent visitors was Deng Xiaoping who saw the zone in January 1984. He proudly commented that he'd visited this '10,000 Yuan village' – meaning that the annual income was US$3,300 or more per household. A Chinese reporter accompanying Deng asked: 'will all Chinese live like this in 50 years?', to which the leader reportedly replied 'a bit longer. Another twenty years beyond that perhaps . . .'. Because Shekou is also being used as a base for China's offshore oil explorations, some local people boast that Shenzhen will not develop into a second Hong Kong, but will more likely be a second Houston. Zhou Nan, a director of the China Nanhai Oil Joint Service Corporation, predicted development of a 'petroleum city' on which tens of billions of dollars would be spent.

In a boastful account in 1983 the *People's Daily* asserted that Shenzhen had already demonstrated some advantages over Hong Kong. It said: 'although the business efficiency of Hong Kong people is relatively high, in fact, whatever Hong Kong can do we in Shenzhen can do as well, or better'. It cited a bed and furniture factory based in Hong Kong which set up cooperative production in Shenzhen and found that 'labour efficiency in Shenzhen was much higher than in Hong Kong'. The paper explained why this is so:

> Although Hong Kong workers master high levels of technical skill, they frequently move from place to place, and things are not quite stable. This not only affects the improvement of labour efficiency, but also affects product quality and the prestige and capability of the product in competing in international markets. In Shenzhen workers are not so mobile and their type of work seldom changes. Therefore it is quite natural that their working efficiency is rather high . . .

So pleased was the Hong Kong furniture-maker, recorded the *People's Daily*, that he moved his factory production lock, stock and barrel from Hong Kong to Shenzhen.

The paper went on to describe other advantages of the Shenzhen system:

> The high efficiency of Shenzhen special economic zone is attributed by some to the workers being young, by others to the strict labour discipline, by others to the fact that directors have management and decision-making rights.

> Most of the newly built factories, shops and hotels in Shenzhen have the decision-making power in their enterprises, and some of them have reformed their personnel and wage system. Since the directors and managers have the power, they have revised labour discipline. If you come late or leave one hour early, 5 per cent of your floating wages [incentive pay] will be deducted. If you stay away from work without leave for half a day, your floating wages will be deducted; and if for one full day, your post wages [basic pay] will also be deducted. Those on night shift duty must not sleep, or play chess or cards, or watch TV. There was an attendant of the Donghu guesthouse who dozed off during night duty, and after being discovered three times in succession, was then dismissed. Aiming at young girls who are fond of dressing up, those units with a greater proportion of female workers have also stipulated that while on duty they are not allowed to wear grotesque clothes, or put on ornaments, or use lipstick, rouge or fingernail polish, or have an unusual hairstyle. A young man in the Friendship restaurant who had long hair and whiskers, was warned either to cut them off or have his wages deducted – he thought it over and finally cut off his long hair and shaved his whiskers. Some shops stipulate that shop assistants must not be seated while receiving customers, or buy articles sold in the shop, or hold long talks with visitors, or smoke, eat or do private work at the counter. And so on . . . (*People's Daily*, 15 January 1983, quoted in BBC Summary of World Broadcasts FE/W1223).

A Shanghai reporter saw benefits for some Hong Kong manufacturers in moving to Shenzhen.

> A certain factory producing paint for ships used to occupy only about 1,000 square metres in Kowloon. After moving to Shekou in the Shenzhen special economic zone, it was

> expanded to cover 4,000 square metres, paying only HK$150,000 annually for the use of land. It is now able to produce 3,000 tons of paint a year, more than double its output when in Kowloon. The wages of skilled workers in Hong Kong are four times higher than those on the mainland. Income tax in Hong Kong is 2 per cent higher than that in Shenzhen. (An Shan, in *World Economic Herald*, Shanghai, 14 November 1983, quoted in the newspaper *Ta Kung Pao*)

Dreams also grew quickly. A prominent official envisaged Shenzhen developing as a centre for training middle management for the whole of China, in effect becoming the 'brain centre' of China.

So much for the statistics and official propaganda. Shenzhen in the late 1980s is certainly a bright contrast and closer to Hong Kong than the rest of China. The consumer society has clearly come to Shenzhen. Apart from the military and the old, who wear uniforms, the young workers disdain conformity and vie with each other to show off bright modern clothes and hairstyles. During the lunch break in a small park in Shekou industrial area workers sat eating western-style snacks and drinking soft drinks with Hong Kong or international brand labels. Adults indulged children with fancy flavoured ice-cream, sticky sweets and playthings such as plastic windmills. Young couples held hands unashamedly and one couple nuzzled lovey-dovey closely together, behaviour still frowned on in 'inland China'. In the nearby supermarket, queues pressed around piles of consumer goods like fans, washing machines and television sets.

Early on, other signs of western-style consumerism began to appear and to worry Communist Chinese authorities, who feared that things might get out of hand. Among the attractions quickly established in the centre of Shenzhen were several disco-dancing rooms. 'We don't consider disco to be spiritual pollution,' said a local official, suggesting that Shenzhen's standards were more relaxed than those of China itself. But standards can't be stretched too elastically. Both the authorities and the managers of the discos were quickly warned by Peking to keep an ear out for so-called 'yellow music'. This means music with lyrics decreed to be lewd, tasteless, or, worst of all, 'politically objectionable'. Among the songs banned were a Taiwanese ballad, 'Wo Shi Zhongguron [I am a Chinese]', a Cantonese song, 'Dream Mother', which has lines about a prostitute, and also an American pop tune, 'I love you more than I can say'; the Culture Ministry regarded its lyrics as causing 'spiritual pollution'.

In some ways these are superficial changes. What matter more are changes in work practices. And Shenzhen has shown China the way. Some of its reforms later became central to China's new economic policies of the late 1980s. China's economic progress has been bedevilled by the twin slogans of the 'iron rice bowl' and 'eating from the same common pot', meaning that Chinese workers are guaranteed their daily rice ration, no matter how hard or how badly they work, and all workers are treated equally, no matter how much enterprise and initiative they show. The system has never worked quite as rigidly as that, of course: Party officials and other functionaries have always lived higher on the hog than ordinary workers; but such privileges have tended only to weaken initiative and enterprise even further. In Shenzhen, new attitudes are apparent. One prominently displayed slogan proclaims in Chinese characters: 'Time is money . . .' a sentiment that is not always evident in the rest of China.

A radical innovation in Shenzhen factories is the abandonment of the two-hour or longer lunchtime siesta. Workers take just a half-hour break for lunch. Discipline generally is much tighter than anyone in state-run factories in the rest of China would dream of. Workers have been sacked for poor performance, and pay does vary according to whether the factory is productive or not.

But the pioneer investors faced more than their share of teething problems. The new boom town was run by a Communist bureaucracy that was too slow-moving and creaky to cope with the massive changes. Early factories were built at the end of mud tracks which turned into quagmires when it rained. Even in 1985 there were only 4,000 telephones in the zone, rather than the 14,000 that had been planned. Installing the telephone system was part of the difficult learning process. The British company Cable and Wireless is the joint venture partner in Shenzhen's Shenda Telephone Company. First of all it found that there were no city maps, so it had to draw its own. Then the allocation of telephone lines had to go through government departments which operate on a strict quota system. Further difficulties occurred when Cocom, the committee of western industrialized countries regulating technology sales to Communist nations, delayed the arrival of spare parts. Then there was a problem in getting trained workers to install and maintain the system.

The human dimensions and demands of changing from a sleepy farming and fishing community to a modern industrial zone also proved taxing. You might not think that running a hotel is a high-tech game, but it imposed unexpected demands on China. At the Shenzhen International Hotel, a joint venture between a Hong Kong businessman and the local Forestry Ministry, the British hotel manager in the mid-1980s compared his property to 'Fawlty Towers', a television comedy programme about a chaotic English seaside hotel. He discovered an order had been placed for 30,000 shower caps, although the hotel already had 20,000 spares in stock; he found women cutting the grass with tiny hand scissors because there were no lawnmowers in the whole of Shenzhen; next he discovered staff taking the hotel's goldfish home for their suppers; and then he found that the 'employee-of-the-month' competition he had organized to discourage complacency wasn't running as smoothly as he had thought, since a coffee-shop waitress told him she was down to win the award for August, though it was only July.

One of the first much-vaunted investments was a failure. Harpers International, a Hong Kong-based subsidiary of

Malaysia's Sime Darby, established a plant to assemble Ford tourist buses and trucks. It was the first foreign motor-car project in China. Unfortunately the Chinese labour force didn't live up to expectations. Managing director Henry P. Lee complained that 'they were mostly farmhands, some of whom had never seen a screwdriver and there was no discipline in the factory' (to Louis Kraar in *Fortune*, 18 April 1983). Harpers abandoned the project and was able to get its investment out. It was not a good opening advertisement for the zone.

Business failures themselves presented unexpected problems which Shenzhen had to struggle to understand. Several companies in the zone with Hong Kong parents went bankrupt. These included the Millie's Group of companies run by Alan Lau, who had a string of factories in Shenzhen making handbags, shoes and jeans. Before his downfall, Lau had assiduously courted local Chinese politicians and entertained them royally with invitations to enjoy the pleasures of Hong Kong. The Shenzhen authorities initially said bluntly that they wouldn't recognize bankruptcies. They had to change their views in the face of hard facts. This was further evidence of the lack of experience of Chinese Communists in handling relatively simple and bedrock concepts like law, business law and modern accounting systems.

All along, the Shekou special zone made faster progress than Shenzhen proper. Being run by a single entity – China Merchants – and one with experience of Hong Kong labour and management practices, helped it to avoid the political infighting and bureaucratic delays in Shenzhen itself. But even in Shekou investors quickly discovered that they had to come to terms with local practices. In theory factories in the SEZs have freedom to hire and to fire, but reality often proved tougher than the promises on paper. Especially in the early days, dismissal of incompetent workers was complicated. As Erling Moesgaard, general manager of China International Maritime Containers (a Shekou joint venture between China Merchants and the East Asiatic Co. of Denmark), gently expressed it, a sacking can take 'a bit of diplomacy'. Chinese traditions also have to be respected in working practices. 'The tradition is that everything must be discussed by everybody first before working practices can be changed,' comments Moesgaard. With these start-up problems it came as a relief to find that workers learned rapidly on the job. However, they were slower to appreciate that being a good worker also involves looking after equipment to make sure that it lasts. Lessons had to be given on the simple maintenance of tools. The container factory found that women were among the best welders, but they ran into resentment from male colleagues. The factory also had problems when world recession had reduced demand for its boxes. In addition, some containers were rejected because they weren't up to quality standards. 'Building simple container boxes isn't exactly state-of-the-art technology,' comments a Hong Kong industrialist scathingly, but realistically pointing out the shortcomings.

As time has gone on, Shenzhen has not only grown fast but has learnt quickly. One of the most impressive factories is that of the China Bicycles Company, a three-way joint venture involving the Shenzhen authorities, Hong Kong (Link) Bicycles, and the US giant Schwinn Bicycle Company. The factory occupies an impressive 70,000 square metres of space, and by the early 1990s will be turning out more than 1.6 million bicycles a year, or a machine every 14 seconds. More than 1,100 workers are dressed in neat uniforms, with the company's logo in different colours indicating which part of the factory they work in – gold bicycles on the breast for management and blue, green, red and silver for other workers. An impressive feature of the factory is the 3.5 km conveyor belt. By early 1989 when this was fully operational it was carrying the completed machines ready packed for shipping out by container. Almost all the production is exported, to North America, Western Europe and even Japan.

The bicycle factory has had its learning problems. From the very start managers were proud that theirs was the only computer-run bicycle factory in China. But in the mid- to late-

80s the conveyor belt carrying the machines frequently had to be slowed down or stopped to keep pace with the workers' speed. It took until the end of the decade before things were running smoothly. The bicycles being turned out in Shenzhen were very different from the typical products to be seen along China's streets. Typical Chinese machines are built so sturdily, jokes a China Bicycles' executive, that 'you could run one into the back of a bus and get up and ride it away undamaged'. Those Chinese bicycles are old-fashioned, 'sit-up-and-beg' models finished in standard black. At Shenzhen the bicycles coming off the belt into their cartons are indistinguishable from top-of-the-line products sold in the big stores in the west. Drop-handlebars, water-bottles nestling on the frame, multi-speed dérailleur gears, BMX models, fashionable colours are the routine, just as they are in the western shops. That's not surprising since China Bicycles is a major supplier to western stores. Sears Roebuck in the USA is a big customer and the factory is making bicycles for Raleigh (UK) under its Triumph label. Under its own Emmelle name, China Bicycles by 1989 was the second largest-selling supplier to the UK market. The retail price range runs from £99 to £390 a machine depending on the sophistication, fashionability and gearing, with the average retail price being £189.99. Locally made Chinese components form more than 60 per cent of cheaper machines, but only 15 per cent of the top quality bicycles.

Executives are talking of going into direct mail-order sales. Discussing the increasing importance of fashion in bicycle production CBC executives expressed confidence in being able to move with the market. 'Next year's colours will be dayglo, very bright and breezy', said Stephen Codron, marketing director for the company, pointing happily to the factory's computer-run paint-spraying machines that can easily cope with the new demand. By the 1990s the company hopes to run its own team regularly in the important Tour de France bicycle race. China Bicycles carved out a niche of its own: the combination of extensive space, a modern computer-assisted factory, plentiful and cheap labour, and Hong Kong capital and supervisors helped to assure quality control and competitive prices; the infusion of US capital and the presence in the factory of former Olympic cyclist and Schwinn senior vice-president, Frank Brilando as consultant has improved technical standards – as well as assuring an in-house share of the US market. This is an unusual combination, tapping western know-how, Hong Kong financial and marketing experience and Chinese basic manufacturing ability.

Most of the Shenzhen factories are quite clearly spillovers from Hong Kong. In its classification of industrial enterprises, the Shenzhen Municipality regarded only 5 of its factories as 'large'; a further 23 were described as 'medium-sized'; the vast majority –1,148 or 97.61 per cent – were 'small'. Given a total industrial workforce of 136,308, this meant that the average factory employed fewer than 120 workers. Bankers and other frequent visitors to the zone praised the speed of development and the growing sophistication of the labour force. 'Girls who a matter of six months before had been scruffy urchins straight from the fields have adapted quickly and look quite attractive with their hair combed, wearing shoes and a dab of lipstick,' said one visitor to the Shenzhen factories. But those who know Hong Kong industry also caution that it's as well not to get too carried away, or to see Shenzhen as a free-wheeling capitalist paradise, still less a place where the first whiff of smoke from a fiery technological revolution can be seen. Productivity is still low compared to Hong Kong, and the Shenzhen electronics factories are only slowly graduating from very simple assembly-line operations to more complicated work that has long been taken for granted in Hong Kong. Other limitations to the development of the SEZ are its poor transport facilities. The port is small and shipping services less regular than Hong Kong's round-the-clock sailings to all parts of the world, while Shenzhen is a three-hour drive along indifferent roads from Canton (Guangzhou), the nearest big Chinese metropolis.

By the 1980s there was a reaction both in Hong Kong and in

China itself against several aspects of Shenzhen life. Many Hong Kong industrialists, driven to move some of their operations out of the colony because of rising land prices and shortages of labour, discovered that they could set up in Shenzhen, or they could go slightly further afield to other southern Guangdong districts like Dongshan. 'There they can do a deal with a local headman for a large piece of land and for labour supplies, without having to go through the political process in Shenzhen itself,' says a British businessman who visits the SEZ frequently. Overheads in Shenzhen, such as electricity prices, were getting costlier and the city's officials had a reputation for greediness. If it was a promising project the Shenzhen authorities might insist on a 50 per cent stake; a local headman would be much more amenable, and quicker, in striking a deal. Labour costs in Shenzhen – US$180 a month in the bicycle factory for example in 1989 – were about a quarter of those in Hong Kong. But outside the zone they might fall to one fifth or lower for similar inexperienced, but eager to learn, workers. Links between Hong Kong manufacturers and southern China as a whole had grown so strongly and rapidly that by 1989 contract workers in Guangdong employed by the colony's industrialists outnumbered the entire industrial labour force in the SEZ by a factor of 15 to 1. Emphasis on joint ventures in the SEZ upset some foreign investments. Before he went out of business, Alan Lau of Millie's Group had complained, asking: 'Why must the Chinese government tie a tall and a short man together and force them to walk; surely they will walk at different paces?' This grumble was echoed in the mid-1980s by S. C. Tam, adviser to Japan's Hokkaido Tokushoku Bank, itself an adviser to the Shenzhen SEZ Development corporation. Tan claimed that joint ventures were not as efficient as wholly foreign-owned companies because of problems in management and cooperation.

The municipality's reputation for greed hadn't gone unnoticed in 'inland China' itself. Li Hao, secretary of the Shenzhen City Chinese Communist Party, declared in late 1988 that 'seeking private gain by abusing one's power, practising extravagance and waste, and law enforcement officers breaking the law' had become three serious phenomena in the Shenzhen SEZ. *Zhongguo Tongxun She* also complained that 'at present, it takes some four months for an entrepreneur applying to operate his enterprise in Shenzhen to receive a business licence because the applicant has to receive the approval of some 37 administrative organs. From making a requisition for land to breaking ground to build a factory in Shenzhen, the applicant has to get the approval of some 22 administrative organs and has to receive some 49 official seals' (quoted in BBC Summary of World Broadcasts, 28 September 1988, FE/0268). Not surprisingly, smart businessmen and greedy officials resorted to ways of short-circuiting the process by giving and receiving gifts. Throughout the late 1980s talk of bribery and corruption was rife in Shenzhen and caused concern in China. In early 1989 road traffic between Hong Kong and Shenzhen was disrupted by a strike of lorry drivers who claimed that Chinese officials demanded bribes of Yuan 100 to 200, plus cigarettes or the pick of the goods to expedite customs procedures. Drivers who argued would face an extraordinarily thorough check.

Equally seriously, an authoritative Peking think-tank weighed in in 1988 with criticisms that Shenzhen was being stifled by traditional Chinese bureaucracy and politicking. The China System Reform Institute, which operates under the State Council's Commission for Economic Reform, declared that comprehensive political and economic reforms were still necessary. Although it acknowledged that Shenzhen enterprises were more market-oriented than those in the rest of China, the report claimed that the SEZ was subject to command-style hierarchy, too much political interference in economic matters and unfair competition brought about by monopolies, personal and political connections and favouritism. Shenzhen, it reported, still used the so-called 'red letter-head' documents to regulate economic business. These documents, traditionally used by Chinese officialdom, are often ambiguous and deliberately uninformative: the idea is that their readers should grasp the spirit of the policy by their understanding of prevailing political winds. The think-tank called for injection of true competition right across the zone. It also wanted to see laws used as the main regulators of economic activity, rather than administrative fiats which could depend on (changing) individual whims. In addition, government departments should be reorganized to allow devolution of power and acceptance of clear responsibilities at each level. Administrative procedures should be standardized so that policy changes could be transmitted swiftly and unambiguously.

Another difficult question concerned financial relations between Shenzhen and the centre. By the end of 1989 the municipality had ambitious plans for creating special areas for electronics and textile production. But Peking was demanding US$200 million to pay for the land, and Shenzhen could not afford such a sum. Demands for financial accountability were an echo of previous arguments within China's ruling hierarchy. Vice-premier Yao Yilin in 1985 lamented that the SEZs were living on 'blood transfusions' from the central government and that two-thirds of Shenzhen's manufactured goods were being sold inside the country. Another sore point is that the SEZs keep all of their earnings, whereas industrial cities like Shanghai surrender 60 per cent of income to the state. It was hardly much consolation that the Shenzhen SEZ came under the special tutelage of Peking and wasn't subject to Guangdong provincial politics. Several times there had been a clean-out of party officials in Shenzhen. But again and again party officials and leaders had shown a special liking for racy non-Communist lifestyles in spite of strictures from Peking.

China Youth News in mid-1988 reported frankly about 'serious social problems' in the Shenzhen SEZ. It said that promiscuity, homosexuality and unwanted pregnancies were on the rise, and attributed them to a shortage of men in the area. There were 250,000 female workers in the zone, but because they were not permanent residents, local men were reluctant to marry them. Without a permit to reside in a certain area, a Chinese cannot live there permanently even if he or she marries a native. 'Here, women are now everywhere', the paper said, 'so the area is called a "Women's Kingdom".' It went on to discuss the frustrations of the women. In spite of the setting up of sports complexes, clubs and dance-halls in some localities, the women were not satisfied. 'With their thirst for love and sex, the newness of these facilities quickly fades.' It quoted one woman worker as saying: 'Who isn't willing to fall in love? After we work all day, who doesn't want to lay one's head against the chest of a man? Even if I'm not married, I'm willing.' Getting married might be difficult, but getting pregnant was proving easier, noted the paper, saying that there were 800 unwanted pregnancies during 1987 in Shekou, where there were 10,000 women workers. Later there was an outcry about the recruitment of women for a massage-parlour in Shenzhen. Women from the city of Changsha, capital of Hunan province, where the advertisement was placed, claimed that the jobs were 'a disguised form of prostitution' – although the firm running the parlour claimed that the masseuses would be fully clothed and observed while at work. Complaints about prostitution were substantiated by one foreign factory executive, who spends most of his working days in Shenzhen. 'Of course I don't get involved, but we have someone who provides for the needs of visiting big bosses. He can usually tell which women are eager to supplement their wages with extra-curricular activities. Out-of-town visitors, especially Party big-wigs, are keen to sample all the delights of the zone.' *China Youth News* had no obvious solution to the problem of the imbalance of the sexes. It balked at the answer of introducing more male workers to the SEZ: there would still be the problem of residence permits.

Clearly, in spite of all the difficulties, Hong Kong and southern China as a whole have been moving closer and closer together, almost in a symbiotic relationship. Hong Kong industrialists need land and labour supplies that are not available in the colony. Shenzhen has so far fallen short of the expectations it raised as an industrial centre, but it has proved popular as a rest and recreation centre both for Hong Kong holidaymakers and for privileged Chinese from all parts of the country who can get the necessary permits. The Hong Kong dollar is the most powerful and most popular currency in use in the SEZ because of its convertibility. (The next most popular currency is the foreign exchange certificate that foreigners are supposed to use in their business dealings in China; least acceptable is China's own renminbi currency.) There is cooperation between the authorities on the two sides of the border. Indeed, it is usually quicker going through Chinese immigration than on the Hong Kong side. One gang of robbers in the town of Sha Tau Kok found to their cost that they couldn't play one side off against the other. They robbed a gold shop on the Hong Kong side of the street, then ran to the Chinese side and dared the British police to catch them. But, recalls a Hong Kong police chief inspector, 'they were promptly nabbed by the Chinese police and subjected to rougher Chinese justice, a bullet in the back of the head, with the bill for the bullet being sent to the relatives of the executed men'.

In the circumstances, the easiest and most logical way of developing the two communities would be to allow Hong Kong to swallow the SEZ to form an expanded and still autonomous Greater Hong Kong. That would solve the problem for Shenzhen of the lack of port facilities; and for Hong Kong flat land in Shenzhen would offer the very best site for a new airport to relieve congested Kai Tak without the expensive solution of levelling land and building bridges off Lantau island. A merger would allow the more flexible and experienced Hong Kong economic and industrial interests a wider area of operation. Shenzhen SEZ is already separated from the rest of China by a fence, security patrols and special entry requirements. The status of Shenzhen in relation to Hong Kong is made amply clear to visitors who want to know which direction they are facing. 'Look at the television aerials,' is the immediate answer; 'they are all pointing south, tuned in to pick up programmes from Hong Kong.' Hong Kong is still the first choice of Chinese seeking a better life away from the rigidities of Communist rule, and Shenzhen is only a poor second best.

But any suggestions of a greater Hong Kong embracing Shenzhen are greeted with horror in official circles. 'Heavens above, no, no,' declared a senior figure in the Hong Kong government. 'That would be seen as proof of Peking's interference in Hong Kong, and would sink confidence in the territory.' On the other hand, the heavy-handed attitude frequently shown towards Shenzhen by Peking, the constant politicking, the corruption and the clammy grasp of the party bureaucracy don't augur well for an 'autonomous' Hong Kong after 1997.

The Walled City: Remnant of the Past

Walking along Tung Tau Tsuen Road in the heart of hugger-mugger overcrowded Kowloon it is impossible to avoid the feeling that someone is smiling, even grinning at you. It is not the old woman and her tiny grand-daughters, too busy slurping their *congee* (Chinese porridge) to notice the rest of the world; it is not the old men, clacking away and completely absorbed in their game of mahjong; it is not the harassed mother with one child slung papoose-style on her back and another mardily in tow as she goes shopping; it is certainly not the constant jostling crowds on all sides. But out of the corner of your eye you can glimpse not one but several broad, toothy grins. It is natural to stop and turn to see who has recognized you. But there is nobody. Yet you are right about the grins: there is not just one, but ten or more, on plates, in bowls, neatly arranged in baskets like some exotic fruit. The disembodied grins belong to sets of false teeth, peppermint-toothpaste-white, gleaming from glistening gums of porcelain so healthily pink you'd never see them in anyone's mouth. They may not be as healthy as you think, since these are the shop-windows of illegal dentists who have set up shop here on the perimeter of the Kowloon Walled City.

This is perhaps the pleasantest way of introducing one of the grimmest and grimiest eyesores of Hong Kong. The illegal dentists' windows offer a warning that this is the fringe of Hong

Kong proper, where the wideboys and sharp practitioners meet the underworld. The very name is a historical hangover, since there haven't been any walls for years and most people wouldn't dignify the settlement with the grand name of city. Yet it is an important and, in its own grubby way, historic piece of land. It says a lot about the relations between China and colonial Britain. In the minds of sceptics it raises important questions about how Hong Kong will fare under Chinese colonial rule.

The best thing that can be said about the Walled City is that it is going to be pulled down. Britain and China have set aside their differences over who owns it, and have agreed that it should be demolished and turned into a public park.

After the teeth, the next thing any visitor notices is the banshee whine from the jet engines of aircraft passing overhead. The Walled City is only yards away from the final flight-path to runway 13 at Kai Tak airport. The aircraft screaming overhead are just completing their 47-degree turn before they straighten up to hit the runway. 'If anything went wrong during those last few seconds before touchdown, it would be the biggest disaster imaginable,' says a senior Cathay Pacific pilot, who worries about less experienced colleagues from airlines that don't fly to Hong Kong frequently.

He has good reason to worry. Government census-takers who moved in immediately after the agreement between Britain and China to knock down the city found that the population was fewer than popularly estimated: a mere 33,000 people in 500 buildings, comprising 8,000 premises and 9,000 households, plus 1,000 industrial and commercial businesses, including 160 doctors and dentists. Previous estimates had put the population as high as 50,000. Even so, this makes the Walled City, less than a hundredth of a square mile in area, the most densely populated piece of land in the world, 3 million people per square mile. This is twenty times greater than the population density of other, only normally overcrowded, areas of Hong Kong. For comparison with the rest of the world, it is about 3,000 times the density of the most heavily populated European country.

From the outside, the Walled City looks like a decomposing layer-cake of apartments, much like the rest of Kowloon. The first inkling of its complexity comes when the guide suddenly disappears. You follow where he was last seen and stumble into a 'street' inside the Walled City. What might be called 'avenues' are little more than five feet broad; normally streets are two or three feet wide. It's difficult to convey the dinginess and festering decay of the inside of the Walled City. A rotten sour smell pervades every nook and cranny. From the moment you step in until the moment you emerge with relief into Hong Kong proper you rarely see daylight. There is just one old house and courtyard, formerly the *yamen* or office of China's magistrate (serving today as a centre for the aged), from which you can see the open sky.

A walk in the Walled City is a real journey through darkness. An imaginative circus or fairground entrepreneur couldn't devise some of the horrors of the place. Only inches above your head there are spiders' webs of wire and cables held together, it often seems, only by real spiders' webs tying up the dirt and grime of decades. It is advisable to wear a waterproof cap to avoid being drenched by the constant drips of water. You also have to watch you don't slip into the puddles of slime and mulched rubbish. Walls are damp and seemingly in the terminal stages of leprosy. Very quickly you lose any sense of direction. It is possible to go in at ground-floor level, wander through the warren-like passages and come out on the sixth floor without apparently having climbed any stairs. These dwellings are built honeycomb-fashion, one backing on to the next without rhyme or reason. They continue a full fifteen storeys high. Police once discovered a heroin factory whose owners had hidden drugs by pushing them through loose bricks in the walls: it took the authorities more than half a day to find the other side of the wall, so chaotically constructed are these dwellings.

The strangest thing about a journey through the badly lit twisting alleyways is the eeriness. It's quite unlike any other place on earth, not like Calcutta, or Dhaka or the slums of

South America, where there is a sense of being jostled by life all the time. In other slums, even if you can't see people, you can hear them, their shouts ringing out, the arguments, laughter and tears of real life. But here the strongest sound is the drip-drip-drip of water and the pattering of feet as rats and other scuttling creatures escape from you. But then, all of a sudden, you may encounter someone or something. It may be a prostitute sidling past, or muffled murmuring coming from a little corner shop selling cigarettes, bread and other necessities. The journey through darkness may be enlightened by a dim glow coming from a factory that's little more than a hole in the wall, making machinery parts, or sweatshop textiles or plastic or bean-curd with its peculiarly cloying rancid smell, or perhaps something else that the denizens would like to keep out of the eye of the police or other authorities.

The special secret of the Walled City is that it has long been a no-go area, a limbo between the city and swamp life. Illegal immigrants, prostitutes, drug syndicates, criminals and Triad groups have long flourished inside, helped by the fact that until the mid-1970s the police kept a wary distance. Even immediately before the announcement of the demolition notice, the authorities' grip was a loose one. Inhabitants don't talk easily. One resident, when asked who controlled the Walled City, declared 'It's the fist people, those who have gangs and force at their disposal.' It was said in the 1970s that cherished dogs did not roam the Walled City alleys because good black chows would fetch HK$2 a catty (not quite a kilo) in the 'fragrant flesh' (dog meat) restaurants. Another claim was that before the establishment of the Independent Commission Against Corruption police received bribes of up to HK$160,000 a day to stay out of the Walled City.

Some businesses have flourished in selling legitimate goods to Hong Kong proper. Low labour costs give small factories an edge, and one speciality of the area is in supplying of cocktail sausages and other party snacks to major luxury hotels in Hong Kong. 'Next time you nibble a cocktail sausage in the Mandarin

Hotel, you should remember that it has probably come from the Walled City,' says a senior government official. Officials now take pains to downplay the idea that the Walled City ever deserved its reputation as a den of thieves. They suggest that their census-takers encountered no illegal immigrants, that the grip of Triads has been overstated, that no one admitted to being a prostitute. To this a senior government secretary who knows the Walled City responds: 'Well, they would say that, wouldn't they? You shouldn't believe everything officials say.'

The reason why the Walled City is different from the rest of Kowloon – and why the colonial authorities sought China's blessing for its demolition – is that its status was long disputed. The controversy dates back to the last years of the nineteenth century, when Britain expanded its colonial rule over Hong Kong. At the time of the Convention of Peking (which extended Hong Kong's boundaries from Boundary Street to the New Territories), the Walled City was an administrative and military centre for the Chinese government. Photographs at the turn of the century show a placid fortified area enclosing typical single-storey Chinese dwellings. The then Colonial Secretary, J. H. Stewart Lockhart, reported on the Walled City during a commentary on the newly leased territory:

> Kowloon is situated about a quarter of a mile from the seashore. It is enclosed by a stone wall built in 1847 [the construction had actually started in 1843] forming as nearly as possible a parallelogram, measuring 700 feet by 400 feet, and enclosing an area of six and a half acres. The wall is built of granite ashlar facing, is 15 feet in width at the top, and averages in height 13 feet. The wall has six watch towers, at present occupied by family dwellings, and two gateways [plans actually showed a total of four gateways] with doors made of wood and lined with iron sheeting. The parapet wall is built of granite and has 119 embrasures. It is approached by four flights of stone steps.

Clearly, this was a place of some distinction. The *Hongkong Weekly Press* in 1904 carried a report that the entrance to the Walled City would 'allow of two carriages and pairs passing each other if they met . . . Kowloon might . . . be styled the City of Cannons. Everywhere one goes one strikes up against ancient dismantled guns . . . The houses here have been of a very superior class and the streets are wide and commodious.' The civil population within the Walled City, according to Stewart Lockhart, 'does not engage in trade, there being no shops of any kind within the city'.

The Walled City was connected to Kowloon City pier by a wide road through the suburbs. Construction of the city wall in the 1840s seems to have been triggered off by the British presence in Hong Kong. At about the same time, a school was set up, and the Chinese magistrate attributed its foundation precisely to the coming of the British: since Kowloon had become a point of interaction with barbarians, he declared, the inhabitants needed to be fortified morally. Under the Convention of Peking lease, jurisdiction within the Walled City was reserved to China. The actual words of the Convention were these: 'Within the City of Kowloon [the Walled City, though some historians have snidely commented that the British negotiator Claude MacDonald had no clear idea what it meant] the Chinese officials now stationed there shall continue to exercise jurisdiction except so far as may be inconsistent with the military requirements for the defence of Hong Kong.'

When the British actually took possession of the New Territories in April 1899 the Convention was unamended. But there had been an outcry among the colonial authorities. They regarded it as intolerable that China should have a toehold within British territory. The more conscientious officials thought that the Chinese presence would make it impossible to clean up the squalor in the suburbs outside the walls. The road between the city and the pier and along the beach offered plenty of gambling houses, an activity illegal in Hong Kong itself. The outrage of the *China Mail* was great. It declared that this was

> the pestiferous haunt of the worst type of Kwangtung [Guangdong] criminals, the refuge of thieves, robbers and murderers fleeing from Hong Kong's minions of the law. We have no personal knowledge of Sodom and Gomorrah, but judging from what we learn of these places in Scriptural narratives and what we know from actual experience of Kowloon city and Chinese Sham Shui Po, we should say that if there were points in favour of either of the couples, Sodom and Gomorrah held the odds.

According to the *Hongkong Telegraph* in 1890, 'it is notorious – too notorious, alas – that the wretched agglomeration of Chinese hovels known as Kowloon City is the favourite [gambling] rendezvous of a considerable number of the British and foreign community, persons occupying prominent positions in the Colony.'

So by Order in Council in 1899 Britain also took over the Walled City. In this Order the British colonial authorities revoked previous provisions and declared:

> Whereas the exercise of jurisdiction by the Chinese officials in the City of Kowloon having been found to be inconsistent with the military requirements for the defence of Hong Kong, it is expedient . . . that the Chinese officials within the City of Kowloon should become part and parcel of Her Majesty's Colony of Hong Kong for all purposes during the continuance of the term of the lease.

The Chinese officials were duly expelled.

After this Order the position in British law was clear: the Walled City was part and parcel of the leased New Territories, subject to British jurisdiction like the rest of the colony. But the Chinese never relinquished their claims on the area and protests were heard from both Kuomintang (Nationalist) and Communist Chinese rulers. In practice, the colonial rulers pussy-footed in the face of these Chinese protests. In 1934 the government gave notice to a number of Walled City inhabitants, mainly pig-breeders, that they would be removed for sanitary reasons; compensation would be paid. The aim was to turn the city into 'a place of popular resort and antiquarian interest'. At the time there were only 436 residents within the walls. They protested. So did the Chinese Nationalist government: China issued separate protests after each evacuation order. It took until 1940 before all the buildings within the Walled City were demolished, apart from the old *yamen* plus a private dwelling and a former school building. When the Japanese occupied Hong Kong the Walled City was deserted. The Japanese occupiers in 1943 took down the walls and used the material as foundations for the extension of Kai Tak airport.

After the war people returned to the Walled City – a flood of them, mostly squatters who were refugees from the turmoil in China. The sudden influx of people into Hong Kong, a human tidal wave, made rational planning for any part of the colony difficult. The authorities were hard pressed to retain law and order and essential services for the swollen population of the war-ravaged city. The coming to power of the Communists north of the Shum Chum (Shenzhen) river also created a delicate situation. The British authorities at one time were afraid that the Communists might not stop at the Hong Kong boundary in their anxiety to roll up the whole map of China. Even when it was clear that Hong Kong would be left alone, tension remained. One attempt was made in 1948 to resettle the squatters, but it provoked a riot in the Walled City. As if responding to a cue, the Chinese in Canton burned the British consulate to the ground. Students in Shanghai also held two-day protest strikes. Such actions reinforced the natural caution of the colonial officials in dealing with the Walled City.

By this time the unwalled Walled City was rapidly losing any remaining charm. Land reclamations had in effect moved it further and further from the sea. New waves of refugees meant that it became overcrowded and overgrown with the flotsam and jetsam not integrated into normal society. Sir Alexander

Grantham, Hong Kong's Governor from 1947 to 1957, described the Walled City as 'a cesspool of iniquity, with heroin divans, brothels and everything unsavoury'.

Until 1959 criminal suspects living in the city – though few were actually caught – were deported to China rather than charged. This was because of fear that there would be a new dispute with China over who really had jurisdiction there. And sure enough, in 1963 the war of words with Peking was rekindled. There was a plan to demolish part of the Walled City to extend a nearby housing estate. The British Chargé d'Affaires in Peking was promptly informed that 'The City of Kowloon is China's territory and within China's jurisdiction, and this has all along been so in history'. China gave its support to the 'Kowloon City Anti-demolition Committee'. The only occasion when the government acted really effectively occurred in 1975, when it successfully demanded that the tops of two buildings be lopped off because they were obstructing the flight-path to the airport.

The decision of 1987 – with China's blessing – to tear down the Walled City and turn it into a public park has interesting historical echoes. British cabinet papers of the 1940s, opened to the public gaze thirty years later, indicate that a garden was one of the suggestions made by the British in the 1940s in an effort to solve the long-running problem. A Foreign Office paper dated 27 October 1948 says

> The Secretary of State will recall that we attempted to sidestep the Chinese claim for jurisdiction over the Kowloon Walled City by proposing that the site be turned into a Garden of Remembrance under Anglo-Chinese trusteeship. The Chinese refused the solution and made a series of counter-proposals, of which the least objectionable seemed to be to make over the whole site as a compound for the official residence of the local representative of the Chinese government. All the solutions, however, have been abortive because of the Chinese government's refusal to shelve its claim to jurisdiction of the Walled City.

The British and Hong Kong authorities were clearly worried about opportunities for mischief-making if China's claims to territory were accepted. The Foreign Office paper continued:

> The conclusion was reached that it would be absolutely inconsistent with military requirements to comply with the Chinese request [that the Walled City be allowed as an official Chinese residence]. Apart from these grounds the Hong Kong government for their part felt that, if an enclave under Chinese jurisdiction was to be maintained within the limits of the leased territory, it might become a refuge for Chinese malefactors and agitators, to their great embarrassment.

Other British official papers suggested referring the question to the International Court or even handing the Walled City over to the United Nations.

Possibly the most interesting attempt to demonstrate China's jurisdiction occurred in August 1983 when the new director of the Hong Kong branch of Xinhua, the New China News Agency, effectively China's leading official in Hong Kong, went on a walkabout in Kowloon. He reiterated China's claims to rule the Walled City. More controversially, however, he praised the squalid stinking Walled City as an example of self-rule, adding: 'If residents of the Walled City could manage their own affairs, by the same token, so could Hong Kong people.'

Certainly there could hardly be anything less attractive as an advertisement for self-rule than the Walled City in the 1970s and early 1980s. It was a *laissez-faire* society, with none of the redeeming features of an established government. Hong Kong itself has often been described as a *laissez-faire* economy, a charge which leading officials like Sir Philip Haddon-Cave have been quick to deny. Looking at the Walled City it is easy to understand why. It offered the only remaining refuge and safe haven for illegal immigrants: if they reached the 'safety' of its alleyways, they were not likely to be turned in to the authorities.

The area offered accommodation at lower prices than were available in Hong Kong proper. There was also the opportunity to run a business free of the restraints imposed by the government outside. On one visit I saw some of the variety: Here a seven-year-old boy is in charge of a machine hissing and spewing out Barbie doll legs; there men in shorts stand over vats of bean-curd. A radio blares 'All I have to do is dream'!

Inside the city there are none of the amenities such as proper water supplies that the inhabitants of the rest of Hong Kong take for granted. Most inhabitants get their water from wells or from street standpipes. And one of those wells is neatly tucked away under a bed, and owned by a Triad gang leader, a reminder of the power of the fist people. The safety of the water supplies is *not* assured. Another well has fish swimming in it, 'so we can tell that the water is still usable', says a resident. 'If the fish died, we'd know that we shouldn't use the water.' The city does have electricity supplies. That is because China Light and Power Co. is a private profit-making company, not bound by government protocol. All in all the Walled City is a dirty throwback to medieval times. Yet this was the place praised by China's unofficial but generally acknowledged representative. It showed – yet again – the distance the Chinese have to travel to appreciate what Hong Kong really offers.

Jackie Pullinger, a British evangelistic Christian, has done much in trying to rescue people of the Walled City from their squalid lives. She holds regular prayer meetings to try to get people to turn towards Jesus Christ. At one meeting about forty young Chinese had gathered in a bare meeting room somewhere in the warren of lanes within the Walled City. Like many charismatic gatherings it was open-ended: some of those present stretched out their arms and told how grubby their lives had been before, and witnessed to their conversion when Christ had entered their existence. At the end of the session they all filed out. 'Now they have to decide whether they are really committed to Christ or whether they will steal to buy the drugs they are dependent on,' said Jackie Pullinger, fully aware of the awful choice ahead of them.

But the decision to demolish the place did produce some unexpected twists. By early 1989 one block comprising about a third of the Walled City was deserted, the emptied apartments carefully padlocked and the stairwells patrolled by security guards. The chief guard is the proud keeper of hundreds of sets of keys neatly collected like military campaign medals on the walls behind him. Inside one tiny flat, a half-empty packet of household cleaner has been discarded, along with a greasy calendar with the days ticked off until 21 April 1988, when the family left. The cramped kitchen, about 6 feet by 2, also houses the Asian-style lavatory, a porcelain hole in the floor. The living room, tattily bare apart from the discarded items and fresh spiders' webs, is about 8 feet by 10.

Surprisingly for Hong Kong, where there is always angry resistance whenever hillside squatter huts are marked for tearing down, the exodus from the Walled City is going on with hardly a murmur. This is probably because the tenement owners are being compensated to the tune of about HK$300,000 (US$39,000 or £23,000) for a typical 300-square-foot dwelling. Tenants are being given alternative accommodation in government flats, cramped but offering a breath of fresh air after the Walled City. There is general relief to be going, moving from the margins to Hong Kong society proper, to homes after hovels.

On my last tour, I overheard a lively debate between a small shopkeeper and the government official about 'our storeroom upstairs'. Some people are haggling for better compensation, claiming that living rooms are in fact storerooms and part of the commercial premises, and therefore entitled to the superior compensation that businesses attract. But that is about the limit of the complaints. 'We will be glad to go,' says a sprightly elderly woman managing a tiny electrical shop and feeding her small grandson at the same time. 'Everything here is dirty and cramped and there are three generations living in two small rooms. With the compensation we may be able to buy a proper flat and a bigger shop.' Some complaints have been sparked off among Hong Kong residents that the compensation is too generous. In particular, some regular dentists and doctors licensed to practice in Hong Kong are jealous of the compensation being offered to the illegal practitioners in the Walled City. One man is generally supposed to own 102 separate pieces of property. A senior police officer says this landlord cheerfully expects to collect HK$51 million in compensation. But when confronted with this story residents and officials alike are reluctant to talk. Pressed, they suggest that 'It's not one man but a company', or 'It's not as many pieces of property as you suggest.'

An old couple did surprise officials and other inhabitants alike when, on the appointed day of removal, they took just a single large suitcase each to the edge of the Walled City. Asked by the driver of the huge pantechnicon who had come to collect them and their household effects where they wanted to go, they replied 'To Kai Tak airport'. There they strode right up to the Qantas check-in and presented tickets to Australia, first-class, to join their children already there.

But what will happen to the rat's nest of the Walled City? Officials are keeping mum. Nothing will be torn down until everyone is out – by early 1991 at expected rates of progress. But the leading suggestion is that the whole city will then go up in smoke in one gigantic explosion (or implosion), perhaps with just the old *yamen* preserved under a steel net for history's sake. The government secretary who suggests this method of demolition says 'It will probably be the world's biggest single explosion.' Ah yes, Hong Kong always has one eye on the *Guinness Book of Records*.

12 China's Triumph: the Unequal Treaty of 1984

In September 1982 the British Prime Minister Margaret Thatcher visited China and Hong Kong and insisted on the validity of the nineteenth-century treaties under which Britain had gained possession of Hong Kong. Treaties, she insisted, could be varied, but not broken, and she talked of Britain's 'clear responsibility', 'moral duty', and 'commitment' to Hong Kong. Only two years later the same Prime Minister travelled back to the Chinese capital for a simple fifteen-minute signing ceremony under which she promised that Britain would hand Hong Kong over to China; at midnight on 30 June/1 July 1997, the British Union flag will be lowered and China's red flag with its five yellow stars will be raised as Peking gains sovereignty over Hong Kong.

In those two years Britain had negotiated the handover of the brightest remaining jewel in its once world-wide empire 'on which the sun never sets'. China had threatened, browbeaten, cajoled and bullied and had achieved the rewriting of the nineteenth century 'unequal treaties'. In some ways the talks between China and Britain offered a mirror-image of those of the nineteenth century. It was a Great Power agreement just as unequal as those of the last century. This time Britain, popularly shown as the proud lion in nineteenth-century cartoons, was the unequal partner. Its once-proud world-embracing vision had become dim; these days the government in London had enough problems to occupy it in its own misty island and on the continent of Europe. Occasionally, as in Thatcher's Falklands

War victory, the British could muster enough strength to mount a military expedition in favour of far-flung kith and kin. But the will was lacking to defend British rule over Asians 12,000 km (7,000 miles) away; and, more important, Britain was not prepared to challenge the burgeoning power of China on the China coast. In spite of the highflown phrases of commitment to Hong Kong, some influential figures in Whitehall and Westminster were always eager to find an easy way of surrendering colonial rule. Prospects of increased trading opportunities in an expanding Chinese economy would make any deal more palatable and sweeter. For China, the agreement meant the return of 'face' lost by those original treaties. ('Face' is a peculiarly Asian concept involving self-respect and honour, or shame where 'face' is lost.) For the people of Hong Kong there was little consultation, no proper role in the negotiations and no alternative but to accept what the powers had offered.

In the nineteenth century Hong Kong had been a mere island with a few humble fisherfolk and farmers on it. Too bad for the 5.5 million people living there by 1984, that by then the territory had a lot more at stake. Supporters of the agreement say that China's promises will allow Hong Kong to continue its own lifestyle without interference from Communist China: Peking promised that Hong Kong's capitalist lifestyle would be allowed to continue for at least fifty years after 1997. China's strongman Deng Xiaoping has boasted that the 'one country, two systems' agreement could serve as a model for other alienated territories like East and West Germany, or North and South Korea. Deng is particularly keen to offer it as a model to tempt Taiwan, the offshore island of 19 million people that still styles itself 'the Republic of China' and claims to be the legitimate government of all China, to return to the embrace of the Motherland. But there are a lot of ifs, buts, and maybes about the Sino-British agreement, a lot of problems to be solved and a lot of questions to be answered.

Hong Kong has its reasons for distrusting Mother China. For

the Hong Kong people what is at stake is not just face but freedom, income, livelihood and lifestyle. The course of the negotiations showed how exposed the local nerves were. The mood plunged from confident optimism at the start of the 1980s to gloom and despondency when first the rulers in Peking spoke of embracing Hong Kong. By 1984 when China and Britain struck their deal, there was a resigned feeling that Hong Kong should make the best of what it had got. Five years later the mood had turned to anger and a sense of betrayal by both Peking and London.

The Background

The 1970s and the very early 1980s, economic and financial scandals notwithstanding, were Hong Kong's finest times. The territory had demonstrated to the world what could be achieved through liberal economic policies, hard work, imagination and a hunger for a better life. These virtues all helped to turn a refugee city into a burgeoning international metropolis, one of the great cities in the world. Undeniably Hong Kong had plenty of warts and blemishes, but it was a shining example both to China, lethargic and trammeled by Communist dogma, and to Britain, lacking the imagination and energy to live up to the demands of a welfare state. During the 1970s Hong Kong was fortunate in being free from the political tremors that had shaken it earlier.

Indeed, the absence of political turmoil and trauma and the very obvious fruits for everyone – including China – of economic progress lulled many people into believing that Hong Kong could continue for ever untouched. Several influential figures waxed eloquent about the very special role of late twentieth-century Hong Kong. In his farewell budget speech as Financial Secretary, before he moved on to be Chief Secretary, Sir Philip Haddon-Cave spoke of Hong Kong as 'the international city', the financial centre for the whole of the Asia-Pacific basin and one of the world's major trading and manufacturing centres. Lord

Kadoorie expressed his own confidence, and pointed out the special benefits that colonial Hong Kong brought to China.

> China has a declared interest in moving into the next century, catching up on western technology. This great city has become the Free Zone of China, the new point of contact between the two ideologies. Hong Kong exists because it is needed and because, under an efficient administration and a sound legal system, it can provide those services essential for the modernization of China . . . with the will to make it work, Hong Kong could become the greatest single trading centre the world has ever known, radiating prosperity, providing employment and setting new standards of life. (*China Light and Power Annual Report*, 1982)

Sensible and sensitive Hong Kong officials remembered the troubles of 1956 and of the Chinese Cultural Revolution of the 1960s, when riots had really rocked Hong Kong. Then, Communist-inspired youths carrying Chairman Mao Zedong's Red Book had taunted Hong Kong policemen: 'Aren't you Chinese too?' Prominent local Chinese received messages through the mail inscribed 'Chinese traitors, where will you run to?' or 'Have you forgotten your Chinese surname?' Only on Peking's orders did things calm down. There was recognition that Hong Kong depended on China, most of all for life-sustaining supplies of water and food. There was a realization that if Peking wanted to, it could easily take over Hong Kong.

In the shorthand of the times, 'a Chinese takeover is only a telephone call away'. An official amplified what he meant: 'all the Chinese have to do is pick up the telephone and say "we're coming", giving us – we hope – some notice to clear out, and that would be more or less the end of British rule. There's no way we could resist China's demands.' But as the 1970s wore on and the economy boomed, there was hope that China might leave Hong Kong alone for its own sake. Those hopes were boosted in March 1972 when China's Permanent Representative at the United Nations (and later Foreign Minister) Huang Hua asked that the question of Hong Kong should be removed from discussion by the United Nations committee dealing with decolonization. China, said Huang, would settle the Hong Kong question in its own way at a time suitable to it. In a letter to the committee he wrote:

> The questions of Hong Kong and Macao belong to the category of questions resulting from the series of unequal treaties which the imperialists imposed on China. Hong Kong and Macao are part of Chinese territory occupied by the British and Portuguese authorities. The settlement of the questions of Hong Kong and Macao is entirely within China's sovereign right and do [*sic*] not at all fall under the ordinary category of colonial territories covered by the declaration on the granting of independence to colonial countries and people . . . the Chinese government has consistently held that they should be settled in an appropriate way when conditions are ripe . . .

Since China had refused Portugal's offer to surrender Macao, why should it want to take back Hong Kong? the ever-optimistic asked.

As Deng Xiaoping came to power in China, dedicated to modernizing the country, hopes began to grow that Hong Kong might be able to survive any deadline such as 1997 when the British Lease on the New Territories expired. These hopes were further encouraged as cooperation between Hong Kong and China grew. The most popular way of describing the relationship was as a 'three-legged stool', in which the British, the Chinese and the local Hong Kong legs were equally important to keep a flourishing experiment going and profitable to everyone. The British provided the stability and the framework of law and government to preserve Hong Kong as a separate capitalist entity from China; Hong Kong got its supplies of food and water from the mainland; the mainland got from Hong Kong its biggest slice of hard currency earnings and a source of learning about the outside world without having to taint its own Communist system (see chapter 10).

The Hong Kong colonial arrangement was a unique one. The island of Hong Kong and a tiny part of the mainland had been handed over supposedly 'in perpetuity' to Britain, according to the old treaties. But the larger part of the colony, comprising more than 90 per cent of the land area, was subject to a ninety-nine-year lease due to expire on 30 June 1997. In the early 1970s no one was prepared to talk about the tricky and ticklish issue of the lease. Officials in the Hong Kong government didn't want to; businessmen and others were too busy making money to stop to consider 1997. When businesses were typically recovering the value of their investments in three to seven years, 1997 was more than a lifetime away. 'Time for several fortunes to be made and lost before then,' was the way one businessman dismissed the issue in the early 1970s. By the later years of the decade, as the economy continued to grow at 10 per cent a year, Hong Kong saw itself becoming more prosperous in per capita income terms than the United Kingdom by the mid-1990s.

This prosperity gave rise to an audacious hope that Hong Kong would be allowed to continue in its existing unique way for ever, or at least until well after 1997. If there were legal or practical difficulties, it was confidently asserted, Britain and the new pragmatic China would find a way of solving them. A senior lecturer in law at Hong Kong University, Peter Wesley-Smith, who became an expert in the subject through researching for his book on the 1898 leasing of the New Territories, argued ingeniously that there should be no real problem over the 1997 date. According to his argument, all the treaties bringing Hong Kong under British rule are invalid in the eyes of the Chinese. But if this is the case, the 1997 expiry date for the New Territories lease has no particular significance for China. China could have taken back all of Hong Kong at any time over the previous thirty years or so, but had not done so.

The problems, in Wesley-Smith's view, concerned Britain, but he even tried to wave this difficulty away. He noted that in British law its right to govern the New Territories was settled by the Order-in-Council after the 1898 treaty. Thus, conventional wisdom would indicate that Britain has the politically embarrassing task of going to China to ask for an extension of the lease. But, Wesley-Smith argued, the Order-in-Council was a *sufficient* but not a *necessary* declaration of British rule. He claimed that the British government had other ways of making its decisions known which the courts would accept. Declarations of war, for example, were Acts of State that the courts would not challenge. In Hong Kong's case an executive certificate stating that the New Territories continued to be part of Hong Kong after 1997 would suffice. And he added:

> What if there is no executive certificate? The determination of the government to stay on in the New Territories will be obvious by the simple fact that it has not departed. It is neater and more satisfying and more apparently 'legal' to have a formal document announcing the decision, but if the political circumstances do not permit formal documents the courts can look for other indications of government intent. 'Business as usual' is enough. (Wesley-Smith put forward these views in a speech to the Rotary Club of Hong Kong, 16 February 1982, entitled 'Hong Kong and 1997: The Options')

This was an ingenious argument, but Wesley-Smith left unsolved the obvious political problem of how China's 'face' could be saved if Britain simply announced or made it apparent that it would be 'business as usual' after 1997. And he also ignored the highly material and practical question of what to do about land leases and mortgage payments as 1997 approached. Would the banks be prepared to continue to grant mortgages on land everyone assumed would revert to China after 1997? Since fifteen years was the normal maximum term for mortgages in

Hong Kong, it was freely expected that difficulties would arise as 1997 minus fifteen years came closer. (This is in fact what happened. Banks did extend the term of mortgages beyond 1997, but Hong Kong's nervousness grew as 1997 minus fifteen years approached.)

The next major step came when China's strongman Deng Xiaoping himself threw out a few crumbs of hope to businessmen and others wishing to see Hong Kong's status quo prolonged after 1997. In 1979 Sir Murray MacLehose (now Lord MacLehose), the Governor of Hong Kong, paid the first official visit by a Governor to the Chinese capital. Deng and everyone in the capital were all smiles, and the strongman made his famous statement that investors in Hong Kong should 'set their hearts at ease'. In his annual policy speech in October 1980 MacLehose adopted a confident tone, declaring:

> there is nothing in this rapidly evolving situation which we have to fear. But naturally it involves new problems as well as new benefits. It is therefore important that we should keep in close touch with the provincial government of Guangdong and find ways by which any new problems can be solved by mutual cooperation. This we are doing.

The following year in his annual address to the legislative council on 7 October 1981, his last one before he retired, Governor MacLehose again painted an optimistic picture:

> I note with satisfaction the steady development of economic cooperation between agencies of the Chinese government and Hong Kong businessmen in Hong Kong, in Guangdong, and in other parts of China. I am convinced that at this time the best contribution we can make to our own future is the fostering of the growing economic links that exist with our neighbour. These are complementary to our very large economic interests in other parts of the world.

The generally optimistic mood continued until early 1982. In mid-1981 the stock market hit a record high of 1,810 on the Hang Seng index. Property values soared ever upwards. Month after month record deals were announced in which reputable business houses paid new world-beating prices for land. In 1981 a consortium, in which the respectable and hitherto staid Hongkong Land Company teamed up with the highflying and mysterious Carrian group (see chapter 8), agreed to buy a hotel site on Kowloon's 'Golden mile' of Nathan Road for the princely sum of HK$2.8 billion (worth at that time almost US$500 million). Then Hongkong Land bid an even more breathtaking HK$4.76 billion for a piece of land on the waterfront side of Connaught Road for a building that would house the new unified Hong Kong stock exchange. The sky, it seemed, was the limit. Banks and foreign businesses continued to flood into Hong Kong and to pay record rental prices so that Hong Kong chased Tokyo and Manhattan for the doubtful honour of being the most expensive place in the world to buy or rent offices or homes. Some foreign executives were paying upwards of US$4,000 a month for a single apartment.

Lord Kadoorie and the China Light and Power Company (which he chaired) were also doing their best to persuade China to allow Hong Kong to continue as a separate entity through a very controversial scheme. Approached by the Chinese provincial authorities in Guangdong, China Light cooperated in a feasibility project to build China's first nuclear power station at Daya Bay not far from Hong Kong's borders. This would be a massive project, consisting of two linked 900-megawatt reactors, and would cost, at 1981 prices, an estimated US$5 billion. Even with the most rapid final agreement and construction it would be the early 1990s before the plant was opened. According to the agreed scheme, China would largely pay for the plant by supplying electricity to Hong Kong. To get the international loans as well as to pay off the debt in foreign currency, Kadoorie reasoned, Hong Kong would have to remain independent of China until at least the early years of the twenty-first century –

since if Hong Kong were part of China it would not generate the hard currency earnings to repay the loan. Privately, some senior China Light officials admitted that 'we need a nuclear plant on the doorstep like we need a hole in the head'.

By 1982 some nervousness had set in: 1982 after all was 1997 minus fifteen years. The property bubble was pricked. Another factor was the impending visit by British Prime Minister Margaret Thatcher to the Far East in September 1982, starting in Japan, then going to Peking and other parts of China and finally to Hong Kong. This would be the time, commentators in the colony declared, when she would discuss the future of Hong Kong. Businessmen began to mutter, as the date of the visit approached, that she ought to get some hard guarantees that Hong Kong would be allowed to remain as an independent entity well beyond the 1997 date. As evidence of the rather twitchy nerves in the colony, the local dollar lost ground against the US unit and slipped below HK$6 to the American dollar. (After Thatcher's visit the currency hit a then all-time low of 6.96 to the US unit and had to be propped up by the government.)

It will long be a matter of argument as to whether Thatcher played her hand badly, whether she was provoked by the Chinese, or whether what followed was inevitable, repairing the damage of history. Businessmen and others in Hong Kong pressing for a clear message about the colony's future got it, but not quite in the form they had hoped. The message from Thatcher's visit was clear enough – that China was going to regain sovereignty over Hong Kong, with the implication that this would be done by 1997 or perhaps even sooner. The Prime Minister left behind a tense atmosphere both in China and in Hong Kong. Some critics claim that she was misled by her experiences in Japan, where her combative stance had been understood and appreciated. Her schoolmarmish manner was not appreciated by her Chinese hosts. Some members of the British entourage noted that the Prime Minister was suffering from a heavy cold which may have made her harsh and irritable.

Another factor was that she went to Asia flushed with the victory in the Falkland Islands War, and in no mood to yield sovereignty over outposts of the British empire. Whatever the reason, whether Thatcher misunderstood or simply departed from her foreign Office brief, her statement in China and in Hong Kong that the nineteenth-century treaties concerning Hong Kong could be altered but not abrogated went down badly with China.

The joint statement issued after Thatcher and Deng Xiaoping had discussed Hong Kong's future was relatively bland: 'The two leaders of the two countries held far-reaching talks in a friendly atmosphere on the future of Hong Kong. Both leaders made clear their respective positions on the subject. They agreed to enter talks through diplomatic channels with the common aim of maintaining the stability and prosperity of Hong Kong.'

But there was an edge to some of the Chinese comments. Xinhua, the official New China News Agency, stated on 24 September, immediately after the Deng-Thatcher statement, that the Chinese government's position on the recovery of the entire territory of Hong Kong was unequivocal and known to all. This was an echo of the comment of Chinese Premier Zhao Ziyang to the press the day before – and immediately before Thatcher began her talks – that China would regain sovereignty over Hong Kong. His statement was seen by British officials as a betrayal of the spirit of the Sino-British talks.

When exactly the Communist rulers in Peking decided to recover sovereignty over Hong Kong is a moot point. In early April 1982 Deng met former British Prime Minister Edward Heath, who later said he had been told that Deng intended to allow Hong Kong people to govern Hong Kong after China gained sovereignty: China's new constitution, then under discussion, would provide for the creation of Special Administrative Regions that could allow maintenance of Hong Kong's existing system. Throughout early 1982 a procession of prominent Hong Kong people visited Peking and were received by top Chinese leaders. The wooing of Hong Kong had clearly begun. But the first public indication that China regarded 1997 as an appropriate date came on 16 July 1982, when Peng Zhen, Vice-Chairman of the Standing Committee of the National People's Congress, stated that reunification of China would be based on the principles of 'respect history, respect the reality and look forward to the future'. It wasn't as enigmatic as it sounded, especially since Peng also appealed specifically to compatriots in Taiwan, Hong Kong and Macao to study Article 30 of the draft constitution providing for the establishment of Special Administrative Regions (later this became Article 31).

In the minds of Chinese political leaders 1997 had probably stood out for a long time as the appropriate date for China to reabsorb Hong Kong. However little they may be aware of what really makes Hong Kong tick, the Chinese leaders are not political fools, and they knew that 1997 posed problems for the British. Inquiries by this author suggest that Governor MacLehose in 1979 was told clearly that China did intend one day to resume sovereignty over Hong Kong; presumably the Governor passed on this information to his political masters in London. Whether he was given any more specific information about when exactly China wanted to take control of Hong Kong is not clear; he could make a good guess. The revised 1981 British Nationality Act (that came into force in 1983), slamming the door against residence in the UK by 2.6 million Hong Kong Chinese entitled to hold British Passports could have been written specifically with an eye on 1997, as if inspired by a Deng revelation. But there were other older clues. In *The Times* (of London) of 23 October 1972 Louis Heren recorded the result of an interview with Premier Zhou Enlai:

> few problems were seen to exist between Britain and China, although the future of Hong Kong would have to be decided. A state must enter into negotiations when a treaty expires. Now that full diplomatic relations existed between the two countries Britain naturally would have to negotiate at the appropriate time. Territories taken from China were bound to be returned. This is not a new procedure, but

> unlike India over Goa, it was not Chinese policy to embark upon such matters with undue haste. China has territory known as Macao. The Soviet Union has tried to provoke China into taking it back by force, but China would not be provoked over Macao or Hong Kong. It would eventually call for negotiations. In a changing world this matter would have to be settled, but it did not have to be considered now. The treaty expires in 1997.

Just in case this were not clear enough, and the mention of 1997 did not offer a clear enough signpost to Chinese intentions, the French news agency Agence France Presse reported in May 1979 an interview with China's Assistant Foreign Minister Song Zhiguang (in the *South China Morning Post* of 8 May 1979). When asked about the future of Hong Kong and Macao Song responded: 'there is no pressing need to settle these questions in the immediate future. A solution to these problems will come later. Hong Kong's lease expires in 1997. We have eighteen years to settle the problem and we are not in a hurry . . .' The minister also advised Hong Kong industrialists not to worry. Because of fears about the New Territories lease, said Song, industrialists 'have fears and some have even thought about cancelling certain major investments. But the Chinese have reassured the industrialists by telling them that if they carried out their investments they would suffer no loss'. On the other hand the minister reiterated that 'Hong Kong is part *of China*'.

When British Prime Minister Thatcher took her stand on the original treaties, and later compounded the issue by declaring at a press conference that if countries tried to abrogate internationally binding treaties it was 'very serious indeed', China reacted strongly in a series of statements. Xinhua was quick off the mark, claiming, on 29 September, two days after the press conference, that 'patriotic students' in Hong Kong disagreed with the British Prime Minister by demonstrating and carrying banners proclaiming 'down with unequal treaties'. The next day, a Chinese Foreign Ministry spokesman said:

> The treaties concerning the Hong Kong area signed by the British government and the government of the Qing (Ching) dynasty in China in the past are unequal treaties which have never been accepted by the Chinese people. The consistent position of the government of the People's Republic of China has been that China is not bound by these unequal treaties and that the whole Hong Kong area will be recovered when conditions are ripe. Both the Chinese and British sides hope to maintain the prosperity and stability of Hong Kong and therefore will hold discussions through diplomatic channels.

The Xinhua agency was less restrained, and the following day attacked Thatcher's position and also rebuked her for saying that Britain had a moral responsibility to the people of Hong Kong. 'The government of the People's Republic of China alone is in a position to make a statement to that effect,' the agency said. A week later senior officials at China's Foreign Ministry indicated that the recovery of sovereignty over Hong Kong would take priority, though China would make efforts to guarantee the stability and prosperity of the territory. The battle for the future of Hong Kong had begun in earnest.

Hong Kong Opinions

The visit of the British Prime Minister to China at least opened the door to talks about Hong Kong's future. But it was some time before the actual talks got started. The two sides first got together on 12 July 1983. In the meantime, two things were clear: China was determined to drum home the message that it wanted Hong Kong back as an integral part of China; and many of its 'compatriots' inside the British-run colony were reluctant to hear the message. Opinion polls must always be viewed with scepticism because the sample of people questioned may be partial or limited or because the question may be loaded. But there was a steady consensus of people saying they would prefer no change. Businessmen and others made it clear that they wanted to continue the system and lifestyle they were enjoying. People on housing estates interviewed by this author in 1982, 1983 and 1984 were more ambivalent: unanimously they considered themselves to be good and proud Chinese; they didn't much like the British rulers, and still less liked being part of a British colony; but nor did they like Communist China or its ways. Before the Thatcher visit a major telephone survey carried out by Survey Research Hong Kong for the Hong Kong Reform Club in March 1982 showed approval for British-run Hong Kong. This was the choice of 70 per cent of those interviewed; a further 15 per cent wanted Hong Kong to become a trust territory; a mere 4 per cent wanted Hong Kong in the words of the question 'to be taken back by China and under Chinese administration'. When it came to what Hong Kong people thought was likely, there was scepticism about whether the territory could actually remain under British jurisdiction. Only 43 per cent thought that the maintenance of the status quo would be the probable outcome, and a further 33 per cent expected Hong Kong to be a trust territory. At this stage, only 6 per cent of the people interviewed expected that Hong Kong would be taken by China and placed under Chinese administration. Within the general survey the younger people, the professionals and the more educated expressed the greatest willingness to emigrate rather than stay in a communist-run Hong Kong.

When they were asked why they liked Hong Kong as it was governed by Britain, the main reason cited was that they were used to Hong Kong and its lifestyle and preferred its freer life and high standard of living. The only areas where China scored over Hong Kong were in its better and more spacious environment, with fresher air and a more relaxed atmosphere. Lack of freedom, the lower standard of living, and limited availability of goods were held against China. When it came to a straight comparison of the Hong Kong and Chinese systems, the preferences were plain: 60 per cent of the Hong Kong people liked

Hong Kong's economic system and only 19 per cent disliked it: asked about China's economic system, only 15 per cent liked it and 47 per cent disliked it.

When it came to an assessment of the various freedoms in Hong Kong and China, the British territory scored high, chalking up 87 per cent in favour of its freedom of speech, 91 per cent for freedom of religion, 65 per cent for freedom of residence, 87 per cent for freedom of choice of work and 89 per cent for personal liberty. On each count China scored miserably, with a majority of the Hong Kong people believing that China has not got enough freedom of speech (66 per cent said so), or choice of work (59 per cent), or personal liberty (56 per cent). A large number also believed China lacked freedom of religion (46 per cent) and freedom of residence (42 per cent). Since the 'don't knows' were many, China was left with only 11 per cent thinking it had enough freedom of religion, 30 per cent freedom of residence, a mere 11 per cent for China's freedom of choice of work and only 15 per cent believing personal liberty in China was sufficient. (The reason given for the use of a telephone survey was that 93 per cent of the Hong Kong population lives in a dwelling with a telephone.)

An ambitious attempt to seek the opinion of businessmen was made by Dr Kenneth W. Y. Leung of the Hong Kong Baptist College in May 1982. He polled business companies by questionnaires sent through the mail. Answers came back from 545 companies (19 per cent of those polled), with estimated total investments of more than HK$6.7 billion in the territory and more than 100,000 employees. Leung summarized the views of the businessmen on how they wanted Hong Kong's future government to turn out.

> The top five 'best possible arrangements' have three things in common: (a) the status quo of Hong Kong is maintained; (b) Peking only indirectly reclaims its sovereignty over Hong Kong; and (c) Britain is allowed to continue to govern Hong Kong legally. As can be expected the two

least preferred 'best possible arrangements' do not contain any of the above elements. On the contrary, these solutions share exactly the opposite characteristics: (a) the status quo of Hong Kong is not maintained; (b) Peking directly and explicitly reclaims its sovereignty over Hong Kong; and (c) Britain has a limited involvement only in the administration of Hong Kong's internal affairs. The suggestion that Hong Kong become a Special Economic Zone of China with its own laws and lifestyle was only the seventh most popular, with 6 per cent backing it.

Another influential and revealing poll was taken in mid-June 1982 on behalf of the Hong Kong Observers, a local pressure-group. The Observers were once described in a government report as an 'enigma whose ultimate objectives are by no means clear'; they themselves claim the task of setting out 'to pressure our unelected and unrepresentative government to be more responsive to the needs of Hongkongers'.

The Observers took a year over the project and interviewed 1,000 people aged between fifteen and sixty face to face, about a wide variety of questions. The aim was to present a profile of the community and to seek awareness of topical questions, as well as to gather views on the 1997 issue. An attempt was made to seek a wide cross-section of the community and 'to ensure that the research design was rigorous and would be able to withstand the most stringent scrutiny'. The Observers commented:

> Hongkongers have been stereotyped as rude, noisy, lacking in civic awareness, obsessed with money, anxious to emigrate to the west and shortsighted in their general outlook. These idiosyncracies are said to have been acquired because of the awareness that they are living in a borrowed place on borrowed time . . . The findings show that the aspirations of this community is [*sic*] similar to those of people in developing countries – Hongkongers want a future. And money is not *the* most important thing in life. Nor do all

> the people want to leave, even if they had the chance. There are obvious trends revealed too: the younger, better educated generation are far more critical, more demanding.

A large majority, 86 per cent, liked living in Hong Kong, but among these 56 per cent expressed dislike of some aspects of life in the territory. Only 2 per cent professed an unmitigated dislike of life in Hong Kong. Dislikes were mainly housing (19 per cent), traffic (15 per cent), crime (13 per cent), overcrowding (12 per cent), and the hectic pace (6 per cent). A large majority, 89 per cent, said they regarded Hong Kong as home, 41 per cent because they were born or had grown up in the territory, but only 11 per cent gave as their reason the fact that they felt a sense of belonging. There was obvious confusion on the questions of ethnicity, nationality and roots. Although 65 per cent considered their roots to be in Hong Kong, only 33 per cent said they were 'Heung Kong yan' (Hongkongers); 61 per cent said they were Chinese and 24 per cent said their roots were in Britain. Those in the fifteen to thirty-four age-group were quicker to assert that their roots were in Hong Kong; while those who said their roots were in China came mostly from the thirty-five to sixty age-group. Regardless of whether they thought Hong Kong was home, 57 per cent said they would emigrate if given the chance and 36 per cent said they would not.

People interviewed by the Observers tended to hold critical views. More people thought the government was doing a good job (36 per cent) than thought it was not (24 per cent) – but not a majority. The areas in which those polled said the government had done well were housing (30 per cent), welfare (22 per cent), education (12 per cent), and the medical system (12 per cent); at the same time housing topped the list of bad performances (24 per cent), followed by crime control (17 per cent) and traffic (15 per cent). The government organizations that most people had heard of were the district board and city district office, but only 30 per cent were aware of these and only 8 per cent mentioned the legislative and executive councils as available to them. (This tallied with another poll commissioned by the Hong Kong government and carried out in January 1982, which discovered that almost half of Hong Kong's adults did not know that the executive council existed.)

Asked about five possible solutions to the 1997 issue, from maintenance of the status quo to return of Hong Kong to China or the territory becoming an independent city-state, there was a clear vote for the continuation of the status quo, with 63 per cent choosing this. Return of Hong Kong to China was the least preferred solution. When asked how acceptable they thought each of the five solutions would be, a similar clear preference for the status quo emerged, chosen as acceptable by 95 per cent; 64 per cent felt that Hong Kong under British administration but Chinese sovereignty was acceptable: 42 per cent were prepared to accept the idea of Hong Kong becoming a Special Economic Zone of China; 37 per cent regarded independence as acceptable; and only 20 per cent chose a return to China as acceptable. The minority 5 per cent who didn't like the status quo gave as their reasons poor administration, low standards of welfare, inflation, the fact that the lease issue was not solved and that Hong Kong *should* belong to China. Thus the clear consensus among most groups of Hong Kong Chinese was for 'business as usual'. Many of the people interviewed had been to China.

These popular views coincided with suggestions put forward by most of the business community as well as by some of the bigger pressure-groups. At this time the idea of *gangren zhigang* (Hong Kong to be governed by Hong Kong people) had not been put forward as a possible solution. One popular idea was that the term of the lease should be extended, and generally a thirty-year extension was mentioned. Jack Chi-chien Tang, chairman of South Sea Textile Manufacturing Co., mentioned this when talking in September 1982 to the *Asian Wall Street Journal*. He also said that a fifteen-to-twenty-year notice period before China took the territory back would be a good idea. Similar views were expressed by several businessmen interviewed by the newspaper on the day Thatcher reached China. But Shun Cha, chairman of Crocodile Garments, a local chain of garment shops and exporters, pointed to the uncertainty already being shown by investors and said:

> the present withdrawal of Hong Kong investors should clearly signal to China that if they wish to continue to see Hong Kong prosper, they really should give confidence to Hong Kong people about their future. Perhaps China can say we will give Hong Kong a twenty-five year prior notice for taking Hong Kong back. This way people will have plenty of time to get out. If China says nothing, people will feel safe [putting] their money into Hong Kong. If it says 'starting from today we'll give you twenty-five years' people will have time to get out.

The wish to put off the evil day of the Chinese takeover was also supported by Louis Cha, publisher of *Ming Pao*, an influential Chinese-language paper. 'Eventually China will resume control of Hong Kong, but that will be a long, long time from now, maybe in fifty or eighty years' time. For the time being, my own feeling is that Hong Kong's status quo will continue beyond 1997, but it won't last forever.' Fung Hon-chu, chairman of Li and Fung, an old-established trading and exporting company, said: 'the best [outcome of the Thatcher trip] would be an indication that the present lease would be extended. [Next best would be] a sensible compromise on the part of China . . .'

Some businessmen tried to make a distinction between sovereignty, which they were prepared to concede, and the administration or management of Hong Kong. Jimmy McGregor, then the director of the Hong Kong General Chamber of Commerce, added his voice to the pleading for the continuation at least of the economic status quo. There must be 'clear evidence of British commitment to the continuation of the economic status quo', he urged:

> In other words [there needs to be continuation of] British administration under a British legal system and [an assurance that] the Hong Kong authorities will be able to follow far into [the] next century the same economic policies developed here without basic interference . . . People tend to confuse sovereignty with management. Sovereignty is ownership, and management is something very different. We have the situation already that the British authorities have management responsibilities for Hong Kong in the wider sense. I find it very difficult to believe that Britain somehow controls this territory or has it in ownership. The *de facto* situation is that Chinese sovereignty is already fully understood and recognized. The *de jure* situation needs to be rectified.

Of the leading lights in the territory, only Mrs Elsie Elliott (now Mrs Tu), an urban councillor, was more or less relaxed about the return of Hong Kong to China.

> I don't see how Mrs Thatcher can come up with any answer from Beijing because she has no basis on which to ask for any kind of extension. I would think that the most she could do is assure the people of Hong Kong that fifteen years is quite a long time. And there's no reason whatsoever why we shouldn't go on with our business as normal. By the end of the time, if Hong Kong does go back to China, China may be willing to allow the people of Hong Kong to live more or less as they live now.

Businessman and Macao hotel and casino owner Stanley Ho was even prepared to accept a solution under which China should take back the New Territories, but leave the originally ceded area of Hong Kong and Kowloon to be run by Britain. In an interview with this author, he said he thought that if an agreement was made allowing Hong Kong the free use of the Kwai Chung container port and of Kai Tak airport, a truncated

Hong Kong could continue to flourish. (Kwai Chung is clearly in the New Territories and therefore part of the leased area, but there are some doubts about the position of Kai Tak airport, with its runway built on reclaimed land jutting into the sea. Some experts thought that if the lines setting out the boundary of Kowloon peninsula were extended to the sea, then all or more of Kai Tak probably came within the ceded rather than the leased area – but of course there would still be tricky jurisdiction problems in terms of traffic overflights and air approach to the airport.) But most people were not so ingenious as to imagine a Hong Kong cut off at Boundary Street and without the New Territories. In the Hong Kong of the 1980s one side of Boundary Street looked much the same as the other. There are houses, a school, playing fields, shops and offices. Boundary Street is the same as many others in congested Kowloon and the ugly urban sprawl continues for many blocks on either side. There would be a major difficulty in setting up checkpoints and customs points along an ordinary street. There would also be the nightmare problem of deciding who would be allowed to cross and reside on the Hong Kong side, and who would be left on the Chinese side.

For a largely refugee colony, many of whose inhabitants have fled from China and specifically from Communism, there were good reasons why a continuation of Hong Kong under British administration (if not sovereignty) was preferred. Ronald Li Fook-shiu, then chairman of the Far East Stock Exchange and later of the new unified Stock Exchange of Hong Kong, was prepared to be the most specific and was quite blunt in his expressed views. He urged, in an interview with this author, 'they should hold a very nice ceremony in which England will surrender sovereignty of the whole territory back to China, and China should lease the whole lot back to England for a period of years, renewable'. He was adamant that London should be given full control, including flying the British rather than the Chinese flag: 'you cannot run a bus with a backseat driver'. He gave his reasons eloquently: 'the British have a track record.

They have run Hong Kong well. China has not got a track record. China hasn't even got a proper legal system. If China wants to show that it can run a free enterprise zone, let it open up Amoy (Xiamen) or Shanghai and do its experiments elsewhere rather than muck up the situation here. Let China show it can do it, then we might be confident about China taking over.' Perhaps to soften the impact of his harsh words, Li insisted that he was a good Chinese and stressed that 'there should be no shame in allowing Britain to manage Hong Kong. Britain is leasing bases to the USA, so is Germany, so is the Philippines, so if these rich countries can do it, why should China be ashamed? It should treat Hong Kong like a boat, like a bareboat charter. If a company takes a bareboat charter, it has the right to put its own flag on the funnel. Does the owner suffer shame thereby?' Li also had sharp words for Britain, warning that it 'should not treat the people of Hong Kong like whores by selling them down the drain'.

After the Thatcher visit and the announcement of China's tough line, there was recognition at least among some of the pressure groups that the question of the unequal treaties and the lease did pose a problem, particularly for Britain. In the view of the Hong Kong Belongers' Association, a group of professional men and women, including civil servants: 'Hong Kong is a fine example of pragmatism at work.' Hong Kong's population, the group noted, 'is comparable with those of Denmark and Switzerland and bigger than those of the Irish Republic, Norway and New Zealand. Yet Hong Kong people shudder at the thought that for the sake of political expediency they might be sold out as a chattel' (open letter to Margaret Thatcher, 6 August 1982). The Belongers thought that, in accord with a Chinese proverb, 'the one who tied the bell round the tiger's neck is the one to untie it', the onus was on Britain to set the situation right. The Hong Kong Observers acknowledged that 'it would be more useful for Hongkongers to start thinking of how we can be of benefit to China than to cling to the blinkered belief that the status quo can be maintained. It cannot. Change is inevitable. The British administration will not continue until the year Dot' (statement in October 1982). The Observers were anxious to get dialogue started with China. Writing after the British Prime Minister had visited China, but before the formal talks had begun, the Observers saw the task for people living in Hong Kong as

> to ensure that the inevitable handover of administrative responsibilities is a gradual process, carried out with minimum disruption . . . What the British administration must do therefore is to set realistic targets for localization, and groom Hongkongers to assume the responsibilities of the Commissioner for Securities, Commissioner against Corruption, Commissioner for Labour, Transport Secretary, Economic Services Secretary, Attorney General, Chief Justice, Financial Secretary and Chief Secretary. At the same time the administration must let the public have a say in policy-making. The appointment system cannot continue as the cornerstone of a responsive administration. It must be replaced by an elected system so that people who are directly accountable to the public can advise and direct bureaucrats. A more representative and open administrative structure is necessary because it is the only way in which all sectors of the community can understand the need to assume social responsibility; we cannot leave it to others to maintain stability and prosperity. Hong Kong is our home. If we want to keep it stable and prosperous, we must be responsible for its management . . . we ask investors who have been kept in business by millions of white and blue collar workers, and middle class technocrats and professionals, who have built a career in Hong Kong's prosperous environment, not to precipitate a self-fulfilling doomsday prophecy.

Squaring Up: The Talks Begin

The first task was to get negotiations started and to work out a framework under which Hong Kong people could be confident of a reasonable future. The negotiations surrounding the talks were supposed to be kept strictly confidential, a requirement that the British team and all those involved with it more or less strictly and honourably abided by.

China had made its position plain. Britain's problem was that it was on the defensive and was forced to react to Peking from a position of weakness. Throughout the 1970s and early 1980s British officials had steadfastly refused to talk about Hong Kong's future after 1997; even on a deep background basis. Whitehall clearly wanted as smooth a ride as possible, wherever that took the people of Hong Kong.

The initial British position was to take a firm, unyielding stand on sovereignty and to hope to trade it for continued British administration. There was one – very small and not very influential – school of thought in the Foreign Office in London which argued that the best way of dealing with the Chinese was to concede sovereignty over Hong Kong to China immediately, and to hope that this spirit would inspire China to similar reciprocity. But such appeasers lost the day. They were overruled on the grounds that if Peking was given an inch it would take at least a mile and would not dream of reciprocating. It was acknowledged that ultimately sovereignty would have to be yielded to China. But, the British team argued, Hong Kong's unique system needed a set of rules. Confidence was delicate and could easily be destroyed. The British were working towards advocating a package deal, under which sovereignty over the whole of Hong Kong would be surrendered to China, the 1997 date thus being removed as a potential catalyst for change, but British administration would be allowed to continue for some time, preferably an unspecified time into the future. Under this sort of plan China's role in Hong Kong could gradually be increased without creating a crisis or impairing the delicate flower of confidence. But it proved not to be a starter, because China wouldn't accept continued British administration or management of Hong Kong.

Although also supposedly bound by confidentiality, China

continued both during and before the negotiations proper to give the most sensitive details of its plans to selected individuals or groups. At the time it looked as if Peking clearly didn't understand what made Hong Kong tick; but, more likely, China was just determined to recover Hong Kong and had decided to bludgeon this thought into the consciousness of the British negotiators and the people of Hong Kong.

As early as October 1982 senior Chinese officials more or less said as much. In the *Financial Times* (of London) on 11 October 1982 an unnamed official promised there would be no less freedom in Hong Kong after China controlled the territory. He indicated that British experts might help to administer Hong Kong, though Peking would have ultimate control. The same message came through loudly and clearly during a visit to China in late 1982 by the present author. Chinese officials saw themselves as putting right one of the great wrongs of history. The wound ran deep. One official even suggested 'What have the British contributed to Hong Kong; we can do better – they are our people.'

The main markers were laid by Liao Chengzhi, then head of the Hong Kong and Macao Affairs Office. On 20 November 1982 he told a visiting delegation of the Hong Kong Factory Owners Association that the idea was that Hong Kong people should govern Hong Kong after China regained sovereignty over the territory. He also promised that Hong Kong's stability and prosperity would be maintained, that its system and lifestyle would not be changed, and that it would continue to be a free port and a financial centre.

The following month China's National People's Congress, the country's law-making body, promulgated a new constitution. A clause in this, Article 31, allowed for special administrative regions to be established. In April the next year Liao referred to this provision when he told a Hong Kong academic group that Hong Kong would have its own mini-constitution and have self-administration as a special administrative region. The next month businessmen and industrialists from the New Territories were in China. Liao met them and sternly told them that China would not agree to any idea that Hong Kong was a 'three-legged stool', with Britain playing the role of one leg. He informed them that Peking would have its own practical plan for Hong Kong ready in about two years. To soften this blow he assured the group that officials in China would not come to take over Hong Kong. Possibly responding to internal political pressures (reputedly from hawkish factions in the army arguing that China should not take a soft line), China's Premier Zhao Ziyang told the Sixth National People's Congress in June 1983 that China would recover sovereignty over Hong Kong 'at an opportune moment and take appropriate measures to maintain its prosperity'. Four days later, Liao died suddenly and was replaced by Ji Pengfei, a former Foreign Minister.

In case the message hadn't been properly appreciated, in Hong Kong Xinhua director Xu Jiatun said on 17 June that Chinese sovereignty over Hong Kong was not negotiable; he also suggested that China would take appropriate measures to maintain Hong Kong's prosperity in the transitional period before sovereignty was recovered, as well as afterwards. A few days later, on 25 June, Deng Xiaoping met Hong Kong delegates to the National People's Congress and the Chinese People's Political Consultative Conference and told them that China's policy towards Hong Kong had not changed and that it was being handled at the very highest level, with head of state Li Xiannian and Premier Zhao in charge.

All this was before Britain and China had sat down to serious talks. In early July, a joint statement from the Chinese government and London stated that the second phase of talks about Hong Kong's future would start in Peking on 12 July 1983. The Chinese negotiating team would be led by Yao Guang, a Vice-Foreign Minister, and other members would be Li Jusheng, second director of the Hong Kong branch of Xinhua, and Lu Ping, adviser to the West European Department of the Chinese Foreign Ministry and Secretary General of the Hong Kong and Macao Affairs Office. Sitting on the British side would be Sir

Percy Cradock, the British Ambassador to Peking, supported by Sir Edward Youde, Governor of Hong Kong and Robin Maclaren, political adviser to the Hong Kong government. China continued to take a tough line towards Hong Kong. Governor Youde declared on returning from London on 7 July that he represented the people of Hong Kong in the negotiations: 'who else?'. The very next day the Chinese Foreign Ministry hit back, asserting that Youde was taking part in the negotiations only as a member of the British team. China expressed displeasure that the Hong Kong executive council was being given details of the confidential negotiations in the capital. The first round of the second phase of the negotiations occupied two days and at the end a brief joint statement was put out describing them as 'useful and constructive'. After the next round, two weeks later, the communiqué simply described the talks as 'useful', this time omitting the word 'constructive'.

The next information breakthrough came not from the negotiations nor from any inspired leak from the negotiators, but from the Chinese direct to some visitors from Hong Kong. Those privileged to be given the information were a group of post-secondary student union activists who had been in Peking. They returned at the end of July 1983 with the message that Hong Kong would be a special administrative region of China, and that local people would take part in drafting the outline of the territory's future laws, though the draft would have to go to the National People's Congress. The students were also given details of how Hong Kong would function as a special administrative region of China. It would keep its capitalist system, they reported. Peking would not send its committed Communist cadres to Hong Kong. The mayor or chief executive of Hong Kong would be elected by Hong Kong people, but he would have to be 'a patriot who supports China's reunification'.

According to the students, China also promised not to intervene in Hong Kong's internal affairs apart from defence and diplomacy, and to allow Hong Kong to manage much of its own foreign affairs. The existing legal framework would continue and Hong Kong's own police would manage law and order. In addition, people with different political backgrounds would be able to express their own views, provided they didn't cause sabotage. Finally, Peking would not interfere with Hong Kong's social reforms. The outline given to the students was later confirmed by urban council member Dr Denny Huang who went to Peking shortly afterwards and met Chinese leaders. On 15 August Hu Yaobang, General Secretary of China's Communist Party, named the date for the Chinese recovery of sovereignty over Hong Kong – 1 July 1997. He also stated that China had 'a complete set of policies' to maintain the prosperity and stability of Hong Kong. Hu's message did not come through any of the regular mouthpieces or through the negotiations. Typical of the diplomatic game that China was playing, it was given to a group of Japanese journalists visiting the Chinese capital.

Meanwhile, negotiations had run into rough water. The statement at the conclusion of the third round of talks in early August was terse: neither 'useful' nor 'constructive' appeared, indicating that no progress had been made. Sure enough, on 16 September Xinhua strongly criticized the Hong Kong government, accusing it of whipping up local public opinion in favour of a transitional phase in which there would be a British presence in Hong Kong after China had taken over. As the Hong Kong government had said nothing on how the talks were going, this was the expression of a peeved China pushing its hard line. The pressures continued. Five days later, China's Foreign Minister Wu Xueqian accused Britain of having a 'rigid' attitude at the talks, and said this must be changed if progress was to be achieved. This was the day before the fourth round of negotiations got under way. When these finished, 'useful and constructive' was again missing. The British Prime Minister Margaret Thatcher conceded that 'great financial and political uncertainty' existed concerning Hong Kong's future.

Hong Kong now began to show its own exposed political nerves. For some time economic indicators such as the Hong

Kong dollar and the stock market had shown sensitivity to the talks in China and to rumours from elsewhere. Before the 1997 discussions opened, the local Hong Kong dollar had traded in the range of $5.25 to 5.70 against the US currency. By the time of Thatcher's visit the local currency had slipped below $6 against its US counterpart. The stock market also recorded its biggest single-day fall for seven weeks while Thatcher was in Hong Kong. The Prime Minister typically brushed aside the stock market movements, saying that fluctuations were to be expected in a place that was as sensitive as Hong Kong. 'I would not conclude too much from what happened in one day,' she commented. At that time, some local economic commentators jokingly prophesied that the dollar would fall to $7.50 and the stock market would drop to 750 as measured by the Hang Seng index.

The joke turned sour on 24 September 1983, the last Saturday of the month. Reacting to the terse statements from the Chinese capital and to Thatcher's comments about uncertainty, crowds swarmed the Hong Kong supermarkets and stripped the shelves nearly bare. Almost everything, from meat to canned food to rice, detergent, baby powder, cooking oil, even toilet paper was sold out. The Hong Kong dollar plummeted to a record low of $9.55 against the US currency. Some banks ran out of US dollars to sell. Panic had clearly set in. The Hong Kong people were speaking most eloquently of their fears of a Chinese takeover. The stock market meanwhile had dropped the previous day by nearly 64 points to 785.48. Hong Kong's Financial Secretary, Sir John Bremridge, was recalled urgently from the United States where he was due to attend the annual meetings of the International Monetary Fund and the World Bank (as an adviser to the British government, not as a representative of Hong Kong). China did not relax its pressure. On the last day of September Ji Pengfei, the head of the Hong Kong and Macao Affairs Office, said that China would make a statement concerning the future of Hong Kong by the end of 1984 if the talks had not reached agreement by that time. He went on to denounce as 'liars' anyone who said that the Hong Kong people were not in favour of China taking sovereignty over Hong Kong. A spokesman for the Chinese Foreign Ministry followed this up on 4 October by criticizing Prime Minister Thatcher. 'Inappropriate remarks made by British leaders cannot lead to a reasonable solution of the question but serve to make the talks more difficult,' said a spokesman responding to remarks in which Thatcher said that under different circumstances Hong Kong would have been another Singapore. The next day the *People's Daily* accused Britain of breaches in confidentiality in the talks because details had been divulged to the executive council. On 10 October the *People's Daily* urged Britain to be more realistic and to relinquish its colonial attitude towards Hong Kong. The treaties governing Hong Kong were invalid, the paper repeated, but China would still wait until the New Territories' lease had expired before taking back Hong Kong because 'it is not a question of patience but of us respecting the outcome of history'.

Urgent consultations involving Bremridge, the Bank of England and economic and financial experts in Hong Kong produced some fruit in mid-October when the Financial Secretary announced that the Hong Kong dollar would henceforth be linked to the US currency in an unusual way, effectively setting the exchange rate at Hong Kong $7.80 against the American currency. Bremridge refused to use the term 'peg' to describe the arrangements, because the ingenious scheme still allowed the Hong Kong dollar to float freely on currency markets.

From mid-October 1983 onwards, Hong Kong's two note-issuing banks, the Hongkong and Shanghai Banking Corporation and the Chartered Bank (now the Standard Chartered Bank) have had to deposit US dollars with the government in exchange for the Hong Kong dollar notes they issue at a rate of 7.80 local units per US dollar; conversely the government is willing to surrender US currency in exchange for local dollars at the same rate. When issuing notes in the past, the banks had merely taken from the government certificates of indebtedness and had credited the government account with an equal amount in Hong Kong dollars. Under the new system, arbitrage works to ensure that the open market rate is more or less effectively anchored to about 7.80 to the US dollar. If the rate drifts too far away, then there is profit to be made by going to the government to buy or sell US dollars at the 7.80 rate. Bremridge was quick to point out that the government's exchange reserves contained more than enough dollars to ensure effective backing of the note rate issue.

At the start there were a few hiccups. The local dollar was quoted at 7.95 to 8 against the US unit, until bankers got used to the new system. Once the situation settled down there have been few upsets. Of course, the system is not completely fool-proof; if there were a major political shock, so that people did not want to hold Hong Kong dollars at any price, it would almost certainly collapse. Another disadvantage is that instead of the currency, interest rates have to take the economic strain, and were pushed to record highs of over 17 per cent in 1984 before settling at record lows in 1985. The new system also ties Hong Kong closely to the progress of the US economy. However, John Greenwood, economist for GT Management, and founding editor of the bimonthly *Asian Monetary Monitor*, who was the main advocate consulted by the government pressing the note link, says that the system would have worked whatever exchange rate was set. 'This system is as good as the gold standard. It operated for hundreds of years before central banks were invented,' Greenwood said, adding that the only amendment he would make would be to allow the general public to buy or sell local dollars directly at the 7.80 rate.

In mid-October 1983, it was evident that some progress was made between Britain and China. The fifth round of talks began on 19 October and British Embassy diplomats were describing them as 'the most important and most substantive meetings' to date. After the two days of discussion had ended, the words 'useful and constructive' reappeared in the joint communiqué. Hong Kong's Governor Youde said that there would be informal contacts between the two sides before the next round of talks. From the Chinese side, Deng Liqun, director of the Propaganda Department of the Central Committee of the Chinese Communist Party, also confirmed that there had been some progress when he said at the end of October that the latest round of talks had shown 'some improvements' on previous meetings.

In fact the Chinese were responding to a letter from Margaret Thatcher in which she suggested that the issue of sovereignty should be set aside for the time being to allow more constructive discussion of other issues. This was rightly seen by China as a concession that effectively settled the sovereignty issue. Not until nearly six months later, in April 1984, did Britain publicly concede that it would have no role in Hong Kong after 1997.

Sources at the formal sessions of the talks subsequently admitted that the set-piece discussions, normally taking three to four hours a time, never achieved very much. They were given over to set speeches, during some of which the Chinese displayed histrionics rather than diplomacy. A lot of time was spent in translating the remarks and there was precious little time available for constructive discussions. The Chinese side spoke in Putonghua (Mandarin), and their words were then translated into English, while the British side used English throughout, and their words then translated into Chinese. All this, even though all the leading British negotiators spoke and understood Chinese, and a number of the Chinese side spoke English. Another hindrance to fluent discussion was the fact that both sides used the leader of the team as the conduit for their opinions. In addition, in the heavily charged political atmosphere both sides were wary of making any commitment that might not be backed up by their government. This was especially so on the Chinese side, over whom the figure of Deng Xiaoping loomed large. 'It became clear,' said one of the British team later, 'that it was Deng who was calling the shots. Other members were terrified that they might say something that could later be disowned by him.' This was a very real worry. Deng did speak out, and in 1984 went back sharply on the assurance of Ji Pengfei that troops of the People's Liberation Army would not be stationed in Hong Kong after China recovered sovereignty. Deng said China *would* station troops. Such is the awe in which Deng is held in the Chinese capital, although he has no formal position in the Chinese government.

On a British Broadcasting Corporation radio phone-in programme in October 1983 Mrs Thatcher said that the fifth round of talks (in mid-October) had been 'very constructive and went much better, and I believe we are reaching a better basis of understanding of what it is that has made this remarkable success in Hong Kong and how we should arrange for it to continue'. Hong Kong did get some support from other countries. Visitors in November 1983 included Japanese Prime Minister Yasuhiro Nakasone and Gaston Thorn, President of the European Economic Community Commission. Thorn declared that it was 'in nobody's interests – and certainly not China's' to put Hong Kong prosperity at risk. The Japanese Prime Minister was told by Hu Yaobang that China would guarantee the absolute safety of all foreign economic investment in Hong Kong.

China was continuing to spray out its thoughts on Hong Kong's future publicly in spite of the pledges of confidentiality. Ji received a group from the New Territories and told them that Hong Kong's existing systems would remain unchanged for fifty years after 1997; he added that this promise would be included in a mini-constitution (subsequently called the 'Basic Law') for Hong Kong. At the start of December Peng Zhen explained that China's constitution would not require Hong Kong to adopt socialism when it came under China's sovereignty. When the official talks resumed the words 'useful and constructive' appeared again with unimaginative monotony. A Chinese source was quoted as saying in mid-November that 'talks have entered a more detailed phase' and in the *South China Morning Post*, he also said 'at the beginning, the British wanted to gain as much as possible on the issue of sovereignty and administration'.

The atmosphere in Hong Kong was becoming more settled. The dollar, effectively anchored to the US currency, settled just below the 7.80 peg. Interest rates were still high, which didn't give much encouragement to the stock market. The market moved nervously up or down in response to a particular statement or gem of information vouchsafed to a group of visitors in Peking. Stories continued about money being taken out of Hong Kong and of passports from other countries being available to Hong Kong residents who were prepared to invest selected sums, normally ranging upwards of US$10,000. A lot of these countries were exotic islands like Tonga, Fiji, Costa Rica, not exactly the places to which Hong Kong industrialists would naturally flock. In fact, some rich factory owners did look abroad, but had to come back home disappointed. Nowhere, a typical industrialist reported, would they be able to replicate the kind of conditions they enjoyed in Hong Kong. They had looked at the west coast of the USA and at a number of islands in the West Indies. For a start, the labour there would not be prepared to work as hard and dedicatedly as their local Cantonese, and they would certainly not respond to Cantonese owners.

China kept to its stance that the talks were a matter for the British, not for the Hong Kong government. Then senior member of the legislative council Roger Lobo (now Sir Roger Lobo) announced in February 1984 that members were going to ask for a full-scale open debate on the talks before a final agreement was signed. Reaction from China was carefully hostile. Liang Weilin, chairman of the Guangdong Provincial Chinese People's Political Consultative Conference, who was visiting Hong Kong, said: 'they can debate anything, past or present, local or foreign, from the south sky to the north land . . . but the Hong Kong issue is a matter between the British and Chinese governments.' In March 1984, Jardine Matheson and Co., Hong Kong's oldest trading company, announced it was moving its holding company to Bermuda, another British territory. The Hang Seng index plunged by 73 points the next day.

Members of the legislative council were later to upset China even more. In a position paper made public in May they openly took issue with the way the talks were going and demanded safeguards for Hong Kong and its people. Before that happened, Britain had already conceded the game. Foreign Secretary Sir Geoffrey Howe visited China in April. Before returning to London he came through Hong Kong and on Good Friday, 20 April 1984, made the portentous announcement that Britain had not only promised to surrender sovereignty, but would play no part in governing Hong Kong after 30 June 1997. The Hang Seng index, a nervous barometer of the local mood as reflected through the Hong Kong stock market, fell by 160 points in the two weeks after Howe's statement, a drop of about 15 per cent. In the eyes of Britain and China, however, the talks were obviously progressing satisfactorily. Chinese representatives continued to drop hints and promises of what would be in the agreement, trying to allay local fears. Further promises took a more specific content. After Ji Pengfei had disclosed in November 1983 that China would leave Hong Kong's internal structure virtually unchanged for fifty years after 1997, Xu Jiatun promised that the future mini-constitution for Hong Kong, special administrative region of China, would be reviewed 'to reflect adequately the views of the Hong Kong people'. He added: 'Hong Kong people of various levels will be consulted when the draft is ready, and all views on the principle of reunification of China will be welcomed.' In January 1984 Zhou Nan replaced Yao Guang as chief Chinese negotiator. Both teams had new heads, as Sir Richard Evans had taken over from Cradock as British Ambassador in Peking and team leader. Zhou told reporters cheerfully: 'China is becoming more prosperous day by day. So Hong Kong's future must be bright.' He was not prepared to go into detail about the talks. But Ji was making more promises. Apart from repeating that Hong Kong's social and economic system would remain largely unchanged and that Hong Kong 'will enjoy a high degree of autonomy', he added that the legal system would remain 'basically' as it was, 'except for legal articles that are colonial in character and harmful to China's sovereignty'. Hong Kong would remain a free port and a financial and trading centre with an open foreign exchange market and stock market. Official jobs would be done by local people, not by people sent from 'inland China' (the term China was using for itself). Foreign nationals would be allowed to work in both public and private organizations.

Ji's grand promises still left a number of questions, starting with whether China could be trusted to keep its promises. In May, on the eve of a debate in the British House of Commons, members of Hong Kong's executive and legislative councils saw gaps that needed filling. A group of them flew to London to make their voices heard. They demanded clarification of the status of British passport-holders who had the right of residence only in the dependent territory of Hong Kong. The request was seen as a demand for the right to settle in Britain or elsewhere with the assistance of the British government, and rejected as unrealistic by most British members of Parliament. The Hong Kong team suggested that essential ingredients of the basic law should be expressed in the formal agreement between Britain and China and that Parliament should not ratify the agreement until the terms of the basic law were known.

In addition, the unofficials asked for some way in which Britain could retain a residual status in Hong Kong after 1997 'to provide the assurance' that the agreement would be kept. They warned of the dangers of China interfering in Hong Kong's administration before 1997, in which case 'the allegiance of the police force and the civil service would be seriously impaired'.

For this intervention the members came under fire in both Britain and China. The Xinhua news agency criticized them strongly: 'the statement is considered as an attempt to obstruct the conclusion of an agreement by the Chinese and British governments on the Hong Kong issue at an early date. It is therefore detrimental to Hong Kong's stability and prosperity, and runs counter to the views and wishes of Hong Kong compatriots.' The left-wing press in Hong Kong claimed that the request would violate Chinese sovereignty, and since the basic law is to be written into the Chinese constitution, it would be a domestic issue of no concern to London or the British Parliament. In London former Hong Kong Governor Lord MacLehose was reported as saying that the intervention was ill-timed and ill-considered. Former British Prime Minister Edward Heath joined the Chinese and left-wing press in Hong Kong in claiming that the members of the councils represented 'nobody but themselves' and were not speaking on behalf of the people of Hong Kong. More telling was the comment that the unofficials had left it too late before speaking out.

This was not the end of conflict between China and the Hong Kong executive and legislative councils. At the end of June three locally respected members went to Peking where they met Deng Xiaoping himself. It was a meeting attended by much fanfare, with television cameras dancing attendance as the three members, Sir Sze-Yuen Chung, the senior member of the executive council, banker Q. W. Lee (now Sir Q. W.), chairman of the Hang Seng Bank, and Swire Group director Lydia Dunn (now Dame Lydia), went in to see Deng. Their leader Chung was wearing a tie with the characters of Hong Kong written on it. Lydia Dunn (whose surname in Chinese is the same as Deng's) epitomized the sleek high fashion of sophisticated Hong Kong, as if showing up dowdy provincial China. Unlike his fashion-conscious Prime Minister Zhao Ziyang, who frequently wore a western-style suit with a collar and tie, Deng was wearing the typical dull Mao suit and chain-smoking cigarettes. He was clearly unimpressed by his visitors. The fact that leader Chung used an interpreter to get from his Cantonese to the Putonghua (Mandarin) spoken in China did not help mutual admiration. Deng dispensed with the chit-chat that normally graces such occasions and launched into a tirade, even as the television cameras whirred and reporters held their notebooks open to catch the trivia that precedes such meetings. Headlines in the Hong Kong newspapers the next morning told how Deng had treated the three: 'Humiliation!', said the *South China Morning Post*, adding 'Deng turns on the Umelco three'. Another newspaper said the three were given a 'Deng-lashing'. Deng told the unofficials bluntly that they represented only themselves, not even the legislative council.

The Chinese leader told them that the question of Hong Kong would be solved between Britain and China without involving any 'third party', an implication that Hong Kong itself was a third party. He knocked over any idea of a three-legged stool. 'No three legs, only two legs.' Deng lectured the trio: 'you should make use of this chance to understand more about Peking, the People's Republic of China and our Chinese people, as it will be very useful to you.' Referring to the three merely as 'Hong Kong residents', Deng made it plain that the Chinese leadership considered it knew what Hong Kong wanted.

> In the past two years we have conducted extensive discussions with public figures from Hong Kong and we know very well what is really in the minds of Hong Kong residents . . . Our proposal for two systems to be practised in one country has taken into full consideration the actual conditions in Hong Kong. I believe that the people of Hong Kong have the ability to administer Hong Kong well. The Chinese are by no means short of talent.

His lecture revealed a mixture of proud determination that China was about to end the colonial era, along with an impatient arrogance that he was right and should not be contradicted:

> As far as sovereignty is concerned, it will be resumed in 1997 regardless of the Sino-British talks and reactions from all sides. I have told the British Prime Minister that if major unrest occurred in Hong Kong before 1997, we would reconsider the timing and ways of taking back Hong

Kong . . . Generally speaking you said Hong Kong people don't have confidence. Actually it is your opinion. It is you who have no faith in the People's Republic of China . . . You do not believe Chinese have the ability to rule Hong Kong; this is because you are still under the influence of old colonialism. The Chinese people are not incapable. One and a half centuries ago, foreigners looked down on Chinese . . . After the establishment of the People's Republic of China the image of China has changed . . . Today, people with a yellow face are no longer abused wherever they go. No matter how he is dressed . . . or what his position is, every Chinese should be proud of being a member of the Chinese race. This is a question of confidence.

Hong Kong people can rule Hong Kong. Singapore is ruled by people with a yellow face and it is said that it is being ruled quite well . . . Members of the future Hong Kong government and its affiliated bodies should basically be patriots, but [they] can include other people who have different positions. Foreigners can serve as advisers.

Patriots must respect the [Chinese] race and should wholeheartedly support China's recovery of sovereignty over Hong Kong. It does not matter which ideologies they believe in, be it capitalism, feudalism or even slavism. They need not support socialism.

You said 'Peking people ruling Hong Kong'. You may say they are Peking people, but I would call them Hong Kong people and their mission is to rule Hong Kong well. I have said many times that Peking would not send people to Hong Kong. If you said patriots are Peking people, that's all right.

The central government has a power. No matter how they are nominated or elected, Hong Kong officials will be appointed by the central government. This is a procedure.

The *Far Eastern Economic Review* carried a cartoon showing Deng with a whip in his hand standing over cats among which were the faces of Chung, Dunn and Lee, with the comment: 'It doesn't matter whether the cat is black or white, as long as it obeys its master.' This was a reference to Deng's famous dictum about capitalism – that it didn't matter whether a cat was black or white as long as it caught mice. Commentator Harvey Stockwin in the *South China Morning Post* wrote on 1 July 1984: 'Deng brutally [but thoughtfully] ripped away the curtain of reasonableness and moderation with which the Middle Kingdom customarily likes to surround itself . . . Deng told the three members of the council to come back and learn, but his TV image made the invitations redundant as he indicated that already China Knows Best.'

Deng was clearly taking a keen personal interest in the talks. A few days before meeting the unofficials he saw a delegation of Hong Kong businessmen. He was clearly exasperated by a comment from Jack Tang, chairman of the Hong Kong General Chamber of Commerce, referring to unhappy memories of the Cultural Revolution. Deng reassured the businessmen that political turmoil wouldn't be repeated and then added: 'would you want me to burn incense in front of Buddha and swear an oath as well?'

By mid-June progress had been made, but the talks were running up against Deng's deadline that the agreement be initialled by the end of September 1984 (just in time for Chinese celebrations of the thirty-fifth anniversary of the creation of the Communist People's Republic on 1 October 1949). There was the threat that if agreement were not reached China would simply announce and execute its own deal. A working group was set up in Peking to get down to the nitty-gritty details and draft the actual language of an agreement. On the British side the team was now led by Dr David Wilson (later to succeed Youde as Hong Kong's Governor), Assistant Undersecretary of State at the Foreign and Commonwealth Office, who was a former political adviser in Hong Kong. Supporting him were Robin Maclaren, political adviser to the Hong Kong government, Fred Burrows, a Foreign Office legal expert, and the Hong

Kong government chief law draftsman Jerry Nazareth. For China, a Foreign Ministry official, Ke Zaishuo, was the leader. All seemed to go smoothly, but the next month a sudden dash to Hong Kong by Richard Luce, the Foreign Office Minister with special responsibility for the territory, indicated that once more snags had occurred. A major stumbling-block was China's suggestion that a joint commission or liaison group should be set up to study Hong Kong's administration during the transition period, up to 1997. The natural fear in Hong Kong was that, if set up and operating in Hong Kong as China proposed, the group would be an alternative government. Other disagreements revolved around the status of the agreement itself. On individual questions, like the passports of Hong Kong people, land and aviation, there were still tricky issues. When Luce passed through, the Hong Kong stock market again showed a typical bout of nerves and the Hang Seng index fell below 800 points, a fall of 10 per cent in the week. The strain also showed on the Hong Kong dollar. A heavy wave of selling in London drove the rate down to 7.90 against the US currency. The government-influenced bank cartel hiked prime lending rates by 3.25 per cent to over 17 per cent, 4 percentage points above rates in the US.

By the end of July some senior officials were beginning to whisper that it might be better to have no agreement at all than a bad agreement. Given that hitherto every official on the British side had maintained a stiff-upper-lip silence, heeding the promise of confidentiality, it looked ominously as if a breakdown might be in sight. It took a visit by Foreign Secretary Sir Geoffrey Howe to China to break the deadlock. In a five-day visit at the end of July 1984 Howe made 'substantial progress'. The Chinese leaders were even more lyrical. Foreign Minister Wu Xueqian declared that the visit was a 'breakthrough', and Zhou Nan, Assistant Foreign Minister and head of the Chinese negotiating team, quoted from a Sung dynasty poem: 'Just as the weary traveller despairs of finding a road, lo, a village appears and the shade of willows and riotous flowers beckons.'

British officials connected with the talks congratulated themselves on the fact that London's stubbornness and refusal to accept a second-rate agreement finally had led to Chinese concessions. Obviously, these officials said, the refusal to budge had eventually been communicated to Deng himself, who had taken over and agreed to some of the British demands. In a statement Howe himself said: 'I am glad to say that very substantial progress has been made. We have agreed: first, the framework and key clauses of an agreement which will preserve Hong Kong's unique economic system and way of life; secondly, that this agreement and its annexes will all be legally binding; thirdly, satisfactory provisions for liaison and consultation after the conclusion of the agreement.'

Howe had agreed to creation of the liaison group, consisting of five representatives each from Britain and China. But China had made concessions on the group's activities. The group was to meet at least once a year in each of the three cities, London, Peking and Hong Kong, before setting up its base in Hong Kong in 1988. China promised that the group would have no power, no advisory role and no part to play in the administration of Hong Kong, and it would remain in existence even after China takes sovereignty over Hong Kong until the year 2000. In a farewell speech Deng Xiaoping told the British Foreign Secretary: 'I thank you for what you have done for the settlement of the Hong Kong question, and I thank Mrs Thatcher for her great concern.'

After Howe had held a press conference the Hong Kong stock market rose by 26.59 points, the biggest jump for three weeks. Wu Hon Fai, president of Hong Kong's Gold and Silver Exchange Society, said: 'I think this statement is worthy of our rejoicing.' But there was still work to be done. Agreements were lacking on three issues: passports, land and civil aviation, and the working group still had to fight against time, hammering out often disputed clauses, sentences, phrases and even individual words in both Chinese and in English. But on 26 September 1984, after frantic work, the document was ready for initialling – in Peking by Britain's Ambassador Sir Richard Evans and Zhou Nan, China's Vice-Foreign Minister. The British negotiators had at least managed to persuade China to make a detailed commitment to its promises, and not just to enunciate vague assurances of the continuation of capitalist Hong Kong and urge people to 'please trust China's word'.

The two sides had different terms for the documents. In Britain it was issued as a White Paper and termed 'The Draft Agreement between the Government of the United Kingdom of Great Britain and Northern Ireland and the Government of the People's Republic of China on the future of Hong Kong'. The version put out in English by Xinhua has an identical text, but the cover describes the deal simply as the Sino-British 'Joint Declaration'.

Margaret Thatcher flew to Peking shortly before Christmas 1984 for the ceremonial signing of the agreement. The mood was very different from that of her previous visit in 1982, which had brought mutual recriminations and upset the nervous Hong Kong economy. The three-month delay between the initialling and the British Prime Minister's visit to China for the signing was taken up in making sure the deal would be acceptable in Hong Kong. In legal theory, only the approval of the British Parliament and the Chinese National People's Congress were needed. But Britain had promised that the deal must be acceptable to the people of Hong Kong. An assessment office was set up there to gather the opinions of the Hong Kong people. Two monitors were appointed by the British government to observe its work and report to Foreign Secretary Howe. They were Sir Patrick Nairne, Warden of New College, Oxford, who used to be a British civil servant, and Justice Simon Li, a Hong Kong Supreme Court judge. Critics complained that the assessment office was something of a charade because whatever Hong Kong people thought of the deal, they had no power to vary its terms in any way or even change a word of it. The introduction of the British White Paper made that clear: 'The alternative to acceptance of the present agreement is to have no agreement. In this case the Chinese government has made it plain that negotiations could not be reopened and that it would publish its own plan for Hong Kong.' Given this condition and the fact that all the propaganda was urging people to support the agreement, the conclusion of the assessment office, published on 29 November 1984, had its own ring of inevitability. The office reported that 'all but a few' of the 3,557 submissions acknowledged the inevitability that Hong Kong would come under China's sovereignty from mid-1997.

> The proposition that an agreement between Britain and China on the future of Hong Kong is preferable to there being no agreement is generally understood and accepted . . . Furthermore, although anxieties and reservations have been expressed by many who have submitted their views, the detailed provisions of the draft agreement have been welcome, whilst the assurances that they will be implemented have been noted.

The leading councils also gave their approval to the agreement. In the legislative council only two out of twenty-nine non-official members abstained from voting; no one voted against. One member, J. J. Swaine, a Queen's Counsel, criticized Britain for going to the negotiating table 'with one hand tied behind her back' because its policies on nationality and immigration had closed the door to people from Hong Kong. He questioned whether elections held in Hong Kong would be fair and was afraid about infiltration from China. He concluded that he 'could not endorse the agreement or commend it to the people of Hong Kong'. Another member, K. C. Chan, also expressed fears about interference from China and said that local people did not trust China.

Subsequently one member of both the legislative and executive councils, T. S. Lo, resigned his seats in criticism. Only one member of the urban council abstained and all eighteen district boards endorsed the deal. Out of 430 representative bodies, including residential bodies, trade unions and religious organizations, 334 approved the agreement and only 33 opposed it. The Hong Kong Bar Association refused to approve the draft, mainly because it was unhappy with the British Nationality Act. This Act, effectively shutting the door of Britain to Hong Kong people who held British passports by right of being born in a British territory, brought anger and a feeling of betrayal, which the assessment office noted. 'A feeling that the United Kingdom had failed in its moral obligations towards the two million Hong Kong British Dependent Territory citizens led to expressions of frustration and sometimes anger . . .' But the assessment office tried to sum up the favourable feeling: 'the calmness with which the draft agreement was received and the reasoned response to it underlines its overall acceptability. There is a general feeling of relief and a wish to build Hong Kong's future on the foundation provided by the draft agreement.'

Margaret Thatcher's visit to China was a brief one. Her Royal Air Force VC-10 aircraft took her halfway round the world merely for a ceremony, on 19 December 1984, which lasted fifteen minutes. (She completed the round-the-world trip by going on to Washington for talks with President Reagan and then back to London for Christmas.) Prime Minister Zhao Ziyang, disgraced in the aftermath of Bloody Peking Spring in 1989, signed for China. He was wearing a sober western suit, whereas Deng and President Li Xiannian were dressed in Mao suits. Champagne toasts were drunk and self-congratulation was the order of the day, 'this historic day', as Chinese leader Deng called it. After that ceremony all that was required was for the legislative bodies of both countries to rubber-stamp their agreement, and on 1 July 1997 Hong Kong, the only bright jewel left in the British empire's crown, will become Hong Kong, China.

The Details of the Agreement

The basis of the agreement between Britain and China is that Hong Kong should be allowed to continue more or less as it is –

as a freewheeling capitalist trading and international financial centre – for at least fifty years after 1997. Britain will give up all its claims over Hong Kong and China will assume sovereignty over the whole of the territory. Top-level British administrators will leave, but Chinese from the mainland will not come in their place. Instead Hong Kong people will be allowed to rule themselves, except in defence and foreign affairs, which will be the prerogative of China. Hong Kong's current executive, legislative and judicial systems will basically remain in place.

The achievement of the British negotiators was to persuade China to commit itself in writing to a series of specific promises on the future shape of Hong Kong. The attitude of the Chinese at the outset was to try to get their promises accepted on trust without being written down and without being too specific. The British White Paper giving the full text of the agreement and its annexes notes that 'the whole makes up a formal international agreement, legally binding in all its parts. An international agreement of this kind is the highest form of commitment between two sovereign states.' The document contains the Joint Declaration, plus Annex I expanding on it, Annex II dealing with the Sino-British Joint Liaison Group, and Annex III with land leases. Then there is an exchange of memoranda on British Dependent Territories citizens, namely Hong Kong residents entitled to Hong Kong British passports.

The basic Joint Declaration takes only three pages. In it China states that from 1 July 1997 Hong Kong will be a special administrative region of China under Article 31 of the constitution. In Clause 3 of the eight-clause declaration China then makes a series of specific promises:

> (2) The Hong Kong Special Administrative Region will be directly under the authority of the Central People's Government of the People's Republic of China. The Hong Kong Special Administrative Region will enjoy a high degree of autonomy, except in foreign and defence affairs which are the responsibility of the Central People's Government.

(3) The Hong Kong Special Administrative Region will be vested with executive, legislative and independent judicial power, including that of final adjudication. The laws currently in force in Hong Kong will remain basically unchanged.
(4) The Government of the Hong Kong Special Administrative Region will be composed of local inhabitants. The chief executive will be appointed by the Central People's Government on the basis of the results of elections or consultations to be held locally. Principal officials will be nominated by the chief executive of the Hong Kong Special Administrative Region for appointment by the Central People's Government. Chinese and foreign nationals previously working in the public and police services in the government departments of Hong Kong may remain in employment. British and other foreign nationals may also be employed to serve as advisers or hold certain public posts in government departments of the Hong Kong Special Administrative Region.
(5) The current social and economic systems in Hong Kong will remain unchanged, and so will the lifestyle. Rights and freedoms, including those of the person, of speech, of the press, of assembly, of association, of travel, of movement, of correspondence, of strike, of choice of occupation, of academic research and of religious belief will be ensured by law in the Hong Kong Special Administrative Region. Private property, ownership of enterprises, legitimate right of inheritance and foreign investment will be protected by law.
(6) The Hong Kong Special Administrative Region will retain the status of a free port and a separate customs territory.
(7) The Hong Kong Special Administrative Region will retain the status of an international financial centre, and its markets for foreign exchange, gold, securities and futures will continue. There will be free flow of capital. The Hong

Kong dollar will continue to circulate and remain freely convertible.
(8) The Hong Kong Special Administrative Region will have independent finances. The Central People's Government will not levy taxes on the Hong Kong Special Administrative Region.
(9) The Hong Kong Special Administrative Region may establish mutually beneficial economic relations with the United Kingdom and other countries, whose economic interests in Hong Kong will be given due regard.
(10) Using the name of 'Hong Kong, China' the Hong Kong Special Administrative Region may on its own maintain and develop economic and cultural relations and conclude relevant agreements with states, regions and relevant international organizations.

The Government of the Hong Kong Special Administrative Region may on its own issue travel documents for entry into and exit from Hong Kong.
(11) The maintenance of public order in the Hong Kong Special Administrative Region will be the responsibility of the Government of the Hong Kong Special Administrative Region.

The annexes repeat these provisions and expand on some of them. One of the most important allows for promulgation by the National People's Congress of China of a basic law 'stipulating that after the establishment of the Hong Kong Special Administrative Region the socialist system and socialist policy shall not be practised in the Hong Kong Special Administrative Region and that Hong Kong's previous capitalist system and lifestyle shall remain unchanged for fifty years'. The annex clearly states that 'the government and legislature of the Hong Kong Special Administrative Region shall be composed of local inhabitants'. English, in addition to Chinese, may be used in government and in the courts. Though the basic law would provide the legal framework, the agreement lays down that 'the laws previously in force in Hong Kong [i.e. the common law], rules of equity, ordinance, subordinate legislation and customary law, shall be maintained, save for any that contravene the Basic Law and subject to any amendment by the Hong Kong Special Administrative Region legislature'.

Underpinning this system China has also committed itself to an independent judiciary.

> The courts shall exercise judicial power independently and free from any interference. Members of the judiciary shall be immune from legal action in respect of their judicial function ... judges ... shall be appointed by the chief executive acting in accordance with the recommendations of an independent commission composed of local judges, persons from the legal profession and other eminent persons. Judges should be chosen by reference to their judicial qualities and may be recruited from other common law jurisdictions. A judge may only be removed for inability to discharge the functions of his office, or for misbehaviour, by the chief executive acting in accordance with the recommendation of a tribunal appointed by the chief judge of the court of final appeal, consisting of not fewer than three local judges. Additionally, the appointment or removal of principal judges [i.e. those of the highest rank] shall be made by the chief executive with the endorsement of the Hong Kong Special Administrative Region legislature and reported to the Standing Committee of the National People's Congress for the record ... The power of final judgement of the Hong Kong Special Administrative Region shall be vested in the court of final appeal in the Hong Kong Special Administrative Region which may as required invite judges from other common law jurisdictions to sit on the final appeal.'

Similarly the Hong Kong Special Administrative Region government will be allowed to make rules and regulations enabling lawyers from outside the region to work in Hong Kong. And the Chinese have promised in the annex to the Joint Declaration that 'the appointment and promotion of public servants shall be on the basis of qualifications, experience and ability'.

Autonomy in financial matters is also specifically promised to Hong Kong. Apart from the provision that the Central Government in China will not levy taxes, the annex says firmly that Hong Kong 'shall use its financial revenues exclusively for its own purposes and they shall not be handed over to the Central People's Government'. The legislature must approve taxation and public expenditure proposals. Auditing of public accounts will be continued. Elaborating on the capitalist structures, the two governments agreed that the Hong Kong Special Administrative Region 'shall be a separate customs territory' with a free port and free trade policy.

The annex specifically mentioned continuation of Hong Kong membership of the General Agreement on Tariffs and Trade and empowers the Hong Kong Special Administrative Region to 'establish official and semi-official economic and trade missions in foreign countries' with only the requirement to report the setting up of such missions to China 'for the record'. Apart from promising that the Hong Kong dollar should be the local legal tender and continue to circulate freely, the detailed annex says that the Hong Kong Special Administrative Region government

> may decide its monetary and financial policies on its own. It shall safeguard the free operation of financial business and the free flow of capital within, into and out of the Hong Kong Special Administrative Region. No exchange control policy shall be applied . . . the authority to issue Hong Kong currency shall be vested in the Hong Kong Special Administrative Region government. The Hong Kong Special Administrative Region government may authorize designated banks to issue or continue to issue Hong Kong currency under statutory authority, after satisfying itself

> that any issue of currency will be firmly based and that the arrangements for such issue are consistent with the object of maintaining the stability of the territory.

The only change will be that currency bearing colonial references or showing the Queen's head – or as the annex puts it, 'Hong Kong currency bearing references inappropriate to the status of Hong Kong Special Administrative Region of the People's Republic of China' – will be gradually withdrawn and replaced. In 1985 both the note-issuing banks, the Hongkong and Shanghai Banking Corporation and Standard Chartered Bank, changed the wording on their banknotes to delete 'objectionable' references to 'the colony', promising instead to pay the bearer of the note 'at its office here'. Hong Kong coins still bear the head of the British sovereign and one- and two-dollar coins carry a crowned lion rampant bearing an orb.

Hong Kong will also have its own control over both shipping and aviation – which represents something of an advance, as previously the shipping register has been that of the UK and aviation rights in and out of Kai Tak international airport have been negotiated by Britain. Complaints have frequently been made that use of the British shipping register meant that it was too expensive for Hong Kong shipowners to fly a British flag (because of crewing demands and high wages), and that aviation rights unduly benefited British carriers. The detailed agreement lays down that the Hong Kong Special Administrative Region will be responsible for shipping management and regulation, including regulating conditions for seamen. Private shipping businesses and shipping-related businesses and private container terminals 'may continue to operate freely'. The Hong Kong government will maintain a shipping register and issue certificates 'under its own legislation in the name of "Hong Kong, China"'. Foreign warships would need China's permission to enter Hong Kong, but other foreign vessels will enter the port under Hong Kong's own laws. In air services, Hong Kong will be responsible for its own civil aviation. Flights between Hong

Kong and China will be arranged between China and the Hong Kong Special Administrative Region government. Air services from China to the rest of the world, including stops in Hong Kong, will be the responsibility of China. But the annex states that 'for this purpose the Central People's Government shall take account of the special conditions and economic interests of the Hong Kong Special Administrative Region government'. For flights not touching China proper, the Hong Kong government itself will have the authority to arrange air service agreements as well as to license airlines incorporated or having their principal business in Hong Kong.

Before the British and Chinese governments sat down to negotiate, a prime fear concerned freedom of education. The annex to the agreement addresses this problem and lays down that

> the Hong Kong Special Administrative Region shall maintain the educational system previously practised in Hong Kong. The Hong Kong Special Administrative Region government shall on its own decide policies in the field of culture, education, science and technology, including policies regarding the educational system and its administration, the language of instruction, the allocation of funds, the examination system, the system of academic awards and the recognition of educational and technological qualifications. Institutions of all kinds, including those run by religious and community organizations, may retain their autonomy. They may continue to recruit staff and teaching materials from outside the Hong Kong Special Administrative Region. Students shall enjoy freedom of choice of education and freedom to pursue their education outside the Hong Kong Special Administrative Region.

Foreign affairs of course are the responsibility of China itself. But the annex to the agreement allows the Hong Kong Special Administrative Region government's representatives to participate as members of Chinese delegations in negotiations directly affecting Hong Kong. In addition, says the agreement, 'the Hong Kong Special Administrative Region may on its own, using the name "Hong Kong, China", maintain and develop relations and conclude and implement agreements with states, regions and relevant international organizations in the appropriate field, including the economic, trade, financial and monetary, shipping, communications, touristic, cultural and sporting fields . . .' Foreign consular and official and semi-official missions may be established with the approval of China itself. These may include consular and other missions of countries that have no formal diplomatic links with China itself, though states not recognized by China will only be allowed to establish non-governmental institutions. The UK, according to the agreement, will have a consulate general in the Hong Kong Special Administrative Region.

The agreement also lays down that Hong Kong will be responsible for its own public order and pledges that 'military forces sent by the Central People's Government to be stationed in the Hong Kong Special Administrative Region for the purpose of defence shall not interfere in the internal affairs of Hong Kong Special Administrative Region'. The cost of the garrison of the People's Liberation Army will be met by the Chinese Central Government itself. Clause XIII of Annex I allows sweeping freedoms for Hong Kong people under Chinese sovereignty. It says

> the Special Administrative Region government shall maintain the rights and freedoms as provided for in the laws previously in force in Hong Kong, including freedom of the person, of speech, of the press, of assembly, of association, to form and join trade unions, of correspondence, of travel, of movement, of strike, of demonstration, of choice of occupation, of academic research, of belief, inviolability of the home, the freedom to marry and the right to raise a family freely. Every person shall have the right to confidential legal advice, access to the courts, representation in

> the courts by lawyers of his choice, and to obtain judicial remedies. Every person shall have the right to challenge the actions of the executive in the courts. Religious organizations and believers may maintain their relations with religious organizations and believers elsewhere, and schools, hospitals and welfare institutions run by religious organizations may be continued.

The clause adds that relations between political organizations in Hong Kong and those in China itself 'shall be based on the principles of non-subordination, non-interference and mutual respect'.

The final clause of the first annex deals with rights of residence. Hong Kong identity cards giving right of abode will be issued to Chinese people born in Hong Kong or resident there for more than seven years, and to people of Chinese nationality born outside Hong Kong of such nationals. In addition, other people ordinarily resident in Hong Kong for more than seven years and who have Hong Kong as their permanent residence, will be able to get Hong Kong identity cards. Besides these, other people with right of residence only in Hong Kong before the Special Administrative Region was established will be able to get Hong Kong identity cards. As regards issuing of passports, there is a distinction between Chinese nationals and non-Chinese. The clause states that Chinese people with permanent Hong Kong identity cards will get 'passports of the Hong Kong Special Administrative Region of the People's Republic of China'. All other Hong Kong residents will get 'travel documents'. The Hong Kong Special Administrative Region government will have its own immigration control. Freedom of travel is also promised: 'unless restrained by law, holders of valid travel documents shall be free to leave the Hong Kong Special Administrative Region without special authorization'.

Annex II deals with the establishment of a Sino-British Joint Liaison Group 'in order to ensure a smooth transfer of government in 1997'. The group is seen as a way of helping the two powers 'to continue their discussions in a friendly spirit and to develop the cooperative relationship which already exists between the two governments over Hong Kong with a view to the effective implication of the Joint Declaration'. The terms of reference of the group are carefully laid down:

(a) to conduct consultations on the implementation of the Joint Declaration;
(b) to discuss matters relating to the smooth transfer of government in 1997;
(c) to exchange information and conduct consultations on such subjects as may be agreed by the two sides.

The agreement lays down specifically that 'the Joint Liaison Group shall be an organ for liaison and not an organ of power. It shall play no part in the administration of Hong Kong or the Hong Kong Special Administrative Region. Nor shall it have any supervisory role over the administration.' From 1 July 1988 the group's principal base has been in Hong Kong, and it will continue to operate until 1 January 2000.

The final annex of the declaration deals with the tricky subject of land leases. Land became complicated because of the different status of the various parts of British Hong Kong. With Hong Kong island and the Kowloon peninsula 'ceded in perpetuity' to Britain there was no difficulty for the colonial authorities in providing long leases of land. St John's Anglican Cathedral was given the freehold of the site, and other prominent central locations were leased in the early days for periods of 999 years. Subsequently, 99-year leases were the rule. In the New Territories, however, the fixed term of British colonial rule created difficulties, and leases could only be granted until mid-1997 – minus a few days to allow for repossession of the land. Ever-shortening land titles in the New Territories had been a major factor pressing the British government to address the issue of Hong Kong's future after 1997. The annex tidies up the situation. It allows land leases not containing right of renewal and expiring before 30 June 1997 (apart from short-term tenancies and leases for special purposes) to be extended to a period expiring not later than 30 June 2047 without payment of additional premium, but with an annual rent of 3 per cent of the rateable value of the property. From the time of the ratification of the Joint Declaration until mid-1997 new land leases may be granted by the British Hong Kong government for terms running to 30 June 2047. These will bear a premium rental until mid-1997, after which lessees will have to pay an annual rent of 3 per cent of the rateable value. But total land granted in this way, apart from public rental housing, will be limited to fifty hectares a year. This provision reflected China's fears that the Hong Kong government might lease out large amounts of land and thus leave nothing for the Hong Kong Special Administrative Region government.

A related fear was that Hong Kong might spend all its reserves before 1997, thus leaving nothing for the new Special Administrative Region government. Repeated pledges by senior Hong Kong government officials that the Hong Kong reserves belong to Hong Kong and couldn't be salted away by Britain apparently did little to reassure China. To allay Chinese fears, the two sides agreed that from ratification of the Joint Declaration (in mid-1985) until mid-1997 income from land sales should, after deduction of the average cost of preparing the land, be shared equally between the British Hong Kong government and the future Special Administrative Region government.

One of the biggest and most difficult issues was that of nationality and passports. Under pressure from Hong Kong, Britain sought a continuing relationship with Hong Kong holders of British passports. This is a complicated issue. The population of Hong Kong, almost 5.8 million by 1989 (not counting the Vietnamese 'boat people' refugees), uses many different kinds of passport or travel documents. A very small number, about 160,000, are full citizens of western or Asian countries. About 60,000 of these are white expatriates, and the rest come from neighbouring Asian countries like the Philippines, Japan, Malaysia and Thailand. Of the Hong Kong Chinese, a majority were born in Hong Kong or have become naturalized British subjects, and are eligible for British Hong Kong passports. This category of people today are entitled to hold British Dependent Territory Citizens' passports, although only a million of these documents have actually been issued. At the time of the agreement there were about 2.8 million Hong Kong Chinese, and by 1989 their number had swollen to 3.28 million according to the House of Commons Foreign Affairs Committee on 30 June 1989 (though there was some confusion about the actual number, and in the space of a few minutes in the House of Commons in June the Prime Minister and the Foreign Secretary gave slightly different figures: Thatcher said 3.5 million; Howe said 3.25 million). The remaining Chinese in Hong Kong – 2.32 million by 1989 – are immigrants from China. For their first seven years in the colony, these people carry a Document of Identity. After that, they have a right of abode and qualify for a Certificate of Identity. A further small number of Hong Kong residents are people of Indian, Pakistani or Eurasian origin who have no rights to passports from India or Pakistan and who also carry BDTC passports. About 12,000 out of the 20,000 Indians and Eurasians living in Hong Kong are in this category.

For the British passport holders, their position, citizenship and residence rights have been fraught with the complications of successive British immigration laws. Until 1962, Hong Kong Chinese with British nationality had the same rights as UK-born Britons. In 1962, in response to immigration pressures, the British government introduced the concept of 'right of abode'. The Hong Kong Britons retained what was superficially the same British passport as other Britons carried, except that the Hong Kong documents did not have the magic words 'Holder has right of abode in the United Kingdom' printed on page 5. The controversial 1981 Immigration Act (effective in 1983) did not change anything as far as residence rights were concerned. But to the Hong Kong Chinese it was highly symbolic of the snub they had received: it showed that they were regarded as 'second-rate citizens' by London. Their passport was the new BDTC version with the qualifying words: 'Hong Kong' clearly visible on its front cover. Recognizing the distinction, many governments, such as Japan, insist that Hong Kong Chinese must get a visa to enter their country, even though 'full' British citizens do not need visas. As a further complication the BDTC passports are now being changed, with Peking's agreement, into British National Overseas (BNO) travel documents in readiness for 1997. Another aspect making the passports, citizenship and residence issue a minefield is that China regards *all* Chinese in Hong Kong, whether carrying British passports or not, as Chinese nationals.

In tackling these issues Britain and China exchanged memoranda. Britain declared that from mid-1997 all BDTCs will cease to be BDTCs. This was obvious enough, since the dependent territory of Hong Kong could no longer exist as a British domain. However, Britain promised that such people 'will be eligible to retain an appropriate status, which without conferring the right of abode in the United Kingdom, will entitle them to continue to use passports issued by the Government of the United Kingdom'. These will be BNO documents.

These promises still leave untidy loose ends. For Chinese BDTCs there is the problem that the British protective writ will not run far.

> Under the Nationality Law of the People's Republic of China, all Hong Kong Chinese compatriots, whether they are holders of the 'British Dependent Territory Passports' or not, are Chinese nationals . . . The above Chinese nationals will not be entitled to British consular protection in the Hong Kong Special Administrative Region and other parts of the People's Republic of China on account of their holding the above-mentioned British travel documents.

For the non-Chinese there is the danger of statelessness. According to the British memorandum, 'no person will acquire BDTC status on or after 1 July 1997 by virtue of a connection with Hong Kong'. Non-Chinese Hong Kong residents may not themselves technically be stateless, since they will hold British travel documents. But their children and grandchildren born in Hong Kong after mid-1997 will not be entitled to a British passport (since it will no longer be a British territory) and will have no automatic right to acquire a Chinese one. There are ways for non-Chinese to obtain Chinese passports. But it is not easy and can't be done simply by being born or living in Chinese territory. (Some foreigners complain that China practises a racist policy.) Non-Chinese BDTCs also ask what kind of citizenship rights a passport carries when it offers no right of residence in the country issuing it. They claim that this is effective statelessness. The British government has avoided rendering many people stateless only by a careful form of words.

Britain was anxious to avoid giving non-Chinese BDTCs full British passports. That would give them a privilege over Hong Kong Chinese British-pass-port-holders. To give full British passports to everyone, a solution that common sense, decency and morality would have urged, was decreed politically impossible. China – British officials claimed in excusing themselves – would have reacted sharply and portrayed any large-scale grant of full British passports as an attempt to steal its citizens. During the debate on the Hong Kong Bill the Thatcher government relented a little, allowing descendants of non-Chinese BDTCs to retain the British connection – but not as full citizens of Britain.

Much effort, time, thought, argument, reams of paper and miles of red tape had gone into the search for a settlement of 'the Hong Kong question'. In Hong Kong government offices there were so many telex and other messages flowing in and out to and from London and Peking that they had to be kept in different coloured folders to indicate where they originated and which way they were going. But for all the champagne toasts and smiles from the British and Chinese leaders in Peking's

Great Hall of the People on 19 December 1984, this was not the end of the debate. It left a couple of niggling questions. Will the agreement work? Can Peking be trusted?

13 WILL IT WORK?

THE agreement between Britain and China promising Hong Kong at least another fifty years of unbridled capitalism under Peking's rule was greeted with relief, even with acclaim. The prospect of continued happy money-making was welcomed by most of the fat cats of business and banking. Many ordinary Hong Kong inhabitants didn't much mind either: living in the poorer public housing estates they felt they hadn't derived much benefit from *gweilo* (literally pale ghost, meaning foreign) masters. One young Hong Kong Chinese woman in a Mark II housing estate asked: 'What have the British ever done for us? At least now we will be ruled by our own Chinese people.' But as the countdown to the Chinese takeover started, so nagging doubts began to set in. By 1989, even before the bloody Chinese crackdown on the naïve pro-democracy movement in the heart of Peking, the sceptical but educated and mobile Hong Kong middle classes increasingly began to worry about whether they could trust either China *or* Britain. Peking seemed determined to get its own way over key points like 'democracy', 'elections' and who was a 'patriotic' Chinese; the Thatcher government was more interested in performing the modern diplomatic equivalent of the ritual *kowtow* in order to stay in China's good books. Blood in Tian'anmen Square simply reinforced the doubts.

'All Will be Well!'

But back in 1984 there had been no mistaking the joy over the deal between Britain and China, especially in the business community. Some businessmen even dreamed of Hong Kong becoming the centre of a huge megalopolis embracing the whole of the Pearl river delta as far as Canton and fulfilling itself as the 'financial capital of the Far East' (in the words of former official Sir Philip Haddon-Cave). Derek Davies, editor of the *Far Eastern Economic Review*, a magazine which had often asked trenchant questions during the negotiations, produced a signed article so full of praise of the agreement that it might have been drafted for him by one of the British government officials. He commented that the majority of Hong Kong people had welcomed the agreement, but that there were 'dark voices prophesying doom emanating from London'. (He was referring to press criticism.) He added, 'Of course we must expect commentators living in a highly political backwardly developing country like Britain today to fail to come to grips with the reality of a sophisticated, fast-growing city such as Hong Kong and to make judgements according to the somewhat primitive ideological labels they tend to stick on countries and peoples.' Warming to his task as salesman for the agreement, Davies noted that Hong Kong had survived and prospered 'during the worst excesses of the cataclysmic upheavals and experiments in social engineering which the monomaniac Chairman Mao Tse-tung (Mao Zedong) inflicted on China', and had even 'evolved a symbiotic relationship with its giant host nation'. Hong Kong's deep-water port, its hard currency earnings, flows of investment, capital, technology and managerial know-how, said Davies, mean that 'perhaps second only to Japan, Hong Kong is a source of knowledge for a China anxious to learn'.

Davies concluded that Hong Kong could help China achieve some of its dreams. 'To suppose that Hong Kong could be a modern antibiotic now to be reinserted into China, to help accelerate the cure of the Marxist disease and aid recuperation by modernization, playing a part out of all proportion to its size in putting China back on to its traditional search for peace, stability and prosperity – the Confucian Golden Mean – is no longer a mere opium dream.' Other Hong Kong newspapers added their voices in support. The *Hongkong Standard* was enthusiastic about being a part of China. The expatriate-owned *South China Morning Post* also saw it as an era of new opportunity.

From business and banking there were calls that Hong Kong should now put its worries behind it and get on with the job it knew best – making money. Michael Sandberg, then chairman of the Hongkong and Shanghai Banking Corporation and a member of the territory's executive council, agreed with editor Derek Davies that Hong Kong has a vital role to play in China's development. The banker reversed the question typically asked about Hong Kong's future, and asserted that people should ask 'not what China will do to Hong Kong, but what can Hong Kong do for China'. Sandberg added:

> Hong Kong has amply demonstrated the capacity of an overwhelmingly Chinese community to prosper in the world's markets and create a rapidly rising standard of living. The economic progress of Taiwan and Singapore drives home the message that those Chinese abilities are by no means an isolated or unrepresentative example. Nor can there be any suggestion that such material progress, bringing in its wake much-needed social and welfare advance, is not the sort of thing that average Chinese communities really want – the pretence would be absurd. It all adds up to a huge challenge facing China to explain why its own mainland population should not achieve at least as much.

The banker also made light of criticisms that China might not keep its word, saying that there are no guarantees in life anywhere in the world. 'What guarantees are there that there will be a democratic capitalist market in West Germany in 1997?' he asked. In this he was echoing the thoughts of Sir John

Bremridge, then Financial Secretary, who imagined subversively that 'it is possible that by 1997 China will be capitalist and Britain will be a Marxist state under the rule of Arthur Scargill and his ilk'. Sandberg agreed that China might seek to subvert the agreement, but added; 'What would be the point? Why spend two years of hard bargaining to set up the agreement and then break it? That would be to kiss goodbye to the prospect of bringing Taiwan back to the fold of a united China. Of course, you may ask whether a marriage is going to last, but it is a strange question to ask whether someone is going to keep his word just after he has proposed' (conversations with the author, early 1985).

Other bankers and businessmen considered that the agreement meant that Hong Kong could now plan for a long-term future. Bill Brown, the area general manager of Standard Chartered Bank, commented: 'Industry and commerce can now plan ahead over an extended time-horizon. Hong Kong is a going concern as British Prime Minister Margaret Thatcher aptly emphasized.' Simon Murray, chief executive of Hutchison Whampoa, concurred: the signing of the agreement 'induces a great sigh of relief as the uncertainties of the last two years are put to rest and we can get on with running our lives and futures again'. Ngai Shiu-kit, president of the Chinese Manufacturers Association, added an optimistic Chinese view, declaring that 'the uncertainties of Hong Kong's future are largely clear. Businessmen will be able to evaluate their plans realistically for the future.'

Simon Keswick, chairman of the old-established trade concern, Jardine Matheson and Company, and of its sister property group, the Hongkong Land Company, also supported the agreement, which he said 'has our unqualified support'. In March 1984, as we have seen, Jardines caused a stir by announcing that it was creating a holding company to be based in Bermuda, a British colony not threatened by a Chinese takeover. Keswick claimed however that the move was not because the company was pulling out of China. Far from it. Jardines wanted to remain a 'British' company in a British jurisdiction. Keswick visited Peking 'to satisfy China that we are happy to do business there'. The Jardines' chairman suggested that the economic uncertainty from 1982 to 1984 was caused by the business cycle 'complicated by politics'. He commented that 'Hong Kong has regular cycles in which it always overdoes things in one way or another'. Keswick confidently claimed that this was only a phase. 'If a bank takes deposits, it must lend or go bust. Liquidity is the key. It starts the froth. I don't believe that the Chinese like leaving money on deposit for long.' With the agreement worked out and a future stretching beyond the year 2000 Keswick predicted that Hong Kong would benefit from the influx of 'an army of people coming from abroad to do business with China'. He praised the Hong Kong Chinese because they have 'a great work ethic and instructive commercial sense', and foresaw the territory continuing to flourish because of the 'lack of government restrictions, the fact that the fittest survive and Hong Kong is the gateway to the biggest market in the world'.

Victor Fung, managing director of Li and Fung, an old-established local Chinese trading concern in Hong Kong, also predicted growing economic cooperation between the territory and China, with Hong Kong showing the big mother country the way forward. The Chinese, he claimed, are naturally 'more competitive than the Koreans'. If China can extend the range of its industrial activities then 'they will kill the Koreans as regards competition'. In addition, he pointed out, China was changing rapidly internally, its domestic market was growing and would grow further and faster as economic reforms began to bite. Fung pointed out that even if only 10 per cent of China grows rapidly, 'that is a market of 100 million people, or twice as big as Korea'. Hong Kong would naturally benefit from this growth, since 'Hong Kong is one huge trading company for China'. Warming to his subject, Fung predicted that the next stage of Hong Kong's development might well prove to be the era of the Japanese, American and other foreign investors, doing business in Hong Kong itself and using the territory as a link with China.

Five years after the joint agreement, Hong Kong officialdom and big business professed themselves highly satisfied. New Governor Sir David Wilson was the best spokesman for the optimistic view. He claimed that the period of the 1950s and 1960s when China and Hong Kong were a mystery to each other was an unnatural time, 'particularly when you remember that Hong Kong was founded as a gateway to China'. Since the improvement in relations, he said, economic links had strengthened and expanded: 'China now sells to Hong Kong more than fifteen times the amount it sold in the mid-seventies. We are China's largest market. China has come from nowhere to become Hong Kong's second market. Hong Kong is also China's largest source of foreign investment – larger indeed than all other sources combined. And China has huge and growing investments in Hong Kong. As for travel, Hong Kong people now make some 14 million visits a year to China; and over 400,000 Chinese visitors come annually to Hong Kong. There are through trains, ferry services and direct flights to Hong Kong from more than twenty cities in China . . .' (speech to the Royal Institute of International Affairs, London, March 1988).

Governor Wilson put his faith in the idea that Hong Kong and China are so linked that 'an increasing number of Chinese cities and provinces are developing a close vested interest in Hong Kong's continuing economic success and economic autonomy'. Wilson brushed aside the view that China wouldn't abide by the provisions of the joint agreement.

> I believe that the Chinese government are fully aware of the value of Hong Kong, and of the benefits that they can and do obtain from it. I believe that they also recognize that this value and these benefits will only continue if Hong Kong is permitted to maintain its present way of life and its present way of doing business. It is for this reason that they devised the imaginative concept of 'One country, two systems' and were prepared to set out in such detail how the separateness of the Hong Kong SAR would be preserved for fifty years after 1997.

Economically, as Hong Kong surged towards the critical 1990s, the faith of the optimists seemed justified. There were hiccups, such as the October 1987 stock market crash, but the economy has gone from strength to strength. The boom has spread beyond the territory's borders and southern China has benefited from unprecedented prosperity spilling over from Hong Kong. Ties with the mainland are increasing by the day. But in Hong Kong's typical timescale, the seven years until the complete Chinese takeover is a long time, longer than most businessmen are used to thinking about. The really critical arena is the political one, and here, though the rulers are reluctant to admit them, doubts have begun to appear. Hong Kong may be a simple place dedicated to the pursuit of a straightforward religion – money-making – but the handover of power is more complicated than in any other colony. The complexities stem from the peculiar nature of colonial rule and the unique hybrid creation proposed for Hong Kong's government after June 1997.

Government after 1997

Departure of British colonial rulers is nothing new. Over the past four decades Britain has folded its imperial tents and departed from dozens of countries to the playing of new anthems and flying of new flags. These 'new' countries have (mostly) managed to get along better without their British masters. What is different this time is that Hong Kong is not being offered *independence*. It will be a Special Administrative Region of an aspiring twenty-first century Great Power, China, autonomous but *not* independent.

Hong Kong is still, as chapter 6 showed, a peculiarly colonial place. Moreover, between now and 1 July 1997 Hong Kong will have to undergo more sweeping personnel changes than many colonies achieving independence. In country after country, even in sophisticated India, British civil servants stayed on in positions of power, transferring their allegiance to the new government.

But in newly autonomous Hong Kong senior British civil servants will have to leave and Hong Kong Chinese will take over all the top jobs. Expatriates may remain as advisers in the civil service, as judges and in senior ranks of the police force *if* such expatriates can be found willing to work under Chinese who were previously junior to them, and in the special circumstances of Hong Kong after mid-1997.

In the immediate aftermath of the Sino-British declaration, its heady promises of a legislature 'constituted by elections' and of executive authorities being 'accountable to the legislature' led some local leading lights to believe that they might at last get the democracy that Hong Kong had never had before. They talked of 'one man, one vote' territory-wide elections, of political parties and popular government. Plans were made in 1989 for several political parties, a development previously opposed by the authorities for fear that it would only pit the Communist Party against the Taiwan-based Kuomintang, both of which have long been covertly active in Hong Kong.

Not everyone was in favour of such ideas. Businessmen in particular pleaded that the successful boat should not be rocked. Helmut Sohmen, Austrian son-in-law of Sir Yue-Kong Pao and an appointed Legco member, argued that the existing system had served Hong Kong well. Direct elections, even of a small number, to the legislative council, would tend 'to denigrate the role and the remarkable work of past and present councillors who were appointed or indirectly elected, and in the public mind will be relegated in future to second or third rank behind their directly elected colleagues'. He questioned whether the experience of other countries was in favour of full-time politicians.

> As has happened in other countries, professional and full-time politicians will gradually replace the part-time legislators coming from a variety of backgrounds and bringing balanced and objective views to bear on the solution of problems. Hong Kong will be the poorer for it; we shall be

> sacrificing pragmatic sense and the chance to refine and strengthen our peculiar Hong Kong institutions – which have proven so successful in good and bad times – on the altar of expediency to achieve what is probably a misplaced feeling of greater security in facing the future.

Sohmen claimed that 'democracy means government by discussion, but it is only effective if you can stop people from talking'.

The most forceful advocate of a more democratic system was Martin Lee Chu-ming, a lawyer, a Queen's Counsel and the son of a former Kuomintang general. He attacked the big business interests and argued that:

> some of the people of Hong Kong are selfish and want to preserve their own vested interests. They claim that Hong Kong owes its success to them, because without their money and investment, the economy of Hong Kong will collapse. Now they want to run our government and rule the rest of the people. They want to deny to their fellow citizens their right to participate in the administration of their own affairs through a democratic electoral process. They claim that direct elections will lead to social unrest that will in turn ruin our successful economy. They advocate the rule of the elite, the oligarchy of the rich. But have they asked themselves whether they are qualified to rule? What training or experience in politics do they have more than the common people? If they do not trust the people of Hong Kong, why should the people of Hong Kong trust them? (Speech to the Hong Kong Legislative Council, November 1986)

Lee went on to claim that the best part of the capitalist system that China sought to preserve for fifty years after 1997 was the rule of law, and 'that means that every person is equal in the eyes of the law'. Responding to the challenge of why suddenly, after a hundred years, there should be a clamour for democracy, he said:

> The answer is simple: we owe our freedom not to the Hong Kong government, but to the British government, which is a democratic one. If the Hong Kong government should ever abuse its powers by locking people up without trial, questions would be asked in the British Parliament. But in 1997, when we sever our ties with Britain and return to the motherland, can we be sure our freedoms will be safeguarded by the National People's Congress (NPC) in China, which has a Communist system and where the Communist Party is in practice above the law? There are still many people in China who are imprisoned without trial, which is against the laws of China. Yet questions are never asked in the NPC about such government abuses.

Lee also took issue with people who claimed that all that was necessary was an independent judiciary and the rule of law. He said the judiciary would not remain independent if the executive tried to interfere. 'Our judges will either become martyrs or they will have to resign. If the rule of law or independent judiciary are to remain, we must have an executive body that is accountable to the people, so that those in power have to abide by the law, knowing they are there by the will of the people expressed through a democratic electoral process.' Democracy, according to Lee, is not the antithesis of prosperity. He claimed there was 'something inherently dangerous' about a political system under which the rich controlled the government. Such a government by the rich of the rich and for the rich would perforce be corrupt. 'For all over the world business deals are often transacted through *guanxi* or connections.' More than anywhere else in the world, said Lee, *guanxi*, nepotism and corruption rule the roost in China. The introduction of these corrupt practices into Hong Kong would kill the good reputation of the territory. Investors would lose confidence. The economy would falter and even the rich tycoons would leave when prosperity faltered. Lee wanted 25 per cent of Legco to be directly elected in 1988. This would give time to expand the system in 1991 and have a fully democratic framework in place in good time for 1997.

An important intervention was made in April 1987 by Sir Sze-yuen Chung, the senior appointed member of the executive council, who spoke out strongly against any direct elections in 1988. He declared that political developments must be carried out within the limits of the Joint Declaration and must 'converge' with the basic law being drafted by China for the Hong Kong Special Administrative Region. Chung, equally controversially, went on to say that Britain would be handing over Hong Kong's administration to China in 1997 – *not* to the Hong Kong people. He added that Hong Kong is not an independent country and must accept that the views of the British and Chinese governments are more important than those of the Hong Kong inhabitants. In consequence the people might not get the political system they wanted – even if it was demanded by the majority of them. He pointed out that the Joint Declaration promised only that the SAR legislature was to be constituted by elections, and did not say whether these would be direct or indirect. An elected Legco member, Dr Conrad Lam Kui-shing, lamented that Chung sounded more like a Chinese official than a member of the executive council. Indeed, Chung's comments followed the claims just a week beforehand of China's leader Deng Xiaoping that universal suffrage and direct elections to a representative assembly would not be beneficial to Hong Kong.

Much more important were China's interventions, guiding the debate – and decisions – in a careful 'Big Brother' bullying way. Li Hou, Secretary-General of the Hong Kong Basic Law Drafting Committee and the second-ranking Chinese official dealing with Hong Kong and Macao issues, argued in May 1987 for only gradual change.

> The existing political system in Hong Kong, except where modification is necessary as stipulated by the Sino-British Joint Declaration, should be changed as little as possible. The less change the better. It is mandatory to keep the advantages of the existing political system in Hong Kong which have proved effective. There is no need to effect an enormous change in a hurry. Otherwise the stability and prosperity of Hong Kong may be jeopardized. (From a report by *Liao Wang* overseas edition, monitored by the BBC and published a month after Li Hou gave his views)

Li also cited a letter from Chinese Premier Zhao Ziyang, written in 1984 to students at the University of Hong Kong. Zhao declared that China was dedicated to democracy: 'safeguarding the people's democratic rights is a basic principle guiding our country's political life. Therefore, the introduction of a democratic political system in the Hong Kong SAR, or as you put it, "governing Hong Kong in a democratic way" will be a completely natural development.'

Of the signs of China's thinking, Deng Xiaoping's speech in April 1987 to the Basic Law Drafting Committee (which was not published in full until September of the same year) contained some of the best clues. The ideas of Humpty Dumpty – 'When *I* use a word, it means just what I choose it to mean – neither more nor less . . . The question is which is to be master – that's all' – have clearly not fallen from grace in China's ruling circles. On the question of direct elections, which he called 'a general election', Deng asked:

> Will a general election necessarily be good for Hong Kong? I do not believe so. For example, I also said in the past that Hong Kong affairs would naturally be managed by Hong Kong people in the future. However, can they be elected by a general election? Our opinion is that the people who are to manage Hong Kong affairs should be those Hong Kong people who love both the motherland and Hong

> Kong. Can a general election guarantee that such people will be selected? (*Ta Kung Pao*, 20 September 1987, monitored by the BBC)

Deng went on to make another important 'clarification':

> Do not think that since Hong Kong affairs will be managed by Hong Kong people and be entirely free from interference from the central government, everything is therefore all right. This is not permissible, and this idea is unrealistic. The central government will not interfere in the Special Administrative Region's routine affairs, nor does it feel a need to. But what if something happens in the Special Administrative Region that threatens to jeopardize the country's fundamental interest? Will this not happen? Will Peking have to step in then? Will things that jeopardize Hong Kong's fundamental interests not happen in Hong Kong? Can one imagine that Hong Kong would ever be entirely free from disturbance and destructive forces?
>
> I think that such self-assurance is unfounded. If the central government gives up all its rights and powers, there would be chaos and Hong Kong's interests would be adversely affected. Thus the central government's reservation of certain powers could only be beneficial to Hong Kong. We should soberly consider this: will Hong Kong encounter problems that cannot be solved without Peking acting on its behalf? In the past, whenever Hong Kong has encountered such problems it has always had Britain to count on. There will be problems that you cannot solve without the central government acting on your behalf . . .

In other words, Peking intends to keep a fatherly eye on Hong Kong, constantly ready to intervene.

With China's dislike of democratic elections made clear, British Hong Kong backed away. In his opening address to the new session of the legislative council in October 1987, Governor Sir

David Wilson stressed the importance of links with China: 'They have become an increasingly significant factor in our day-to-day lives. In addition to the many personal contacts between people in Hong Kong and the people on the mainland, we have a wide range of official and institutional channels for exchanges of ideas on matters of common interest.' The Governor referred to the first draft of the basic law, which he described as 'another key building block in the creation of a clear structure for our future'. In February 1988 the Hong Kong government produced a white paper shelving any direct elections until 1991. The white paper admitted that there was clear support in Hong Kong for direct elections to Legco, and it fudged and played with evidence, claiming that there was no clear opinion about how or when they should be introduced. So it proposed that in 1991 ten seats on the fifty-six-seat Legco should be filled by direct elections.

The government's plans provoked outrage from Martin Lee and those who supported direct elections in 1988. An open letter from eight Legco members including Lee accused the British government of going back on its promises. 'During the parliamentary debate on the Sino-British Joint Declaration on the question of Hong Kong, Sir Geoffrey Howe [the British Foreign Secretary] assured Parliament that a "solidly based democratic government" would be developed in Hong Kong. He also said: "During the years immediately ahead, the government of Hong Kong will be developed on increasingly representative lines."' The Legco members claimed that the beginning of direct elections in 1988 was

> the first but absolutely necessary step towards the development of a democratic government in Hong Kong before 1997, which is vital to Hong Kong's continued existence as a capitalist system. For without democracy in Hong Kong, there is no hope that the future government of the Special Administrative Region of Hong Kong will be able to defend the rights and freedoms of the Hong Kong people or to

> protect Hong Kong's interest in a situation involving a conflict of interests vis-à-vis the central government. Without democracy, the policy of 'one country, two systems' and 'Hong Kong people ruling Hong Kong' is doomed to fail.

Lee was personally scathing about Prime Minister Margaret Thatcher and the British government. In Hong Kong by 1988 Thatcher was no longer called 'the iron lady' but the 'rusty lady'. Lee said: 'There's a sense of betrayal. We feel we have been sold down the river by the British government for its own interests of trade.' He accused Britain of 'reneging on its promises. The intellectual people believe that even today, it is the Chinese government that really governs Hong Kong via the British administration.'

In a House of Commons debate just before the white paper was produced in Hong Kong, several British Members of Parliament called for at least partial direct elections in 1988. Former British Prime Minister Edward Heath claimed that 'unless action is taken quickly now', Britain would be unable to hand over any form of experienced representative government by 1997. But Sir Geoffrey Howe was not moved. He denied accusations that Britain wanted good relations with China at the expense of Hong Kong, claiming that such charges were 'a grotesque distortion'.

According to him the most important thing was to get the best foundation for Hong Kong's future stability and prosperity. 'It certainly cannot be founded on confrontation between Britain and China.' Decisions about Hong Kong should be 'in line with the destination commended by the People's Republic of China', Howe claimed. Indicating the lack of interest in the subject among British MPs, fewer than 50 of the 650 MPs attended – and this was a record turnout for a Hong Kong debate. Only a matter of days after publication of Hong Kong's white paper on representative government Howe was in Moscow urging the Soviet Union to withdraw its troops from Afghanistan and to help facilitate the emergence of a genuinely representative government in Kabul.

As debates in the Basic Law Drafting Committee and other bodies continued, the heady expectations of an autonomous Hong Kong governing itself after 1997 began to be hedged with qualifications. There was just one straw in the wind for these optimists who claimed that Hong Kong can take over China after 1997 rather than vice versa. In elections for delegates to China's National People's Congress, Hong Kong television personality Lisa Wang came out top of the poll for representatives of Guangdong province. Guangdong had set aside 20 seats for Hong Kong and Macao representatives in its delegation. Of course this was a Communist election, so there were only 20 candidates for 20 posts. But Miss Wang scored 743 out of 745 possible votes and came ahead of Xu Jiatun, Director of Xinhua, the New China News Agency, and in effect China's representative in Hong Kong. He scored 737 votes.

The work of the Basic Law Drafting Committee charged with the task of producing Hong Kong's constitution after 1997 also confirmed Peking's wish to take over a Hong Kong as little changed as possible. The first draft was produced in 1988, a revised version in 1989 and the document is to be approved by China's National People's Congress (NPC) in 1990. The 59-member committee had a majority of mainland members (36 against 23 from Hong Kong), but it was never necessary for Peking's men to vote together to overrule the Hong Kong members of the committee, who showed themselves split and squabbling over most issues. Only lawyer Lee and Szeto Wah, an elected Legco member representing teachers, lobbied consistently for democracy. The resulting draft law was summed up by in a headline in the *Far Eastern Economic Review*; 'The Kowtow Constitution' (27 January 1989). Democracy was very firmly postponed at least until the year 2012. Both the Chief Executive of the Hong Kong Special Administrative Region (SAR) – the successor to today's British Governor, and the key post in Peking's view – and the majority in the legislature will be indirectly elected at least until then. The Chief Executive, who will serve a five-year term, will be selected by a 400-member committee (rising to 800 members for the second term) of businessmen, professionals, workers and politicians from Hong Kong and the mainland.

The SAR's legislature will have 27 per cent of its first membership directly elected, rising to 38 per cent in 1999 and 50 per cent in 2003. The drafters suggested that a referendum be held in 2011 to decide whether the Chief Executive and entire legislature should be elected by universal suffrage – but then drew such restrictions as to make such a referendum unlikely. The proposal for a referendum must be approved by the Chief Executive, two-thirds of the legislature and the NPC standing committee – *and* must be supported by 30 per cent of the qualified voters. The timetable for democracy was the brainchild of Louis Cha, owner of *Ming Pao* newspaper, who pleaded for cooperation rather than confrontation with Peking. 'People are afraid of 1997 and the Communist way of doing things. The way to keep China out is by being useful to Peking. We can't keep them out by force or any democratic structure.' Hong Kong businessman Cha Chi-ming had added the referendum clause, so it became known as the Cha-Cha clause.

The abiding impression of the draft was that China – as Deng Xiaoping had suggested – intends to keep a continuing careful grip on the Hong Kong SAR, and to do this principally through the Chief Executive. Peking must approve the Chief Executive and all people for senior positions in the SAR government. Deng has said that all these office-holders must be Chinese 'patriots', another Humpty Dumpty word. China also retains considerable reserve powers. The NPC standing committee has power to interpret the basic law. Peking can also send laws back to the SAR for revision. In another much-criticized part of the draft, the SAR government is ordered to strive for a balanced budget, to avoid deficits and to maintain a low taxation policy. Hong Kong and British government officials criticized these clauses as being inconsistent with the promise of the Joint Declaration that the SAR government will have financial autonomy. And there is a loophole allowing Peking to declare a state of emergency in Hong Kong even against local wishes and to rule the territory directly.

Other clauses in the draft basic law threaten Hong Kong's freedom. Article 23 provides for laws prohibiting secession, sedition or divulging state secrets. This could make it illegal for magazines to publish anything, even readers' letters, suggesting independence for Tibet or Taiwan; and the term 'state secrets' has been interpreted by several countries to cover almost anything that the government wishes. Article 30 of the draft allows freedom and privacy of communication, but subject to the authorities' right to censorship to meet 'the needs of public security', another expression that can mean anything a government decrees it should mean.

Hong Kong's Chief Justice, Sir Ti Liang Yang, drew attention to a possible conflict between the basic law and China's socialist constitution. Yang was a vice-chairman of the Basic Law Consultative Committee before his appointment as Chief Justice (the first Chinese) in 1988. Article 31 of the Chinese constitution allowed the setting up of Special Administrative Regions. According to the Chief Justice,

> Section 31 says where you set up a special region and then special rules will apply. Now I personally have always been a little unhappy about Section 31 because I take the view that if you apply the normal rule of interpretation you would say that, even though it is a special region applying different rules, it still has to come within the main Constitution . . . So you can arguably say that on the strict rule of interpretation all that is stated in the general principles of the Constitution ought to be read with the Basic Law. But all that I know is that we have an assurance from Peking that this is not so. (answer to a question at the Foreign Correspondents' Club, Hong Kong, June 1988)

One obvious conflict is that the Hong Kong SAR will be following a capitalist economy, whereas China is constitutionally a socialist state.

The best that could be said for the later versions of the basic law is that China had shown some willingness to listen and to learn. Originally, Peking had threatened to sack all retiring Legco members and start with a completely fresh team. Li Hou in 1988 suggested that 1 July 1997 wouldn't simply be a straightforward 'changing of the guard'. He declared: 'the existence of sovereign right cannot be a show' (quoted in the *Financial Times*, 10 February 1988). After talks with Governor Wilson in Peking, China agreed that Legco members elected in 1995 would serve until 1999. Optimists also noted that the basic law first draft had been modified on two important points. Originally the NPC standing committee had power to *revoke* SAR laws; and in the later draft references applying Chinese laws to the SAR 'which gave expression to national unity and territorial integrity' had been deleted. However, the NPC standing committee retains the power to interpret the basic law.

Is it too late for further changes? Joseph Cheng, lecturer at the Chinese University of Hong Kong, thought by 1989 that China's hardline attitude indicated there was little room for manoeuvre. 'The Chinese have probably given up any pretence of listening to the Hong Kong people since the charade has not stopped the emigration tide,' he said, referring to the exodus of Hong Kong residents.

One factor colouring Peking's attitude and making it anxious to vet the system and players is its belief that Britain makes big gains from Hong Kong. Even the Sino-British agreement and Whitehall's constant and careful massaging has not removed China's suspicions. It is true that certain British interests and agents do well out of Hong Kong. The Ministry of Defence maintains a useful and cheap training ground for its troops in Hong Kong, a relief from being under fire in Northern Ireland or on the front line in Germany. British Airways has profited immensely from its favoured Hong Kong landing rights. A selected number of British-run companies like Jardines, Swires and the Hongkong Bank make good money out of Hong Kong and provide a superior living style for young Britons. But the surprise should be that British companies don't do better. In any case, the days when the British *hongs* ruled the Hong Kong roost are long over. Local Chinese businessmen – most of whom are Peking's best friends – are the richest people in the colony.

Can the new political system work? One of the most knowledgeable commentators, Richard Margolis, deputy political adviser to the Hong Kong government at the time of the agreement and now a merchant banker, claimed that Hong Kong's success was built on confidence, implying credibility and durability. The durability of Hong Kong's existence had not been altered by the Sino-British agreement, but the credibility had. Margolis commented:

> The real price which Hong Kong has to pay for the Joint Declaration is that it can no longer receive free of charge the assurance of tolerable standards of government which the link of authority to Britain has provided, since the Joint Declaration is founded on the premise that all links of authority with Britain must be cut in 1997. Without making any value judgements about the system in China, it is a fact that the whole history and tradition of government in China – imperial, republican and Communist – is quite different from the British-inspired, common-law based system which exists in Hong Kong.
>
> Hong Kong will therefore have to bestir itself in a way it has never previously needed to do in order to ensure that the same standards are maintained after 1997. Some of the time and energy previously devoted to business will have to be diverted to this task . . . Hong Kong's interests are not well served either by those who prostrate themselves before China and tell China's leaders only what they wish to hear, or by those who believe that we should charge at the Chinese government head-on and try to cudgel them into living up to their promises. Chinese leaders have to be persuaded of the wisdom of granting real autonomy to Hong Kong – persuaded that they have nothing to fear

> from trusting Hong Kong people to manage their own affairs and persuaded that obsessive concern with sovereignty, when the question has already been settled by the Joint Declaration, damages their own interests and credibility. (*Far Eastern Economic Review*, 25 June 1987)

Much will rest on the ability of the Chief Executive and the senior government officials to put Hong Kong interests first, and to resist any pressures from Peking. They can cite the joint declaration promising Hong Kong autonomy, but that may be of little use the way China plays politics. Not all the signs are hopeful. By 1989 not very much was clear about the character of the first Chief Executive – except that Peking would get whoever it wanted for the job. Some speculation suggested that a local businessman would be the candidate. At various times the names of Sir Yue-Kong Pao, though he will be in his late seventies, David K.-P. Li, by then in his early fifties, chief executive of the Bank of East Asia, and Vincent Lo Hong-shui, head of the Shui On group, were advanced. Later suggestions from China were that a bureaucrat might be chosen. The prospect of a representative of either of these categories providing firm Hong Kong leadership seem limited. Businessmen in particular have shown themselves the first to curry favour with Peking. The forty-year-old Vincent Lo claimed in early 1989: 'I was educated in Australia. I understand democracy and want it for Hong Kong. But I don't want democracy for its own sake. I want it for the stability and prosperity of Hong Kong. I think that if we remain prosperous and do not go too much for political confrontation China will stay out' (interview in the *Financial Times*, 17 February 1989).

There were also considerable doubts about the tough-mindedness of leading Hong Kong Chinese bureaucrats. Governor Wilson and leading officials tried to claim that the local Chinese officials were of top quality. But some senior expatriates in private conversations expressed considerable reservations. The pace of localization, originally too slow, had been pushed too hard, claimed one high-level official. Another government secretary discussed the qualities and shortcomings of the senior Chinese one by one. His view was that they were all good middle-level administrators, honest, but in the end limited. 'The best of them have got 90 per cent of what it takes. They may grow into the jobs and get the remaining 10 per cent. But none of them is of sufficient steel to be able to stand up to Peking's steamroller tactics' (conversations with the author). Another Hong Kong expatriate bureaucrat claimed in 1988 that there were 'dangers in Chinese culture' which were already becoming evident with recent promotions in Hong Kong. 'In the old Chinese mandarin system, when a man reached the top he was supposed to enjoy the fruits of office. The difficult decisions and the hard work were done lower down the ladder. This was certainly *not* the British tradition. But there are signs of it happening now. Selected top officials don't want to take difficult decisions.'

All of China's behaviour indicates that it will take a much more activist role in Hong Kong than Britain ever played. The statements of Deng Xiaoping make this clear. In addition, at various crucial times China's officials have made unsettling remarks, indicating that they were determined to be the masters of Hong Kong. Hardly was the ink dry on the agreement than Xu of Xinhua heavy-handedly reminded Hong Kong that Peking would not tolerate anything that smacked of independence. Later Lu Ping, a deputy director of the Hong Kong and Macao Affairs Office under the State Council, declared that for Legco to debate the draft basic law would be 'absolutely inappropriate. The Legco is a law-making body under the British government. It is inappropriate for it to discuss the laws made by the Chinese government.' His colleague Li Hou had already declared that the British Parliament should not discuss the draft because it was 'a matter for China'. In 1989 Li intervened to criticize Hong Kong's handling of Vietnamese 'boat people' refugees, more than 20,000 of whom had fled and taken shelter in the colony. He said it was an insult that Chinese illegal immigrants were handcuffed and locked up, whereas Vietnamese illegals were not; he claimed that the disparity might lead to racial disputes. Li harshly told Britain that no Vietnamese refugees or illegals would be allowed to become SAR residents after 1997, so Britain had better settle the problem.

There are plenty of indications that China doesn't really trust Hong Kong people to rule themselves. There has been a build-up of Peking's cohorts within the colony. Xinhua, the New China News Agency, had expanded its staff to more than a thousand people by the late 1980s, more than double the figure of a few years before. The news-gathering and journalistic side of the agency's operations are small; the agency has long been Peking's *de facto* consulate-general in Hong Kong. In 1985 Xinhua announced that it was a department of China's State Council as well as a news agency. In the years after the signing of the Joint Declaration it further enlarged its staff in Hong Kong and developed into what is generally regarded as a 'shadow government'. The agency's executives have become active in the community, playing a key role in encouraging sympathetic pro-Chinese candidates to stand for election to Hong Kong's various local councils.

Another activity has been the courting of key figures on the mutual aid committees that run the housing estates; such people have been assiduously invited to receptions, and Xinhua has been on the lookout for likely leaders in every aspect of Hong Kong's life. It invited Wat Chiu, a leader of an association of street hawkers, to join the Basic Law Drafting Consultative Committee, a large group of people advising the Basic Law Drafting Committee. His group, happily for Peking, promptly came out against early direct elections.

By the late 1980s there was increasing scepticism about whether the concept of a special, autonomous future for 'Hong Kong, China', was workable. Professor S. E. Finer of Oxford University had warned in 1984 (at a Hong Kong University seminar in December) that it was hard to think of a Communist Party anywhere in the world that had been prepared to share power. Anti-Communists pointed to parallels between Hong Kong and Tibet. Chinese troops had marched into Tibet in 1950 to 'liberate' it and to unify China. In 1951 a seventeen-point autonomy programme had been promised to Tibet. Among other things: 'The Tibetan people have the right of exercising national regional autonomy under the unified leadership of the Central People's Government' (point 3). 'The central authorities will not alter the existing political system in Tibet. The central authorities will not alter the established status, functions and power of the Dalai Lama. Officials of various ranks will hold office as usual' (point 4). 'The policy of freedom of religious belief laid down in the common programme of the Chinese People's Political Consultative Conference will be protected. The central authorities will not affect any change in the income of the monasteries' (point 7). 'In matters relating to various reforms in Tibet, there will be no compulsion on the part of the central authorities. The local government of Tibet should carry out reforms of its own accord, and when the people raise demand for reform, they must be settled through consultation with the leading personnel of Tibet' (point 11). The similarities with the promises made to Hong Kong are obvious, and Peking has kept a tight grip on Tibet, sent its own people in to run the government, mostly Han Chinese, not Tibetans, suppressed the local Buddhist religion, and several times, including twice in 1988, ordered its troops to fire on civilians demonstrating for more freedom.

An example closer to home of China's determination to get its own way, of Britain's insistence of putting its own commercial interests first *and* of local legislators' unwillingness to stand up to Peking came over the Daya Bay nuclear plant, just across the border from Hong Kong. More than a million Hong Kong inhabitants signed a petition objecting to the plant. A few vocal members of the legislative council called for a special session to discuss it. But the majority of Legco refused even to allow a debate. They accused the minority who wanted the debate of 'ulterior motives', and of being potential trouble-makers. China's attitude was straightforward enough: Jiang Shengjin, its top nuclear specialist, declared that China would purchase the power generator for Daya Bay from Britain provided that Hong Kong bought electricity. Otherwise China would buy all the equipment for the US$4 billion plant from France. The plant would in any case be built. 'Hong Kong is like a theatre packed with people, but without proper exits,' says a leading member of a pressure group worried about the nuclear project. Hong Kong's unease was not helped by the discovery in late 1987 that 316 steel bars were missing from the bottom of the reactor's foundation shaft, which was below the required safety standard. Zhang Mingchang, Deputy Director of the Nuclear Power Bureau, said: 'The organization and modern management of the exotic construction projects are very good, with the exception of quality control which still lacks perfection' (interview by *Zhongguo Xinwen* monitored by the BBC, 12 October 1987). And all this unease was before China's bloody spring of 1989.

Perhaps surprisingly, Legco member and businessman Helmut Sohmen also questioned whether 'one country, two systems' would work for long. He compared China's takeover of sovereignty over Hong Kong to a business merger. 'The "one-country – two systems" slogan was a highly imaginative political solution to a potential negotiating deadlock,' declared Sohmen.

> It not only worked wonderfully as such, but created a stock of goodwill that will help facilitate the discussions about the very real practical problems of the proposed merger. Because that is really what the Sino-British Joint Declaration is all about: Hong Kong's merger into China, its integration into a national system with simply *other* objectives and ambitions – it does not matter whether they are similar, better, or worse than those previously pursued by Hong Kong or the United Kingdom. And like any corporate merger where there is subordination rather than fusion into a new company, Hong Kong will necessarily become like an operating division of the larger entity. No matter

> what philosophies moved previous management, how strong the original corporate identity was, or how well Hong Kong's logo was recognized in the world, the ultimate result of that merger will still be the same as it normally is in the commercial world: submersion . . . I cannot honestly see a territory of 5.5 million people further develop, or over any length of time maintain, a really separate system or existence as an integral part of a one-billion people-community. I cannot see a 'high degree of autonomy' being anything else but the effort to maximize overall marketing power through the maintenance of a different brand name, to be emphasized or toned down as changing conditions warrant. It certainly should not be seen as an expression of corporate generosity that would allow self-determination to the operating division or create inherent divisional rights that are not dependent on or embedded in corporate Group policies or strategies. (speech at a lunch given by Dr Eike Braeklo, the German Consul-General in Hong Kong, 26 May 1988)

It was honest of Sohmen, but his views didn't say much for the integrity of politicians in China or Britain, and pointed up the sheer impracticality of believing that tiny Hong Kong could hope to change the huge mass of China.

The optimists who see Hong Kong changing China forget that the colony is so minute – a mere 0.5 per cent of China's population – and so *different* from the rest of China – for a start with per capita income about thirty times greater than China's – that the adjustments involved in becoming fully a part of China would be painful, and almost all the pain would fall on Hong Kong. There will be business opportunities for some, but hardship for many.

Denis Chang, former chairman of the Hong Kong Bar Association and a member of the Basic Law Consultative Committee, pointed out some of the characteristics of the new regime from China's perspective:

> China sees the 'realization of sovereignty' or *tixian zhuquan*, in terms of real and effective control based on 'leadership of the centre'. This is a conception of sovereignty whereby the centre permits no dilution of power that has not been consciously and exclusively granted . . . seeing those powers that have been reserved to Peking not as residue but as a reservoir. Above all, China's view of 'one country–two systems' allows no place for any system of government (*zhengti*) that competes with the basic political structure of the state (*guoti*) . . . The traumatic lessons of history coupled with the exciting possibilities offered by China's recent open-door policy, have driven today's leadership in Peking to recognize the practical necessity and the relative advantages of decentralization – without, however, ever ceasing to assert forcefully the unitary character of the Chinese state. For old habits die hard, and even the more recent 'liberalizations' allow only a careful measure of autonomy outside of a centre which still retains the means of control at every critical juncture. This is not surprising in a vast country where dispersionism has been regarded as an enemy of national unity and another name for chaos (*hunluan*). (from *Basic Law, Basic Questions: The Debate Continues*, Review Publishing Co., Hong Kong, 1988).

Derek Davies, about to be promoted to editor-in-chief of the *Far Eastern Economic Review*, had by 1988 repented of some of his previous optimism about Hong Kong's future:

> the provisions of the Joint Declaration continue to be eroded. London's promises of political reforms have, under Chinese pressure, been broken. This has involved the manipulation of 'soundings' and surveys of public opinion, at least two-thirds of which is thought by experts to be in favour of direct elections in 1988 . . . This manipulation has been accomplished with a cynicism breath-taking even by the standards of British colonial history . . . (7 April 1988)

Is it too late? Can China be persuaded to be more generous in granting full autonomy? Who can persuade Peking? Not Britain, nor Governor Wilson, according to most observers. The general perception in Hong Kong is that Britain is anxious to scuttle away from any responsibilities. Foreign Secretary Sir Geoffrey Howe declared in Parliament that 'Hong Kong prospers when Peking and London are in harmony'. Governor Wilson was criticized by one of his own senior colleagues as 'ever the consummate diplomat, always seeking to fudge rather than to stand up for a principle. A good governor of Hong Kong after eighteen months in office would have distinguished himself by good public argument standing up for Hong Kong. Sir David hasn't.' Only after Peking's crackdown in Tian'anmen Square did the Governor stand up and argue against Prime Minister Thatcher that Hong Kong Chinese BDTCs should be given rights to live in Britain.

Leaving the Sinking Ship

The passports question was a particularly sore point. Even though the importance of the 1981 Immigration Act was symbolic rather than real, since the significant changes had been made twenty years before, the message seemed clear to the three million Hong Kong British: this was telling them firmly that whatever happened in the negotiations between Britain and China there would be no place in Britain for them. Salt was rubbed in the wound when residents of Gibraltar and the Falklands Islands, in Hong Kong's eyes much less valuable citizens of the declining empire – though of course smaller in number and 'kith and kin' of the first-class British – were given full British passports.

Britain's attitude contrasts sharply with that of Portugal towards its Chinese subjects in Macao (and indeed of France towards its Melanesian and Polynesian subjects in the Pacific). Portugal is issuing full Portuguese passports to up to more than 100,000 Chinese. This will allow them to live and work in Portugal and any other European Community country, including Britain. France also showed generosity by promising full

French passports to Hong Kong Chinese who had worked loyally in French companies in the territory.

As a measure of its meanness, Whitehall showed it was ill-prepared to reward loyalty. In January 1989 it was announced that of 500 civil servants who had applied for British citizenship for being 'loyal to the Crown' a paltry 8 would get it. When challenged that this attitude was unfair, visiting Foreign Office Minister Lord Glenarthur replied pleasantly 'But there are many things in life that are unfair.'

China has been prepared to reassure visitors, mostly foreigners, that their investments in Hong Kong will be safe. For example, then-Premier Zhao Ziyang saw John Swire, at that time chairman of the Swire Group, in Peking in March 1987 and reassured him about Hong Kong's need for international investment after 1997. The Premier said: 'The Chinese mainland needs to absorb foreign investment, so how can Hong Kong reject foreign investment? Hong Kong needs investment by local Chinese as well as foreign investment, including British investment . . .' (*Wen Wei Po*, 11 March 1987). More startlingly, in March 1988 Xu Jiatun, director of the Hong Kong branch of Xinhua, announced that 'the modern capitalist system is a great invention of human civilization.' He ventured criticism of both Karl Marx and Mao Zedong, declaring that

> apparently, the capitalism in Marx's time was only the initial stage of capitalism. In the contemporary era, capitalism has changed and developed tremendously. In the past we thought that capitalism would soon be doomed. It now seems that modern capitalism still has considerable room for development. The principal changes of modern capitalism find expression in the fact that it has a relatively legal structure, which ensures an environment of free competition and which enables the productive forces to develop further. Moreover, it has also developed a middle class . . . (interview with Peking-based *Jingji Shehui Tizhi Bijiao*, quoted in *Wen Wei Po*, 20 March 1988)

Xu said of Mao, 'because he never went abroad to have a look and because he didn't understand modern capitalism, he adopted a series of "Leftist" lines and policies so that our socialist construction suffered major setbacks. We have extricated ourselves from our series of "Leftist" lines and policies. We have started to sober up and have awareness.' The Xinhua director also threw in some comments about his own Communist colleagues, complaining that 'They always judge capitalism by old standards. They do not notice its changes. Had I not worked in Hong Kong for four years, I would probably have entertained the same idea as those comrades. In short, some of our colleagues know too little about and are too fearful of modern capitalism.' Xu added that unless the legal and operational structures of modern capitalism were mastered, it would not be possible to carry out the socialist modernization programme properly.

Most such propaganda from China has been directed towards foreigners rather than local Hong Kong Chinese, though rich and powerful Hong Kong businessmen have been wined and dined royally in Peking. But Peking's bullying tactics have done little to reassure Hong Kong's nervous professionals and executives. Their worries are further increased because they can see a China that doesn't have the legal safeguards available to them in Hong Kong or in the West. China remains a very unequal society, in which some offenders can be punished with a bullet in the back of the head (with a bill for the bullet sent to their relatives) while others who are well connected can get off lightly. In 1988 a minor party official was executed for embezzling about $10,000, while a senior party boss who had been convicted two years previously of being a ringleader in a huge US$1.5 billion smuggling racket was appointed deputy mayor of Canton.

Some Hong Kong inhabitants have already fallen foul of China's legal system. In one celebrated case in 1986, the son of a defendant accused of fraud in Shenzhen was detained for a short time, almost as a human ransom for his father's offence.

Lee Yee, editor-in-chief of the *Nineties*, an independent Hong Kong journal, commented on the fairness of the trial.

> In Shenzhen the accused was isolated and opposed by all other participants in the case, who were themselves united under party leadership. Moreover, the Public Security Bureau, the prosecutor's office, the court and the plaintiff were united in a scramble after the defendant and his family to persuade them to turn over HK$100,000 (the amount allegedly involved in the fraud). (*Asian Wall Street Journal*, 3 February 1986)

The defendant was detained and isolated for six months before the trial, and his accusers never appeared in court to give evidence, let alone be cross-examined.

Growing numbers of Hong Kong Chinese are distrustful of Peking, so distrustful that they are seeking to leave. More than 45,000 left, mainly for Australia, Canada and the USA, in 1988 alone, and another 50,000 expect to go in 1989. Governor Wilson tried to play down the emigration, claiming that since Hong Kong has become more and more international, there had long been a movement of its people abroad. He claimed that the historic net outflow had been about 20,000 a year. The Governor also claimed that some of the emigrés, having established their foreign residences and obtained their foreign passports, had come back to Hong Kong. Writing in the *Harvard International Review*, Wilson claimed: 'Of those leaving because of a lack of confidence in the Joint Declaration quite a few, having obtained their "insurance policy", have returned because they prefer Hong Kong's lifestyle and the opportunities provided by its dynamic economy.' Later, speaking in London, he added: 'To the Hong Kong Cantonese, Hong Kong is superior to most other places in the world' (Answer to a question at the Royal Institute of International Affairs, March 1988).

According to most management consultants and others at the sharp end of the problem, the Governor was being too optimistic.

A survey by the Hong Kong Institute of Personnel Management in 1987 showed that the number of executives leaving Hong Kong exceeded those arriving by 760 per cent. Government, including the police, and the financial sector were among those worst-hit. In the nine months to 1 January 1988, 3,344 civil servants left Hong Kong, including five at director level. This was a sharp rise of 34 per cent on the previous full year. T. P. Cheng, interpreter for Britain at the talks with China, also announced in 1987 that he was leaving Hong Kong. The police force was experiencing manpower problems in the critical middle ranks. The Hongkong Bank also lost more than 8 per cent of its Chinese executives in a single year. Other banks were badly affected. An executive of one prominent head-hunting firm said: 'It's what they call "baby bankers"; people with less than ten years' experience, who are leaving.' To the Hong Kong Management Association, the situation in early 1988 was serious enough to merit setting up a service to try to lure local managers back. 'The brain drain has become so serious that we had to do something,' the association's marketing manager Rick Tam said. Evidence of the anxiety to get out can be seen in several key places, in the queues outside the American, Australian and Canadian consulates, and outside a police station in Causeway Bay where Hong Kong Chinese apply for the certificates of 'no criminal record' that forty-five countries demand before they will give residence permits. Applications for the magic piece of paper are running at more than 50,000 a year.

The tragedy for Hong Kong, and for China as well, is that the professional and managerial executives who are getting out are the very people who have helped to build modern Hong Kong. Foreign investors and rich men may supply the capital, but the managers are needed to make it work. This exodus came during an economic boom which saw Hong Kong's most rapid growth for many years. Apologists for the agreement said that the rapid economic growth was a mark of confidence that people have faith that the Joint Declaration will work. But

Hong Kong has always operated on a shorter time-span than most other industrialized countries. And this growing unease about the uncertain future was all before Deng Xiaoping let loose his troops on his own people in June 1989.

14 Fallout from the Bloody Peking Spring

The sight on television screens in their own cosy living rooms of tanks and guns mowing down unarmed civilians pleading for democracy shook Hong Kong people, Chinese and expatriate alike. Rose-tinted shades were ripped from millions of eyes; the Chinese Communist Party was seen in a colder, clearer light; Deng Xiaoping, often romanticized in the West and in expatriate Hong Kong as a cuddly lovable figure, was revealed as a tired, power-hungry old man unable to recognize the ideals of his own youth in the students' demands. The very pillars of the community who had previously sung the praises of the 1984 Joint Declaration changed their minds when they witnessed the savage ruthlessness of the Chinese leaders. Helmut Sohmen, Legco member and son-in-law of Sir Yue-Kong Pao, who had previously (see chapter 13) welcomed the idea of Hong Kong being fully absorbed into China, a profitable business merger, was now among the first to condemn Peking: 'If they treat their own people like this, how might they treat the people of Hong Kong?' he asked, and called for an immediate leaseback of the colony to Britain. Simon Murray, managing director of Hutchison Whampoa, who had looked forward to prosperity and stability in 'Hong Kong, China', lamented 'This is an enormous blow and is tremendously damaging. This place is shocked with anger, outrage and sadness, though we should have learned the lesson of [Peking's interventions in] Tibet.' China's own Communist-run organizations in Hong Kong were quick to place newspaper advertisements condemning the violence.

Ta Kung Pao, a pro-Communist Hong Kong newspaper wrote: 'The day of 3 June 1989 is one that all Chinese wept for because of the tragedy in Tian'anmen, and will go down in Chinese history. Those who have committed this error will come under the judgement of history' (4 June 1989). Another paper actually funded by Peking, *Wen Wei Po*, appeared for a week with its title-block (masthead) in black instead of the traditional red. The paper denounced its paymasters the Communist leadership as 'murderers' and 'robbers of the people'. Among the hundreds of thousands of demonstrators who marched in protest was Richard Margolis, Britain's deputy political adviser in Hong Kong during the drafting of the Sino-British agreement and now a merchant banker. He said 'The agreement was built not on trust but on confidence. Though we might not *trust* Uncle Deng, that was a non-existent commodity, we had confidence that the Chinese would keep their promises because they could see on which side their bread was buttered. That confidence has now been shattered.'

Sometimes Hong Kong's expressions of sympathy with the students and protestors in Peking were touching. A spontaneous campaign was begun to give blood for the victims in Peking. About 500 hawkers from Hong Kong island promised to give three days' earnings to support the pro-democracy movement.

But soon a colder reality set in. Hong Kong people quickly realized that they were themselves very much in the firing line. The search for a new place to live outside the gunsights of the Chinese Communism was resumed in greater earnest. One government official *sotto voce* gave his opinion that if they had been Cantonese protestors in Tian'anmen Square, 'they wouldn't have been there to have been mown down. They would have escaped to fight another day. There's a tough realism about the Cantonese which isn't always seen in northern China.' The Hong Kong realists pointed out that Peking would take no notice even of Hong Kong's 5.8 million united people speaking with one voice. 'We are a prudent people,' one added. A survey taken in July by the Federation of Hong Kong Industries found that three out of every four industrialists planned to leave Hong Kong before 1997. The survey also showed that 40 per cent were rethinking their investment plans in Hong Kong and 30 per cent were re-examining their China operations.

The Canadian consulate in Hong Kong ran out of application forms for immigrants. Other mainstream countries that had already offered residence to large numbers of Hong Kong Chinese, such as Australia and the USA, found the queues outside their doors six times as long as before the bloody Peking spring. Singapore announced in July that it was lowering the requirements for the admission of immigrants from Hong Kong. When news spread that Singapore was prepared to take up to 25,000 people over the next five to eight years the consulate was forced to close its doors as thousands tried to obtain application forms. Consulates of other unlikely places began to be beseiged with applications for foreign passports, including faraway islands like Tonga, Mauritius, Jamaica, Belize. Only Britain of the major democracies was not a popular choice. In an opinion poll Britain came out bottom of the heap. If given the chance, only 6 per cent would go to Britain. Britain is not popular partly because of its climate – 'four seasons in one day' – but also because of its refusal to accept Hong Kong British as full British. Since 1983 more than 200,000 Chinese have left; few for Britain. In 1988, 24,500 went to Canada, 11,700 to the USA, and only 1,150 were accepted by Britain.

There are different views about what might happen in China in the years leading up to 2000. According to students of history, what happened in Tian'anmen Square in June 1989 was a minor and not so bloody event in Chinese historical terms. In 1864 in Nanking, 100,000 civilians were massacred by the Imperial Army. This was only a single episode in the fifteen-year civil war called the Taiping Rebellion in which 20 million people are estimated to have died. In 1927 Chiang Kai-shek's Kuomintang (Nationalists) killed at least a thousand civilians in cracking down on the Left in Shanghai; tens of thousands died in southern China in the repression that followed. Mao's China also saw the deaths of millions of people. Some were the victims of starvation as a conseqence of stupid economic policies which had gone wrong; others were people who stood in Mao's way and were disposed of either individually and quietly or, as during the Cultural Revolution, in large-scale terror campaigns. British diplomat turned banker Margolis commented:

> In the league table of Chinese violence Tian'anmen Square stands out for stupidity rather than brutality. Twice just when the protest movement seemed to be running out of steam, Deng and his gerontocratic colleagues helped fuel the popular anger, first by declaring martial law, then by sending in the troops. Having murdered, they then pretended that no massacre happened yet revelled in the 'bravery' of the 'heroic' soldiers. This was stupidity compounded by savagery. (*Conversation with the author,* July 1989)

The evident unpopularity of the Communist Party was clear in the size of the demonstrations in the centre of Peking and the variety of people who supported the student cries for democracy and sheltered the demonstrators. This leads some respected China-watchers to predict that the days of Communist Party rule may be numbered. Father Laszlo Ladany goes so far as to say, 'What we saw in the streets of Peking may be the painful birth of a new baby of democracy.' In the past Ladany has spoken out critically against the Communist party and has not been known for his optimism. He points to the way in which the cry for democracy was taken up right across China, in Shanghai, in Xi'an, Nanking, Chengdu, Canton.

He also notes that although the Chinese media has been quick to reprint a multitude of expressions of support from military and provincial leaders, some of them have been less than fulsome. Messages have been issued in the name of the regional commands without the personal name of the commander attached. Typically they also contain whole-hearted messages of support for Deng Xiaoping and expressions like,

'We will study carefully the statements of prime minister Li Peng.' In Chinese Communist-speak this is a barely polite rejection. Visitors to southern China in mid-year said it was obvious that provincial authorities there didn't want to get themselves into trouble with Peking, but were unhappy about the crackdown and anxious about its implications for themselves.

Guangdong and the other southern Chinese provinces like Guanxi and Fujian have done especially well from the economic reforms and from closer ties with Hong Kong, their main supplier of investment and provider of economic livelihood. But those reforms themselves are in question simply because the Chinese economy, not to put too fine a point on it, was already in a dreadful mess as the twenty-first century approached. The mess was only compounded by politics.

China has changed rapidly over the past twelve years, since Mao died and Deng assumed power, and superficially most of the change has been for the better. Evidence of an unprecedented economic boom is clear enough: statistics show steady double-digit growth. There were myriad small signs of progress in China of the late 1980s, such as the constant Peking traffic jams, in which even the imported Mercedes and Volvos found it hard to get out of second gear; the policeman sporting fashionable platform-heeled shoes with loud purple socks; the crocodiles of hand-holding toddlers brightly dressed in new clothes; the fast-growing forests of television aerials in most towns; the factories and glitzy houses worthy of new entrepreneurs springing up all over southern China; and the multi-coloured piles of fresh fruit and vegetables and department-store ranges of consumer goods sold from barrows and cars in hundreds of 'free markets' in China's cities.

But there was a price to pay for the progress, including a 1988 inflation rate officially underestimated at 18.5 per cent – 30 per cent in the towns. Production of basic commodities like grain, cotton and edible oil has fallen, and output of coal, oil and steel has risen only marginally. In some areas, notably Shanghai, factories were on half-time because of power shortages.

Alarmed by these signs, conservatives led by Premier Li and supported behind the scenes by the tough old Marxist Chen Yun got the upper hand and demanded the reassertion of discipline and central control in 1988. If anything, their tough measures made matters worse.

All this has been compounded by the unrest. China's *Economic Daily* said in an editorial in July 1989 that the turmoil had caused 'enormous losses'. Alarm bells began to ring over the growing size of the state budget. This in itself was fuelling inflation and further threatening economic reforms. Finance Minister Wang Bingqian sounded like a voice crying in the wilderness when he urged state firms to be more efficient and private ones to pay their taxes. At the same time, an optimism in Hong Kong that the future lies with entrepreneurial China has led to some seditious dreams of 'a capitalist southern Chinese state. We could take on the whole world and tell the Northern Marxists to go to hell.'

The political background to the crackdown further complicates the issue. According to Ladany, 'Deng was saved by his enemies.' The old men around Deng, President Yang Shangkun, Chen Yun, former President Li Xiannian, Peng Zhen, all in their eighties, have scores to settle against Deng. All are hardline Party centralists and have all expressed opposition to reforms. Li Peng, younger at sixty-one, is regarded as a puppet without a power base of his own.

Chen Yun quickly said that it was necessary to take a step backwards in order to take two forward. In an 'internal' speech on 22 May Premier Li Peng declared that the unrest in China was 'the result of the long-standing, unchecked spread of liberalization' aimed at introducing 'the so-called democracy, freedom and human rights of the West'. Li is a Soviet-educated engineer, who speaks Russian and is known to favour big Soviet-style industrial schemes. According to the Hong Kong newspaper *Ming Pao*, Li said of the 'trouble-makers': 'If we retreat still further, we shall have to give China to them.'

Another sign of the intention to tighten the central grip and swing away from the west came in a speech reportedly made by Yao Yilin, a Vice-Premier and member of the key Politburo Standing Committee. He was supposed to have told officials that Premier Li wanted to get closer to the Soviet Union. Because China was a poor country it needed to change its investment strategy and make it 'suitable for Chinese conditions'. This meant that large-scale borrowing from the USA, Japan and Hong Kong was not suitable, and Peking should 'mainly talk to the Soviet Union'. However, such is the Byzantine world of Chinese politics that some commentators claimed that release of the speech was an attempt by Yao to discredit Li Peng.

Deng has tried to signal that he wants the reforms to go on. The appointment of Shanghai Party boss Jiang Zemin to be Zhao's successor as Party Secretary-General points to some of the contradictions and to the hole which Deng has dug for himself. Like Li Peng, Jiang is a technocrat without a real power base of his own, though he was successively mayor, then Party head in Shanghai, a grassroots position that Li Peng has never experienced. Like Li, Jiang has good *guanxi*. He is rumoured to be the son-in-law of former President Li Xiannian, just as Li is the adopted son of China's beloved Premier Zhou Enlai. Like Li, Jiang studied in Moscow, at the Stalin Automobile Factory. As mayor of Shanghai, Jiang had impressed foreign businessmen and diplomats as an energetic man who would get China's largest industrial city moving again. One reason for his success was that he speaks English (as well as Russian) fluently. Another is that he has a populist touch. He travelled on a crowded city bus to show his sympathy with complaints against the state of public transport and visited people angry about poor housing. But when it came to the bottom line Jiang still hadn't done much to improve the economic chaos that passes today for what was once China's international city.

More importantly, he knew on which side his own bread was buttered. In 1988 as head of the Shanghai party, he emphasized the need for ideology. He claimed that 'thought work', Chinese Communist gobbledegook meaning indoctrination, had been neglected. 'The more reform develops, the more political thought work must be strengthened.' He also attacked 'the worship of money, extreme individualism and extreme democracy'. As Ladany says, 'None of the new leaders could be recognized as Liberal. Jiang in 1989 closed down Shanghai's *World Economic Herald*, the most lively weekly in the city.' He also warned Hong Kong in July: 'We practise our socialism – you may practise your capitalism.' Hong Kong should not seek to 'transplant' capitalism into China: 'the well water does not interfere with the river water'. But the Secretary-General does not have blood on his own hands, so foreign visitors may feel they can safely shake one of them.

The immediate prospect is that China's leaders will try to resume the economic reforms selectively, but will put the lid on anything that smacks of political freedom of expression. If there is any conflict the political lid will be kept on at all costs. During this time there will be lots of infighting and sniping among the leaders as old hardliners like Chen Yun try to restrain the reforms. Hong Kong in particular has already felt the effects of Peking's wish to have its bread buttered on both sides. On the one hand, after the Chinese leaders had recovered from the shock of events, they were reassuring Hong Kong that they would keep their promise to respect the 1997 agreement, and that Hong Kong would be allowed to continue its own autonomous lifestyle; but on the other hand there were stern warnings that the Hong Kong people must behave themselves. 'Certain Hong Kong people have wantonly ignored Chinese laws and support and encourage the turmoil in Peking,' said a letter in the Peking press.

It is not clear whether foreign investors after 1989 will be quite so patient with Peking as they have been, or prepared to play ball entirely on China's terms. 'China has been treated very leniently compared to the Soviet Union,' says a Peking-based western diplomat. 'We have turned a blind eye to political repression. No one knows how many political prisoners there are in China: estimates run from 100,000 to one million, but the West has largely kept quiet. Businessmen have been prepared to sit and wait for weeks and then sell technology on China's terms. There will be resistance now.' Without foreign assistance China's economy will drift into a bigger mess.

These confusions and contradictions are an important reason why Ladany predicts that democracy may be on the way. That's no immediate consolation. One signal for change will be Deng Xiaoping's death, especially since there is no assured successor and the Communist leaders are likely to squabble. Mainland Chinese are probably prepared to wait. Time in China is not measured in days and minutes as it is in the West. The student protestors have fled the country or have gone underground and will patiently wait for their day to come after the repression is over.

There was a moving patient certainty in the message of student leader Wu'er Kaixi (the hunger-striker who sat in pyjamas to argue with Li Peng). 'A black sun has appeared in the sky of my motherland and republic,' he wrote.

> Under this black sun, on a day in June that should have belonged to a season of fresh flowers, my people, my countrymen, my classmates and my beloved comrades-in-arms fell. Blood from the bullet wounds moistened the tracks of tanks from an army of beasts, painting the earth of the republic. But under this black sun and in this land of red, bunches of flowers still opened, still in full bloom! My republic will always be beautiful! But still the cold light flashing from bayonets revealed the stupid cruelty of fascism. The fascists, pretending a happy appearance or dignity, used their big heels to crush these flowers that had survived a disaster, because they were afraid. They feared these beautiful flowers, they intend to strangle a life. They are aged.
>
> But our life is young, stubborn and uncrushable. What's

> more, in my motherland of 9.6 million square kilometres, these fresh flowers will one day open proudly under a red sky. Black sun, I'm going to shoot you down! Wu'er Kaixi. 15 June 1989. On the run.

The message was smuggled out from Hong Kong, and the student leader went first to Paris – just as the young Communist Deng was in exile in France in his youth – then to the US.

Democracy may come on the mainland. But can Hong Kong wait? Unlike China, it is used to dealing in a western business system where the days and minutes count. And in particular the days and minutes are ticking away towards 30 June 1997, when Britain hands over the colony to China. The millions of Hong Kong Chinese have an awkward choice to make: should they sit tight, try to get on with their ordinary lives and trust China, perhaps hoping that by 1997 things will have changed? Or should they try to emigrate? Even if the regime and system of government in China does change, it may not please Hong Kong. Hardline rule may be protracted, say by an army take-over to save the country from splitting up into chaos. China after all is a complicated country, where regional feelings are strong; throughout the nineteenth and early twentieth centuries, central domination was challenged by individual rebellions. Or there might be breakdown into chaos. And even if democracy comes, it might not be to Hong Kong's immediate benefit. Other democratic governments have pursued populist promises which haven't always made good business sense. The Chinese Communist government in 1987 and 1988 failed to bite the bullet of price reform because it was afraid of a popular outcry against higher prices. A new democratic government might not have the same view of the usefulness of Hong Kong that the Communists had.

Hong Kong can certainly be accused of wanting things both ways. The colony's businessmen and bankers want to be left separate from China to enjoy their own autonomous lifestyle; but they also want to make as much profit as possible from dealing with China. While wishing to be free of the embrace of the Communists, some Hong Kong leaders wanted to continue pushing the democracy struggle. In spite of Peking's warnings, some Hong Kong democracy activists were planning to bombard all China's fax machines with their messages.

Less fairly Hong Kong was accused of hypocrisy in its treatment of Vietnamese refugees who had fled in their leaky boats to find landfall in Hong Kong. By the middle of 1989 there were more than 50,000 Vietnamese in Hong Kong. For years the government has tried to discourage them. It has penned them in camps. Small children were born and had to live their whole lives in these dingy prisons, though they could hardly be guilty of any crime. In mid-1988, the government decreed that any new Vietnamese arrivals would be counted as 'economic refugees' and therefore not entitled to a haven unless they could *prove* that they were fleeing from political persecution. The United Nations High Commission for Refugees complained about the Hong Kong screening procedures. The government took still tougher measures. In May 1989, arriving boatloads were made to stay on their boats on the Soko Islands at the extremity of Hong Kong's territorial waters, with no proper water supplies or provisions. Officials talked of refusing any haven to future boat people. This hostile attitude had the full backing of Hong Kong Chinese, who objected to any proposals to let the Vietnamese out of their prison encampments or to build new camps near them. 'It is the classic refugee mentality,' said one long-term British resident in the colony. 'The attitude is, "I'm all right, I've got in, don't let anyone else in." Yet these same people are clamouring to be accepted in richer countries. Hong Kong economic refugees are rich, the yacht people, yet they won't offer a crust to the bedraggled boat people.'

What could be more hypocritical? the critics said. Here were thousands of Hong Kong people clamouring to escape, economic refugees seeking a better life, yet the colony denied even the minimum refuge to the Vietnamese. Why should anyone have sympathy for Hong Kong? The charge was unfair because back in 1979 the rich western countries had agreed to accept Vietnamese as refugees. Hong Kong was not present nor a party to the deal and accepted refugees on the strength of Britain's promise as one of the countries offering them a home, So it was the failure of Britain and the rest of the west to fulfil their promises by accepting the Vietnamese that caused the crisis. Hong Kong routinely hands back Chinese seeking economic freedom.

Britain's reputation in Hong Kong slumped to an all-time low with the refusal of the government of Margaret Thatcher to offer full passports to the 3.28 million Hong Kong Chinese who by 1989 were British subjects. Though Governor Sir David Wilson himself personally pleaded with Thatcher, though the respected businesswoman Dame Lydia Dunn, the senior member of the Hong Kong executive council, warned that Hong Kong might become ungovernable unless Britain were prepared to offer a refuge, Thatcher was unmoved. Foreign Secretary Sir Geoffrey Howe went to Hong Kong specifically to tell the colony this home truth. There would be no 'insurance policy' of a mass award of British passports. For his pains he was accused of speaking 'bullshit' and insulting the intelligence of Hong Kong Chinese. In spite of Howe's refusal, a local campaign was begun in July 1989 to get British passports for as many people as possible. It was supported by pillars of the establishment including the Hongkong Bank, Jardines, Swires, Hutchison as well as the Stock Exchange, the General Chamber of Commerce and other organizations. Simon Keswick, then chairman of Jardines, said the Foreign Office had 'the vision of a bat', and both Keswick and Simon Murray compared Howe's assurances over the agreement to Neville Chamberlain waving his piece of paper after meeting Hitler in Munich in 1938.

The most generous thing that the Thatcher government will contemplate is more 'flexibility' within the existing Immigration Acts to admit Hong Kong Chinese who have loyally served the Crown or whose jobs would put them at particular risk. About thirty widows of Hong Kong Chinese who fought and died in Britain's service during the Second World War will – belatedly

– probably be allowed British passports. Even before the Tian'anmen Square massacre a small number of senior civil servants had been secretly approached and told that if they stayed in their jobs until the handover they would be given British passports on production of their special code number. Such were the cloak-and-dagger methods the Thatcher government was already resorting to.

The Foreign Affairs Committee of the House of Commons in June 1989 urged the government to give assurances to 'a larger number of key people in the Hong Kong civil service, the police or indeed in any area of public life' that they would be able to settle in Britain in or after 1997. Members of the committee said they hadn't done sums on the numbers involved, but 'it would be thousands not hundreds or tens'. But, evidently, not hundreds of thousands or even tens of thousands. The Conservative-dominated committee, like the Thatcher government, set its face against mass immigration to Britain. This was not surprising since, according to Westminster sources, the government whips had been used to making sure the committee voted the right way. The best that the committee could suggest was that Britain should work with other members of the European Community, Australia, Canada and the USA to give assurances that Hong Kong would not be forgotten in the event of an 'Armageddon scenario'. In that event the accommodation of 'even several million people from Hong Kong would be quite possible if shared amongst the international community', the committee said.

The Conservative government's line on passports was supported by the Labour opposition. Gerald Kaufman, the Shadow Foreign Secretary, went to Hong Kong immediately after the Tian'anmen Square massacre. He found a colony which in some ways was very British, including ball-by-ball radio commentary on the cricket test match between England and Australia and a cenotaph to the war dead similar to that in many British cities. He listened to the impassioned pleas of the 'brave and determined representatives of the Hong Kong people', but in the end he said that he couldn't agree to changes in Britain's Immigration and Nationality Acts. He added: 'Moreover, such a change would be regarded as permitting entry into the crowded British Isles of a huge group of people, who, simply because of their numbers, would be hard to absorb.' Just to add insult to injury Kaufman claimed to have found a counter-charge against Hong Kong's impassioned arguments – the Vietnamese boat people huddled in Hong Kong and not admitted to the colony at large. (Kaufman gave his views in *The Times*, 13 June 1989.) In the House of Commons the Labour Shadow Foreign Secretary even took issue with the government's willingness to accept more flexible entry of key Crown servants, declaring that a Labour government might not consider itself bound by any promises made.

The only major party leader prepared to accept and argue that the Hong Kong Chinese had a right to full British passports was Paddy Ashdown of the Social and Liberal Democrats. Interestingly, Ashdown is the only senior British politician who has direct experience of living in Hong Kong. He served in the Far East with the Royal Marines Special Boat Squadron before entering politics. But he wasn't completely alone in his pleas for the Hong Kong Chinese. He was supported by an almost unanimous chorus of leading articles in Britain's newspapers from *The Times* and the *Daily Mail*, both normally Conservative supporters, to the *Independent*. *The Times* thundered in a long leader entitled 'The Hong Kong crisis: Duty and Honour' that 'The course which would meet Britain's obligations and safeguard against a mass exodus would be to restore the right of abode to all 3.25 million, but to operate, as of this year, an annual quota system . . . Convulsions in Chinese history have often been associated with the most appalling massacres. Britain could not merely "deplore" blood flowing along Kowloon's Nathan Road' (*The Times*, 8 June 1989). The *Independent* drummed out the same message:

In the wake of the massacres in Peking, Britain has been

shamed into promising 'flexibility' towards the would-be immigrants from Hong Kong. This appears to mean that, though it will return the colony to whatever group of gentlemen, statesmen, madmen, or butchers happen to be ruling China in 1997, it will attempt to protect the stability of its own administration by promising passports to whichever bureaucrats and businessmen are needed to keep the place ticking over for the eight years which remain. These might be, at a guess, policemen and prison officers, financiers and firemen, company directors and anybody in official circles lucky enough to have a hand in drawing up the list. A cynical exercise, it will still be thought to go too far by some MPs in London, those legislators who would rather see Hong Kong tear itself to shreds than vote to vary the Nationality Act to help non-Caucasians . . .

The issuing of British passports to British subjects in Hong Kong would bring with it three practical and urgently needed benefits. It would lower the anxiety level of those who stayed; would remove the bitterness now building up towards the departing British government; and would encourage China to rule more benignly for fear of depopulating its possession. In sum, the issue of passports could prevent Hong Kong from becoming ungovernable – at least from London – before 1997, and could preserve lives and liberties after that date. Only the most selfish and callous of governments would reckon those lives and liberties were outweighed by the votes which it feared to lose as a result.

A lone, though distinguished, Conservative Member of Parliament, Sir Eldon Griffiths, supported and thanked *The Times*. He pointed out that as a junior minister he had been responsible for helping resettle Ugandan Asians threatened with massacre by Idi Amin.

I can attest that the vast majority of these newcomers

> absorbed quickly and peaceably into our society. They have also contributed, valuably, to British commerce, industry – and culture . . . I recently have met large numbers of the Chinese immigrants who have settled in southern California. Most are technicians, small businessmen and students. And one cannot speak too highly of their intelligence and industriousness; they are proving, again and again, the varieties that give rise to a message that was chalked by an unknown immigrant on the plinth of the Statue of Liberty: 'We came not empty-handed here, we brought a rich inheritance.' (Letter, *The Times*, 10 July 1989).

The 'economic' argument against acceptance of large numbers of Hong Kong Chinese was seized by politicians anxious to keep Britain's door slammed shut against immigrants. But the economic evidence was by no means clearcut. Professor Bernard Corry of Queen Mary College, London, in a report commissioned by the *South China Morning Post* Sunday edition, found some costs in mass immigration of Hong Kong Chinese to Britain. Public spending on housing, schools, education and roads would have to increase. There would also be the danger of congestion in south-east England with higher house prices and local labour-market bottlenecks. But against these costs, there would be a large number of benefits if Hong Kong Chinese were admitted in large numbers to Britain.

- Economic growth would be stimulated. The construction industry in particular would boom. Consumer electronics would bloom. Britain's textile industry would be reborn.
- Britain's balance of payments would enjoy the injection of financial capital from the wealthier immigrants. This might be helpful in strengthening the pound or allowing interest rates to fall.
- By the same token, the trade account and manufacturing industry could be revised through relocation in Britain of Hong Kong's export-oriented industries.

- Britain's labour force would increase instead of facing contraction. Similarly the 'dependency ratio' of non-workers to workers in Britain's population would fall.
- Above all, arrival of Hong Kong immigrants could inject new skills and energy into the British economy.

Corry did not examine the political implications or explore the arguments about 'social tension'. But the economic message was clear: provided that proper planning was done and the immigrants' arrival spread over several years, then the coming of several million Hong Kong Chinese, far from damning the British economy, could rejuvenate it. But the Conservative politicians had set their face even against exploring the arguments. Home Secretary Douglas Hurd claimed that Britain was 'an overcrowded island' – although Hong Kong's density of population is *twenty times* greater than that of Britain and that had not stopped Hong Kong from going from strength to strength.

Nor was the government disposed actually to put the issues before the electorate. In a television programme linking Hong Kong and London, there was vigorous condemnation from several outspoken Britons of the idea of mass immigration. But when the issue was put to the vote, about 60 per cent said they would agree to offering the Hong Kong Chinese a home. Foreign Secretary Howe, also in the studio, simply repeated his message that Britain 'could not' offer passports to more than three million Hong Kong British people even on the expectation that most of them wouldn't come. A television critic, John Naughton of the *Observer*, commented that Howe 'also made it clear that if it came to a confrontation between the UK and China, Britain's preferred option would be to go to lunch leaving a recorded message saying "we surrender"'.

Howe's best offer was to press Peking to abide by its promises in the Joint Declaration and to speed up Hong Kong's progress towards democracy. The Foreign Affairs Committee had recommended a string of British actions, including introduction of full direct elections before 1997; a Bill of Rights to protect the basic rights of Hong Kong citizens; and a joint constitutional court in Hong Kong to interpret the territory's laws in accordance with the legal principles that prevail in Hong Kong, rather than entrust the interpretation of the basic law to Peking. The committee also urged that Peking should be asked not to station People's Liberation Army troops in Hong Kong after 1997. In the heady anger after Tian'anmen Square, the British government seemed to be all for quick democracy for Hong Kong. But then doubts began to set in and officials fretted about Peking's reaction if Britain went ahead and introduced democracy without consulting China. Would Peking accept this after 1997? Perhaps it would be best not to anger China. In September the Peking hardliners returned to their thuggish bullying. China insisted that it would station PLA troops in the colony after 1997. It accused Hong Kong and British officials of interfering for suggesting otherwise. Premier Li Peng said that Hong Kong people would not be allowed to become 'special nationals' of China and bluntly said that China's constitution would take precedence over basic law.

Between them, Britain and China are doing their best to make sure that 'Hong Kong, China' starts life with all the disadvantages possible. Throughout the 1980s, during the negotiations, in the agreement and subsequently, there has been a common pattern (as has been demonstrated throughout this book) of Chinese bullying and British *kowtow*ing in response. China deliberately refused to listen to the views, wishes and feelings of Hong Kongers. It was open to Britain to encourage Hong Kong to speak up – or even to let the Hong Kong government do so. The British Foreign Office also set too much store by the idea that China was becoming more liberal and international. One problem, say British Conservatives, is that Britain has been behaving as a responsible late twentieth-century member of the international community, whereas Deng's China has responded like a thug, or perhaps barbarian would be the more appropriate term. However, is it gentlemanly Britain or merely a cowardly or calculating one – since there is no profit in trying to challenge China? (Argentina and the Falklands were different: a weaker opponent and a war victory to cheer the electorate.)

The other view, taking into account the meanness of Thatcher over passports, is that Britain as the twenty-first century approaches has the narrow moral view of a rather greedy small-town grocer who can count her pennies but has no grand international vision, still less any commitment to a noble ideal like protection of British subjects against bullies. The one word missing from political discussions of the plight of the Hong Kong Chinese was 'honour'. Only Ashdown and the press (and the British people) seemed concerned about it. In this case honour and practical considerations go hand in hand. Unlike almost every other member of the once-proud empire, the 5.8 million people of Hong Kong have been deliberately denied a choice. India, Ghana, Jamaica, the Solomon Islands, Tuvalu, possessions with populations ranging from hundreds of millions to 8,300 (Tuvalu), have negotiated for their *independence*, allowing them to shape their own destiny, to fly their own flags, play their anthems, sit at the United Nations and be courted by China and the UK. Hong Kong, the brightest jewel the British empire has ever seen, with a population of nearly six million, bigger than the populations of Israel, Ireland, Denmark, Libya and almost as big as Switzerland, was denied this right of independence. If honour and morality had anything to do with it, then the people should have been permitted their own say. At the very least the colonial power would have allowed them to choose their own safe haven if they did not like the deal. But that's not the way the world works. Especially not when dealing with the People's Republic of China.

By mid-1989 unease in Hong Kong about the handover had reached fever pitch. The danger is that by 1997 Hong Kong will have bled nearly to death by the steady trickling away of its lifeblood, the younger entrepreneurs and the middle-class managers and intellectuals who are not prepared to take a chance on China's munificence, nor to trust its promises.

What is perhaps most shocking is to hear British ministers and officials talking of what they will do in the case of the 'Armageddon scenario' – if the PLA tanks and troops seen in glorious action in 1989 in the centre of Peking came trundling down Nathan Road. British officials concede: 'Yes, then, we would have a moral obligation to look after the Hong Kong people.' What scandalous handwashing! By then it would be impossible to evacuate more than a few jumbo-jet loads of the beleaguered people. China or its puppet government in Hong Kong would have demanded that everyone trying to leave should have exit visas, so that the hyprocritical British could lament happily, knowing there was nothing they could do. Posthumous British passports cost little. A few Hong Kong people might escape in their own boats, but it is a long way by boat from Hong Kong to anywhere in the west.

The best, the most honourable *and* the most practical solution would be for the UK to offer full passports to all its British subjects in Hong Kong. It would be possible after that for Britain to try to work out its own insurance policies or tradeoffs with the European Community countries, with the Commonwealth or the USA. But Britain should accept that Hong Kong is part of its empire, and it bears the responsibility. The passports would be an insurance policy encouraging the Chinese to stay in Hong Kong in the hope that by 1997 China will have changed and become a tolerant and tolerable master. If large numbers did nevertheless go to Britain, it would be to Britain's advantage, not disadvantage.

The Hong Kong migrants today are not impoverished demoralized boat people. They would leave taking assets, energies, abilities, to their new home, as businessmen, doctors, engineers, teachers (whom the British Ministry of Education reported to be keen to attract to make up for a shortfall of homegrown British teachers). Far better for Britain to get its share of these than to see them fleeing to Canada, Australia, and the USA, leaving Hong Kong with the old folk, the poor, the unskilled, the very young and the sick. With full British passports, knowing that they could get out at any time, the majority would want to stay on in Hong Kong as long as they could. Hong Kong Chinese did look round the world for a better home and most of them found there was nowhere else they could replicate the special magic that is Hong Kong, noisy, overcrowded, gaudy, glittering, but home and a money-making machine, a place where the poorest person can still dream of fulfilling his or her ambitions.

One disgruntled former Hong Kong executive council member in 1985 had been incensed at Britain's '*kowtow*ing to China'. He chuntered: 'There is no obligation to *return* Hong Kong as you see it to China. Hong Kong as you see it is a creation of much-maligned British colonial officials and refugee Chinese who fled from China. The only obligation is to return a barren island with hardly a house on it.' Hong Kong at the start of 1989 was the greatest glory of the British empire, the world's first international city. It would be the supreme sad but savage irony if the bloodstained Chinese rulers and the timorous small-town grocers running Britain between them reduced Hong Kong by 1997 to a superficially modernized twentieth-century island, full of grand buildings but essentially barren.

Sources and Acknowledgements

General

Hong Kong is a remarkably open city and especially kind, at least on the surface, to journalists. It is generally easy to see almost everyone and anyone, from the richest mega-zillionaire and highest-ranking official to the ordinary person in a public housing block or clerk behind a desk. The Governor – almost alone – rarely gives formal press interviews. Almost a decade ago my colleague Charles Smith and I tried to obtain a couple of sentences on the record from the then Governor Sir Murray MacLehose for a *Financial Times* survey of Hong Kong. A flimsy document went back and forth to Government House for endless changes, the repositioning of a comma, the change of an article, the dotting of an 'i' or crossing of a 't' until HE (His Excellency) was happy that his words were sufficiently bland and anodyne. Since those days even HE has got used to having a thicket of media microphones thrust into his face every time he appears in public, and to undergoing the rigours of press conferences on his foreign visits to explain Hong Kong and its problems.

After I had migrated to Tokyo, Chief Secretary Sir Philip Haddon-Cave helped rekindle my interest in Hong Kong's uniqueness. He declared roundly over a lunch *à deux* that Hong Kong offers the only surviving *living* Chinese culture in the world, in the same phrase damning the suppression of traditional ways in China, their sanitization in Singapore and the fact that they are exotica in alien soil in North America. At that time

Haddon-Cave was Acting Governor. Only after we walked out of the restaurant did I notice a lone bodyguard who had been carefully observing him from a distance. Together the two men strolled on foot back to the office.

But it is not only the chief executive who can wander freely unharmed and unhindered through the centre of this most international but intensely Chinese city. On a recent visit in the space of a single day I spotted property king Li Ka-shing jostled among a throng of people who didn't give him a second glance in their common anxiety to jaywalk safely to the other side of Pedder Street; saw former Stock Exchange chief Ronald Li standing disconsolately on a street corner; bumped into China Light and Power Co. chairman Lord Kadoorie in the lobby of the Mandarin Oriental Hotel; and watched Hongkong Bank chairman William Purves in smiling conversation outside the Hong Kong Club. The very openness of Hong Kong is in marked contrast to China, where leaders are sheltered behind bolted doors, where Chinese journalists are told what to write and where foreigners are left to pick over the entrails of Communist actions and statements. Freedom to meet and talk in the British colony is only partly a consequence of its compact size – after all, much tinier Singapore conforms in many ways to China's closely guarded secretiveness. Whether the more accessible Hong Kong businessmen actually reveal very much is a different issue. Some conspiratorial Chinese business practices have defied the best efforts of government regulators to understand them, let alone successfully prosecute their infringements of the law.

All this means that I have been able to rely, much more than authors writing on other countries, on personal interviews. Over fifteen years' writing and reporting about Hong Kong, a good number based in the colony, I have met and interviewed most of the major and many of the minor players in government, banking, business and industry. Such is their accessibility that Gordon Wu stands out as the only person who did not respond to my requests (repeated in his case) for an interview. On those occasions in this book where quotations have been attributed to someone without a source given, they come either from a face-to-face interview with me or from a 'public' occasion, such as a press conference, widely reported in a variety of newspapers; the context usually indicates which. This does not apply to the quotations in the history chapters, where I have relied on a variety of primary and secondary sources (as well as interviews with personalities still surviving).

What is perhaps surprising is that dynamic Hong Kong is not well-served by books trying to explain its fascination. There are a good number of histories, though no complete history written in the last two decades, and a spate of partial, mainly political, studies written during and since the negotiations between China and the United Kingdom over the colony's future. Of the guide books the *Insight Guide to Hong Kong* of Apa Productions (Hong Kong, 1985) is by far the best with its sumptuous photographs, though it is marred by silly mistakes, including a claim that Britain pays an annual rent of HK$5,000 to China for the New Territories' lease. Every year the Hong Kong government produces its yearbook, an essential source (and very good value at a mere HK$42 for *Hong Kong 1989*), jam-packed with facts and figures, though frequently written in a tedious bureaucratic style. Hong Kong the modern metropolis had to wait until 1988 for Jan Morris to produce *Hong Kong: Xianggang* (Viking, London), a typically idiosyncratic *tour de force*, though she rather neglects the economy and nearly ducks the vital political question. Perhaps the problem is that Hong Kong moves too quickly for everyone.

CHAPTERS 1 AND 14: The Slaughter of Six Million Hopes; and Fallout from a Bloody Peking Spring

Thanks to David Rothkopf and International Media Partners' audacious idea of producing a daily newspaper in Peking for the four days 3–6 May 1989 of the Asian Development Bank meeting, I was on hand to watch the student protests and see how they tapped a popular vein. This allowed me a series of revealing interviews with leading Chinese (while Zhao Ziyang's gentler line – though no promises – was being tried) and also with visiting finance ministers and bankers who met Zhao and Li Peng and other members of the inner leadership. Father Laszlo Ladany (whose *The Communist Party of China and Marxism 1921–1985*, C. Hurst and Co, London, 1988, is an excellent source) was courteous and in a twinkling way helped steer me through elementary Chinese politics.

For anyone trying to keep up with China the BBC *Summary of World Broadcasts*, part 3, the Far East, published six days a week from Caversham, is essential material.

CHAPTERS 2 AND 3: A Very Chinese International City; A Raucous Kaleidoscope of Sights, Sounds and Smells

Captain Martin Willing was only the most helpful of several Cathay Pacific Airways' pilots who went out of their way to offer visits to the flight deck, discussions of the whys and wherefors of Hong Kong and, particularly, information on how to land safely on a difficult shore. When I asked him about the perils of the approach to Hong Kong, Martin Willing responded by producing a novelette of an imaginary CX 801 flight approaching Kai Tak on a stormy typhoon-visited night with visibility minimum and fuel low after the long flight from Vancouver. It's nice to be in such safe hands, a factor often forgotten in the ballyhoo of which airline has the most scrumptious food or winning, smiling crew. Cathay's airline magazine *Discovery* provides nuggets of information about what is going on in Hong Kong.

Christopher Hilton was ever helpful in suggesting whom to see, what places to visit. He also has a genius for finding interesting restaurants in the most unlikely places, which helped my appreciation of the culinary variety that Hong Kong has to offer.

As I tried to touch all bases in Hong Kong, the Government Information Service provided information and helped arrange some visits. John Yaxley, in his incarnation as Director of Industry, lined up various factory owners for me, and later as Deputy Financial Secretary was a mine of witty information about many aspects of Hong Kong. Without the help of Caritas International I probably wouldn't have begun to understand the viewpoint or the problems of the people on the housing estates. Discussions in vigorous Cantonese between young social workers, mothers, old folk and teenagers on the estates were just as stimulating – though offering differing views – as those in boardrooms or government offices.

Several people helped me to appreciate Hong Kong's special qualities. Sir Michael Sandberg offered the lavish hospitality of his box when he was chairman of the Royal Hong Kong Jockey Club (as well as chairman of the Hongkong Bank). Several officers of the Royal Hong Kong Police Force at different levels of seniority provided views on the Triads. *Triad Societies in Hong Kong* by W. P. Morgan (published in 1960 by the Hong Kong government) still offers the best grounding on the rituals of the pernicious societies. As to *fung shui*, the Rev. E. J. Eitel's work (spelt *Feng-shui* and first published in 1873) is still a good starting-point. Examples, both humdrum and exotic, of the way Hong Kong Chinese try to live in conformity with *fung shui* can best be gathered through talking to people or reading the newspapers.

CHAPTERS 4 AND 5: Barbarians Invade the Celestial Kingdom: The Birth of the Hong Kong Colony; A Smug Hastings in the East: 1841–1950

It is fascinating to open old historical accounts of the China coast before the British colonists came. Macartney's account of his travels to the court of Emperor Ch'ien-lung, the Son of Heaven, is particularly revealing. Other members of the party such as John Barrow also added perceptive details. But not all of these accounts are available in modern editions. Macartney's journal is available in *An Embassy to China: Being the Journal Kept by Lord Macartney during his Embassy to the Emperor Ch'ien-lung,*

1793–1794 edited by J. L. Crammer-Byng (Longmans 1962), but the second edition of John Barrow's *Travels in China* was issued in 1806. Quite the best book dealing with the opening up of China to the foreign barbarians is Christopher Hibbert's *The Dragon Wakes: China and the West, 1793–1911* (Longmans, 1970; paperback edition Penguin, 1984), a masterly study. *Foreign Mud* (*Anglo-Chinese Opium War*) by Maurice Collis (Faber, 1946) provides a chatty, sometimes day-by-day, account of the opening up of China in the 1830s. For a Chinese viewpoint the Foreign Language Press in Peking has issued a series of accounts translated from the *History of Modern China* series (Shanghai People's Publishing House). The most relevant is *The Opium War* which presents an aggressive uncompromising view, with its first chapter headed 'The Covetous British Invaders'.

As far as Hong Kong itself is concerned, Geoffrey Robley Sayer produced a two-volume study, *Hong Kong 1841–1862: Birth, Adolescence and Coming of Age* (Oxford University Press, 1937; reissued Hong Kong University Press, 1980) and *Hong Kong 1862–1919: Years of Discretion* (Hong Kong University Press, 1975). The earlier work starts with the stories of Elizabethan sailors' attempts to reach China, but then, disappointingly, omits Macartney and plunges into the struggles of the 1830s to open up China. More than half of the book is given over to the story of the effort to set up the colony and Sayer's chapters are ruled by the Hong Kong governors' reigns. The later Sayer book is skimpier and was only published eleven years after the author's death.

The role of Hong Kong's main modern historian was taken over by George Beer Endacott, who published the standard work *A History of Hong Kong* (Oxford University Press, 1964). Endacott also wrote a number of other informative volumes including *Government and People in Hong Kong, 1941–1962: A Constitutional History* (Hong Kong University Press, 1964), and *Hong Kong Eclipse*, a study of the Second World War years, published after his death (Oxford University Press, 1978). Endacott can be dull. He himself wrote that his story of the colony 'has been told mainly as seen through the eyes of the governors and the Colonial Office'. He too used the Hong Kong governors as his milestones, but included separate chapters on social and economic conditions in the colony and on topics such as education. I also read through selected files in the Public Records Office, notably Series CO 129, the Governor's Dispatches and Replies from the Secretary of State for the Colonies, Series CO 131, Minutes of the Hong Kong Executive and Legislative Councils and Sessional Papers.

Much more lively are accounts of more limited periods of Hong Kong's history. H. J. Lethbridge dips into a number of aspects of Hong Kong life as varied as the Tung Wah Association; the question of caste, class and race in pre-war Hong Kong; a profile of Colonial Secretary Sir James Haldane Stewart Lockhart; and the careers of two adventurers in his *Hong Kong: Stability and Change* (Oxford University Press, 1978). Peter Wesley-Smith's *Unequal Treaty, 1898–1997* (Oxford University Press, 1983) is a highly detailed but always lucid study of the negotiations leading up to the New Territories' lease.

Paul Gillingham's *At the Peak: Hong Kong between the Wars* (Macmillan, 1983) is a joy to read; it shows very colonial Hong Kong in light yet deadly serious mood through the use of newspapers, books and a series of enlightening interviews with the survivors of those times. Two books, *Captive Christmas: The battle of Hong Kong – December 1941* and *Captive Years: the Occupation of Hong Kong 1941–1945* (both published by Heinemann Asia in 1979 and 1982 respectively) are based on radio and television broadcasts put together by writer Alan Birch and producer Martin Cole.

The most vigorous of the early histories is that of Rev. E. J. Eitel, former Inspector of Schools in Hong Kong, whose history, entitled *Europe in China*, was first published by Kelly and Walsh in 1895 and was reissued by Oxford University Press in 1983. Many of the materials Eitel used have since disappeared. His book is an exemplar of the self-confident Victorian colonial mission to bring civilization to the far-flung natives.

For the later period I have been able to rely on interviews with prominent figures who are still alive. Lord Kadoorie kindly provided many illuminating thoughts and experiences of Hong Kong before and after the Second World War. He has an unrivalled knowledge and memory of both Shanghai and Hong Kong in their heyday and it is a pity that no one has yet persuaded him to provide a full and detailed account. David Macdougall, Colonial Secretary immediately after the war, provided me with several hours of fascinating detail on the problems of putting the colony on its feet again. Eric Himsworth also gave helpful comparisons of the pre- and post-war years and helped me to appreciate the mammoth task of economic reconstruction and renaissance.

CHAPTER 6: Kindly but Colonial Paternalism

The Hong Kong government yearbooks provide the bare facts on how the colony is organized. Norman Miners' *The Government and Politics of Hong Kong* (4th edition, Oxford University Press, 1986) is the standard indispensable work, a goldmine of information.

CHAPTERS 7 AND 8: The Hong Kong Dragon Catches up with the West; Global Financial Centre with a Small-town Mentality

The most helpful documents are the Hong Kong government's annual budget and the supporting documents that come out every year, including the 'Economic Background' and 'Economic Prospects', plus the Financial Secretary's opening and closing speeches. These have the advantage of topicality over books, which tend to be out of date before they are published.

I have benefited from the constructive attitude of successive financial secretaries – Sir Philip Haddon-Cave, Sir John Bremridge and Sir Piers Jacobs, all very different in character, in being prepared to talk reasonably freely to journalists.

In addition, the rapid growth of the financial services spawned the growth of what British Chancellor of the Exchequer Nigel Lawson condescendingly called 'city scribblers', analysts and commentators on the markets and on the economy. Their reports sometimes provide helpful stepping-stones to judging financial and economic progress. The columns of the *Far Eastern Economic Review* and the *Asian Wall Street Journal* have also been invaluable. In particular, I should thank Alan Smith, managing director of Jardine Fleming, far too senior and far too knowledgeable to be called a mere city scribbler, but with an informed, sometimes irreverent but always thoughtful view of Hong Kong and its business practices. *The Official Report of the Securities Review Committee May 1986* is a valuable inquiry into the way the stock market worked.

CHAPTER 9: Captains of Finance and Business

My task was made easier in putting together these profiles by countless reports of the city scribblers, but also by having met the principals in each of the four companies. Their annual reports provided valuable nuggets if the reader will search hard to find them. *The Thistle and the Jade*, edited by Maggie Keswick (Octopus Books, 1982), to celebrate Jardines' 150th anniversary, was helpful. The Hongkong Bank also has a massive history in four volumes, written by Professor Frank H. H. King (Cambridge University Press), but only the first volume was available at the time of writing, and at £60 it is an expensive source.

CHAPTERS 10 AND 11: China's Takeover of Hong Kong; Hong Kong in China: China in Hong Kong

For economic details I have relied heavily on personal visits and interviews, though the *South China Morning Post* was invaluable in keeping track of the rapidly changing relations. Several people facilitated visits to Shenzhen. For the Walled City, Caritas, the Hong Kong government, the Royal Hong Kong police and Jackie Pullinger all took me on visits. Jackie Pullinger has written *Crack in the Wall: The Life and Death of Kowloon Walled City* (Hodder and Stoughton, 1989). It is bittily written but extremely moving.

CHAPTER 12: China's Triumph: The Unequal Treaty of 1984

Daily newspapers, mainly the *South China Morning Post*, and the weekly *Far Eastern Economic Review* were useful, though this meant wading through hectares of newsprint, not all of lasting value. Joseph Y. S. Cheng brought the most interesting documents and speeches together in *Hong Kong in Search of a Future* (Oxford University Press, 1984); unfortunately this was published *before* the Joint Declaration.

CHAPTER 13: Will it Work?

Frank Ching's *Hong Kong and China, for Better or for Worse* (The China Council of the Asian Society and the Foreign Policy Association, New York, 1985) was an instant guide to the issues of the Joint Declaration. *Basic Law, Basic Question: The Debate Continues*, edited by William McGurn (Review Publishing Co., 1988) takes the question forward to publication of the first draft of the basic law. Much more important were literally hundreds of conversations with officials, businessmen, bankers and ordinary people of all shades of opinion in Hong Kong. To them, my humble thanks.

I should add a brief note on spellings of Chinese names, an infernal problem. I have tried to follow the most common transliteration and added a variant in brackets. This has generally meant using the Wade-Giles system for historical characters and Pinyin for modern people. I steadfastly refused to use Pinyin for common places like Peking, Canton and, indeed, Hong Kong.

Many people have helped at various stages in the preparation of this work. My agent June Hall suggested the project in the first place. At Penguin Books Peter Carson, Eleo Gordon and editor Judith Flanders set aside their normal production schedule to get this book out as quickly as possible after the bloody Peking spring. Harriet Barry, copyeditor, made important suggestions about organization as well as protecting me from the dreaded horror of sentences left with hanging participles.

But without the help of two people in particular I could never have written about Hong Kong. Time after time after I had moved to Tokyo, Christopher Hilton gave me the freedom of his home in Hong Kong, my base for exploring the fascinating aspects of the territory. He also was generous with advice, and provided frequent inspiration from his well-stocked malt-whisky cupboard. He is the most hospitable person I know and I owe him many grateful thanks.

The greatest contribution of all was made by my wife, Michelle. She shared many of my adventures and kept reminding me of the importance of our friends on the housing estates, in the Walled City and the refugee camps. Only she knows how many times she rescued me when I was getting lost in piles of papers, notebooks and taped interviews and pointed me again on the right road. Only she could have interpreted my scribblings and squigglings and turned them into typewritten prose that Penguin could understand. Often, too, her good sense produced valuable suggestions that enlightened my meandering writing.

Index